Seedtime for the Modern Civil Rights Movement

Seedtime for the Modern Civil Rights Movement / *The President's Committee on Fair Employment Practice, 1941–1946*

Merl E. Reed

LOUISIANA STATE UNIVERSITY PRESS

Baton Rouge and London

Copyright © 1991 by Louisiana State University Press
All rights reserved
Manufactured in the United States of America
First printing

00 99 98 97 96 95 94 93 92 91   5 4 3 2 1

DESIGNER: Patricia Douglas Crowder
TYPEFACE: Linotron 202 Aldus
TYPESETTER: Graphic Composition, Inc.
PRINTER AND BINDER: Thomson-Shore, Inc.

LIBRARY OF CONGRESS CATALOGING-IN-PUBLICATION DATA

Reed, Merl Elwyn, 1925–
    Seedtime for the modern civil rights movement : the President's
Committee on Fair Employment Practice, 1941–1946 / Merl E. Reed.
      p.   cm.
    Includes bibliographical references and index.
    ISBN 0-8071-1617-3 (cloth)   ISBN 0-8071-1688-2 (pbk.: alk paper)
    1. United States. Committee on Fair Employment Practice—History.
2. Discrimination in employment—Government policy—United States—
History.   3. Afro-Americans—Employment—History.   I. Title.
HD4903.5.U58R44   1991
331.13'3'0973—dc20   90-39656
                                                                CIP

The paper in this book meets the guidelines for permanence and durability of the Committee
on Production Guidelines for Book Longevity of the Council on Library Resources.⊗

for Martin and Mary Ann

Contents

Preface

My interest in the President's Committee on Fair Employment Practice as a research project began shortly after Edward Weldon, regional archivist at the then National Archives and Records Service (NARS) branch in East Point, Georgia, called my attention to the records of the FEPC's southeastern regional office (Region VII) in Atlanta. After more years of research than I care to remember, what began as brief glimpses of the southern shipyards, federal agencies, and Pennsylvania black workers during World War II developed into a history of the FEPC itself. I am indebted to Archivist Weldon and to his successor, Gayle Peters, and staff. At that time FEPC materials had not yet been microfilmed, and the policy of dispersing relevant federal records among the National Archives' regional branches was a boon to me. I also appreciate the guidance rendered by Joseph Howerton at the National Archives in Washington, D.C.

Individuals in several other federal facilities were helpful, including the Library of Congress, the U.S. Department of Justice, the Franklin D. Roosevelt Library, and the Harry S. Truman Library. I also wish to thank archivists and staff people at the Catholic University of America, Washington, D.C.; the Southern Historical Collection, University of North Carolina; the Robert Muldrow Cooper Library, Clemson University; the Richard R. Russell Library, University of Georgia; and the Chicago Historical Society. Finally, Sandy Ross, son of FEPC Chairman Malcolm Ross, kindly invited me to his home to examine a small collection of his father's papers.

Colleagues who are willing to spend untold hours reading and critiquing a manuscript are always appreciated, and I am greatly indebted to Gary M. Fink and John M. Matthews. Both made valuable suggestions, though their participation in no way relieves the author of full responsibility for any shortcomings in this work.

Finally, a word about the usage of names. The FEPC was primarily, though not exclusively, concerned with discrimination against Americans of African descent. Since World War II, as the nation passed through the civil rights revolution and beyond, four different names have identified this group: Negroes, blacks, Afro-Americans, and African-Americans. Each in its time had a special meaning and relevance, all were accepted by the race as desirable, and I use these interchangeably.

Abbreviations

BSCP   Brotherhood of Sleeping Car Porters
DJ-FOI   Department of Justice, Freedom of Information
F   Film (precedes a number)
FDRL   Franklin Delano Roosevelt Library
ND   Department of the Navy
R   Reel (precedes a number)
RG 228   Records of the Fair Employment Practice Committee,
           National Archives
  FR   Field Records, RG 228
  HR   Headquarters Records, RG 228
WD   Department of War

Seedtime for the Modern Civil Rights Movement

Introduction

The President's Committee on Fair Employment Practice (FEPC) was the subject of bitter controversy among contemporaries, and it has not been ignored or neglected by historians. From the beginning, the agency attracted dedicated champions and bitter opponents. Its supporters comprised a determined minority, including racial, ethnic, religious, and liberal groups scattered across the country, with their widest following in the Northeast. But there were enemies everywhere. Although strongest in the South, the opposition was nationwide and included all classes of whites, from blue- and white-collar workers to the occupants of corporate boardrooms, from opinion makers to politicians at all levels of government. Attacked and defended in newspapers and magazines, the committee was also discussed and analyzed in scholarly publications throughout the war period.[1] It was the most controversial federal agency in the nation during the war and perhaps in modern American history.

1. Seldon Menefee, *Assignment: U.S.A.* (New York, 1943); Charles S. Johnson *et al., To Stem This Tide: A Survey of Racial Tension Areas in the United States* (Boston, 1943); Gunnar Myrdal, *An American Dilemma* (New York, 1944); Herbert R. Northrup, *Organized Labor and the Negro* (New York, 1944); John A. Davis and Cornelius A. Golightly, "Negro Employment in the Federal Government," *Phylon,* VI (1945), 337–46; Louis C. Kesselman, "The Fair Employment Practice Movement in Perspective," *Journal of Negro History,* XXXI (1946), 30–46; John A. Davis, "Non-discrimination in the Federal Agencies," *Annals of the American Academy of Political and Social Science,* No. 244 (March, 1946), 65–74.

In the immediate postwar years, the FEPC was not forgotten, most notably in the writings of individuals who served on the President's Committee or who were closely associated with it. Such were Malcolm Ross's interesting but rambling account of his committee stewardship, Sarah Southall's challenge to industrial leaders to take up the agency's unfinished tasks, and Walter White's autobiography with its many references to the committee's work. Robert Weaver's authoritative book on black labor, virtually a reference work on that subject, made frequent comment on the FEPC. As a wartime agency created in response to threatened mass demonstrations by members of America's largest minority racial group, the FEPC also attracted political scientist Louis G. Kesselman, who was interested in wartime reform movements. More impressive, however, is the unpublished doctoral thesis of sociologist William Bradbury, who in 1952 provided a detailed description and analysis of racial discrimination in the federal service from Reconstruction to 1947. Bradbury noted that the FEPC had "considerably greater" prestige "in government than in industry," making possible "informal settlements" of complaints of discrimination. The fear of sanctions by supervisors and the belief that the president supported the FEPC also influenced the behavior of government hiring officers.[2]

In 1953, the only full-scale historical treatment of the FEPC appeared. The author, Louis Ruchames, relied heavily on the committee's published reports, its hearings, and newspapers. He also received valuable editorial, but apparently little oral, input from some of the committee and staff members. His book is a moving and sympathetic story of the committee's activity, rendered mostly in the rhetoric and judgment of the war years. Indeed, the FEPC's appeal in the early 1950s was still so powerful that Ruchames speculated, as he described the defeat of a bill for a permanent FEPC by a Senate filibuster in 1945, that reconstituting the committee could still be possible.[3]

2. Malcolm Ross, *All Manner of Men* (New York, 1948); Sarah E. Southall, *Industry's Unfinished Business* (New York, 1950); Walter Francis White, *A Man Called White: The Autobiography of Walter White* (New York, 1948); Robert Weaver, *Negro Labor: A National Problem* (New York, 1946); Louis C. Kesselman, *The Social Politics of FEPC: A Study in Reform Pressure Movements* (Chapel Hill, 1948); William Chapman Bradbury, Jr., "Racial Discrimination in the Federal Service" (Ph.D. dissertation, Columbia University, 1952), 44–45.

3. Louis Ruchames, *Race, Jobs, and Politics: The Story of FEPC* (New York, 1953), 213–14.

It was the civil rights revolution, however, that led to new writing and interpretation beginning in the 1960s. Although none of these works dealt with the President's Committee as an entity in itself, larger studies of the New Deal, World War II, the Truman administration, African-Americans, individual states during wartime, and national politics touched on the emerging civil rights movement and the role of the FEPC. Consequently, attention turned from the romance of an embattled agency engaged in a moral battle in the nation's capital against evil forces to a harder look at the FEPC's significance. In a 1961 study of wartime Indiana, for example, Max Cavnes concluded that the real impetus for action against local job discrimination, whether by the federal or the state governments, came through the initiative of Indiana's black leaders. In responding to discrimination, the FEPC was effective mainly by using investigative powers, which in the hands of skilled field representatives made it possible "to cajole and persuade" employers to alter discriminatory policies.[4]

One of the more important features of the postwar civil rights struggle was the appearance of mass movements and charismatic leadership. Herbert Garfinkel's 1969 work on the March on Washington Movement (MOWM) and the pivotal role of A. Philip Randolph in forcing concessions from the reluctant Roosevelt administration provide a reminder that the creation of the FEPC, like the passage of the Civil Rights Act over two decades later, was not a casual occurrence. The MOWM, though remaining active, gradually faded into the background as World War II progressed. Randolph, not unlike a later charismatic civil rights leader, attempted to rekindle the spirit of MOWM through new issues and another organization called the Committee for a Permanent FEPC, but the war emergency and the fervor it produced were ending, and the mantle of leadership passed from him.[5]

By the mid-1960s, most writers had begun to question the FEPC's effectiveness as an agency fighting against discrimination. They were certain, however, that the FEPC had important long-range consequences. Lerone Bennett, Jr., thought that the agency had not accomplished much. Nevertheless, he believed, the committee was signifi-

4. Max Parvin Cavnes, *The Hoosier Community at War* (Bloomington, Ind., 1961), 135.
5. Herbert Garfinkel, *When Negroes March: The March on Washington Movement in the Organizational Politics for FEPC* (Glencoe, Ill., 1959).

cant because it had provided "a point of focus which changed the climate of race relations and the vision of Negro leadership." For once, the federal government had performed "a decisive act . . . on behalf of the Negro citizen." Henceforth, the strategy of black groups would change, he noted. They would begin seeking decisive federal intervention in all matters involving civil rights. The conservative black leadership would also begin supporting a greater militancy in bringing about change. Richard Dalfiume went even further. He agreed with a number of writers who described the war as a "watershed" or "turning point" for the civil rights movement after which blacks would no longer accept discrimination without protest. Dalfiume believed that segregation in the armed services, an issue ignored in FDR's executive order, was just as important as discrimination in defense industry employment in assessing the causes for black protest and for the creation of the FEPC. But Dalfiume was less impressed with the committee itself. Its establishment was a victory for the president rather than for the MOWM leaders. With the FEPC, Roosevelt was able to undercut Negro opposition to the war and to his handling of racial matters.[6]

For historian August Meier during the 1960s, the judgment was also still out. Approaching the subject from the perspective of civil rights strategies for black employment, Meier believed that the FEPC "established a precedent for considering job discrimination a denial of civil rights." The agency was also a forerunner of numerous postwar fair employment practice laws in the states and of the federal Civil Rights Act of 1964. Meier made no comment, however, on the agency's effectiveness during the war period. He did find that the MOWM had long-range significance. Although never held, the march focused the black protest movement on economic problems and revealed the importance of "mass action by the Negro working class."[7]

Another historian, Barton Bernstein, exhibited the greatest skepticism. For him, the FEPC made no significant contribution "to the wartime advancement of the Negro," though the agency might have

6. Lerone Bennett, Jr., *Confrontation: Black and White* (Chicago, 1965), 179, 184; Richard Dalfiume, *Desegregation of the U.S. Armed Forces: Fighting on Two Fronts, 1939–1953* (Columbia, Mo., 1969), 118–21; Richard Dalfiume, "The 'Forgotten Years' of the Negro Revolution," *Journal of American History*, LV (June, 1968), 90, 94–95.

7. August Meier, "Civil Rights Strategies for Negro Employment," in Arthur M. Ross and Herbert Hill (eds.), *Employment, Race, and Poverty* (New York, 1967), 184–85.

accomplished more had it received a larger budget. If there were any gains by blacks, they resulted more from the labor shortage than from any federal effort. On the other hand, Bernstein saw Executive Order 8802, which created FEPC, as "the greatest achievement in American history for organized Negro action."[8] Thus did scholarship during the 1960s concentrate a good deal on the long-range effects and little on the actual work of the FEPC during the war.

In the early 1970s, interpretations remained much the same. Harvard Sitkoff, in two works published during that decade, believed like Bernstein that Executive Order 8802 was "the single greatest Negro victory since the Civil War." It had occurred "because of uncompromising Negro leadership." According to Sitkoff, Roosevelt's reluctance to grant concessions to blacks "helped unleash an even greater militancy" that served to make civil rights "a major national concern," but old-line leaders quickly "retreated from their earlier militancy and began to entrust white liberals with the job of winning the Negro his rights." Meanwhile, during the war, the FEPC, along with White House advisers David Niles and Jonathan Daniels, provided a "wailing wall for minorities" that proved very powerless but was "handy as a safety valve."[9]

Writing also in the early 1970s, Richard Polenberg cited many factors that served to make the FEPC ineffective, including "lack of funds, personnel and authority." More than his predecessors, except for Ruchames, Polenberg commented on the internal working of the committee itself. He believed the FEPC was hampered because it took no action until the filing of a formal complaint of discrimination, yet workers were "reluctant to file charges," and blacks particularly did not apply for jobs at plants known to reject them because of race. Lacking statutory authority, the FEPC could not compel compliance with its directives. Although the agency could request that war contracts be canceled when there were violations of the executive order, this option was a very weak weapon. Upon examining White House documents from the war period, Polenberg also had doubts about the

8. Barton J. Bernstein, "America in War and Peace: The Test of Liberalism," in Barton J. Bernstein (ed.), *Towards a New Past: Dissenting Essays in American History* (New York, 1968), 297–98.

9. Harvard Sitkoff, "Racial Militancy and Interracial Violence in the Second World War," *Journal of American History*, LVIII (1971), 675, 678; Harvard Sitkoff, *The Depression Decade* (New York, 1978), 323, Vol. I of Sitkoff, *A New Deal for Blacks: The Emergence of Civil Rights as a National Issue*, 3 vols. projected.

resolve of the FEPC's white leadership after the reorganization that brought in Monsignor Francis Haas and Malcolm Ross as chairman and deputy chairman in 1943. Both men rejected segregation as a cause for committee action, Polenberg charged. This charge was true, and many contemporary black leaders also criticized Haas and Ross over the segregation issue. Nevertheless, the agency received no authority in the executive order to deal with segregation except when discrimination in employment resulted therefrom. Finally, citing the FEPC's struggles with the Philadelphia Transit Company and the railroads as activities that secured concessions for blacks, Polenberg yet believed that "the most substantive gains" occurred as a result of manpower shortages rather than because of FEPC action. "When manpower grew scarcer in 1943," he noted, "many of the obstacles to Negro employment collapsed."[10]

Like Polenberg, labor historian David Brody believed that, despite the FEPC's contributions, labor shortages "played the more important part in breaking down discrimination in employment." Nevertheless, he argued, Executive Order 8802 was a "major advance, not only for the immediate accomplishments of the FEPC, but as the first step in making public policy an instrument against racial discrimination." In addition, other agencies helped the FEPC. The War Labor Board (WLB) stopped "wage differentials based on race," the United States Employment Service (USES) refused work orders specifying race, and the National Labor Relations Board (NLRB) refused union certification to those excluding minorities. Thus, according to Brody, a precedent was established for the "use of public policy against discrimination in the postwar period" at both the state and federal levels. The FEPC was important because it demonstrated "the mechanics of wartime reform" in an administration that shaped "policy by a close calculation of the relative power of claimant groups." The balance among these contenders was altered by the war in a way that gave "disadvantaged groups . . . a more strategic position to press their claims for reform." As an example, Brody cited the MOWM, which before 1941 never would have been a threat to the administration.[11]

10. Richard Polenberg, *War and Society: The United States, 1941–1945* (New York, 1972), 116, 117, 120–23.

11. David Brody, "The New Deal and World War II," in John Braeman, Robert Bremner, and David Brody (eds.), *The New Deal: The National Level* (Columbus, Ohio, 1975), 274–76, Vol. I of Braeman, Bremner, and Brody (eds.), *The New Deal*, 2 vols.

Meanwhile, August Meier and Elliott Rudwick, in tracing the use of nonviolent direct action in Afro-American protest, offered a provocative interpretation of the civil rights movement from the Depression to the 1960s that indirectly affected any assessment of the FEPC. The use of direct action, they claimed, went far "back into black history." It clustered at certain periods, however, and "only seldom [did] it achieve a major role in black protest." Yet such tactics "were continuously reinvented by blacks in response to shifting patterns of race relations." Meier and Rudwick saw the Great Depression as the "watershed" for direct action, and at that time and during the war, with the formation of the Committee on Racial Equality (CORE), direct action also involved a "self-conscious interracialism" that was a "significant new departure" in American reform. Nevertheless, direct action was "essentially an indigenous creation of the Negro Community." To the authors, "the evidence of history" suggested that the force of nonviolent direct action in the black community would have led to the "sit-ins and other demonstrations of the 1960s . . . even if Gandhi's revolution had not developed . . . even if CORE and Randolph's 1941 March [which led to the creation of the FEPC] . . . had never existed."[12]

Another historian, Neil Wynn, after studying the role of black Americans during World War II, directly challenged Louis Ruchames, who claimed that the FEPC had demonstrated how laws could change mores and customs. Ruchames failed to produce any evidence, and he admitted that the definitive results of FEPC activity could never be known. Wynn noted that blacks made considerable economic gains after 1942 both in the quality of jobs as well as in numbers employed, and like most of the postwar historians, he concluded that wartime labor shortages rather than FEPC activity produced these changes. Limited budgets, the absence of enforcement powers, and inadequate staff compared with other federal departments made the FEPC's position even more hopeless.[13]

By the late 1970s, the attention of historians began focusing more

12. August Meier and Elliott Rudwick, "The Origins of Non-violent Direct Action in Afro-American Protest: A Note on Historical Discontinuities," in August Meier and Elliott Rudwick, *Along the Color Line: Explorations in the Black Experience* (Urbana, 1976), 378–79, 387–89.

13. Neil A. Wynn, *The Afro-American and the Second World War* (New York, 1976), 48–49, 55, 57–59.

directly on the activity of the President's Committee. James A. Neuchterlein, relying heavily on congressional and presidential records, examined the committee in the context of the political climate in which it had to operate. For three years especially, the FEPC faced a difficult struggle to survive and function; thus it could produce only "mixed results." Obstacles constantly frustrated the FEPC's work, including hostile congressional investigations instigated by southern committee chairmen, adverse rulings by unfriendly bureaucrats, potentially crippling amendments to appropriation bills, and senate filibusters. In the end, attempts by FEPC supporters to create a permanent postwar agency failed. Considering all the handicaps, Neuchterlein pronounced the FEPC's record as "commendable," and he concluded that the struggle over the agency "foreshadowed later, more successful, struggles for the civil rights of black Americans."[14]

Others began more extensively consulting the FEPC's own considerable body of records, hitherto only superficially utilized. Especially important were materials generated by the central office in Washington, D.C., and by the various field offices. In a study of blacks and the United Auto Workers (UAW) in Detroit, Meier and Rudwick found that black organizations, in seeking better job opportunities, used labor shortages and government agencies such as the FEPC as leverage. These organizations particularly "grasped the fact that if any progress was to be made, federal intervention would be absolutely essential." Black militance "was clearly rooted in heightened expectations stemming directly from FEPC pressure." Historian William H. Harris, in a study of black shipyard workers and the boilermakers union on the West Coast, found that the FEPC played a similar role as blacks fought against segregated and discriminatory auxiliary unions.[15]

Finally, Merl E. Reed studied the work of the FEPC in the southern shipyards and in its association with federal agencies in the South. He found that though the committee was instrumental in forcing a large Alabama shipyard to hire skilled black workers, the price for this gain was the creation of a segregated way (the structure on which the

14. James A. Neuchterlein, "The Politics of Civil Rights: The FEPC, 1941–1946," *Prologue*, X (1978), 171–91.

15. August Meier and Elliott Rudwick, *Black Detroit and the Rise of the UAW* (New York, 1979), 112–13, 173; William H. Harris, "Federal Intervention in Union Discrimination: FEPC and West Coast Shipyards During World War II," *Labor History*, XXII (1981), 325–47.

ship is built) for black workers. Considerably greater progress was made in the shipyards of the upper South, but the FEPC could not prevail in the region as a whole. The committee did have a few limited successes in dealing with the United States Postal Service, he discovered. Nevertheless, every level of the bureaucracy, federal, state, and local, resisted the agency.[16]

In the Northeast, however, the results of FEPC activity were different. In Pennsylvania, for example, Allan Winkler, in his account of the Philadelphia transit strike of 1944, found that the FEPC succeeded in getting platform jobs for blacks, but "only with strong executive backing" that involved the use of the army to break a strike of white platform workers. Thus, there were limits to the FEPC's power. In other Pennsylvania industries, however, the FEPC had more success. In a study of that state's black workers during the war, Reed documented FEPC successes on behalf of blacks in public utilities, in U.S. post offices, in shipbuilding, and in the steel mills around Pittsburgh. In the mills, the FEPC's contribution was vital in settling strikes and walkouts as well as conflicts over promotions and upgrading.[17]

The present study focuses on the work of the agency itself, paying particular attention to the FEPC's complex relations with the Washington bureaucracy and the White House. It also explores the internal dynamics of the committee and staff, particularly the role of blacks in formulating and executing policy and their relations with whites in the agency. Leaving the central office in Washington, D.C., the work surveys FEPC's field offices. Additionally, it discusses the FEPC's activity on behalf of minority groups other than African-Americans, particularly Japanese-Americans and various religious minorities. The committee also had both friendly and stormy relations with organized labor.

Most writers since the 1960s have made the judgment that market forces were the sole or primary determinant of the changes in minority employment patterns during World War II. Indeed, it is impossible to deny the importance of labor shortages to the committee's

16. Merl E. Reed, "The FEPC, the Black Worker, and the Southern Shipyards," *South Atlantic Quarterly*, LXXIV (1973), 446–67; Merl E. Reed, "FEPC and the Federal Agencies in the South," *Journal of Negro History*, LXV (1980), 43–56.

17. Allan M. Winkler, "The Philadelphia Transit Strike of 1944," *Journal of American History*, LXIX (1972), 73–89; Merl E. Reed, "Pennsylvania's Black Workers, the Defense Industries, and the Federal Agencies, 1941–1945," *Labor History*, XXVII (1986), 356–84.

work. To conclude, however, that the market made the committee's work irrelevant misses the point. Of course, the full-employment economy provided employment for minorities in services, in unskilled labor areas, and in the semi-skilled, undesirable jobs of heavy industry. In such an economy, the FEPC's services would not have been needed if it had been just another employment agency. But wartime conditions also created labor shortages in the skills and professions, jobs that too often were unobtainable to qualified members of minority groups because of discrimination. The FEPC concentrated on the quality of the job and the qualifications of the worker and on the excuses and subterfuges used to deny such positions to minorities. Of this and other activity there is much to relate that has not yet been told. Nevertheless, the use of the word *seedtime* in the book's title by no means implies that the FEPC was the only force for change. Black activists, CIO unions, radicals, liberal religious groups, other government agencies, and many others, often working with the FEPC, were also part of this wartime movement toward civil rights.

The events leading up to the creation of the President's Committee on Fair Employment Practice (COFEP), the agency's official title during its first two years, have been related many times elsewhere and need restating only briefly. But the acronym COFEP did not stick. Black newspapers often referred to the agency as the "FEP Committee" and the "Labor Board," and by late 1942, occasional reference was made at the White House and the Justice Department to the Fair Employment Practice Committee (FEPC).[18] This last became the committee's official title in May, 1943, when the president abolished the "Old Committee" (COFEP) and created the FEPC or "New Committee" under Executive Order 9346. The committee's formation came after a decade of hope and disappointment over the administration's performance. Although in the 1930s the government put into effect liberal programs that, according to one writer, helped bring about a "New Deal for Blacks," Afro-Americans often experienced bitterness and frustration in dealing with the Congress and the administration. Antilynching and anti–poll tax bills failed to receive official adminis-

18. See memorandum, Jonathan Daniels to Marvin McIntyre, December 14, 1942, in Official File 4246-G, Box 9, Justice Department folder, FDRL, and "Fair Employment Practice Committee" (Typescript, n.d., in Box 45, FEPC, Monsignor Francis J. Haas Papers, Catholic University, Washington, D.C.).

tration support and repeatedly went down to defeat in the face of determined southern opposition.[19]

In addition, no headway was made against segregation in the armed services. During World War I, black soldiers were relegated primarily to segregated common labor. In the postwar years, African-Americans were nearly eliminated from the services. By 1939, there were only 3,645 blacks in the regular army, and the few allowed in the navy served only in the galleys. None were permitted in the marines or air corps. In 1937, the Pittsburgh *Courier* launched a campaign to end segregation in the services. It argued that African-Americans should constitute 10 percent of the forces, and *Courier* editor Robert L. Vann also wanted FDR to appoint two blacks annually to the military academy at West Point. With support from black World War I officers, the Committee for Participation of Negroes in the National Defense was organized in 1938 to seek "a more dignified place in our armed forces" for blacks. World war veterans such as Charles H. Houston, who later served on the FEPC, recounted bitter experiences of unequal treatment during that conflict. The Participation Committee was determined that in future wars the black soldier would have a combat role instead of being confined to labor units.[20]

These and other black leaders sought change through legislation. A law passed by Congress in 1939 authorized the creation of civilian aviation schools to train military pilots under air corps supervision, but the War Department resisted, maintaining that the law authorized but did not direct such enlistments. In 1940, attempts to get congressionally mandated, volunteer, nonsegregated army units also failed. As the presidential election of 1940 approached, segregation in the armed forces became a major issue for Afro-American voters, and the Republican party, eager to recapture those who had been attracted to the New Deal, pledged to end discrimination not only in the armed services but in the civil service and other federal agencies. The Republicans also nominated for the presidency Wendell Willkie, a racial

---

19. Sitkoff, *New Deal for Blacks*, 304–305. For a discussion of the origins of FEPC, see Ruchames, *Race, Jobs, and Politics*, 3–21.

20. Robert L. Vann to the President, January 19, 1939, quoted in Dalfiume, *Desegregation of the Armed Forces*, 21–27, esp. 26; Phillip McGuire, *He, Too, Spoke for Democracy: Judge Hastie, World War II, and the Black Soldier* (Westport, Conn., 1988), 3; Wynn, *Afro-American and the Second World War*, 22.

liberal, attractive to those who later supported the FEPC. Willkie shortly picked up endorsements from some of the black press, including the influential Pittsburgh *Courier*.[21]

As black Democrats worried, the administration by September began orchestrating a series of press releases by the War Department and the White House to reassure Negro voters. Black criticism continued, however, and FDR met on September 27, 1940, with three Afro-American leaders, A. Philip Randolph of the Brotherhood of Sleeping Car Porters (BSCP), Walter White of the National Association for the Advancement of Colored People (NAACP), and T. Arnold Hill of the National Youth Administration (NYA). These men demanded an end to segregation, with blacks integrated throughout the armed forces, but the service chiefs were adamantly opposed to what they regarded as such a revolutionary change.[22]

Other opportunities appeared for the administration to calm black discontent. Through the offices of the liberal southerner Will W. Alexander, the administration discovered that Negro leaders wanted the promotion of Colonel Benjamin O. Davis, a celebrated black career officer who began his career in the Spanish-American War, to the rank of general. They also hoped for the appointment of a black assistant in the office of the secretary of war. Before the election FDR did both, and for good measure he named a black adviser to the Selective Service director. After Davis' promotion to brigadier general, he was assigned to the 9th and 10th Cavalry Regiments with white officers under his command, an action that violated a 1940 War Department memorandum. Judge William H. Hastie became civilian aide to the secretary of war, and Colonel Campbell C. Johnson was named adviser to the director of Selective Service. In addition, the president wrote Randolph, White, and Hill that all the services would be open to Negroes, albeit in segregated units. The Democrats carried the election with votes to spare, but the issue of segregation in the armed forces did not go away. During this time Afro-Americans pursued another major grievance, employment discrimination in the defense industries.[23]

21. Dalfiume, *Desegregation of the Armed Forces*, 28–34.
22. *Ibid.*, 36–40.
23. *Ibid.*, 41–43; Jesse Thomas Moore, Jr., *A Search for Equality: The National Urban League, 1910–1961* (University Park, Pa., 1981), 117; McGuire, *He, Too, Spoke for Democracy*, 10.

While the defense program in the late 1930s brought new jobs for white workers at all levels and skills, black unemployment increased. In May, 1940, FDR set up the National Defense Advisory Commission (NDAC) to oversee defense production. Its Labor Division, headed by Sidney Hillman, with black economist Robert C. Weaver as an assistant, worked diligently against job discrimination but made little progress. Suggestions that industrialists hire black workers were generally ignored. Hillman's attempts to attack the problem through labor leaders in the AFL and the CIO also failed. In January, 1941, Roosevelt abolished the NDAC and created a stronger agency, the Office of Production Management (OPM), which took over Hillman's Labor Division. As complaints of discrimination in defense employment grew louder, Hillman created the Negro Employment and Training Branch, under Weaver, and the Minorities Group Service, headed by Will Alexander.[24]

Meanwhile, black dissatisfaction grew, and Randolph, charismatic president of the BSCP, organized the MOWM. He threatened a massive demonstration in the nation's capital against discrimination in the defense industries and segregation in the armed forces. Such direct action tactics had been used by blacks in local protests during the 1930s, but Randolph's movement involved a mass demonstration of major proportions. It was bold in conception and historic in its ultimate effect. At first leary of such tactics, black leaders such as the NAACP's White eventually endorsed the movement. By March, Randolph announced a date for the march on Washington, D.C.: July 1, 1941. Toward the end of May, as Randolph called for 100,000 participants, the administration became concerned. Having such a demonstration in the nation's capital would be an embarrassment. Roosevelt also feared racial violence. Politically, the march could fracture the Democratic party, whose ranks included both protesting blacks and volatile southern segregationists. The president tried to stop it.[25]

24. National Defense Advisory Commission, press release, October 23, 1940, R45, RG228; Geoffrey Perrett, *Days of Sadness, Years of Triumph: The American People, 1939–1945* (New York, 1973), 148–49; Moore, *Search for Equality*, 90; George Q. Flynn, *The Mess in Washington: Manpower Mobilization in World War II* (Westport Conn., 1979), 5; Carol Riegelman, *Labour Management Cooperation in United States War Production* (Montreal, 1948), Chap. 1; Wynn, *Afro-American and the Second World War*, 44; Gerald D. Nash, *The Great Depression and World War II: Organizing America, 1933–1945* (New York, 1979), 66–70.

25. Meier and Rudwick, "Origins of Non-violent Direct Action," 344; Jervis An-

To demonstrate concern, Roosevelt sent a strong statement to the OPM, praising its work with defense contractors and urging an even greater effort. Discrimination against blacks went on nationwide, and it affected other minority groups. A nation battling totalitarianism could not arbitrarily refuse war work to its own citizens, Roosevelt stated. It must promote unity and build morale "by refuting at home the very theories which we are fighting abroad." The matter was of "grave national importance, and immediate steps" had to be taken to "deal with it effectively." Shortly, administration leaders invited Randolph and White to the White House in an effort to change their minds.[26]

Although the black press welcomed FDR's recognition that blacks were having employment problems, Randolph was bitterly critical of the president. He thought Roosevelt should have spoken out ten months earlier and vowed that the effort to march on Washington would be redoubled. To plead the government's case, the president called in several prominent liberals, but race leaders refused to be dissuaded by Mayor Fiorello LaGuardia, Aubrey Williams, and Eleanor Roosevelt, who met with them on June 13. Finally, on June 18, Randolph and White saw Roosevelt.[27]

The meeting lasted only half an hour, but the group impressed upon the president some significant points. The march was being planned by sober and responsible black leaders, not by elements on the radical fringe. They wanted an executive order denying contracts to companies that discriminated against minorities. Such an order should also instruct government agencies and departments to end their racial bias. In addition, they asked Roosevelt to desegregate the armed forces and to seek from Congress legislation denying access to the NLRB to labor unions that practiced discrimination.[28]

---

derson, *A. Philip Randolph: A Biographical Portrait* (New York, 1972), 248–51; Roi Ottley, *"New World A-Coming": Inside Black America* (Cleveland, 1943), 289; Sitkoff, *New Deal for Blacks*, 317.

26. Memorandum, the President to William Knudson and Sidney Hillman, OPM, June 12, 1941, in Public Relations 5, Final Disposition Report, R45HR, RG 228; Ruchames, *Race, Jobs, and Politics*, 19.

27. Chicago *Defender*, June 21, 1941; Jervis Anderson, *A. Philip Randolph*, 255; Ruchames, *Race, Jobs, and Politics*, 19.

28. Sitkoff, *New Deal for Blacks*, 320; Ruchames, *Race, Jobs, and Politics*, 19–20.

When the meeting ended, Randolph and White began negotiating with the president's representatives. Strongly resisting all the MOWM demands, the administration offered to issue a memorandum instead of an executive order. Randolph and White insisted: without concessions, the march would be held as scheduled. The government offered an executive order prohibiting discrimination in defense industries. When the two men demurred, the administration added the federal agencies. With the omission of desegregating the services, it was only half a loaf, but the black leaders accepted. On the following day Roosevelt signed Executive Order 8802, and Randolph called off the march. The order created the President's Committee on Fair Employment Practice to receive and investigate complaints of discrimination in war industries and in government departments and agencies. For the first time since Reconstruction, the nation had a federal agency devoted exclusively to minority problems. Furthermore, the federal government was now officially involved with discrimination in employment, a matter that would ultimately be established as a civil right.[29]

Among the Afro-American newspapers, only the Pittsburgh *Courier* had attacked Randolph's plan as a "crackpot proposal" from which nothing would be gained. Such marches always failed, it said, because Congress regarded them as "nuisances organized by publicity hounds, job hunters and addelpates . . . [who were] mob minded and misguided." But others had been enthusiastic. Blacks were abandoning "the timid role of Uncle-Tomism no matter what the sacrifice," editorialized the Chicago *Defender*. They would not be satisfied to pray and be "appeased and soothed with vacuous promises." An executive order "should have [been] issued long ago," it insisted. Columnist Charlie Cherokee was certain the march would be a success. The "bandwagon is getting crowded . . . [and] pretty girls selling march buttons are making the colored man on the street march conscious," he noted. Later, after the issuance of Executive Order 8802, cancellation of the march "left things flat," he reported, and the substitute mass meeting "drew only a thousand persons at the Lincoln Memo-

29. Sitkoff, *New Deal for Blacks*, 320; Ruchames, *Race, Jobs, and Politics*, 20; Wynn, *Afro-American and the Second World War*, 46–47; Meier, "Civil Rights Strategies," 184–85.

rial Water Gate," who heard addresses from LaGuardia, Randolph, White, and others.[30]

March supporters were reserved in appraising the president's executive order. Compared with the original MOWM demands, it was disappointing. The Philadelphia *Tribune* wondered how it would be enforced: "There must be forces which make it work." Columnist Marjorie McKenzie believed the enforcement procedures would fail because the committee members would be volunteers without power to hire investigators and there were no punitive clauses to compel compliance. The race was better off with the OPM and Weaver's Negro Employment and Training Branch, she thought. The Chicago *Defender*, disappointed at the executive order's narrow scope and omissions, still struck an optimistic note. Executive Order 8802 was "one of the most significant pronouncements that has been made in the interest of the Negro for more than a century," and the president's action in issuing it was courageous. But for "false leaders" who had misinformed him as to the true "sentiment of the Negro people," he undoubtedly would have acted sooner.[31]

Although proclaimed as a bold new move, Executive Order 8802 was certainly not without precedent. In the 1920s, Massachusetts had prohibited discrimination in the civil service and in public utilities owned by a government. Several New Deal agencies had utilized antibias clauses or interpreted their congressional mandates as requiring nondiscrimination. In 1933 New York State had ordered its public utilities to employ anyone, regardless of race or religion, and the following year Illinois had mandated the inclusion of nondiscrimination clauses in public works contracts. Subsequently, New Jersey and Pennsylvania adopted the Illinois model. New York took further action early in 1941 with the passage of the Mahoney Act. This law made discrimination by public officials or by defense contractors because of race, color, or creed a misdemeanor punishable by fines up to $500. Shortly thereafter, Governor Herbert Lehman appointed a Committee on Discrimination in Employment to operate within the New York State Department of Labor. This body engaged in activity similar to that of the FEPC. Unlike the federal agency, however, the

30. Chicago *Defender*, June 28, 1941, pp. 14, 15, July 12, 1941, p. 15; Pittsburgh *Courier*, June 14, 1941, p. 6.

31. Philadelphia *Tribune*, July 3, 1941, p. 4; Chicago *Defender*, July 5, 1941, p. 1, July 12, 1941, pp. 12, 14.

New York committee had statutory authorization with penalties against violators. In April, 1942, the Mahoney Act was amended to include a wider range of businesses, such as hotels and restaurants, and public places, including beaches.[32]

Nevertheless, with Executive Order 8802 finally in place, black leaders and the press waited expectantly for the appointment of the committee members. These individuals might well determine whether or not the executive order would be workable.

32. Verbatim transcript, committee meeting, May 11, 1942, pp. 5–6, R63HR, Frieda S. Miller, Chairman, Committee on Discrimination in Employment, to Will W. Alexander, May 22, 1941, in Public Relations, OPM, R43HR, and "Power of the President to Issue 9346" (Typescript, n.d., Legal Division, office files of Emanuel H. Bloch, R6HR), all in RG 228; John Beecher, "Problems of Discrimination," *Science and Society,* VII (1943), 44; Kesselman, "Fair Employment Practice Movement," 33–34.

PART I

The Washington Scene

1941–1945

1 / Getting Organized and
Holding Hearings

Although an important victory for the MOWM and black Americans, the creation of the FEPC was only a beginning. Its chairman and four members had to be strong people, and the agency, which lacked enforcement powers, had to become viable. In the ensuing weeks, A. Philip Randolph and Walter White were able to influence the selection of some of the committee members, and they carefully monitored the FEPC's direction and effectiveness. Not all in the black community supported their efforts, however. The Pittsburgh *Courier* had been a constant critic of the MOWM and continued attacking Randolph in subsequent issues. The *Courier* itself claimed credit for Executive Order 8802. The president had yielded, it insisted, not to Randolph's threats but to the long-accumulated pressure of the type exerted by the *Courier* and similarly aroused citizens.[1]

But Randolph and White kept the MOWM intact, dispatched letters and telegrams to the White House, and in a sense negotiated over committee appointments. Five days after Executive Order 8802 was signed, Randolph asked President Roosevelt for a conference. Sidney Hillman, co-director of the OPM, to which the FEPC was attached, met with Randolph and White on July 10. Their first choice for FEPC chairman was Fiorello LaGuardia. Unknown to them, however, the post had already been offered to Mark Ethridge on the advice of

1. Pittsburgh *Courier*, July 5, 1941, p. 6, July 26, 1941, p. 6.

LaGuardia, Hillman, and others at OPM. Born in Mississippi, Ethridge was editor of the Louisville *Courier-Journal*. Widely recognized as a southern liberal, he attended the Southern Conference for Human Welfare at Birmingham in 1938 and was admired by many, though not all, blacks. Lester Granger of the National Urban League had serious reservations about him.[2]

In their meeting with Hillman, the MOWM leaders also discussed the other four committee positions and suggested several names, including two blacks. Although they professed to agree with Hillman's strongly expressed opinion that both the AFL and the CIO must be represented, Randolph and White worried that the two peak federations could dominate a body in which three members constituted a quorum. CIO policies had somewhat mitigated black hostility to organized labor, but most AFL craft unions remained staunchly racist. Randolph and White wanted a seven-member committee that included two blacks. The members should be individuals of national prominence so that the FEPC would command respect. A July 17 amendment to Executive Order 8802 enlarging the committee to five plus the chairman may have been an administration response to their concerns over labor's influence.[3]

By July 18, five members, including the chairman, had been chosen. They were, besides Ethridge, industrialist David Sarnoff of the Radio Corporation of America (RCA), William Green, president of the AFL, and two blacks, Chicago alderman Earl Dickerson and Milton Webster, vice-president of the BSCP-AFL. But a deadlock developed over the labor representation. Green refused to serve unless the CIO sent a delegate of comparable rank. When CIO president Philip Mur-

2. A. Philip Randolph to the President, June 30, 1941, Walter White to the President (telegram), July 8, 1941, Stephen Early to Mark Ethridge, July 9, 1941, and Fiorello LaGuardia to the President, July 18, 1941, all in Official File 4245-G, Box 4, 1941, FDRL; draft of letter to the President to be signed by Randolph and White, July 11, 1941, General Office File FEPC–Transfer and Railroad Hearings, 1941–43, NAACP Records, Manuscript Division, Library of Congress; Wilma Dykeman and James Stokeley, *The Seeds of Southern Change: The Life of Will Alexander* (Chicago, 1962), 256; Moore, *Search for Equality*, 94; George B. Tindall, *The Emergence of the New South, 1913–1945* (Baton Rouge, 1967), 351, 605, 632, 636.

3. Draft of letter to the president, July 11, 1941, memorandum, Charles Fahy, assistant solicitor general, to the Attorney General, July 17, 1941, both in DJ-FOI request, September 15, 1978 (xeroxed copies presently in my possession, to be deposited in Special Collections, Pullen Library, Georgia State University).

ray finally accepted, the representation included labor, blacks, a southerner, and an industrialist of Jewish background who allegedly spoke
for business and ethnic groups. Some undoubtedly were pleased that
one member, Murray, was a Roman Catholic. Having two blacks on
the committee, both with strong civil rights backgrounds, was significant. Subsequently, Murray named John Brophy as his alternate to
the FEPC, and Green appointed Frank Fenton. Brophy had begun in
the labor. movement with the United Mine Workers (UMW), and
Fenton had served as director of organization at AFL headquarters.
Both men later became permanent members.[4]

While Randolph and White could feel some satisfaction with their
efforts, the FEPC appointments brought mixed reactions from the
black press. The organized labor appointees drew caustic comments
from the Pittsburgh *Courier*, which charged Hillman with sabotage in
loading the FEPC with subservient labor leaders and stooges who
would smother investigations and stall remedial measures. Green, it
charged, had "on every occasion ducked and evaded the issue of color
discrimination" in the AFL. Although FDR could have done better
than Mark Ethridge as chairman, the paper continued, the other
choices were excellent. But Ethridge had black support from other
sources. The Chicago *Defender* described him as an "able, brave, stubborn man" with a "reputation of militant liberalism . . . a friend of
the Negro."[5]

When the President's Committee met late in July, the members
may have been "a little at sea as to what they were supposed to do."
At first, they concentrated on administrative organization, a matter
of considerable interest to the OPM's Hillman, Weaver, and Alexander, who attended as observers. The OPM delegation learned that the
FEPC, which was attached administratively to the OPM, was determined to remain operationally independent of that body. The FEPC
would, however, rely on the OPM staff for its investigations, a decision opposed by black committee members, who wanted separate
FEPC regional offices and personnel.[6]

4. Memorandum, LaGuardia to the President, July 18, 1941, draft of letter to the
president, July 11, 1941, both in DJ-FOI; Pittsburgh *Courier*, July 12, 1941, p. 5;
Lawrence Cramer to Mark Ethridge, September 9, 1941, in Public Relations 5, Ethridge file, R45HR, RG 228; Ruchames, *Race, Jobs, and Politics*, 25, 74.
5. Pittsburgh *Courier*, July 19, 1941, p. 1, July 26, 1941, p. 6; Chicago *Defender*,
July 26, 1941, p. 15, August 2, 1941, p. 3; Philadelphia *Tribune*, July 24, 1941, p. 1.
6. Milton Webster to A. P. Tureaud, July 26, 1941, Box 18, BSCP Papers; Chi-

Because the committee members were part-time appointees, hiring an executive secretary to direct operations was essential. The Pittsburgh *Courier* wanted an Afro-American, and Earl Dickerson nominated Howard University Law School dean George M. Johnson, a University of California at Berkeley graduate also supported by White. Believing that a black would have difficulty working with "lily-white" government agencies, the committee, on August 12, chose Lawrence W. Cramer, former governor of the Virgin Islands. Cramer was born in New Orleans and educated in Wisconsin. A handsome, persuasive man "who talked good liberal sense," Cramer to some was a martyr figure, having resigned as governor over the construction of public housing that lacked plumbing facilities. He proved to be a low-key, talented organizer who in the initial months made important contacts with government departments and agencies, kept communications open with civil rights organizations, and presided over the recruitment of staff. After some delay, Johnson became assistant executive secretary in November. As second in command, he attended the committee meetings and exerted much influence over the development of staff functions.[7]

The FEPC needed people with special competencies in the law, in research, and in public and labor relations. As the staff grew, it had an interracial mix reflecting the spirit of the executive order. Idealism and dedication were also important, because the task of challenging union leaders and employers, who were often hostile and prejudiced, could be unpleasant. Assembling a staff took weeks, during which time the black press speculated over individuals who might get positions. Staff appointments were vital to the black community because they provided both input into the FEPC's program and intelligence on its operations. Consequently, while favoring racial balance, blacks fought hard to get positions at every level. The committee initially attracted candidates from labor and civil rights organizations, col-

cago *Defender*, August 2, 1941, p. 1; Philadelphia *Courier*, August 2, 1941, pp. 1, 4; interview with Clarence Mitchell, Washington, D.C., August 24, 1978.

7. Verbatim transcript, committee meeting, July 6, 1942, pp. 42–44, R63HR, Public Relations 5, Cramer file, 45HR, "Official Steps Taken on Discrimination" (Typescript carbon, n.d., in office files of Frank D. Reeves, Defense Training Program, R7HR), all in RG 228; Pittsburgh *Courier*, August 9, 1941, pp. 1, 6; Chicago *Defender*, October 25, 1941, p. 8, January 3, 1942, p. 9; Jonathan Daniels, *White House Witness, 1942–1945* (New York, 1975), 18.

leges, law schools, and the press. Committee members made suggestions, but Cramer relied heavily on Walter White, who quickly established a first-name relationship with Cramer and Chairman Ethridge. Besides George Johnson, White suggested G. James Fleming III, a member of a respected Philadelphia family and a Republican. Formerly managing editor of the Philadelphia *Tribune*, Fleming had authored a manuscript on the Negro press for the Gunnar Myrdal study of American race relations.[8]

Early in 1942, two white southerners, John Beecher and Ernest Trimble, joined the staff. Beecher, an Alabama native and descendent of Harriet Beecher Stowe, strongly advocated social justice for minorities. After taking undergraduate and graduate degrees at the Universities of Alabama and Wisconsin, he supervised migratory labor camps for blacks and advised the Resettlement Administration on labor relations. He had served as an editorial writer for the liberal Birmingham *Age-Herald* and came to the FEPC from the OPM's Labor Division. Trimble, whose family also had abolitionist roots, left the faculty of the University of Kentucky Law School for FEPC field work. Other staff members reflected the ethnic, racial, and professional dimensions of the FEPC's activity. They included four black professionals: Theodore Jones, a certified public accountant from Chicago who became the committee's administrative officer; Maceo Hubbard, a Savannah, Georgia, native with a Harvard University law degree; Clarence M. Mitchell, graduate of the University of Minnesota School of Journalism who had been born in Maryland; and Elmer W. Henderson, an instructor in social anthropology at Dillard University in New Orleans. Also recruited were Jewish educator and social worker Harry I. Barron of Chicago, CIO organizer Daniel Donovan, and anthropologist Dr. Ruth Landes of New York.[9]

8. Walter White to Lawrence Cramer, August 22, 1941, General Office File, FEPC-Gen., 1941, NAACP Records; Lawrence Cramer to Mark Ethridge, August 27, 1941, Ethridge file, Walter White to Mark Ethridge, July 25, 1941, and Lawrence Cramer to Walter White, August 24, 1941, White file, Public Relations 5, all in R45HR, RG 228; Philadelphia *Tribune*, July 14, 1941, p. 3, September 13, 1941, p. 5; Mark Ethridge to Milton Webster (telegram), August 3, 1941, in Box 18, BSCP Papers; Myrdal, *American Dilemma*, xi.

9. Victor Rotnem to Francis Haas, January 3, 1943, Organization Table and Vitae, n.d., both in Box 45, FEPC, Haas Papers; FEPC release, January 31, 1942, in Official File 4245-G, January–July, 1942, Box 4, FDRL; Records of George M. Johnson, director of personnel, Confidential file, Legal Division, R5HR, RG 228; General Office

The FEPC also used the specialists in the Labor Division. Assembled primarily by Weaver and Alexander, these people served the FEPC mainly as field investigators. The mixed racial and ethnic character of the committee's work force often startled official, segregated Washington, D.C., while in the field, especially in the South, FEPC investigators bore insults and sometimes faced physical danger. Blacks worked both as chiefs and as Indians. White secretaries typed letters for black supervisors who also directed the work of white professionals. In the South, one FEPC regional office ignored local custom by utilizing black professionals and clerks in racially mixed work situations. According to an Afro-American professional who had a white supervisor and who supervised a biracial staff, lines of authority were often hazy even though civil service classifications denoted rank.[10]

By late August, the FEPC, under Cramer's guidance, was getting organized. First, however, Cramer had to reassure Randolph and White that the agency would remain independent. Although the executive order put the committee under the OPM, Cramer wrote that "in matters of policy determination and public relations, it was independent of any control . . . except [by] the President himself." Procedural and administrative matters such as budgets and personnel management had to clear through the OPM, but the FEPC's budget would not be part of Hillman's Labor Division. The FEPC shared physical facilities with the OPM, but it was not an administrative arm of that agency. In view of subsequent FEPC struggles with the bureaucracy, its independence was of utmost importance.[11]

Obviously, from its creation the FEPC was an administrative hybrid with serious innate weaknesses, as Cramer's letter to Randolph and White revealed. Worse, the agency, created by executive order under the president's war powers, rested on a shaky foundation, for it was without specific congressional authorization and funding. In begin-

---

File, FEPC branch material, 1941–43, in Box 252, NAACP Records; Pittsburgh *Courier*, November 15, 1941, p. 1.

10. Interview with Clarence Mitchell; interview with John Hope II, Washington, D.C., September 7, 1978; Lewis O. Padgett to Elmer L. Irey, January 14, 1944, in U.S. Govt., Gen., N–Z, R67HR, RG 228; Philadelphia *Tribune*, July 17, 1941, p. 3; Chicago *Defender*, April 29, 1944, in Newspaper Clippings, RG 228.

11. A. Philip Randolph and Walter White to FEPC, August 7, 1941, Lawrence Cramer to Walter White and A. Philip Randolph, August 14, 1941, both in Public Relations 5, White file, R45HR, RG 228.

ning its operations, the FEPC had few bureaucratic precedents to follow, with the possible exception of the NLRB, which, among its procedures, had guidelines for handling complaints of unfair labor practices on a case-by-case approach. Weaver's Negro Training Branch in the OPM, on whose investigative staff the FEPC would rely, worked against job discrimination on a plant- or industry-wide basis. Then, too, the fledgling agency, already operating in new and unfamiliar territory, was staffed generally by outsiders who would have to pick up on their own skills and competence in government service. Against these drawbacks the FEPC's greatest asset was a small but enthusiastic political constituency, and support for its program would grow until the end of the war.[12]

In beginning its work, the FEPC first asked for support from the nation's two major business groups, the National Association of Manufacturers (NAM) and the Chamber of Commerce. NAM president Walter D. Fuller was an outspoken critic of job discrimination. In his commencement address the previous June to graduates of black Lincoln University, Fuller advocated the use of quotas in hiring. Furthermore, the NAM's August newsletter urged the avoidance of "arbitrary prejudice in employment." The chamber, though, displayed no interest. While advocating the use of all available labor and materials in the defense effort, it did not get involved in racial or religious matters. With some exasperation, Cramer reported to Ethridge that the chamber favored using all manpower but would "not take the steps to make that policy effective," and asked the chairman, "Do you have any suggestions?" Having received complaints against several AFL unions, Cramer also asked for help from its president, committee member Green, who agreed to cooperate. The FEPC had no reports of discrimination in the CIO.[13]

In government agencies and departments, racist practices had always existed and had even worsened during the Wilson administration. Bypassing individual agencies, Cramer went to the Council of Personnel Administration, comprised of departmental and agency

12. For a discussion of the origins and purposes of legal agencies, see James Willard Hurst, *Law and Social Order in the United States* (Ithaca, 1977), 82–154.

13. Walter D. Fuller to Lawrence Cramer, August 26, 1941, NAM file, Lawrence Cramer to Mark Ethridge, August 26, 1941, Ethridge file, both in Public Relations 5, R45HR, and Albert Hawkes to Lawrence Cramer, September 29, 1941, Lawrence Cramer to Mark Ethridge, October 7, 1941, both in U.S. Govt., Gen., N–Z, R67HR, all in RG 228.

heads dealing with personnel policy. The council believed that the executive order covered "discrimination [primarily] in defense industries," not in the government. When Cramer strongly disagreed, the council recommended that a letter be prepared for the president's signature, directing each department and agency to take "effective action to eliminate discrimination in the government service." Whether the council made the suggestion seriously is unknown, but Cramer endorsed the idea and persuaded the White House to cooperate. The directive went to thirty-two federal departments and agencies on September 7. Armed with it and the executive order, both evidence of presidential intent, the committee could move persuasively against discrimination in the government. Establishing itself in the bureaucracy was basic to the FEPC's operations. Given its weaknesses, it had to depend heavily on other agencies and departments to enforce Executive Order 8802 in both the public and private sectors. FDR's letter, one of the few examples of positive White House support, gave it a real boost.[14]

Cramer next turned to the major procurement agencies. By fall, 1941, the War Department, the Navy Department, and the Maritime Commission were handling hundreds of millions of dollars in defense contracts, which under the executive order had to contain nondiscrimination clauses. So also had untold numbers of subcontracts involving defense- or war-related work. By 1944, for example, out of $315.0 billion in military contracts, the War Department had $179.9 billion and Navy $83.9 billion. Getting the three procurement agencies to enforce the executive order through the contract system became one of Cramer's priorities. The procurement agencies needed to notify defense contractors about the nondiscrimination policy, Cramer wrote Chairman Ethridge. "If I can succeed in this effort, it may [even] get at the problem of reducing discrimination" under contracts negotiated prior to the issuance of the executive order. If he failed, he pointed out, it might become necessary to ask the president to instruct the agencies by letter.[15]

14. FDR to Mark Ethridge, September 3, 1941, Mark Ethridge to the President, September 26, 1941, FDR file, Lawrence Cramer to Mark Ethridge, August 26, 1941, Ethridge file, all in Public Relations 5, R45HR, RG 228; "Official Steps Taken on Discrimination"; Pittsburgh *Courier,* September 6, 1941, p. 1; Davis, "Non-discrimination in the Federal Agencies," 69.

15. A. C. Koistinen, "Mobilizing the World War II Economy: Labor and the Industrial Military Alliance," *Pacific Historical Review,* XLII (1973), 446; Lawrence

Cramer learned from the procurement agencies that the nondiscrimination clause had been incorporated into most of the agreements. Only a few in the War Department did not carry the clause: those that had been substantially negotiated on June 27 when the executive order was issued and could not be renegotiated without delay in defense production; those for which competitive bids had been submitted before June 27; and those negotiated or advertised before War Department instructions to include the clause had been received by the contracting officers. The nondiscrimination clause, already included in certain types of subcontracts, would be applied to all of these as well. The procurement agencies also agreed to notify the FEPC if local or state legislation or police regulations required contractors to engage in discriminatory practices. Having anticipated resistance, Cramer must have felt considerable satisfaction over what had been accomplished. In the War Department, future liaisons with the FEPC would be handled by the black civilian aide Judge William Hastie, appointed by Roosevelt in October, 1940, in response to complaints of discrimination against Afro-Americans in the segregated army. Cramer hoped for the appointment of comparable officials in other agencies. In view of the role of affirmative action officers put in place decades later, the suggestion was prophetic.[16]

Having touched base with the procurement agencies, Cramer next turned to the problem of enforcement. With no staff and with the budget still under negotiation, the FEPC was powerless to carry out the presidential mandate, but alternatives were available. In establishing enforcement procedures, Cramer informed Walter White, the FEPC would use all existing government agencies "in making primary contacts with employers . . . [and] where the agencies [met] with definite refusal to comply" and exhausted all means of gaining compliance, the committee would act "as a final Board of Appeals" and hold hearings in areas where evidence of noncompliance existed. The

Cramer to Mark Ethridge, August 19, 1941, in Public Relations 5, Ethridge file, R45HR, RG 228.

16. Lawrence Cramer to Assistant Secretary of War Robert Patterson, August 22, 1941, Lawrence Cramer to Wade H. Skinner, assistant general counsel, U.S. Maritime Commission, August 25, 1941, Cramer to Ethridge, August 26, 27, 1941, all in Public Relations 5, Ethridge file, R45HR, Robert Patterson to Lawrence Cramer, August 26, 1941, U.S. Govt., WD, M–W, and Robert Patterson to Chiefs of All Supply Arms and Services, September 24, 1941, U.S. Govt., WD, A–L, both in R67HR, all in RG 228.

committee at its August 11 meeting decided to act as a board of review to hear cases certified to it by the Labor Division. Cramer asked War Department, Navy Department, and Maritime Commission officials to remind the major contractors of Executive Order 8802. The War Department agreed, but Assistant Secretary of the Navy Ralph Bard, reluctant to get involved with enforcement, thought the FEPC should handle the letters. The Navy Department considered the matter for several weeks. By October, Bard announced that his office had contacted all businesses with contracts amounting to $1 million or more, informing them of the executive order.[17]

The contracting agencies could help the FEPC in other ways. They possessed extensive employment statistics, and if such data were made available, the FEPC thought, it might be able to discover patterns of discrimination. The agencies had procurement officers throughout the nation in constant contact with defense industries and other contractors. These people possessed information useful to the committee. Furthermore, Cramer knew that under certain conditions government contracts could be terminated for cause. He explored all of these possibilities in seeking ways to enforce Executive Order 8802. He was disappointed to learn, however, that defense contracts could not be voided because of discrimination. Even the agencies themselves were considerably restricted when contract termination was involved. According to Assistant Secretary Robert Patterson, War Department contracts had clauses giving the government the right of termination only for default in deliveries. In some cases they provided for liquidation damages. So there would be no misunderstanding by the FEPC as to the powers of the War Department, Patterson stressed the limited character of the government's right of termination. Presumably the Navy Department and the Maritime Commission operated under similar restraints.[18]

Cramer found the procurement agencies willing to provide the FEPC with employment statistics. Navy readily supplied information

17. Cramer to Ethridge, August 19, 21, 26, 1941, Cramer to Patterson, August 22, 1941, Ethridge file, Lawrence Cramer to Walter White, August 14, 1941, White file, all in Public Relations 5, R45HR, Ralph Bard to Lawrence Cramer, September 3, 1941, and Ralph Bard to Mark Ethridge, October 8, 1941, both in U.S. Govt., ND, R67HR, all in RG 228.

18. Patterson to Cramer, August 26, 1941, in U.S. Govt., WD, M–W, R67HR, RG 228.

on the total number of employees and the number of blacks working in the navy yards. It also furnished a detailed breakdown of the skilled and semiskilled occupations of black navy yard workers at Philadelphia, Norfolk, Washington, D.C., and New York. Finally, Cramer succeeded in getting somewhat grudging recognition of the FEPC as a board of appeals. Although Bard cautioned that his field inspectors did not try to determine who should be employed by defense contractors, the assistant secretary finally agreed to notify the FEPC when Navy's officers received formal complaints of discrimination. In October, Bard forwarded to Ethridge summaries of five such documents. Cramer's discussions and ad hoc agreements with the various contracting agencies could not guarantee total enforcement of Executive Order 8802, but they did provide the FEPC with a presence in the bureaucracy. It was one of Cramer's many accomplishments as chief operations officer. As time passed, the FEPC through similar arrangements would extend itself into many other areas.[19]

Meanwhile, contact was made with the New York Committee on Discrimination in Employment, set up under the Mahoney Act four months before the FEPC was created. The two agencies, besides their interest in discrimination, shared David Sarnoff, who served in both. The FEPC believed the work should be coordinated to avoid duplication, but a September 10 meeting among Ethridge, Cramer, and Frieda Miller, New York State's industrial commissioner, seemed to put the two agencies at cross purposes. Miller's committee planned to stress education and persuasion. Complaints would be investigated only in unusual cases and then by private agencies such as the NAACP or various Jewish organizations. Cramer demurred. Private groups, he thought, should refrain from investigating discrimination until the government gave the go ahead. Miller stressed instead government's role as mediator. Using the conference method, a government agency should have no commitment to any group. If mediation failed, then the case would be referred to the FEPC. Despite differences, the conferees did agree to consult and avoid a duplication of effort and the harassment of employers. Subsequently, Cramer requested the Labor Division in the OPM to communicate with the New

19. Patterson to Cramer, August 26, 1941, in U.S. Govt., WD, M–W, Charles Piozet, Navy Department director of personnel, to Lawrence Cramer, September 24, 1941, and Ralph Bard to Mark Ethridge, October 13, 1941, both in U.S. Govt., ND, all in R67HR, RG 228.

York committee before investigating any complaints. In time, the committee began turning over cases to the FEPC for investigation.[20]

The first four months, from July through October, were most difficult, and the FEPC's staff had to function in deplorable physical surroundings. Black columnist Charley Cherokee, visiting the offices early in October, noted the absence of "filing cabinets, few desks, insufficient space"; the place was "overrun with mail, complaints and job seekers." In this confusion sat Executive Secretary Cramer "trying to talk to visitors, take telephone calls, interview job seekers, hear complaints, answer mail." There was no privacy. "Cramer in the presence of visitors [referred] to various members of the committee as 'prima donnas.'" Cherokee, often irreverent, also had observations about committee members who came to the central office, "talk[ed] big and stir[red] things up a little and [left] for home again." Because "everybody with a real complaint or an axe to grind [was] saying COFEP [FEPC] is a farce and only lollygagging," Cherokee thought the agency should avoid making the same mistake that the OPM's Robert Weaver had. Weaver had worked hard and had made "history-making gains for Negro skilled labor" but lost face with the public by "making grand optimistic announcements . . . every time three or four colored workers [were] hired or promised a job in a plant of 20,000 workers." Cramer's political sense sometimes led him in the opposite direction: caution and expedience. Addressing the National Urban League's Green Pastures Camp in Milwaukee, he told the group not "to have anyone become overenthusiastic relative to the results" that the FEPC might achieve. Milwaukee was the home of the Heil Company, which employed two blacks as janitors. Julius Heil was also the governor of Wisconsin. Privately, Cramer told James W. Dorsey, vice-president of the Milwaukee NAACP, that the FEPC would probably avoid the Heil situation because of its delicate nature.[21]

20. Lawrence Cramer to John Habbarton, August 20, 1941, summary of meeting in Commissioner Miller's office, September 10, 1941, Lawrence Cramer to Will Alexander and Robert Weaver, September 18, 1941, Victor Einach to Daniel Donovan, April 23, 1942, all in Public Relations 5, Committee on Discrimination in Employment, R45HR, and Cramer to Ethridge, August 27, 1941, Reports, N–Z, R48HR, all in RG 228. See also Dominic J. Capeci, Jr., "Wartime Fair Employment Practices Committees: The Governor's Committee and the First FEPC in New York City, 1941–1943," *Afro-Americans in New York Life and History,* IX (1985), 45–63.

21. Charley Cherokee, "National Grapevine," Chicago *Defender,* September 13,

Despite frustration in the black community over a perceived lack of progress, much had been accomplished. Working quietly, Cramer had established channels of communication with the three most important defense agencies in the government. Using the prestige of a presidential letter, the FEPC had also put the entire bureaucracy on notice that discrimination in employment violated national policy. Cramer's plan of operation, using presidential influence here and the personnel of other agencies somewhere else, employing persuasion and sometimes mild threats of exposure, had established a pattern that the FEPC utilized throughout its existence. Taking the next step, the committee and staff began preparing for a series of public hearings that would publicize the widespread discrimination existing in the nation's defense industries.

FEPC members were divided on holding hearings and disagreed over the seriousness of discrimination and how the problem should be approached. Possibly none of the white members except the CIO's John Brophy appreciated the depth of discrimination that existed and the difficulty of the FEPC's task. Chairman Mark Ethridge, a gradualist in race relations, opposed activity that moved ahead of public opinion. He believed that race relations would improve only over time and through education. Government could not legislate an end to segregation and should not attempt to do so. Based on his experience in the Louisville area, Ethridge could foresee few problems for the FEPC to solve. Only a few investigators would be needed to do the job, he concluded, and these would tackle only difficult situations that the OPM could not adjust. Additionally, the FEPC should avoid publicity because public attention would simply stir up opposition to its work. "I think we can be constructive without being spectacular or without harassment," he wrote Walter White in August. "You who have been in this work so long, must know that . . . the threat of force" will set back the Afro-American's cause.[22]

The two blacks on the President's Committee, Earl Dickerson and

---

1941, p. 15, October 4, 1941, p. 15; William V. Kelley to Lawrence Cramer, September 22, 1941, in Public Relations 5, K file, R43HR, RG 228.

22. Mark Ethridge to Walter White, August 30, 1941, White file, Lawrence Cramer to Mark Ethridge, August 24, 1941, and Lawrence Cramer to Walter White, September 19, 1941, White file, all in Public Relations 5, R45HR, RG 228; Polenberg, *War and Society*, 119–20.

Milton Webster, were southern born and liberal like Ethridge, but the difference between their liberalism and his was as pronounced as the difference in their races. Webster, a tall, blunt-speaking, self-educated former Pullman porter, rose from obscure origins in Tennessee to become vice-president of the BSCP and a leader in the Chicago Republican organization. Dickerson migrated with his family from Mississippi, served overseas as a lieutenant during World War I, took a law degree at the University of Chicago, became a leader in the Chicago Urban League, and in 1933 accepted an appointment as assistant attorney general for the northern Illinois district. In 1939, Dickerson won election to the post of Chicago alderman despite a reputation for being overly intellectual and too independent; he was judged a maverick undeserving of Democratic party support. Unlike most black elected officials, he was also uncompromising on the issue of racial advancement and often crossed swords with Mayor Edward Kelly and his political machine. By one account he was appointed to the committee "as a favor to the Chicago Democratic organization which wanted him out of its hair." With this background, Dickerson joined the President's Committee determined to do battle against job discrimination.[23]

Dickerson and Webster would attack job discrimination frontally. According to them, if quiet persuasion failed, the FEPC should publicly embarrass employers and order them to take affirmative action. Whether Dickerson was the first to propose public hearings, as he claimed, is uncertain, but early in September he persuaded the committee to schedule three, in Los Angeles, Chicago, and New York. As a subcommittee of one, he went to Los Angeles and directed the preparations. Meanwhile, Walter White instructed the NAACP in Los Angeles to render all assistance possible: "Gather . . . exact and spe-

23. Verbatim transcript, committee meeting, May 11, 1942, R63HR, RG 228; interview with Earl B. Dickerson, Chicago, December 11, 1978; Garfinkel, *When Negroes March*, 64–65, 73–74; Sitkoff, *New Deal for Blacks*, 322; Christopher Reed, "Black Chicago Political Realignment During the Depression and New Deal," *Illinois Historical Journal*, LXXVIII (1985), 246, 253–54. See also Arvarh E. Strickland, *History of the Chicago Urban League* (Urbana, 1966), 142, and William H. Harris, *Keeping the Faith: A. Philip Randolph, Milton P. Webster, and the Brotherhood of Sleeping Car Porters, 1925–37* (Urbana, 1977), 40. A more complete vita on Dickerson appears in FBI file 101–76, Chicago, February 9, 1942, in Public Relations 5, Dickerson file, R45HR, RG 228.

cific information so as to have it ready for presentation to the Committee when the hearings begin. . . . Wherever possible, please have the information put in affidavit form." White also asked Los Angeles to help the San Diego NAACP get prepared. "I fear that some of the members . . . [there] have been taken in by Consolidated [Aircraft] and have defended the company because it hired a few Negroes as janitors." The FEPC's Eugene Davidson was placed in charge of the Los Angeles investigation, with staff support from Guy T. Nunn and Clarence Johnson of the OPM's regional minority branch. Later, in preparation for the New York hearing, the NAACP instructed local branches to investigate complaints through their labor and industry committees. White suggested that if defense industries or defense training classes in the area had no complaints but there was reason to believe discrimination existed, qualified blacks should apply for jobs and if refused, then enter a complaint and send it to the NAACP central office. Very early, the FEPC received active support in its work from a network of private organizations, initially black ones and ultimately white and biracial ones.[24]

Complaints of job discrimination in west coast defense industries were legion. Boeing Aircraft in Seattle refused to hire skilled minority workers. In defending itself, Boeing cited its contract with Local 751 of the International Association of Machinists (IAM): "It is our understanding that only those of the Caucasian Race are acceptable to the IAM." Early in September, Lawrence Cramer sent the Seattle complaint to the AFL's William Green without result. A letter from U.S. senator William Wallgren and a War Department directive to Boeing brought additional pressure, but Local 751 remained evasive. The union would "cooperate . . . in all policies which will promote the national defense program . . . insofar as workers eligible to membership . . . are concerned." Noting that the contract preceded Executive Order 8802 and would not expire until July, 1942, union officials

24. Frank D. Reeves, NAACP legal assistant, to D. J. Henderson, East Orange, N.J., NAACP, January 22, 1942, in General Office File, FEPC–New Jersey, 1942–43, NAACP Records; press release, Division of Field Operations, office files of Eugene Davidson, Newspapers, R77HR, verbatim transcript, committee meeting, A.M., January 23, 1942, pp. 27–28, R64HR, and Walter White to Thomas Griffith, Jr., September 3, 1941, Cramer to White, September 19, 1941, both in Public Relations 5, White file, R45HR, all in RG 228; Chicago *Defender*, September 6, 1941, p. 3; Pittsburgh *Courier*, September 20, 1941, p. 1.

proclaimed the legality and inviolability of both the contract and their own procedures.[25]

Pressed further by Boeing, the union leaders elaborated. They would not "accept into membership individuals or groups . . . whom they sincerely and honestly felt [would] not tend to promote or perpetuate harmonious relationships with employers . . . or whose membership might destroy the integral functions of our local lodges." There was a veiled threat to disrupt production if Boeing attempted to hire non-Caucasians. Following Pearl Harbor, Local 751 shifted tactics and began attacking Asiatics. Societies of American-born Japanese were attempting to get jobs for their members, the union charged, and causing great concern among employees. Union procedures would not change to show preference for any minority. If ethnic or religious groups succeeded in forcing their way into the aircraft industry, production would be hampered, went the union line of reasoning. IAM policies at Boeing and also in the San Francisco shipyards thus could not be resolved even in the midst of a national emergency. The FEPC referred the cases to the president, who summoned international union officers to Washington, D.C., and directed them to allow the hiring of qualified black workers in the shipyards and aircraft plants. They complied, ordering two west coast lodges to issue work permits, but blacks still could not join the union.[26]

Meanwhile, the FEPC prepared for the Los Angeles hearing scheduled for October 20 and 21. The committee wanted to get a broad picture of good and bad employment practices and to avoid making accusations of discrimination. Nevertheless, testimony by witnesses revealed shocking evidence of bias. David Coleman of B'nai B'rith reported that Jewish, Portuguese, Afro-American and Mexican-American youth could not find employment in the aircraft industries

25. Jack Steinberg to Boeing Aircraft, June 28, 1941, Boeing Aircraft to Jack Steinberg, July 10, 1941, Bernard E. Squires to President Roosevelt, September 22, 1941, Robert Weaver to Sidney Hillman, September 29, 1941, G. R. Cotton to Boeing Aircraft, October 10, 1941, Closed Cases Referred to Washington Office, A–E, all in F107FR, RG 228.

26. Malcolm MacLean to the President, May 12, 1942, in Public Relations 5, FDR file, R45HR, Boeing Aircraft to Aeronautical Industrial District Lodge #751 (IAM), October 14, 1941, G. R. Cotton to Boeing Aircraft, October 15, 1941, statement by G. R. Cotton, January 16, 1942, Closed Cases Referred to Washington Office, A–E, in F107FR, and hearing, Cook County Plumbers' Union, p. 8, R18HR, all in RG 228; John Beecher, "8802 Blues," New Republic, February 22, 1943, p. 249.

and faced discrimination even in government vocational training programs. The California State Employment Service accepted biased orders from employers, and its interviewers were brutally direct: "You're Jewish, aren't you? . . . Come back in a couple of weeks." Employers took advantage of the second-generation American rule, which required that both parents had to have been born in the United States. This hiring practice adversely affected Jews, Poles, Czechs, Russians, Orientals, and Mexican-Americans, both directly and indirectly. For example, a mechanical training school refused to enroll Jews because of the difficulty in placing them after graduation.[27]

Aircraft industry spokesmen squirmed under tough committee questioning. Vultee Aircraft's industrial relations manager, W. Gerard Tuttle, was particularly vulnerable to criticism. In August, 1940, Tuttle had informed the National Negro Congress that company policy excluded "people other than of the Caucasian Race." A year later, he refused to employ fifteen blacks as janitors. Two weeks before the Los Angeles hearing, however, he told OPM investigator Clarence Johnson that Vultee's policy had changed, but he refused to provide a plan to implement nondiscrimination. Not a single black worked among the company's 6,000 employees, so committee members found Tuttle's assurances unconvincing. Earl Dickerson wanted to know why Vultee asked job applicants about their religion. Tuttle said he thought it was necessary "to know as much about an individual as we can," though he claimed that Vultee never used the information. David Sarnoff seemed mystified: if it conveyed nothing, as Tuttle stated, then it should not be asked, and if it did have some sort of meaning for the company, what was it? The AFL's Frank Fenton thought he saw the real purpose. Companies sometimes tried to separate workers by religious faith as a means of fighting unions, a charge Tuttle vigorously denied. In exasperation, Milton Webster asked if the FEPC could now announce, in view of Tuttle's statements, that Vultee had no restrictions on race. Tuttle remained evasive.[28]

Throughout the hearing, AFL unions generally took a drubbing,

27. Testimony of David Coleman, Los Angeles hearing, R18HR, RG 228; Ruchames, *Race, Jobs and Politics*, 27–28.

28. W. Gerard Tuttle to National Negro Congress, August 2, 1940, quoted in *Proceedings*, October 20, 1941, p. 21, R18HR, testimony of C. A. Pearl, Los Angeles hearing, 75–76, R18HR, and testimony of W. Gerard Tuttle, 479–517, Los Angeles hearing, R19HR, both in RG 228.

and Fenton became increasingly defensive. He opposed the introduction of testimony against the machinists' union by the Seattle Urban League because Boeing Aircraft was not invited to appear, even though earlier he had not challenged testimony against a company whose union was not notified of the hearing. When a witness stated that CIO longshoremen accepted blacks and related how a white member had been suspended for refusing to work with a "Negro brother," Fenton demanded that the testimony be stricken from the record on the grounds that the committee should hear only complaints of discrimination. Over Earl Dickerson's objection, Ethridge ruled that the FEPC accepted as fact that all unions were open to blacks unless proven otherwise.[29]

There were other flareups between Dickerson and the chairman. The black Chicagoan, who approached the hearing as a trial lawyer would, often pressed witnesses with determined single-mindedness and copious, time-consuming reiteration. Concerned about the way businesses handled job interviews, he tried to find out the regional origins of company interviewers, particularly whether they were southerners. Mark Ethridge, who saw no value in reviewing the interviewers, became annoyed. Dickerson continued, making the point that blacks and whites were "working around places together and getting along pretty well together." Ethridge did not believe the President's Committee "ought to go into that." Dickerson strongly disagreed: "This is an educational session, [so] we ought to be able to educate them." Ethridge shot back, "Let me give you a little education. I want to put on the record the fact that Indiana has the largest membership of the Klu [sic] Klux Klan" in the United States. Dickerson thought that the chairman appeared to be "answering my statement about prejudice."[30]

Except for sloppy staff work by FEPC investigator Eugene Davidson, who presented witnesses possessing no direct knowledge of the facts, at times seemed inattentive, repeated questions already asked, and occasionally had to be told by the chairman to stick to the facts and not to interpret, the Los Angeles hearing was a success. The black press was delighted. "AFL 'Color Clause' Exposed; California hearing

29. Testimonies of Bert H. Corona, longshoreman, and B. E. Squires, Seattle Urban League, October 21, 1941, Los Angeles hearing, R19HR, RG 228.

30. Testimony of A. M. Rochlan, 187–216, and testimony of Leland R. Taylor, 267, both in Los Angeles hearing, R18HR, RG 228.

reveals union discrimination," shouted the headlines from the Pittsburgh *Courier*. The *Defender* emphasized industry's shortcomings:
"Big Business Trembles During Los Angeles Hearing; coast probe
shows bias in defense training." Among the aircraft manufacturers,
only Lockheed Aircraft Corporation emerged unscathed. Without
government prompting, Lockheed on its own initiative began recruiting blacks. Later, in a special December press release, Ethridge com-
mended Lockheed for its "sympathetic and intelligent program of
eliminating discrimination." Although employers like Lockheed were
praised, violators yet received no reprimands. Instead, the FEPC
merely recommended that the business community end discrimination. In future hearings, however, it would begin singling out violators, citing specific abuses.[31]

In addition to racial discrimination, the Los Angeles hearing also
uncovered a preference by defense contractors for Protestant employees. But religious job discrimination did not have the impact in the
West, which, with the exception of Mexican-Americans, had few ethnic Catholics and fewer Jews, that it had in the Northeast, where two-
thirds of the population of New York City alone consisted of blacks,
Jews, and ethnic Europeans, large numbers of whom were Catholics.
Consequently, the FEPC's New York hearing in February turned up
considerable testimony about religious, as well as racial, discrimination. The New York Employment Service, unlike its counterpart in
southern California, put its entire managerial personnel on notice in
August, 1941, that "we are not going to fill orders from employers
which contain any discriminatory qualifications." This declaration did
not deter many defense contractors. When the state employment
service refused to cater to their prejudices, employers often patronized
private agencies. In January, 1942, for example, a private, fee-
charging New York agency advertised for six clerks without experience for jobs in a defense industry. A Jewish girl applied but was
informed that Jews were not wanted.[32]

31. Testimony of W. Gerard Tuttle, 479, and testimony of Floyd C. Covington,
426, both in Los Angeles hearing, R19HR, and FEPC News Release, December 4,
1941, Speeches file, Division of Review and Analysis, R75HR, all in RG 228; Pittsburgh *Courier*, November 1, 1941, p. 1; Chicago *Defender*, November 1, 1941, p. 2;
Herbert R. Northrup, *The Negro in the Aerospace Industry* (Philadelphia, 1968), 17–
19; Ruchames, *Race, Jobs, and Politics*, 34–35.
32. Testimony of Rabbi J. X. Cohen, p. 61, Circular (or general order) from New

Private agencies often sorted out job applicants through discriminatory advertising. At the New York hearing, Rabbi J. X. Cohen, having surveyed the Sunday editions of the *Times* and the *Herald Tribune* between April and December, 1941, found that discrimination more than kept pace with the increase in jobs. In April, out of 10,051 advertisements, 2,950, or 29 percent, expressed a religious preference, usually Protestant or Gentile. By November there were 17,839 advertisements, 5,882, or 32 percent, of which were religiously biased. Cohen thought the advertisements represented only a portion of the jobs available. When job applicants were not sorted out through advertising, discrimination still went on at the plant doors. Private training schools sent students resumés that included information on religious affiliation to their corporate clients. Jobs could be found for Christians but less easily for Jewish graduates.[33]

Black workers faced discrimination throughout the New York and New Jersey areas. Isolantite, Incorporated, a New Jersey firm, employed 745 production workers, 80 percent of whom were white women. When a company advertisement in the Passaic *Daily Herald* attracted African-Americans, about 600 white women threatened to leave. Thereafter, Isolantite's advertisements specified a racial preference. Upon discovering that the company was leaving the matter of discrimination in the hands of the chemical and oil workers union, David Sarnoff offered some advice. As an employer of a large work force, he knew that the situation would not be corrected by expecting someone else to handle it. Isolantite should take a chance on impairing the defense program, he recommended, and if the labor union or the workers threatened a walkout, it should call on the FEPC for help. Frank Fenton agreed that Isolantite should hire some blacks and find out what would happen. When he learned that the union was a federal local affiliated directly with the AFL, Fenton threatened to lift its charter if the members discriminated against blacks.[34]

The list of companies summoned to the New York hearing was im-

---

York State Employment Service to section heads, etc., August 14, 1941, read into the record by David Sarnoff, February 10, 1942, New York hearing, R63HR, RG 228; Beecher, "8802 Blues," 249.

33. Testimony of Rabbi J. X. Cohen, p. 61, New York hearing, R63HR, RG 228; Beecher, "8802 Blues," 249.

34. Testimony of John F. Evans *et al.*, Isolantite, Inc., 534, New York hearing, R63HR, RG 228.

pressive. Continental Can in Passaic, with 600 employees, came to explain its hiring practices. Babcock & Wilcox in Bayonne employed 630 blacks out of 6,500 workers. On the advice of employment experts, Babcock's job application forms carried a racial identification because of the alleged existence of "recognized racial aptitudes." If the FEPC objected, Babcock said, it would remove the question. Ford Instrument, of Long Island City, employed only 6 blacks, an elevator operator and 5 porters. The company had hired 60 black trainees but did not provide equal opportunity for advancement despite the urging of the local CIO union. Fairchild Aviation, of Jamaica, preferred a work force of Caucasians and Gentiles. Sperry Gyroscope Corporation, the parent company of Ford Instrument, employed only 21 blacks out of 11,212. Sperry also liked to hire white, Christian Americans. The message was clear: hyphenated Americans, blacks, and Jews need not apply. A Sperry interviewer told Harry Feld, "I think I can use you," but reneged after seeing "Jew" on Feld's application. Even after Pearl Harbor, Sperry continued to advertise for "U.S. Citizens only" and refused to certify a naturalized German-American with a valuable skill.[35]

In mid-January, between the Los Angeles and New York hearings, the FEPC visited Chicago. Although an ordinance there outlawed discrimination in war plants, it was not enforced. Committee members heard familiar testimony. Minorities, particularly blacks and Jews, could not find employment in defense establishments. Among the firms charged in the January Chicago hearing were Stuart-Warner Corporation, Studebaker Corporation, and Nordberg Manufacturing Company, all of Chicago, and Allis-Chalmers Corporation, A. C. Smith Corporation, and Heil Company, all of Milwaukee. After the hearing the committee issued directives ordering each company to cease discriminatory activity and specifying certain action that had to be undertaken as proof of good faith. Near the end of the Chicago hearing, the committee became interested in the activities of AFL building trades unions, and in April a subcommittee headed by Earl Dickerson returned to probe the activities of the Chicago plumbers and steamfitters.[36]

The subcommittee found patterns of discrimination going back to

35. Proceedings, 305, 330, 377–78, 409, 488, New York hearing, R63HR, RG 228.
36. Firms appearing at Chicago hearing, Statistics folder, F3FR, summary of Chicago hearing, U.S. Govt., Aliens in Defense, Mexican workers file, R66HR, and hear-

World War I, when blacks began entering the plumbing and steamfitting trades. White Steamfitters' Local 597 and Plumbers' Local 130 made closed shop agreements with the Plumbing Contractors Association and then found excuses to deny membership to blacks. The plumbers' union books were usually closed, or too many members were out of work. The steamfitters had ritualistic barriers. A union member in good standing had to vouch for any outsider who wanted to join. Beyond this hurdle was a blackball. If jobs with the city were involved, there were other ways to discriminate. After Hugo Williams returned from service in France at the end of World War I, he graduated from Brooklyn's Pratt Institute and took courses in plumbing at Hampton Institute. Williams also had work in draftsmanship. Certified as a plumber after passing a Chicago civil service exam, he was sent to the Chicago Water Department. There Williams was told to join Plumbers' Local 130. Examined orally and in writing by three white union members, he failed.[37]

In 1926, hoping to demonstrate solidarity with the union movement, Afro-Americans formed two organizations, the Cook County Steamfitters' Union and the Cook County Plumbers' Union, but the white unionists never changed. In the 1930s, as New Deal funds became available, the blacks, supported by the Chicago Urban League and with the help of federal quota requirements, got some jobs on government projects over the opposition of the white unionists. Nevertheless, white plumbers and steamfitters did most of the government work even in black neighborhoods. As the defense effort got under way, the federal government required contractors to sign closed-shop agreements. Armed with this power, Steamfitters' Local 597 controlled the jobs at the Great Lakes Naval Station near Chicago. Local 130, emboldened by the closed-shop guarantee, moved in 1939 to cut blacks out of most of the construction projects. Summoned by white unionists to a meeting in December, two black craftsmen, a steamfitter and a plumber, were told by union leaders that whites would stay out of jobs in the ghetto if blacks would promise not to compete in white areas of Chicago. In 1941, Local 130 presented this

ing, Cook County Plumbers' Union, April 4, 1942, R18HR, all in RG 228; Beecher, "8802 Blues," 249; Ruchames, Race, Jobs, and Politics, 35.

37. Hearing, Cook County Plumbers' Union, April 4, 1942, pp. 9, 14, 17, 96, R18HR, RG 228.

"agreement" in writing and demanded black compliance. Upon their refusal, black plumbers were cut out of all defense jobs. With little construction going on in black Chicago, and with Locals 130 and 597 in control elsewhere, black employment opportunities in these trades remained bleak.[38]

In his testimony, William Quirk, business manager of Plumbers' Local 130, claimed the 1939 "agreement" was fair. If black plumbers wanted union benefits, he said, they had to work hard and organize as he and others had done. Earl Dickerson wondered if it was fair in defense work to make blacks wait until all the whites in the union were employed, and he wanted to know if Local 130 had the right to determine which plumbers could work in the whole Chicago area. Quirk cited the closed shop agreement between the plumbers and the plumbing contractors as his authority. Dickerson called Quirk a Hitler, but Fenton defended the plumbers. Over the previous fifty years Local 130 had assembled a body of competent mechanics. According to Fenton, it was a splendid system, not Hitlerism. When informed that many contractors were willing to hire black plumbers, Quirk said the men from Local 130 would walk off any job where blacks worked without union referral. For the FEPC, dealing with the smug and defiant leaders of the Chicago Plumbers' and Steamfitters' unions became a frustrating task, made more difficult because committee jurisdiction covered only defense projects. These unions and their leaders epitomized some of the time-honored traditions of the AFL: brotherhood, quality workmanship, exclusion, and racism. Their tactics may have served union members well in earlier times, but held up to scrutiny during a national emergency and measured against the moral imperatives of an emerging civil rights movement, they were highhanded and unpatriotic. After reviewing the testimony, the FEPC in June warned the two Chicago unions to stop preventing black steamfitters and plumbers from working on defense projects. The FEPC continued to watch the unions and defense industries in the Chicago area for the remainder of the war.[39]

From October until April, the President's Committee had concentrated on hearings on both coasts and in mid-America. As the Chicago

38. Testimony of Edward L. Doty et al., hearing, Cook County Plumbers' Union, April 4, 1942, pp. 14–20, 25, 31, 63, 80, 103, 128, 210, 270, R18HR, RG 228.
39. Hearing, Cook County Plumbers' Union, April 4, 1942, pp. 9, 115, 138, 153, 203, 270, 292, 299, R18HR, RG 228; Chicago Defender, June 20, 1942, p. 6.

plumbers' hearing ended, one more public display was planned later that spring or summer in Birmingham, Alabama. Press coverage had thus far been favorable. The comments of the Amsterdam *Star News*, congratulating the FEPC for doing a good job, were typical. The hearings opened to public view narrow, un-American, un-Christian conduct, it said, but the committee needed more funds, a larger staff, and corrective powers. Even the large dailies, generally indifferent to the FEPC, took notice. The Detroit *Free Press*, in an editorial entitled "No Time to Hate," blamed the prejudice on both war contractors and their workers: "They should rise above petty spites in support of human liberty." Even Walter White and A. Philip Randolph expressed satisfaction with the FEPC's work.[40]

Lawrence Cramer thought the defense industries were responding to the committee. Of "all the firms that appeared" at the Chicago hearing, he told Mark Ethridge, none "so far has indicated an intention to refuse to comply with our directions." The same seemed true for Los Angeles and New York. Sperry Gyroscope and its subsidiary, Ford Instrument, increased their employment of blacks. Ford requested the local NAACP to enroll Afro-Americans for jobs. Both companies were "making a serious effort," according to Cramer, but "their lawyers won't admit that they have in the past practiced discrimination."[41]

In preparing the FEPC's findings and directives, the committee members had to rely heavily on the staff, whose drafts then received committee comment and revision. Most of the committee spent considerable time at this task, though Earl Dickerson probably read the staff recommendations more closely than any other member. Sometimes he thought the findings were too weakly worded. Must this committee "get on its knees to beg these people to do something . . . which they under the law ought to do," Dickerson asked, referring to the use of the words *persuade* and *encourage* in one of the directives. When a contractor was guilty of discrimination, the finding should so indicate, and he should be directed to make reports, argued Dickerson. David Sarnoff saw it differently. While finding merit for a militant

40. Amsterdam *Star News*, March 28, 1942, Detroit *Free Press*, April 14, 1942, quoted in Press Clippings Digest, May 13, 1942, office files of Eugene Davidson, R77HR, RG 228.

41. Verbatim transcript, committee meeting, A.M., May 11, 1942, pp. 7–8, 14–15, R63HR, RG 228.

attitude that condemned the perpetrator and then demanded action, Sarnoff thought persuasion and encouragement were attractive alternatives, particularly in view of the FEPC's weakness. A time would come, he believed, when the committee would have to take more positive action than it felt wise to do now, but that time had not yet arrived. Yet much had been accomplished. The sum total of the FEPC's contributions far exceeded anything Sarnoff had thought possible. There was general acceptance of the agency throughout the country, but Sarnoff insisted the FEPC would get further by exercising restraint than by cracking down at that particular time.[42]

Dickerson persisted. He was talking not about cracking down but about using language in the findings that was direct and realistic. In his view, the Chicago findings should have stated, "We direct you to take these men whenever a vacancy occurs." Sarnoff wondered what the FEPC would do if those orders were disobeyed. Dickerson said he would refer the case to the president. It would give FDR something to think about. "Do you want to put the President in that position?" Sarnoff asked. "Absolutely," was the reply. Dickerson had traveled around the country talking to people in the employment field. His assessment was that in individual cases there had been some success, but the general attitude toward black employment under Executive Order 8802 had changed very little. The FEPC must, therefore, insist on the gradual entrance of blacks into employment channels in order to prove that the races could work together. When the war ended, Dickerson believed, some blacks would be on the assembly lines. With the principle that the races could work together established, blacks with skills would not be dropped. Sarnoff agreed up to a point but noted that the executive order applied only during the war. In the meantime, he continued, more state laws like those in New York and Illinois should be passed, and there should be federal enactments. Dickerson also wanted that kind of action, but he believed it would flow out of the activity under the executive order. Drive 8802 to the point where it failed to carry out its objective, he argued, and people, seeing that the goal must be realized, would be willing to take the next step and support federal legislation. Whether Dickerson changed any minds is unknown, but after the June hearing in Birmingham, tough language began to appear in the FEPC findings.[43]

42. *Ibid.,* 16–18.
43. *Ibid.,* 16–24.

Although Earl Dickerson fretted over the national mood, significant things had been done. The FEPC had taken on some of the largest and most important defense contractors in the country, questioned their employment practices, and exposed them to publicity. The committee had also challenged a major international union and numerous locals. Shortly, it would apply the hearing process to government agencies. Thus far, exposing discrimination had been moderately effective, though contractors feared adverse publicity more than labor unions did. The hearings were especially important, however, because they began radicalizing the private network of racial, multiracial, and religious organizations such as the NAACP, the Urban League, and groups of Jews and white Christians; and individuals became more active through their various organizations. Here were the seeds of the civil rights movement, and the committee's activities seemed to energize them. During the various hearings, many employers commented on the fact that blacks had begun applying for jobs that they had never before dreamed possible.[44]

As the FEPC conducted its hearings, serious problems involving leadership threatened its stability. Equally dangerous for it was a reorganization of the war agencies, including the abolishment of the OPM, that began soon after Pearl Harbor. While the FEPC-OPM investigations in the field continued, the committee and its staff spent most of the time until July deliberating over the future of the FEPC during and after reorganization.

44. For evidence of increasing job applications by blacks, see New York hearing, 409, 517, R63HR, RG 228.

2 / Taking on the Bureaucracy

The year 1942 began in the midst of a national crisis. With its naval power seriously weakened at Pearl Harbor, the United States still had to wage global war on land and on the high seas. Physical and human resources were reorganized as factories shifted to war production. Millions of men and women entered the armed services, creating shortages of manpower in the war industries, and their replacements had to be recruited from within the civilian population. Women workers began entering the labor force in large numbers, but there were hundreds of thousands of minority workers who still could not fully participate in war production because of discrimination.

The FEPC's work was cut out for it, but the agency first had to deal with serious internal problems and with the evolving wartime bureaucracy. The internal problems concerned doubts about the continued service of three important FEPC officials. January brought rumors that Executive Secretary Lawrence Cramer was about to resign. "He is sick and tired of it in more ways than one," especially because the job of helping the race was a "hot spot," reported the Chicago *Defender.* "Heads of government departments are said to resent the quiet manner in which this Quaker-born secretary has kept pressing home the point of complying with the Presidential order." So did industrial leaders and personnel directors in the private sector. "Cramer has been losing friends," the paper continued, and having forfeited the governorship of the Virgin Islands for too zealously promoting the black man's cause, he "is said to feel he cannot constantly play the role of martyr." The *Defender* believed Cramer "had been honest, fearless and indefatigable" and was gratified when he agreed to stay "a while longer."[1]

Meanwhile, David Sarnoff had been embarrassed over charges of discriminatory practices in his own company. The RCA facilities, in Indianapolis and Camden, New Jersey, followed lily-white employment policies. Sarnoff handled the situation in a forthright manner. "On the theory that even staff of organizations like ours which are in sympathy with the spirit" of Executive Order 8802 "need periodic checking," he wrote Cramer, "I have today issued a general order to all RCA Companies, their executives and department heads" to follow the spirit and letter of the executive order. Sarnoff set a tone and an example that he no doubt hoped other business leaders would follow.[2]

Finally, Mark Ethridge surprised FEPC supporters with his resignation as chairman. Although his philosophy differed from more militant committee members, he resigned not for that reason but because of increasing responsibilities at the Louisville *Courier-Journal* as his close associates there went into government service. "I have to negotiate with twelve unions between now and March besides carrying on my other duties . . . as publisher," he wrote Sidney Hillman. Ethridge believed he had done a good job as FEPC chairman. David Sarnoff was his first choice as a successor "if the President would be agreeable." He also suggested three southerners: Edwin R. Embree, Howard W. Odum, and Raymond A. Kent. Despite his cautious conservatism and his obvious failure to grasp the enormity of minority employment problems, Ethridge enjoyed unquestioned support among key race leaders. To Walter White, Ethridge's resignation was "a terrible blow," and he thought the size of the committee should be increased to seven so that "Mark" could stay on. For chairman, White favored Malcolm MacLean, the white president of Hampton Institute. Several blacks in the Washington, D.C., establishment agreed, as did

1. Chicago *Defender*, January 3, 1942, pp. 9, 15, January 10, 1942, p. 15.
2. Arthur Fleming to Lawrence Cramer, December 18, 1941, Lawrence Cramer to Arthur Fleming, January 6, 1942, Fleming file, David Sarnoff to Lawrence Cramer, January 31, 1942, Lawrence Cramer to David Sarnoff, February 6, 1942, Sarnoff file, Malcolm MacLean to Marvin H. McIntyre, February 9, 1942, MacLean file, all in Public Relations 5, R45HR, RG 228; David Sarnoff to All RCA Companies, January 31, 1942, in General Office File, FEPC-Gen., 1942, NAACP Records.

Lawrence Cramer. In a letter to Randolph, White reported that William Hastie, Robert Weaver, and George Johnson also supported MacLean. Presidential Secretary Stephen Early added to the list his own choices: Jonathan Daniels for chairman and Ethridge as vice-chairman.[3] Roosevelt also wanted MacLean. Persuading Mark Ethridge to stay on as a member, he enlarged the size of the committee to seven to accommodate him.

Malcolm MacLean was born in Denver, was educated in the Midwest, and pursued careers in journalism and college teaching and administration until his move eastward to Virginia in the early 1940s. At Hampton Institute, his reforms offended conservative white faculty and trustees, while more radical faculty and students found them inadequate. When he joined the FEPC, his first written communication to Presidential Assistant Marvin McIntyre dealt with political, not agency, matters. Perhaps he thought his appointment made him the president's key adviser on racial problems. His memorandum indicated that a "small storm" was "brewing . . . among Negro leaders," who felt "that things [were] going sour in various government agencies," particularly in the National Housing Administration, where Nathan Straus had resigned and Clark Foreman was ousted after attacks by southern congressmen. Within days of his appointment, MacLean, in the manner of the White House staff, began referring to Roosevelt as "the Boss." Other political advice followed. It is essential, he wrote McIntyre in mid-February, "that the Boss and you be immediately and thoroughly acquainted with some smart politicking by our Republican opponents" in which they "are telling our Negroes that . . . the Boss is . . . [giving them] the run-around." Blacks were complaining because the FEPC had only indirect access to the president through McIntyre. What they wanted, MacLean confided, was an appointment to a policy-making position such as a "Negro secretary or under-secretary or administrative assistant in the White House." He did not advocate such an appointment, however,

3. Mark Ethridge to Sidney Hillman, January 7, 1942, in Public Relations 5, Ethridge file, R45HR, RG 228; Chicago *Defender*, January 24, 1942, p. 9; Walter White to A. Philip Randolph, January 6, 1942, Walter White to Mark Ethridge, January 9, 1942, Walter White to A. Philip Randolph, January 13, 1942, all in General Office File, FEPC–Mark Ethridge, 1942, NAACP Records; memorandum, Stephen Early to the President, December 26, 1941, in Official File 4245-G, January–July, 1942, FDRL.

and his apparently unsolicited advice seemed designed more to ingra-
tiate himself with the White House than to benefit "our Negroes,"
whose interests he allegedly represented.[4]

Chairman MacLean proved particularly adept at answering letters
sent to FDR by citizens and organizations and then forwarded to the
FEPC for reply. Indeed, in his eagerness to please, he may at times
have compromised the committee. In a "Dear Mac" note he sent to
McIntyre shortly after becoming chairman, MacLean included the
draft of a letter he had prepared for the White House "to take the heat
off the President and at the same time not give undue encouragement" to the Fraternal Council of Negro Churches. Protecting the
boss was the committee's job, MacLean stated, "and at the same time
[the FEPC will] . . . make steady progress in practical ways as we
can." MacLean requested White House stationery "for similar jobs to
this." Lawrence Cramer, who also answered letters for the White
House, read MacLean's contribution with "admiration." The statement was, he said, "an excellent one." Letters of this type undoubtedly pleased MacLean's White House superior, southerner Marvin
MacIntyre, who had little sympathy for Afro-Americans and apparently had isolated FDR from this constituency. Earlier, in 1935, Walter White found out that none of his letters to the president on antilynching legislation got past McIntyre's vigilant blocking. Thereafter,
Eleanor Roosevelt hand-carried White's messages directly to the president. On one occasion, after the first lady detained the president for
over thirty minutes at the White House, McIntyre mimicked her:
"Franklin, something has got to be done. The Negroes are not getting
a square deal."[5]

Apparently MacLean also believed that employers needed shielding

4. Sidney Hillman to Harold D. Smith, March 4, 1942, Harold Smith to the At-
torney General, March 17, 1942, both in DJ-FOI; Sidney Hillman to the President,
January 24, 1942, Malcolm MacLean to Marvin McIntyre, February 6, 1942, both in
Official File 4245-G, January–July, 1942, FDRL; Malcolm MacLean to Marvin Mc-
Intyre, February 12, 1942, in Public Relations 5, D file, R44HR, and FDR to Malcolm
MacLean, February 7, 1942, in Public Relations 5, MacLean file, R45HR, both in RG
228; Philadelphia *Tribune*, February 21, 1942, p. 10, February 28, 1942, p. 10;
Neuchterlein, "Politics of Civil Rights," 177.

5. Malcolm MacLean to Marvin McIntyre, August 3, 1942, in Official File 4245-
G, January–July, 1942, FDRL; Malcolm MacLean to Marvin McIntyre, February 24,
1942, Lawrence Cramer to Malcolm MacLean, February 28, 1942, both in Public
Relations 5, MacLean file, R45HR; Polenberg, *War and Society*, 120; White, *A Man
Called White*, 168; Jonathan Daniels, *White House Witness*, 55.

from adverse criticism. Often when they discriminated against individuals it was unintentional, he argued. "A lot of alleged discrimination is not discrimination at all," he told Hampton students, "but arises on the employer's side from ignorance of the fact that there are any Jews or any Negroes who have the skills they so much need." In addition, it was his opinion that ignorance on the part of applicants about procedures for getting defense jobs contributed to charges of discrimination. While MacLean and Cramer, as members of the administration team, were undoubtedly obligated to do public relations work for the White House, both men seemed to take too much satisfaction in their ability to avoid giving "undue encouragement" to earnest citizens whose interests they were supposed to be serving. Furthermore, if MacLean had been paying attention to the hearings, or if he had read the hearing transcripts, he should have known that employers, most of whom had placed discriminatory newspaper advertisements or otherwise had refused to hire Jews or blacks, were scarcely innocent bystanders, ignorant of the job market.[6]

Early in 1942, the administration began a major reorganization as Roosevelt dismantled existing agencies and created new ones to facilitate war production. The OPM was abolished, and the powerful War Production Board (WPB), headed by Sears executive Donald Nelson, took its place. The WPB absorbed Sidney Hillman's Labor Division, but the FEPC's administrative domicile remained undecided. Blacks became alarmed that the President's Committee might suffer the same fate as the OPM. The FEPC had made "searching inquiries" and had "done a good job," editorialized the Chicago Defender. Without authority to enforce its decisions, it had nonetheless "succeeded admirably in focussing the attention of the critical public on . . . recalcitrant industrialists" and had got some promises. The committee had "given hope to millions of Negro workers whose morale would have been irreparably shattered." The administration, however, had no plans to abolish the FEPC. The agency could choose to affiliate with the production board or with the Office of Emergency Management (OEM), a catchall administrative unit run out of the White House.[7]

6. Chicago Defender, March 14, 1942, p. 4.

7. Memorandum, Sidney Hillman to Marvin McIntyre, January 29, 1942, in Official File 4245-G, January–July, 1942, FDRL; Lawrence Cramer to Mark Ethridge, January 27, 1942, in Public Relations 5, Ethridge file, R45HR, RG 228; Chicago Defender, February 7, 1942, p. 14.

Most committee members were impressed with the WPB because of its power. Mark Ethridge thought FDR had given Donald Nelson so much authority that even agencies with cabinet rank, such as the War Department, had to go there with production problems. Because important FEPC activity, including minority employment in war industries, came under the heading of war production, affiliation with the board became especially attractive. The WPB would have control of defense training, also an area of interest to the FEPC. Sidney Hillman assured committee members that the Labor Division under the WPB could be much more helpful than before. The FEPC also had jurisdiction over government agencies, however, and Hillman would accept no responsibility for discrimination in the bureaucracy. Nevertheless, committee members, pressured by rapidly developing events, voted in a telephone poll for WPB affiliation. Only David Sarnoff and Milton Webster opposed the move. Earl Dickerson, obviously uninformed, decided to follow Ethridge, who favored it.[8]

Although supposedly the FEPC could choose, others actually made the decision. Donald Nelson, who had never heard of the FEPC before the reorganization, did not want labor supply functions, including Hillman's Labor Division, in the WPB, whose principal task was the production and allocation of war materials. After a decade of depression, high unemployment, and labor surpluses, Nelson, along with leaders in business and the armed services at the WPB, seemed to view the labor supply as infinite. They pushed war production to the limit. The procurement agencies, in their haste to hand out contracts, showed little concern for regional balance or the availability of manpower. As alarming labor shortages appeared, Roosevelt on April 18 created the War Manpower Commission (WMC) and made Paul V. McNutt its chairman. Hillman's Labor Division left the production board and went to the manpower commission. The FEPC now had a choice between the WMC and the OEM.[9]

8. Sidney Hillman to Marvin McIntyre, February 4, 1942, in Official File 4245-G, January–July, 1942, FDRL; Mark Ethridge to David Sarnoff, January 26, 1942, Cramer to Ethridge, January 27, 1942, both in Public Relations 5, Ethridge file, R45HR, RG 228.

9. Pittsburgh *Courier*, April 25, 1942, p. 1; Flynn, *Mess in Washington*, 16; Riegelman, *Labour Management Cooperation*, 16; Koistinen, "Mobilizing the World War II Economy," 451–54; Alan Clive, *State of War: Michigan in World War II* (Ann Arbor, 1979), 241–42.

Lawrence Cramer never doubted that the FEPC, while keeping its independent status, should join McNutt's manpower operation. Having sounded out Chairman MacLean by telephone, Cramer, without committee consultation, negotiated with Marvin McIntyre and the Bureau of the Budget for an FEPC-WMC affiliation. As committee members arrived in Washington, D.C., for their May 11 meeting, Cramer had an agreement ready to put in writing. Only a few details as to the precise range of the committee's power remained to be worked out. In Cramer's view, the establishment of the WMC was an exceedingly fortuitous event. He was impressed with the WMC's power over government agencies and thought it was important to have representation at WMC staff meetings. Chairman MacLean agreed, assuring the members that the FEPC would be responsible to the White House, not to McNutt. [10]

Earl Dickerson was skeptical. McNutt had discussed a wide range of WMC activities but never mentioned the FEPC, he noted. An affiliation with the OEM was the best way to keep the committee independent, he argued, for the FEPC's mission, unlike the task of the manpower commission, was not to find jobs for people but to remove barriers so that others could put people to work. Furthermore, the WMC was governed by a board with representatives from the very agencies, including War and Navy departments and the Maritime Commission, that had resisted FEPC efforts to enforce the executive order. Dickerson believed they all had preconceived notions about the role of minorities in the war production program. Under the powerful WMC chairman, he warned, "we will be subject to the orders of the man in the front office." Dickerson moved to affiliate with the OEM. David Sarnoff agreed, observing that the FEPC's prestige would be "seriously affected . . . by being first under the WPB and then under Manpower and then something else." The FEPC would, he was certain, gain more esteem as an independent agency. There was little opposition to these views except from the AFL's Frank Fenton, who wanted a manpower affiliation because organized labor had influence there. Dickerson's motion passed unanimously. Chairman MacLean

10. Verbatim transcript, committee meeting, P.M., May 11, 1942, pp. 13–19, R63HR, and Lawrence Cramer to Malcolm MacLean, April 22, 1942, in Public Relations 5, MacLean file, R45HR, both in RG 228. This was the first committee meeting for which a verbatim transcript was made.

communicated the request to the White House, and a conference was arranged with the president for May 25.[11]

When MacLean and Cramer met with him, Roosevelt not only agreed to the OEM affiliation but astonished them with suggestions for additional FEPC responsibilities. He thought it should work directly with the armed forces and with all government agencies and operations having minority problems. Additionally, the FEPC would definitely deal with segregation in the armed forces, one of the most controversial issues in the African-American community. Later that day, committee members listened to the account of Roosevelt's views with equal surprise. "I congratulate you in bringing home the bacon," Sarnoff quipped. "As I understand the statement, it is the doughnut with the hole plugged up." Dickerson called it "a big proposition . . . all those activities with the Army and Navy," and MacLean was "scared to death of it." Outside the committee, however, there was skepticism. At a meeting primarily of black Washington insiders at Cramer's home a few days later, George Johnson, Maceo Hubbard, Robert Weaver, and Truman Gibson all responded negatively: they thought the new agenda could not succeed unless FDR agreed to strengthen Executive Order 8802 and give the FEPC more power.[12]

Roosevelt's performance is difficult to explain, particularly since Lawrence Cramer, who kept in constant contact with the White House, told committee members before the May 25 conference that the FEPC's fate was practically settled. It was to become a subsidiary of the manpower commission. On May 22, three days before Cramer and MacLean met with FDR, Attorney General Francis Biddle noted that the cabinet discussed "the Negro situation which everybody seemed to think was rather acute." In late April, attacks on the black press had come from two diverse sources, a southern white liberal, Virginius Dabney of the Richmond *Times-Dispatch,* and the ultraconservative syndicated columnist Westbrook Pegler. Dabney noted the racial riots around service installations in the South and warned that some individuals (not Dabney) found the alleged intemperate news

11. Verbatim transcript, committee meeting, P.M., May 11, 1942, pp. 21–26, R63HR, and Malcolm MacLean to Marvin McIntyre, May 12, 1942, personal and confidential records of George M. Johnson, R5HR, both in RG 228.

12. Verbatim transcript, committee meeting, May 25, 1942, pp. 10, 17–18, R63HR, RG 228; interview with Maceo Hubbard, Washington, D.C., August 25, 1978.

coverage of the black press to be the cause. Dabney was concerned over white polarization in the South if blacks moved too fast, so he urged them to reject the more radical northern race leaders. Pegler savaged the Negro press, particularly the Chicago *Defender* and the Pittsburgh *Courier,* charging editorial sensationalism and inflammatory news coverage. He compared their journalism to the biased publications of both right and left, the Reverend Charles E. Coughlin's *Social Justice* and the communist *Daily Worker.*[13]

Shortly before the May 22 cabinet meeting, the White House received two reports from the Office of Facts and Figures on the black press and the attitudes of Afro-Americans toward the war. Roosevelt was already concerned about "subversive language" in black newspapers. The office reported that the black press concentrated on the theme of racial discrimination and that Negro morale suffered as a result. The president was also aware of black dissatisfaction with his administration. Blacks were excluded from policy making, and they had no direct contact with the president. As a remedy, F. D. Patterson, president of Tuskegee Institute, had proposed the appointment of a black assistant secretary or undersecretary in one of the departments of government. Roosevelt's sweeping proposals regarding the FEPC may have been a response to these concerns.[14]

Certain blacks were kept far outside the circles of power. Earl Dickerson, though he served on a policy-making body, felt the isolation as keenly as any black leader. However elated he may have been over the president's promises, he was bothered when the chairman and the executive secretary attended important White House meetings that excluded the full committee and especially its two blacks. When the entire body was not available for White House meetings, he told committee members, a black should be present to state the views of Afro-

13. Cabinet meetings, January–June, 1942, in Francis Biddle Papers, FDRL; Patrick S. Washburn, *A Question of Sedition: The Federal Government's Investigation of the Black Press During World War II* (New York, 1986), 85; Lee Finkle, *Forum for Protest: The Black Press During World War II* (Madison, N.J., 1975), 63, 65.

14. Draft of letter from F. D. Patterson, unsigned, February 14, 1942, in Public Relations 5, P file, R44HR, RG 228; Pittsburgh *Courier,* May 23, 1942, p. 14, June 6, 1942, p. 7; Philadelphia *Tribune,* April 11, 1942, p. 2; Washburn, *Question of Sedition,* 81–82. The FEPC was not the first agency that Roosevelt had created without clearly defined powers and duties and with nebulous relationships to other administrative bodies. For an account of FDR's handling of the NLRB in 1934, see Peter H. Irons, *The New Deal Lawyers* (Princeton, 1982), 215.

Americans, because "unless you have been through the mill yourself and have had the sting of criticism and the hurt of rejection, you can't" adequately present the case. There was no recorded discussion. After Dickerson made his point, the group went on to other business. The fact remained, however, that though blacks on the President's Committee served at the policy-making level of government, they were still outsiders.[15]

Whatever FDR's motives in making his broad proposals to the FEPC, he refused to strengthen the executive order because he believed the FEPC already had sufficient power to carry out the mission assigned to it. The Bureau of the Budget disagreed. This powerful body, headed by Harold D. Smith, interpreted the laws and executive orders that created the agencies, advised on the limits of the agencies' responsibilities, monitored their management of funds, and consulted on their internal administration. It also ranked agencies on the basis of their contributions to the war effort. Contrary to FDR's expectations, the bureau refused to authorize the FEPC's funding without amendments to Executive Order 8802. Consequently, Cramer and the staff began to draft a new executive order, advising committee members of their action by telegram. The order would establish the FEPC as an independent agency within the OEM with the power to make findings and issue orders necessary to enforce 8802, to get access to the records of all government agencies for the purpose of investigating violations, and to appoint the personnel and establish the facilities needed in its pursuit of its mission. The proposal reflected Roosevelt's words, but getting his approval was another matter.[16]

On June 9, the President's Committee gave Cramer's proposed executive order on reorganization a thorough airing. During the discussion, David Sarnoff critiqued the committee itself and analyzed Cramer's proposal, which he pronounced inadequate. Sarnoff seemed unaware of the politics surrounding the FEPC's creation, and he naively assumed the committee to be like any other government agency. As yet, he thought, the committee had made no decisions on

15. Verbatim transcript, committee meeting, May 25, 1942, pp. 18–21, R63HR, RG 228.

16. Lawrence Cramer to Earl Dickerson (telegram), May 29, 1942, in Public Relations 5, Dickerson file, R45HR, and George M. Johnson to Harold D. Smith, June 4, 1942, Proposed Plan for Reorganization, office files of George M. Johnson, R4HR, both in RG 228; Larry Berman, *The Office of Management and Budget and the Presidency, 1921–1929* (Princeton, 1979), 14, 25–29.

what it should be, *i.e.*, what its functions should be, how far it wanted to go, how much responsibility it wished to take, and how much status it felt it should have. Whereas the executive orders setting up the WPB and the WMC were broad and comprehensive so that these agencies could do practically anything, "ours was just a statement of intention without any powers." Turning to the FEPC's operations, he found the administrative structure to be inadequate. Chairman MacLean was "a swell guy," but as a part-time appointee he could not perform the necessary tasks. Sarnoff knew of no organization that advanced very far without an individual on the scene directing policies from day to day. If RCA had been run like the FEPC, by an executive secretary with a chairman who came in occasionally to take a look, the company would have failed. The FEPC was fortunate in having Cramer as executive secretary, he admitted, but he also noted that Cramer was not the chairman and presiding officer, the leading mind, the dominating head that battled both private and government agencies. If the committee members agreed to his plan, Sarnoff would make a plea for a full-time chairman. He believed the president would respond favorably because there were precedents in both the WPB and the WMC.[17]

While Sarnoff respected Lawrence Cramer, he found Cramer's leadership wanting. The FEPC, he explained, needed a strong administrative officer with a flare for showmanship who could put the agency forward and give it publicity. "That is not Lawrence Cramer's particular forte," said Sarnoff, who made his criticisms good naturedly and with some humor. Cramer he saw as a thinker, a student, a philosopher, a great man on policy, but "as an administrator he works six times as much as I would . . . and covers a lot of work." Sarnoff thought the FEPC should be reconstituted in order to give certain groups better access. Whereas blacks and organized labor had proper representation, he pointed out, others did not. Sarnoff represented industry and the Jewish minority, but in truth he spoke for neither group. In the hearings he attacked industry as vigorously as did any other member, and as a consequence business felt it had no spokesman. In short, he concluded, the new executive order should be drafted both to give the FEPC the widest possible latitude and power

17. Verbatim transcript, committee meeting, June 9, 1942, pp. 70–74, R63HR, RG 228.

and to define its functions well. Noting that Executive Order 8802 had been issued "very early in the game," Sarnoff, again citing the WMC and the WPB, believed the technique of setting up such bodies had been greatly perfected since then.[18]

David Sarnoff's interesting display of administrative insight and political naiveté was challenged first by Chairman MacLean, whose opinions were "exactly opposite." MacLean viewed the FEPC as an agency handling administrative law, directly parallel to a federal court; it was a policy-forming, deliberative, judicial body. Having a full-time chairman who was a paid employee would cause confusion between that officer and the executive secretary. Such a chairman also would be alienated from the committee, for he would have lost his deliberative power in the group. As for Sarnoff's criticism of Cramer, MacLean strongly and justifiably defended the executive secretary as a skillful negotiator who had won the complete respect and admiration of other officers in the government. This and ensuing discussions over the proposed executive order and the future of the FEPC, while sometimes sharp, revealed a group of capable and dedicated men arguing with candor, occasional needling and rancor, and flashes of brilliance.[19]

The deliberations continued for several weeks. Some committee members struggled with the draft of a new executive order, while David Sarnoff chaired a subcommittee on reorganization. As the committee considered his proposals early in July, the discussion revealed the serious concerns of blacks that reorganization would diminish their influence. Earl Dickerson and Milton Webster vehemently opposed a proposal to enlarge the committee from seven to nine members. Although the larger committee would give other minority groups representation, Webster argued, the problems of nonblack minorities were comparatively unimportant compared with those of African-Americans, whose complaints comprised 90 percent of the FEPC's workload. Expansion would add different points of view and impede progress on the primary problem the commiteee had been created to handle. Sarnoff wanted the two additional members to rep-

18. *Ibid.*
19. *Ibid.*, 91–96; George Johnson to Lawrence Cramer, June 25, 1942, Proposed Plan for Reorganization, office files of George M. Johnson, in R4HR, and Lawrence Cramer to Earl Dickerson (telegram), June 27, 1942, in Public Relations 5, Dickerson file, R45HR, both in RG 228.

resent women and Mexican-Americans, and he suggested author Pearl Buck as a possible appointee, but Dickerson thought these groups did not need representation, for the FEPC was already looking out for their interests. He pointed out that the seven committee members, having worked together for a year, knew the problems. They had progressed from timidity in Los Angeles to daring in Chicago. Adding two people who had missed that experience would thus have a retarding effect.[20]

Sarnoff next proposed the creation of a full-time, salaried vice-chairman. MacLean agreed, because Larry Cramer, who did all the liaison work with the bureaucracy and also managed the staff, had too many responsibilities. Contacting the agencies and then getting them to take over investigative and enforcement work had become one of the committee's most important objectives, MacLean pointed out. A vice-chairman, on assuming these duties, should be salaried and have the prestige of full committee status. This proposal threatened the power balance between blacks and whites on the staff, however, and Dickerson and Webster opposed it. Webster thought salaried committee members might be compromised, and that even if approved, the position should not have committee status. Dickerson predicted that Sarnoff's proposal would produce a strong chairman with a committee of "rubber stamps." Sarnoff remained adamant. "While I would speak with due defference [sic] to Mr. Dickerson's views on matters of law . . . I don't regard him competent to advise me on the subject of organization [because] . . . I have had more experience than he is ever going to have." Dickerson's reply was equally strong. Even if Sarnoff "had a million years of experience in management," he could not "state his views as the final dogmatic position of take it or leave it . . . and make it the action of the Committee." The argument continued, each man citing administrative law and the example of this or that agency. Sarnoff thought the committee was too spread out. "Everybody has all the power . . . [with] each member . . . trying to run" things. "I think you and I have too much to say about it." Dickerson became very direct: "Let me get this to you. . . . I am going to have as much to say as I please." Sarnoff answered, "If you are . . . going to try to run the administration of it, I won't be on the Com-

20. Verbatim transcript, committee meeting, A.M., July 6, 1942, pp. 1–28, R63HR, RG 228.

mitee because I haven't got time to listen to what I regard to be 50 per cent administrative talk."[21]

Two strong personalities had clashed over an important issue. As Chairman MacLean summarized it, Sarnoff wanted one individual, a vice-president or executive secretary, with power to be responsible, under committee guidance, for the whole operation. His solution would ease committee burdens and produce greater administrative efficiency. Dickerson favored "a real change," with a two- or three-man board, each assigned to a specific area and responsible individually to the committee. Their differences were understandable only in the context of the interracial situation within the FEPC. Dickerson sought to preserve and broaden the influence of the "Negro people." A vice-chairman, he thought, would work with the bureaucracy and, in the contemporary mindset, must certainly be white. The kind of administrative board Dickerson wanted would include one or more blacks. At a crucial point he proposed a compromise. At the first meeting, the committee had argued over whether the executive secretary should be black or white. In deciding on a white man, they agreed that a second person, "who would have the background of the Negro people . . . could contribute his judgment and opinions" to the executive secretary. Dickerson proposed a continuation of "that kind of arrangement," with the understanding that George Johnson, as assistant executive secretary, would "be part of the deliberations which cause the Executive Secretary to make his conclusions." Dickerson knew that Johnson had been "put outside the picture" and had not contributed to the ongoing reorganization discussions. He indicated he would support a strong administrative head if Johnson were "part of the alter ego of Cramer in the formation of the program." Sarnoff agreed, noting that the saving grace of Dickerson's proposal was in not asking the executive secretary to be bound by Johnson's advice. In effect, little would change. Dickerson and Webster did succeed, however, in preserving black influence, and they put the committee and Lawrence Cramer on notice that George Johnson, as the representative of "the Negro people," had to be taken more seriously.[22]

During these five months of uncertainty, the FEPC's work went on,

21. *Ibid.*, 28–36; Chicago *Defender*, June 13, 1942, p. 4.
22. Verbatim transcript, committee meeting, July 6, 1942, pp. 36–44, R63HR, RG 228; Chicago *Defender*, June 13, 1942, p. 4.

though outsiders sometimes wondered if anything was being accomplished. "Every man for himself in the mad scramble to get . . . started [on] a plan for 'our Negras,'" jibed Charley Cherokee. Cramer, MacLean, "and other whites who have a name for understanding the Negro, are allegedly busy drawing up recommendations [for the White House] . . . with the help of their Negro advisers." Included in the plan "is a breath-taking enlargement of COFEP with legal staff, field investigators, plush trimmings and calliope." The situation so alarmed A. Philip Randolph and Walter White, whose influence in the committee had apparently waned, that they submitted a jointly signed letter with several detailed questions about staffing, the possible use of sanctions, relations with other government agencies, and funding, among other concerns. Yet Walter White's constant quest for information sometimes exasperated Cramer. In August, 1942, White, in a "Dear Larry" letter, tried to find out how much money would be allotted to the FEPC out of the president's contingent fund. Cramer replied icily, "As I told you in our conversation . . . it would not be wise" to publicize this information. White replied to "My Dear Mr. Cramer" that he would follow instructions and give out no publicity.[23]

Despite reorganization, routine staff work progressed during the spring of 1942. It involved the kind of detailed, often tedious memorandum writing and negotiating, mostly with other agencies, that David Sarnoff so soundly but mistakenly belittled. There was continuous prodding from the FEPC. The War Department finally promised to remind defense contractors in the New York area that discriminatory newspaper advertisements violated government policy. It also agreed to desegregate the buses transporting employees to its Arlington, Virginia, facility and ordered the guards to stop enforcing segregation in the cafeteria. But it took Cramer months to convince that agency to remove a racial identification question from its job applica-

23. Walter White to Lawrence Cramer, August 24, September 2, 1942, Lawrence Cramer to Walter White, August 29, 1942, NAACP file, Walter White and A. Philip Randolph to Malcolm MacLean, April 8, 1942, White file, all in Public Relations 5, R45HR, RG 228; Malcolm MacLean to Walter White and A. Philip Randolph, April 14, 1942, in General Office File, FEPC-Gen., 1942, NAACP Records; Charley Cherokee, "National Grapevine," Chicago *Defender*, May 30, 1942, p. 15, June 13, 1942, p. 15.

tion forms, which it finally did in October, 1942. The Civil Service Commission (CSC) had abandoned such queries in 1940, along with the requirement that applicants submit photographs.[24]

The FEPC also tried to change policy in the civil service, because the service's loosely drawn rules could be easily manipulated by biased government personnel officers. At the heart of the civil service procedure for referring applicants to government jobs was the "rule of three," which permitted hiring officials in the agencies to select any one of the top three candidates appearing on the civil service register. The register listed the scores of each candidate or "eligible," but under the rule of three, hiring officers could ignore the ratings. Two of the three eligibles could be blacks and have the highest scores but still be passed over. The rule of three invited discrimination, and the procedure was so loose that bias could rarely be proved. The FEPC succeeded in getting the rule of three set aside for lower-echelon positions during the war emergency.[25]

After a detailed study of the system, the FEPC also urged that eligibles, if they were refused jobs because of discrimination, be given the same number of chances to reapply as the number of their rejections resulting from bias. The CSC adopted this policy and agreed to investigate violations of 8802 and send copies of all complaints to the FEPC. Yet proving bias remained difficult, and the partial abandonment of the rule of three apparently brought little change as the recruitment of government workers accelerated. In March, 1942, war service regulations that brought all federal agencies under civil service went into effect. During the emergency, tens of thousands of applicants were hired. As the pools of eligibles grew, the system for selection became even more subjective. With the large number of appli-

24. L. B. Swartz to Civilian Aide to Secretary of War [Judge Hastie], October 8, 1942, William Hastie to Lawrence Cramer, February 14, 1942, Lawrence Cramer to Malcolm MacLean, February 25, 1942, Lawrence Cramer to William Hastie, April 18, 1942, Lawrence Cramer to Col. Thomas A. Lans, May 22, 1942, Lawrence Cramer to Marvin McIntyre, May 26, 1942, all in U.S. Govt., WD, A–W, R67HR, RG 228.

25. Lawrence Cramer to Arthur S. Fleming, November 19, 1941, in U.S. Govt., CSC, R66HR, and Lawrence Cramer to Malcolm MacLean, March 24, 1942, in Public Relations 5, MacLean file, R45HR, both in RG 228; Davis, "Non-discrimination in the Federal Agencies," 70; Davis and Golightly, "Negro Employment in the Federal Government," 341; Bradbury, "Racial Discrimination in the Federal Service," 25–26; Gladys Kammerer, *Impact of the War on Federal Personnel Administration, 1939–1945* (Lexington, Ky., 1951), 50–52; Paul Van Riper, *History of the United States Civil Service* (Evanston, Ill., 1958), 438–39.

cants, the CSC stopped listing the numerical ratings of eligibles except when the supply exceeded the demand. Consequently, personnel officers, in the absence of rating scores, had a greater opportunity to make prejudiced decisions without having to justify their actions. Although the hiring of minorities increased with the numerous government positions available, discrimination still remained difficult to prove despite the changes in CSC regulations.[26]

While the CSC and the procurement agencies were marginally helpful to the FEPC, the USES became, sometimes reluctantly, its most important ally. With the federalization of state employment agencies under the operating direction of the USES in December, 1941, the FEPC got better access to the war industries. Under state auspices, local employment officers often had refused to refer blacks to defense jobs, or they offered jobs below the applicant's level of skill. Although federalization did not change such practices overnight, reform was now possible. As Robert Weaver suggested, there was a need for specific directives and an educational program to acquaint USES employees with their minority responsibilities. Conferences between representatives of FEPC-OPM and John J. Corson, the director of the USES, eventually brought agreement that USES personnel would notify employers that biased job specifications violated federal policy. When this action proved inadequate, the FEPC asked the USES to refuse discriminatory requests. Corson was noncommital, but he did agree to supply the FEPC with the names of employers violating federal policy.[27]

Corson was reluctant to make any further changes. He believed that though 8802 required "full participation in the national defense program by all citizens," the policy had not been enforced by the contract agencies and even the FEPC's efforts had been ineffective. The USES faced a serious dilemma. If it followed the policy laid down in the executive order, many employers would stop using the service

26. Elmer W. Henderson to Lawrence Cramer, March 6, 1942, in U.S. Govt., CSC, R66HR, and Malcolm MacLean to Harry B. Mitchell, February 23, 1942, in Public Relations 5, MacLean file, R45HR, both in RG 228; Davis and Golightly, "Negro Employment in the Federal Government," 70; Bradbury, "Racial Discrimination in the Federal Service," 25–26; Kammerer, *Impact of the War*, 50–52; Van Riper, *History of the Civil Service*, 438–39.

27. Robert Weaver to John Corson, December 23, 1941, in office files of George M. Johnson, USES, R4HR, and Lawrence Cramer to David Sarnoff, February 9, 1942, in Public Relations 5, Sarnoff file, R45HR, both in RG 228.

at a time when its effectiveness was essential to the war effort. Corson might have added that local employment officers often identified and sympathized with employers, solicited their good will, and looked upon them as customers whose use of the service justified its existence and their jobs. Corson faced pressure for change within his own agency as well. In New York, USES director Anna Rosenberg sent a strong statement to her personnel on February 10, 1942: "You are not to fill orders from employers holding war contracts which contain any discriminatory specifications. . . . We have no right to fill such orders under the President's order [and particularly] . . . as administrators in a democracy." On March 30, in Bulletin C-27 Corson issued a policy statement that was mostly meaningless: USES employees should take no action, directly or indirectly, encouraging or facilitating discrimination by employers, nor should they enter on any order card a discriminatory specification. In exasperation, the FEPC asked for the names of employers who submitted discriminatory orders. Inexplicably, Corson, who had previously volunteered such information, refused on the dubious grounds that the Social Security Board, the parent organization of the USES, was required by law to keep the records confidential.[28]

Cramer next sought help from the newly created WMC after it took control of the USES. In the meantime, the latter was fashioning its own solution. In July, Bulletin C-45 required the issuance of reports on employers who failed "to eliminate discriminatory specifications" or who "obviously discriminate[d]" even though their orders did not do so. Entered on USES form 510, the reports would be sent to the FEPC and other interested agencies. Having complied with this regulation, the USES could then service the discriminatory orders. Black organizations were outraged. In support of their position, the Pennsylvania Department of Labor and Industry sent the FEPC a strongly worded telegram. President R. J. Thomas of the UAW also protested. Bulletin C-45, he wired Roosevelt, violated 8802 and invited employers to file discriminatory orders.[29]

28. Regional Director, Federal Security Agency, to USES Employees in New York State, February 10, 1942, Lawrence Cramer to Paul McNutt, February 26, 1942, Will Alexander to Guy T. Nunn, March 6, 1942, John Corson to All Personnel of USES, Bulletin C-27, March 30, 1942, Lawrence Cramer to Committee Members, May 4, 1942, all in U.S. Govt., USES, R67HR, RG 228.

29. Lawrence Cramer to Arthur J. Altemeyer, May 26, 1942, Lewis H. Gines, Pennsylvania Department of Labor and Industry, to FEPC (telegram), August 4,

Lawrence Cramer labeled the USES policy a clear violation of 8802 and requested again that all discriminatory orders be refused. Chairman MacLean wondered if "it [might] be too much to expect USES to act as an enforcement agency for" Executive Order 8802, but Cramer vowed to "negotiate this thing through to its ultimate conclusion . . . even though the end [might] be only an expiration of official life." Although Corson refused to change the policy, Cramer's "official life" did not end. Meanwhile, the USES director began to put into effect conciliatory procedures. In September, he outlined a method for transmitting USES 510s (Report of Discriminatory Hiring Practices) to the FEPC, and he enclosed sixty-two of them from employment offices across the nation. Investigating and seeking relaxation of discrimination, however, was the FEPC's problem. In October, Corson rescinded Bulletin C-45 and issued new instructions to USES personnel. As the FEPC had requested, his statement defined discrimination, but it was not broad enough to prevent the referral of applicants to jobs below their level of skill or to stop the processing of discriminatory orders. Corson did urge the USES to counsel employers against discrimination. If unsuccessful, the agency would send a 510 report to the FEPC. It continued to fill discriminatory work orders, nonetheless, until September of 1943, when the WMC, faced with serious labor shortages, ordered an end to the practice. Even then, the dedication and attitudes of USES personnel in each local office remained the key to enforcement. The FEPC got good cooperation from many offices, but it had to monitor closely the practices of others. The USES was helpful, even indispensable, in areas where its officials wanted to stop discrimination. When they were neutral or hostile, especially in the South, their value to the FEPC was limited at best.[30]

In the spring of 1942, the FEPC planned more hearings. Field investigations had revealed extensive discrimination in the nation's de-

---

1942, R. J. Thomas to the President, September 14, 1942, all in U.S. Govt., USES, R67HR, RG 228.

30. Lawrence Cramer to John Corson, July 31, 1942, Malcolm MacLean to Lawrence Cramer, August 22, 1942, Lawrence Cramer to Malcolm MacLean, August 28, 1942, John Corson to Lawrence Cramer, September 29, 1942, John Corson to All USES Personnel, October 22, 1942, all in U.S. Govt., USES, R67HR, and John Corson to Lawrence Cramer, November 14, 1942, Reports 1–1, USES 510s, 1942, R48HR, all in RG 228; Chicago *Defender*, August 29, 1942, p. 1; Bryon Fairchild and Jonathan Grossman, *The Army and Industrial Manpower* (Washington, D.C., 1959), 159.

fense training, and in April, the committee announced its first hearing involving a government agency, the United States Office of Education (USOE), which administered the training programs. Although the FEPC had held open hearings when exposing discrimination in the private sector, Roosevelt ruled that proceedings involving government agencies should be conducted in secret, an order that drew criticism from the national press, which usually ignored FEPC activities. When Cramer tried to reverse the decision, he was rebuffed. The White House, after receiving a copy of the USOE hearing summary, notified him that publication would be "inadvisable . . . at this time." The FEPC also planned a hearing in the South, at Birmingham, and another in the Southwest, in El Paso. Going south involved political risks, some of which Mark Ethridge carefully outlined. But probably not even he foresaw the furor that the Birmingham hearing would create.[31]

Chairman MacLean thought the hearing should begin with testimony from southern employers known for operating without discrimination, to be followed by those who had achieved good results with a mixed labor force. Timid employers might thus be influenced to hire Afro-American workers, and unions that barred blacks from membership or refused to give them referrals to war jobs could be exposed. Finally, "we could call a few sinners" and hold up their transgressions "against the others' virtues." This approach seemed preferable to a direct attack. John Beecher, who had become an FEPC field representative in the South, agreed that the hearing should stress the positive side, but his investigation had turned up eleven defense industries that should be called to task for discriminatory practices. Beecher also wanted to summon five state directors of defense training to explain why federal funds went primarily to facilities for whites. Ethridge agreed to MacLean's format, but he warned committee members "that a hearing in the South is in no sense an ordinary hearing . . . [and] improperly staged . . . could cause the always-present, latent prejudice to flare." The committee should thus focus on the one point "of whether the minority groups are being denied

---

31. Marvin McIntyre to Lawrence Cramer, July 21, 1942, in Personal and Confidential file, Box 20, BSCP Papers; Chicago *Tribune*, January 22, 1942, Minneapolis *Spokesman*, January 30, 1942, both in FEPC Press Clipping Digest, office files of Eugene Davidson, R77HR, RG 228; Philadelphia *Tribune*, April 11, 1942, p. 10, April 25, 1942, p. 20.

employment in defense industries." A "direct frontal attack without groundwork [would] be entirely destructive." Ethridge worried especially about Earl Dickerson's safety, and he tried to persuade the Chicagoan to stay away from Birmingham. He also urged committee members to "refrain from expressing their opinions of the credibility of witnesses" during the course of the testimony.[32]

Dickerson thought the South should be treated like the rest of the country. "The South is part of the United States," he argued, and the Bill of Rights should apply there as elsewhere. Indeed, he continued, the FEPC had a responsibility to the American people to try and give life to the Bill: "I was born in the South, unfortunately; left there early, thank heaven; but have been a close student of the South, taught school in Tuskegee. . . . The white people down South are no tougher than they are any other place." The committee should attack the problem decently and vigorously, certainly not with fear and trembling. If the federal government could not protect the committee members, Dickerson was willing to risk his life: "I can be a casualty. . . . If honestly trying to get some benefits from this area for the 9,000,000 Negroes who live in the South is going to jeopardize my life, I am willing to do it." David Sarnoff supported the sentiments but suggested tempering courage with judgment: "I can sympathize with your deep feelings. You are justified in having them. . . . But if you are going down to Alabama to try the persecution of the Negro race, which has been going ever since the country started, I am not in sympathy. That is not judgment." Dickerson said he did not intend to give that impression.[33]

As Beecher continued his investigation, he discovered firsthand just how close to the surface latent prejudice in the South could be. While working out of Birmingham, Beecher, who was using office space, clerical help, and other facilities of the WPB, received word that all the funds that were to be used to defray the administrative costs of the hearing had been withdrawn under orders from Atlanta banker

32. Malcolm MacLean to Mark Ethridge, March 24, 1942, MacLean file, Mark Ethridge to Malcolm MacLean, March 27, 1942, Ethridge file, both in Public Relations 5, R45HR, and John Beecher to George M. Johnson, April 15, 1942, Administrative Division, Hearings folder, Ala., all in RG 228; interview with Earl B. Dickerson, Chicago, December 11, 1978; Morton Sosna, *In Search of the Silent South: Southern Liberals and the Race Issue* (New York, 1977), 107.

33. Verbatim transcript, committee meeting, May 11, 1942, pp. 47–50, R63HR, RG 228.

Frank H. Neely, recently appointed as the WPB regional director. At an Atlanta conference on April 29, Beecher found Neely highly exercised over hearings that he believed would create dissension and impede the war effort. Neely interpreted Executive Order 8802 to mean that pressure groups and minorities should "cease making demands for the check-off, the union shop, or the redress of grievances based on discrimination . . . [and] join in the effort to achieve full production." Instead, he believed, "the Negro press and the columns of Mrs. Franklin D. Roosevelt" were stirring agitation over racial discrimination—agitation that "had its indubitable origin in the propaganda departments of the Axis nations." During the meeting, Neely flattered Beecher, calling him "very intelligent," and mentioned a number of good jobs, including two deputy directorships, that were open in the WPB regional office. Beecher interpreted this action as "an attempt . . . to influence me unduly." Neely feared a racial outbreak and suggested "some Negro church or school" as the "proper quarters" for the hearing, implying that he would block any FEPC attempt to secure the use of a federal building in Birmingham. Donald Nelson of the WPB, informed of this episode by Malcolm MacLean, apparently delivered a stern reprimand, which led Neely to recant. But the wealthy Atlantan would, as Beecher put it, "do everything within his official power to discredit the work" of the FEPC and "by ugly imputations . . . arouse mob hatred of complainants and committee investigators alike."[34]

There were other pressures. In Jackson, Mississippi, while Beecher interviewed black complainants, two white men entered the community center and sat down. After the conference, Beecher introduced himself and discovered they were Jackson police detectives who thought 8802 was very unfortunate. In Birmingham several prominent individuals suggested that the hearing should be canceled. One man, a representative of Associated Industries of Alabama, offered to photograph Beecher with two other FEPC investigators, Maceo Hubbard and Elmer Henderson, both blacks. Suspecting that the picture would be used to embarrass and slander the FEPC, Beecher refused. Finally, FBI agents questioned OPM officials about the background

34. John Beecher to Lawrence Cramer, April 30, 1942, Malcolm MacLean to Donald Nelson, May 12, 1942, Donald Nelson to Malcolm MacLean, May 14, 1942, Lawrence Cramer to Members of COFEP, May 21, 1942, all in office files of John Beecher, Cramer-confidential file, R77HR, RG 228.

and associations of Cy Record, an investigator from the Labor Division who worked with Beecher.[35]

Together, Beecher and Record covered territory from Georgia to Louisiana. By mid-April, the two men had compiled a list of violators, including shipyards in four states, an aircraft factory, a fuse plant, an arsenal, defense training programs in all the states in the region, a white machinists' union, and the Brecon Bag Loading plant of Talladega, Alabama, owned by the Coca Cola Company. Beecher insisted that Harrison Jones, Coca Cola's executive vice-president, should be cited to appear. The list became even lengthier before the hearing began on June 18. In the shipyards particularly, there were both labor shortages and surpluses because restrictive union policies and management hiring practices overemployed whites, whose numbers were insufficient to operate the yards, and denied defense jobs to unemployed blacks. In New Orleans, these practices, pursued by the boilermakers union and acquiesced to by the huge Delta Shipyard, brought serious delays in production. Beecher and Record were joined in the middle of May by Trimble, Hubbard, Henderson, and Donovan.[36]

As the Birmingham hearing began, Mark Ethridge, the only white southerner on the committee, gave the opening statement. While he warned other committee members to be careful in their remarks, his own rhetoric was scarcely judicious. Among other things, he attacked black leaders who had "adopted an all or nothing attitude" toward racial problems, and he assured his listeners that "no power in the world—not even . . . Allied and Axis [armies together] . . . could now force the Southern white people to the abandonment of the principle of social segregation." The criticism of his remarks was intense, but Ethridge made no apologies except to write privately that his words did not reflect his own racial attitudes. In justifying the speech, he cited New York *Times* columnist Brooks Atkinson's interview with several southern blacks who said they were "not asking for or expecting social equality" within their lifetimes. All of them regarded Wal-

<hr/>

35. Lawrence Cramer to John Beecher, May 6, 1942, John Beecher, Reports file, R48HR, and verbatim transcript, committee meeting, A.M., June 8, 1942, R63HR, both in RG 228.

36. Beecher to Johnson, April 15, 1942, Administrative Division, Hearings folder, Ala., and Field Report, John Beecher to Lawrence Cramer, March 7, 1942, in office files of John Beecher, Unarranged Correspondence file, both in RG 228; Pittsburgh *Courier*, May 30, 1942, p. 1.

ter White and the NAACP "as lacking in realistic understanding of the racial situation" and as possibly injuring "the Negro cause." Ethridge thought Atkinson's piece "bore out all that I have said about the South."[37]

Ethridge sent a copy of the speech to Presidential Secretary Early, with the comment that it had eased tensions at the hearing. FDR assistant Marvin McIntyre was "greatly pleased" with the statement and called it to the attention of President and Mrs. Roosevelt. To Walter White, however, Ethridge seemed to be equating northern black leaders with white southern demagogues like Eugene Talmadge, and he wrote Lawrence Cramer asking for more specifics on what Ethridge had said. White fretted over the "circumstances . . . which caused Mark to make such a statement" yet added that nothing "can change my absolute faith in his integrity and sincerity." Ethridge was less charitable to White. If he really wanted to know what was said, Ethridge wrote Cramer, "he could ask for a copy" of the speech.[38]

Among other blacks, Ethridge's speech produced anger and dismay. A. Philip Randolph thought Ethridge "should quit FEPC." So did the Chicago *Defender* in a bold-faced editorial entitled "Mark Ethridge Must Resign." The Pittsburgh *Courier*'s Horace R. Cayton, who delighted in the fact that the FEPC broke the conventional pattern of race relations in Birmingham, said: "I sat back to read with pleasure the fine words I thought this Southern gentleman was going to say. Boy, that article took me for a ride." Ethridge saw the executive order not as a social document but as a simple expedient to organize manpower, Cayton lamented. The hope he placed "in this group of liberal southerners" had waned. They were acting "as stupid as the British were, and are, in India." As for the reaction of blacks on the committee, Earl Dickerson publicly disavowed Ethridge's statement as a violation of the letter and spirit of the presidential order. When Chairman MacLean introduced the subject at the July 21 committee meeting, he noted that the *Afro-American* was petitioning for Eth-

37. Lawrence Cramer to Mark Ethridge, July 3, 1942, Mark Ethridge to Lawrence Cramer, July 9, 1942, both in Public Relations 5, Ethridge file, R45 HR, RG 228.

38. Mark Ethridge to Steve Early, June 22, 1942, Marvin McIntyre to Steve [Early], June 26, 1942, both in Official File 4245-G, January–July, 1942, FDRL; Walter White to Herbert Agar, July 8, 1942, in General Office File, FEPC-Ethridge, NAACP Records; verbatim transcript, committee meeting, A.M., July 21, 1942, pp. 23–25, R63HR, RG 228; Sosna, *In Search of the Silent South,* 109.

ridge's resignation. Ethridge replied he had already told the White House that when the petition arrived, he would "give it the power of attorney to put [his] name on top of it." Dickerson told Ethridge and the committee that "Negroes [who] considered Mr. Ethridge a strong friend" now felt "he had walked out on them." Blacks had believed "that southern liberals were willing to concede that Negroes had an equal chance in America . . . [but] now that feeling is perhaps gone." Dickerson spoke with restraint, but privately he "rubbed Ethridge off [his] list." Milton Webster also "drastically disagreed" with Ethridge.[39]

After Ethridge's speech, the Birmingham hearing continued with the testimony of academicians, FEPC and OPM field investigators, complainants describing cases of discrimination, union leaders, and defense industry executives. Contrary to MacLean's hopes, there were more "sinners" than "saints" and few examples of good employers except Andrew Higgins, a New Orleans shipbuilder who announced plans to train and employ thousands of blacks in segregated ways in his expanding yards. Black sociologist Ira deA. Reed found no complaints that blacks were being denied defense work but rather that the jobs open to them often did not match their skills. The South was thus importing thousands of white workers while thousands of southern blacks remained unemployed or underemployed. John Beecher testified that the management of one Mobile shipyard refused to upgrade black workers because it was "impractical and utopian." In that city's other shipyard, the Mobile Metal Trades Council (AFL) had eliminated all skilled blacks from their rolls. Frank Fenton, unhappy with testimony reflecting adversely on his federation, tried to discredit Beecher by belittling his methods as an investigator. "Do you confer or investigate?" Fenton asked sarcastically.[40]

Corporate executives in their testimony defended segregation and claimed it was preferred by the unions and their members, while union leader George M. Googe, the AFL's southern representative, attacked FEPC investigators, who, he claimed, refused to give infor-

39. Verbatim transcript, committee meeting, July 21, 1942, R63HR, RG 228; Pittsburgh *Courier*, July 4, 1942, p. 13, July 18, 1942, p. 13, July 25, 1942, pp. 4, 13; Chicago *Defender*, July 25, 1942, p. 1, August 1, 1942, p. 14; interview with Earl B. Dickerson; Ruchames, *Race, Jobs, and Politics*, 41.

40. Address of Ira deA. Reid, 65–73, and testimony of John Beecher, 225–27, June 19, 1942, both in Birmingham hearing folder, RG 228; Ruchames, *Race, Jobs, and Politics*, 38–41.

mation. Googe believed that all cases of discrimination should be adjusted outside the committee when possible, though according to the OPM's Cy Record, when given the opportunity, Googe failed to settle a dispute between the Savannah Metal Trades Council (AFL) and a black union in that city. As David Sarnoff listened to the testimony, however, he wondered why certain companies had been brought into a public hearing and charged with discrimination "when they have a closed shop agreement which forbids them to hire." He concluded, "I think you ought to haul up the union." When the committee expected an employer "to take on the responsibility that goes with violating a [closed shop] contract, I don't think [it] is on fair ground."[41]

Whether or not the Birmingham hearing succeeded was partly the interpretation of the beholder. The Pittsburgh *Courier* believed the "FEPC gets results in Dixie" and quoted Malcolm MacLean's prediction of thousands of new jobs for blacks in the South. One corporate offender, Coca Cola, was quick to make amends. Although its subsidiary, the Brecon Bag Loading Corporation, had been "most vicious" in denying opportunities to blacks, Coca Cola signed an agreement with the FEPC promising immediate abandonment of its discriminatory practices, according to the *Defender*. In Washington, D.C., FEPC employees, in a posthearing mood of jubilation, celebrated the agency's first anniversary with a dinner attended by twenty-two staff and one committee member in the Gold Room of Harrison's Cafe.[42]

To those concerned about the sanctity of the southern way of life, the FEPC's Birmingham hearing was a shocking event. Black professionals testified as experts, black workers accused white unions and employers of job discrimination, and black committee members occupied seats of authority, questioned white witnesses, and sometimes challenged them in a manner unfamiliar to the Deep South. Birmingham whites had not witnessed such a "spectacle" since the interracial Southern Conference for Human Welfare met four years earlier in the municipal auditorium and held nonsegregated sessions until Police Commissioner Eugene "Bull" Connor enforced the city's segregation ordinance. Yet the hearing received generous and generally fair

41. Testimony of George M. Googe and Cy Record, 685–94, and statement of David Sarnoff, 699–700, June 20, 1942, both in Birmingham hearing folder, RG 228; Merl Reed, "FEPC, Black Worker, and Southern Shipyards," 452–53.

42. Pittsburgh *Courier*, June 27, 1942, p. 1; Chicago *Defender*, June 27, 1942, p. 3, July 4, 1942, p. 4.

coverage, according to the FEPC's press clipping digest, though not all editorial opinion was sympathetic. According to Ralph McGill, many outraged editorials centered their wrath on Eleanor Roosevelt, who somehow became a symbol of all the things that southerners perceived to be causing change, including the coming of wartime prosperity, the loss of cooks, yard men, and butlers, and the FEPC. The major press syndicates, the Associated Press and the United Press International, had reporters in Birmingham, as did the Associated Negro Press, but in the large northern newspapers, war news crowded the hearings off the front pages. The southern press was generally hostile, but a few newspapers, including the Birmingham *Age-Herald*, on which John Beecher had earlier served as an editorial writer, remained sympathetic to FEPC objectives. In nearby Anniston, the *Times* ran a story about Beecher, native Alabamian, a man of tremendous talent, intelligence, and integrity, who was heading up the FEPC investigation.[43]

But there were ominous rumblings elsewhere. A newly established magazine, *Alabama*, branded the hearing as "race trials" and a "carnival of reform." It called on southerners to "fight this ominous encroachment on the sacred principles of their homeland." Politicians in the region and in Washington, D.C., quickly mounted attacks on the FEPC. Shortly, Alabama governor Frank Dixon, amid a flurry of publicity, refused to sign a contract with the Defense Supplies Corporation for cloth made by convicts, because it contained the standard nondiscrimination clause required by the executive order. Birmingham police commissioner Connor sent a blistering letter to Roosevelt charging the USES and the FEPC with stirring up trouble when there ought to be unity. FDR referred the letter to Marvin McIntyre with a penciled note: "Mac—What do you think we should do about this? I don't know." In Bessemer, near Birmingham, international representative of the Mine, Mill, and Smelter Workers Union (CIO) Mike Ross was threatened, and some of his officers were physically assaulted for supporting FEPC policies. "Race relations has our southern gentle-

43. Verbatim transcript, Birmingham hearing, June 18, 1942, R17HR, and Press Clipping Digest, July 6, 1942, office files of Eugene Davidson, R77HR, both in RG 228; Tindall, *Emergence of the New South*, 636–37; Thomas A. Krueger, *And Promises to Keep: The Southern Conference for Human Welfare, 1938–1948* (Nashville, 1967), 72–73; Robert J. Norrell, "Caste in Steel: Jim Crow Careers in Birmingham, Alabama," *Journal of American History*, LXXIII (1986), 680; Ralph McGill, *The South and the Southerner* (Boston, 1963), 169.

men all a dither over this coddling of Negras in Washington and the No'th," taunted Charley Cherokee. But it was deadly serious business. The Birmingham hearing became a turning point in the fortunes of the Old Committee.[44]

Still elated, the President's Committee and staff began preparing during June and July for the additional tasks assigned verbally by FDR. The staff structure at central was to remain basically unchanged, but there were plans for twelve regional offices, and permanent appointments were approved for New York, Chicago, and San Francisco. Toward the end of July, Cramer officially notified WMC's Robert Weaver and Will Alexander that the FEPC no longer needed the Labor Division to investigate complaints. Then, on July 30, without warning or consultation, Roosevelt transferred the FEPC to McNutt's manpower commission. Earlier New Deal agencies had occasionally had similar experiences. In 1934, FDR had delivered a shock to members of the NLB when, in the face of pressure from the auto industry, he ended the majority rule principle and permitted management to bargain with more than one bargaining committee. Now it was the President's Committee members who were shocked and dumbfounded, sentiments MacLean expressed to the White House in a futile protest four days later.[45]

The explanation for the president's action lay in events to which none of the committee was privy. One was the ambitions of WMC chairman McNutt, who wanted all of the nation's manpower functions under his jurisdiction. In seeking control of the FEPC, he received help from Budget Director Harold D. Smith, a powerful figure in whom Roosevelt had great confidence. On July 18, the day the Birmingham hearing began, Smith requested a meeting with FDR to

44. *Alabama,* quoted in Chicago *Defender,* June 27, 1942, p. 3; Malcolm MacLean to Lawrence Cramer (telegram), July 24, 1942, in Public Relations 5, MacLean file, R45HR, and Alton Lawrence to Malcolm MacLean, August 14, 1942, in Public Relations 5, I file, R43HR, both in RG 228; Eugene Connor to the President, August 7, 1942, in Official File 4245-G, August–December, FDRL; Charley Cherokee, "National Grapevine," Chicago *Defender,* June 2, 1942, p. 15; Pittsburgh *Courier,* August 15, 1942, p. 1; "The Negro in Industry," *New Republic,* October 18, 1943, p. 539; Norrell, "Caste in Steel," 680; Ruchames, *Race, Jobs, and Politics,* 43.

45. MacLean to McIntyre, August 3, 1942, in Official File 4245-G, January–July, 1942, FDRL; Lawrence Cramer to All Staff Members, July 22, 1942, Lawrence Cramer to Will Alexander and Robert Weaver, July 22, 1942, both in office files of Eugene Davidson, and memoranda to and from Lawrence W. Cramer, all in R77HR, RG 228; Irons, *New Deal Lawyers,* 212.

discuss pressing questions about the committee's functions. He saw serious policy problems if the FEPC operated as an independent agency under the OEM, with expanded jurisdiction into nonwar industries and with broader enforcement powers. He was concerned that FEPC hearings, findings, and directives might affect the relationship between government agencies and war contractors. In a meeting with FDR on July 21, Smith warned that the proposed executive order would enlarge the committee's duties and increase its staff "from 21 persons to approximately 225—[with a budget] increase from $70,000 pr [sic] annum to slightly less than a million dollars." When Smith told FDR "that the Committee proposed to assume jurisdiction over discriminatory hiring practices in states, counties and municipalities and in business enterprises manufacturing for interstate commerce," Roosevelt exclaimed, "They can't do that." FDR believed that the FEPC should handle complaints of discrimination by informing the injured party that "the matter had been referred to the proper official of the governmental unit." The complainant should "deal with that official . . . [in order] to correct the practice which led to the complaint." The president thought the FEPC should be transferred to manpower, Smith noted, and its objective should be "complete utilization of the available manpower of the country." Smith did suggest an increase in committee staff from the present twenty-one to sixty or seventy-five people. It should be noted that neither Smith, a Kansan, nor upper-echelon budget officers under him, many with strong southern ties, had any fondness for the FEPC.[46]

The storm of protest following the Birmingham hearing came in an election year, and the Democrats badly needed southern votes. If the budget director and the ambitious WMC chairman had raised any doubts in the president's mind about maintaining the FEPC's independent status, the controversy after Birmingham surely sensitized his political instincts. To accommodate southern critics, he transferred the FEPC to the manpower commission in order to control and weaken it. Charley Cherokee suggested that several other interesting elements were involved in the transfer, but not all were subject to documentation: the triumph of Will Alexander over MacLean and Cramer "in the struggle for power among whites who get prestige for

46. Harold Smith to the President, June 18, 1942, in Official File 4245-G, January–July, 1942, and conference, July 21, 1942, in Conferences with the President, 1941–42, Harold D. Smith Papers, both in FDRL; interview with Clarence Mitchell.

administering to Negroes"; a personal triumph for Weaver over FEPC rivals Dickerson, Webster, and Johnson; the bitter repercussions from the Birmingham hearing; objections to the announced Texas [Southwest] hearing; and the formation of a clique of seven congressmen to vitiate the FEPC and protect white supremacy.[47]

The FEPC had been functioning about a year. Despite inexperience and dissension inside the committee, shortages of funds and staff, and uncertainty during administrative and bureaucratic upheavals, it had made progress with government agencies and departments in preparing to enforce the executive order. Its public hearings, including Birmingham, were successes, and they gave significant insight into the kind of job bias the FEPC had to eliminate. Several months later, Cy Record reported "some numerical progress [in] employing Negroes" by several large firms that had been called to testify at Birmingham. By July, the committee and its staff had fashioned a creditable plan for reorganization. Before Birmingham, much of the FEPC's success probably could be attributed to the fact that the administration, for the most part, had left it alone. After the transfer to the WMC, the FEPC would fare poorly, with its status undermined, its morale shaken, and its future uncertain.[48]

47. Flynn, *Mess in Washington*, 157–59; Ruchames, *Race, Jobs, and Politics*, 46–47; Neuchterlein, "Politics of Civil Rights," 177; Charlie Cherokee, "National Grapevine," Chicago *Defender*, August 15, 1942, p. 15.

48. Clarence Mitchell to George Johnson, February 5, 1943, Reports, D–M, R48HR, RG 228.

3 / Destroying the Old Committee

Although naval victories in the Coral Sea and at Midway Island in May and June, 1942, were turning the tide of war, the struggle in the Pacific was far from over. In the Atlantic and the Gulf of Mexico, German submarine wolf packs marauded along the coastline despite some Allied success in checking their activity. The toll in sunken ships was appalling. Meanwhile, preparations were under way for a fall offensive in North Africa. On the home front, there were continuing resource and manpower shortages, yet bias persisted against minority workers. The task ahead for the FEPC was enormous.

After the FEPC's transfer to the manpower agency, the *Defender* reported that the committee members, including Mark Ethridge, would resign in protest of the transfer. Charley Cherokee began referring to McNutt as the "officially designated Patron Saint of Negroes, supplanting Papa [Harold] Ickes and surpassing Brother [Wendell] Willkie." Committee members, instead of resigning, negotiated for months with Paul McNutt and his spokesmen. The FEPC's overriding goal was the preservation of its independent status and its right to appeal to the president. Both had been promised, but implementation remained uncertain. Manpower already handled racial and minority employment problems through its Labor Division. Would these matters now be addressed by two separate branches under the WMC umbrella? If combined, who would be in charge? Despite previous cooperation between the FEPC and the Labor Division, the committee remained wary of Robert Weaver's Negro Training Branch and Will Alexander's Minorities Group. Under manpower, would the FEPC retain its public relations function, hold hearings, and issue findings? Earl Dickerson and Milton Webster were especially concerned. They had just won an important battle over the FEPC's internal reorganization, only to begin all over again with the WMC. Then there was the president's earlier promise to expand FEPC activity. Earl Dickerson avidly pursued this issue: "If the new jurisdiction conferred orally by the President is not to be assured," he wrote, "then let this fact come either from McNutt or the President himself."[1]

Chairman MacLean had absolutely no intention of pressing FDR. The committee was "shocked," he wrote McIntyre, particularly since the president's action "seemed to be a reversal, without discussion or warning," of the understanding "of a few weeks ago." He nevertheless gave McIntyre assurances: "So far as I am concerned, I obey orders. You know that." MacLean was most apprehensive over the reaction of the Negro press. Thinking of a way to save the situation, he proposed a "fireside talk to minorities," with a "special section on the Japanese" and "another on Latin Americans," explaining why the Southwest hearing, scheduled for July, had been canceled. Unless something was done quickly, "all hell [would] break loose." MacLean avowed stoutly, "I and others can take it, but I don't want the Boss to have to." In forwarding MacLean's letter to FDR, McIntyre, who was regarded by some as an evil genius in the FEPC's White House misfortunes, confessed his confusion, "since I did not know that the transfer had been made." In response, FDR instructed McIntyre to get MacLean and McNutt together to "talk over this whole thing because I think it is a lot of smoke and very little fire, in which case I will not have to answer McLean's [sic] letter."[2]

When MacLean met with McNutt at the White House on August 13, public relations was still his main concern. The NAACP, in an August 7 press release attacking the transfer, had feared that Congress

1. Chicago *Defender*, August 8, 1942, p. 4, August 22, 1942, p. 15; Malcolm MacLean to Paul McNutt, August 14, 1942, Proposed Plan for Reorganization, official files of George M. Johnson, R4HR, and Earl Dickerson to Committee, n.d., in Public Relations 5, Dickerson file, R45HR, both in RG 228.

2. Malcolm MacLean to Marvin McIntyre, August 3, 1942, MAC [McIntyre] to the President, August 6, 1942, FDR to MAC, August 3, 1942, all in Official File 4245-G, January–July, 1942, FDRL; Lawrence Cramer to Ernest Trimble (telegram), August 19, 1942, in Public Relations 5, Trimble file, R45HR, RG 228.

would block funding if the FEPC was part of the WMC. It had blamed "Southern enemies" and the Birmingham hearing for the transfer. To neutralize the criticism, MacLean prepared a form letter for White House distribution and asked for McNutt's approval. "It ought to be sent out immediately," he wrote, "so that the attack by the Negro press and other organizations may be changed as rapidly as possible to acceptance" of the president's decision. Thus MacLean deferred to the WMC chairman even before they had worked out an operating agreement. Having gotten the clear message that the White House expected cooperation, MacLean did obey orders. The WMC transfer "strengthens rather than weakens" the FEPC, he wired committee members. "If Committee and staff abandon defeatist attitude and take positive one we shall move farther and faster than heretofore." In his official letter-writing duties for the White House, Lawrence Cramer also defended the transfer as a "change for the best."[3]

"With great reluctance," MacLean also sent McNutt a copy of the FEPC's proposed executive order, which reflected "what the President [the previous May] told us he wished us to undertake." The committee opposed these new responsibilities, he wrote, and would "be very relieved not to have this Order issued." He hoped the committee would "return under your direction to its already heavy job" of eliminating discrimination in defense industries and government agencies. Despite his claims of speaking for the committee, MacLean expressed only his own sentiments. Not a shred of evidence supports his assertion that committee members opposed the new executive order. MacLean's deference may have communicated erroneously to the WMC chairman that the committee was ready to capitulate on every major issue and accept without question McNutt's complete authority.[4]

Meanwhile, "various communications" received at the White House led Roosevelt to detect more than "a little fire" over the con-

3. Press Service of the NAACP, Public Relations 5, NAACP file, and Malcolm MacLean to Earl Dickerson, August 13, 1942, in Public Relations 5, Dickerson, both in R45HR, MacLean to McNutt, August 14, 1942, Proposed Plan for Reorganization, office files of George M. Johnson, R4HR, and Press Service of the NAACP, September 18, 1942, in Public Relations 4, R47HR, all in RG 228; Pittsburgh *Courier*, September 5, 1942, p. 2.

4. MacLean to McNutt, August 14, 1942, Proposed Plan for Reorganization, office files of George M. Johnson, R4HR, RG 228; Malcolm MacLean to Marvin McIntyre, August 14, 1942, in Box 20, BSCP Papers.

troversy. Three weeks after the transfer, a White House press release attempted to explain the transfer, this "widely misunderstood" action, more fully. It was FDR's intention "to strengthen—not to submerge—the Committee, and to reinvigorate—not to repeal—Executive Order 8802." The FEPC would thus be stronger because of the WMC's extraordinary powers to mobilize the nation's manpower. "It will have the friendly supervision of . . . Mr. McNutt, whose grasp of the whole problem of manpower utilization will be of great assistance." The FEPC, he assured the nation, could continue to refer all matters it judged as requiring Roosevelt's attention. In this case, however, FDR's masterful powers of persuasion failed to allay the profound misgivings about the transfer. A. Philip Randolph, the NAACP, and the press remained unconvinced. The upcoming negotiations between the committee and the WMC would reveal how misleading Roosevelt's assurances really were.[5]

By the end of September, the committee members were certain that McNutt's "friendly supervision" in reality meant the loss of the FEPC's independence. Meetings with McNutt and his staff, followed by WMC memoranda interpreting what had been discussed, fueled their apprehensions.[6] The committee fought back, unanimously adopting three proposals for McNutt's consideration: first, the FEPC would receive jurisdiction over everything relating to minority groups, including the staff of the Labor Division; or second, the FEPC would take over all work under the executive order, in which it would function only as an appeals board; or third, the FEPC would recommend to the president that the committee be disbanded. All three proposals were politically or administratively unpalatable to McNutt and the administration. Total FEPC jurisdiction would destroy the Labor Division and weaken McNutt's control. Making the FEPC an appeals board or abolishing it would raise a furor among minority groups. The Chicago *Defender* erroneously reported on September 19 that McNutt had approved a plan that included independent status for

5. White House press release, August 17, 1942, in Public Relations 3, R42HR, RG 228; Pittsburgh *Courier*, August 29, 1942, pp. 1, 5, September 5, 1942, p. 9; Chicago *Defender*, August 22, 1942, p. 1.

6. According to the *Courier*, the full committee was scheduled to meet with McNutt for the first time on September 11 (Pittsburgh *Courier*, September 5, 1942, p. 4). During the period between July 21 and September 30, no verbatim transcripts of the committee meetings appear in the FEPC records.

the FEPC and enlarged activities with additional field offices. McNutt actually dealt with the proposals by ignoring them.[7]

Manpower, in the meantime, signaled its determination to monitor all committee activity and dominate the agency. Even a simple field decision to charge an employer with discrimination could not be made without WMC approval. Since WMC regional, state, and area directors were usually political appointees close to local power structures, FEPC field activity would be stifled. "We have to fight this thing out . . . on the basis that we have sole responsibility . . . in determining what is discrimination," Dickerson vowed. MacLean disagreed. Dickerson was making "a purely academic argument" over an issue in which both sides had good intentions. If fighting with the WMC started immediately, MacLean warned, the FEPC would never get the cooperation mandated when FDR made the transfer. Milton Webster found the discussion over power pointless. "Any damn thing the Manpower Commission wants to do they can do," he stated flatly. "McNutt is the whole boss . . . and as long as that is so, we are running around in circles trying to find out whether or not" the committee has any power. Perhaps considering advice from the press that the committee resign in protest, Webster was "just hanging around here to see what [was] going to happen."[8]

The WMC was also suspiciously vague about the roles of Robert Weaver and Will Alexander, both slated to become assistants to the chief of operations, General Frank J. McSherry. MacLean purportedly had "spelled out the situation" very clearly to McNutt: if Weaver and Alexander were put under McSherry, they would have "absolutely nothing to do, whatsoever, with the work of FEPC in the field or in Washington." In the past, the FEPC had disagreed with these men over methods of dealing with discrimination. The Labor Division, using the mass approach, worked at the management level in plants and industries. Meetings were held with corporate leaders and their personnel directors, the WMC representatives quietly trying to persuade these men to hire minority workers. The FEPC took a very different approach. It investigated individual complaints and con-

7. Verbatim transcript, committee meeting, A.M., September 30, 1942, R63HR, RG 228; Milton Webster to Mark Ethridge, October 7, 1942, in Box 20, BSCP Papers; Chicago *Defender*, September 19, 1942, p. 1.

8. Verbatim transcript, committee meeting, A.M., September 30, 1942, pp. 3–16, R63HR, RG 228.

fronted employers with charges of discrimination. When this approach failed, it might schedule public hearings. Large defense contractors, especially, hated publicity and usually sought to avoid it, though some fought back, attacking the FEPC and activating their elected representatives. Politically sensitive administration leaders preferred the quiet ways of the Labor Division to the FEPC's public activity. "Soreness is developing over the plan to transfer all the staff dealing with Negroes and other minorities in Manpower to the" FEPC, White House adviser Jonathan Daniels informed Marvin McIntyre on September 15. It may have been carefully planned, he wrote, "but I have more regard for the wisdom of Dr. Will Alexander in this matter than for all the more radical defenders of the Negro." Regrettably, it appeared to Daniels, Robert Weaver and "the fine Alexander influence" were on the way out.[9]

Although Robert Weaver's relatively lengthy service in the New Deal's so-called Black Cabinet probably made him one of the most respected race representatives in Washington, D.C., black leaders such as A. Philip Randolph and Walter White, in demanding the issuance of Executive Order 8802, wanted better results than Weaver's Negro Training Branch had delivered. Once established, however, the FEPC duplicated many of the Labor Division's activities. According to columnist Horace Cayton, Weaver's office never had good relations with the new agency. Charley Cherokee thought Weaver accomplished more than any force in breaking down traditional prejudice against semiskilled and skilled blacks yet faulted him because he often issued news releases that were "too eloquently optimistic" about job openings for black workers. Earl Dickerson was considerably less complimentary. They tried their method for over a year and a half and failed, he declared, for up to June, 1941, when the FEPC was created, very little had been accomplished. In the final analysis, Dickerson thought, corporations would not employ blacks out of good will, and "if they do, they will give a Negro chemist a job carrying a broom." The FEPC could improve this situation if the president and the WMC would only provide the ammunition.[10]

9. *Ibid.*, 22; memorandum, Jonathan Daniels to Marvin McIntyre, September 15, 1942, in Box 28, Jonathan Daniels Papers, Southern Historical Collection, University of North Carolina; Meier and Rudwick, *Black Detroit and the Rise of the UAW*, 156–57.
10. Verbatim transcript, committee meeting, September 30, 1942, pp. 20–24,

At a committee meeting with WMC deputy chairman Fowler Harper on September 30, it became clear that Paul McNutt wanted the FEPC totally under his control. In response to committee proposals, Harper made several points. First, the FEPC could not directly supervise its own field personnel. Instead, there must be one staff and one operation supervised by WMC regional directors, who were under the overall direction of the WMC's chief of operations, General McSherry. They and McSherry could veto FEPC recommendations on the conduct of field operations, the appointment of field personnel, and the holding of hearings. The FEPC could appeal only to the superior authority of McNutt. Second, when the FEPC moved against discrimination in the government bureaucracy, the WMC chairman would notify the appropriate agency heads. Finally, the FEPC could not investigate individual complaints of discrimination in any areas with industries already preempted by the Labor Division. In Milton Webster's words, McNutt was truly the "whole boss."[11]

WMC control over the appointments and removals of field personnel particularly incensed Earl Dickerson. "Now wait," he interrupted Harper. "The Committee is being stripped down to its last legs. We are being taken for a ride. . . . The clothes are off the Committee, and now you are going into the corpuscles." For the first time in history, Dickerson noted, blacks sat on a policy-making committee of the federal government. This signified real progress and a possible breakthrough for service on other important bodies. One prerogative of the FEPC was the appointment of its staff, a function in which blacks had never before participated. It might seem like a small thing, said Dickerson, but he thought it worthy of attention. Taking this prerogative away from the committee would be the same as taking it "from the Negro people." He left the September 30 meeting totally pessimistic about the FEPC's future. The problem was FDR himself. "The disagreement . . . rests with something fundamental that can't at this conference, or at this table be corrected," he stated at the end of the meeting, "and that is when the transfer was made, and made subject

---

R63HR, RG 228; Pittsburgh *Courier,* January 17, 1942, p. 13; Chicago *Defender,* January 24, 1942, p. 15, March 21, 1942, p. 15.

11. Verbatim transcript, committee meeting, P.M., September 30, 1942, pp. 49–72, R63HR, and Fowler Harper to the President's Committee on Fair Employment Practice, October 1, 1942, Proposed Plan for Reorganization, office files of George M. Johnson, R4HR, both in RG 228.

to someone else, that is an act which Mr. Roosevelt did and only Mr. Roosevelt can make that."[12]

Dickerson's concern about black participation in committee appointments was perfectly justified, and the ability to affect policy and influence patronage was an important advantage for blacks in the government. Indeed, the patronage system was as old as the federal bureaucracy itself. At the FEPC's inauguration, Walter White of the NAACP successfully named several individuals for staff positions. Lester Granger of the National Urban League wrote Cramer about the need for a strong Negro executive director in the FEPC's proposed regional office in New York City. Several well-qualified people were available, Granger stated, but he would not make any suggestions unless asked. Some committee members were approached directly about jobs, Milton Webster by a perfect stranger. "A good many people will be integrated into the staff in the very near future," Webster wrote in response to a Mrs. Bessie Gilbert of Baltimore. "Get in touch with me in Washington," D.C., before the Monday meeting, "because the jobs are being gobbled up pretty rapidly." One prominent individual, the white Alfred Baker Lewis, volunteered. A wealthy socialist who for many years had supplied funds for Norman Thomas, Lewis offered to serve without compensation as an FEPC field investigator. Cramer thought that his "list of arrests" for "distributing leaflets and a few things like that" were "not too bad," but John Brophy believed putting unpaid individuals on the staff would harm morale. Lewis' application was processed along with others, but his offer was ultimately passed up.[13]

As the confrontation went on, public indignation mounted in the press and in letters from organizations and individuals. Some attacked McNutt personally. This outcry came from the FEPC's growing constituency, an increasingly interracial network of supporters, exerting pressure before the upcoming November elections. These groups included several metropolitan councils for fair employment practice in

12. Verbatim transcript, committee meeting, P.M., September 30, 1942, pp. 83, 94, RG 228; Earl Dickerson to Lester B. Granger, October 8, 1942, in Series 1, Box 16, FEPC 1942–43, Records of the National Urban League, Library of Congress.

13. Lester Granger to Lawrence Cramer, July 22, 1942, Central Files, Public Relations, G file, R43HR, and verbatim transcript, committee meeting, October 26, 1942, p. 71, R63HR, both in RG 228; Milton Webster to Bessie Gilbert, November 20, 1942, in Box 20, BSCP Papers.

cities such as New York, Cleveland, Detroit, Chicago, and San Francisco. In addition to messages from Walter White, telegrams from NAACP branches urging the FEPC's independence poured into the White House from the East Coast to the Midwest and from Tennessee to Oklahoma. Ernest Angell's Council for Democracy, which was studying problems of black workers in industry, sent a strong protest. A white woman who belonged to an interracial group in Syracuse, New York, asked for the restoration of the FEPC's powers. Numerous Jewish groups and individuals, Protestant organizations, and various CIO unions gave their support to the committee. The list of church groups included the Pennsylvania Council of Churches; the Albany (New York) Ministers' Association; the Andover Newton Theological School; the Board of Education of the Methodist church in Nashville, Tennessee; the Bronx Clergy Association; the Detroit Council of Churches, representing 500 parishes; the Department of Christian Social Relations, Episcopal Diocese of Long Island; the Federal Council of Churches of Christians in America; the Interdenominational Ministerial Alliance of St. Louis; the New Haven Council of Churches; the National Baptist Convention; the North Dakota Conference of the Evangelical Church; and the United Christian Council for Democracy. Many individual congregations also expressed their support for the FEPC.[14]

Except for Chairman MacLean, all the committee members opposed WMC controls. Mark Ethridge accused the manpower agency of making the FEPC ineffectual by interfering with its power to investigate and hold hearings. Unless the committee could go into a place like Birmingham, in the face of all the pressure from senators, congressmen, governors, and other powerful figures, it would have little effect and "might as well not be in existence." To Milton Webster the situation was hopeless. As if speaking for McNutt, he said sarcastically, "Before you have hearings, see me about it and I will decide whether or not you are going to have them." Fowler Harper disavowed any

14. James M. Yard to Lawrence Cramer, June 30, 1942, XYZ file, E. W. McFarland to Malcolm MacLean, July 3, 1942, MDC file, Cleveland Metropolitan Council to the President, August 15, 1942, CMC file, all in Public Relations 5, R45HR, Bay Area Council Against Discrimination to the President, August 21, 1942, and Ernest Angell to Lawrence Cramer, September 4, 1942, both in Public Relations 5, R42HR, and Agnes Lindberg to the President, October 19, 1942, Public Relations 5, L file, R43HR, all in RG 228; Philadelphia *Tribune*, August 2, 1942, p. 1; Public Relations, Churches file, R46HR, RG 228.

interference with FEPC investigations and hearings, but General McSherry's attitude reflected the real WMC. His own people could carry on certain overall negotiations to eliminate entire practices and policies of discrimination, he believed, and accomplish the purpose better than plunging in immediately with a case of some individual who could not get a job. Cramer and Ethridge worried about the "dualism" of function between the FEPC and the Labor Division. After a second reading of Harper's proposals, Ethridge believed "the Committee [would] become a semi-detached agency and that the real director of operations [would] be Dr. Weaver, working through General McSherry." Although Ethridge professed to have "no feeling about Dr. Weaver or Dr. Alexander," such an arrangement would surely hamper the FEPC's work, he thought. Dickerson summed up their dilemma. If stripped of all those functions and left only with the right to appeal to the operations chief and to McNutt, he told Harper, the FEPC would have power left not to do anything but "only to go to somebody."[15]

Shortly after the September 30 meeting, McNutt, in an exclusive interview with the Associated Negro Press, promised that the FEPC would be strengthened, but he refused to answer specific questions until the budget was approved. As public protests intensified, however, he began to yield. Finally, on October 26, Fowler Harper announced the abolishment of the Labor Division. The investigative staffs of the Negro and Minority branches would be turned over to the FEPC as "the operating agency" within the WMC on all matters of discrimination covered by the executive order. Although the "one staff" concept survived in the field, the FEPC received the power to appoint its own field investigators, who would then be assigned to the WMC regional offices. The WMC's regional directors could object to FEPC appointments through channels, but they had to follow the committee's operations bulletins and instructions in dealing with its personnel. The FEPC's central office in Washington, D.C., would be in direct contact by letter, wire, and telephone with its field examiners, though copies of all communications had to be sent to the WMC. The demise of the Labor Division meant, of course, that Robert Weaver's tenure would also end. When the Chicago *Defender* highlighted these

15. Verbatim transcript, committee meeting, September 30, 1942, p. 61, R67HR, and Mark Ethridge to Lawrence Cramer, October 6, 1942, in Public Relations 5, Ethridge file, R45HR, both in RG 228.

events with the headline "Weaver Loses U.S. Post," George Johnson delivered a mild rebuke to publisher John Sengstacke for "misinterpreting the substance of the agreement" with the WMC. "It is, in my judgment, unfortunate to emphasize personal issues at a time when all our energies should be directed toward making a united effort."[16]

The WMC's protracted resistance to the FEPC undoubtedly sprang from several motives. McNutt's desire to control all manpower functions certainly dovetailed nicely with administration wishes to keep the troublesome FEPC under wraps. Then, too, a bureaucratic power struggle was going on within the WMC between its Labor Division and the President's Committee. Nevertheless, it was a significant victory for the FEPC in which the upcoming election no doubt played a part. But there was one important qualification. All hearings had to be approved in advance. On this question McNutt refused to yield. Having won other important concessions, the committee capitulated on this point. Chairman MacLean, especially, did not want to continue the battle. He "would rather be reversed" before a decision was "sent into action and into publicity . . . [than] spanked in public afterward." Milton Webster did not "like the whole thing" and cast the one negative vote. David Sarnoff could understand the president's desire to have as few agencies as possible, but there was no denying that the FEPC's independent status was gone. Sarnoff also sympathized with McNutt, who would bear the responsibility for the FEPC's failures but share little of the glory if it succeeded. If he were in McNutt's shoes, Sarnoff indicated, he would want some degree of authority over the FEPC's operations. Whether it could function in accord with the original intentions of 8802 Sarnoff did not know, but he went along with the agreement.[17]

With the operations agreement completed after nearly three months of argument, the FEPC requested an annual budget of

16. Memorandum, Relationship of the President's Committee on Fair Employment Practice to the WMC, Fowler Harper to Paul McNutt, October 24, 1942, office files of Malcolm Ross, Extra Copies files, R1HR, George Johnson to John Sengstacke, October 30, 1942, in Public Relations 5, Johnson file, R45HR, all in RG 228; Pittsburgh *Courier*, October 3, 1942, p. 1.

17. Verbatim transcripts of meetings between September 30 and October 26 do not appear in the FEPC records. Earl Dickerson was absent from the October 26 meeting at the time the vote was taken on the operating agreement. Verbatim transcript, committee meeting, October 26, 1942, pp. 2–20, 92–95, R63HR, RG 228; Pittsburgh *Courier*, October 31, 1942, p. 1, November 7, 1942, p. 6; Chicago *Defender*, October 31, 1942, pp. 1, 14.

$497,000 to staff a central office of forty-eight, with fifty-two field personnel. Committee members never doubted that the WMC would honor the agreement. Paul McNutt had a liberal record on the race issue. In 1941, for example, he warned political and business leaders in Philadelphia to end racial discrimination, and he repeated this message frequently in 1942, once during an appearance in Harlem. Shortly thereafter he approved a controversial hearing involving the southern railroads, and in December he told several hundred railroad executives at a New York meeting that they must end their bias against minorities. Nonetheless, there were alarming delays in implementing the FEPC-WMC agreement. When two months passed without the approval of funding, the Bureau of the Budget could be blamed, but McNutt and his staff were responsible for other delays. By January, Labor Division personnel were still with the WMC, and none of the files had been merged. General McSherry ignored repeated requests to distribute the FEPC's Operations Bulletin, which established guidelines for the relationship between FEPC personnel and WMC regional directors. Disputes flared up in the field over FEPC activity. Meanwhile, backlogs of work piled up in the central office as complaints of discrimination and USES 510s continued to arrive. In November alone, 775 cases were reported. By mid-January Cramer reported to the Budget Bureau that over 7,000 complaints against 1,500 companies, unions, and government agencies had been handled by the FEPC. Because of inadequate staff, only 10 percent of these had been thoroughly investigated.[18]

Yet the protracted hassle with the manpower commission only partially distracted the staff. Beginning in July, 1942, they sifted through the Birmingham testimony and prepared summaries, findings, and directives against various offenders. Earl Dickerson seemingly read every word, chastising the staff for its leniency. Even the committee

18. Verbatim transcripts, committee meetings, November 23, 1942, p. 2, January 9, 1943, p. 63, and February 8, 1943, pp. 48–50, R64HR, Lawrence Cramer to Frank McSherry, December 7, 1942, Reports 1-1, USES 510s, 1942, 48HR, Harry Barron to Eli E. Cohen, December 5, 1942, in Public Relations 5, Jewish Occupational Council file, R45HR, L. B. F. Raycroft to Lawrence Cramer, December 10, 1942, U.S. Govt., WMC, George Johnson to Ira deA. Reid, March 8, 1943, U.S. Govt., USES, R67HR, and Theodore Jones to Lawrence Cramer, December 14, 1942, Office Memorandum, J file, R1HR, all in RG 228; Flynn, Mess in Washington, 152–53, 159; Meier and Rudwick, Black Detroit and the Rise of the UAW, 111–12; Lawrence Cramer to Robert M. Barnett, January 19, 1943, Reports, FEP 1, R48HR, RG 228.

had "been too much yielding to the status quo," he scolded. In one case, he thought an admiral should be fired for failing to cooperate. Mild-mannered John Brophy did not find fault with "your spanking an admiral but I do object to your spanking me." In the fall of 1942, as the negotiations with Harper and McNutt dragged on, the committee decided to increase the number of its field examiners, appointing four and approving seven others.[19]

With the October 26 operating agreement completed, the committee took up important business. It responded to blacks and the UAW in Detroit by ordering a hearing on area defense industries, particularly the automobile industry, where black women were refused employment. The committee agreed tentatively to hold other hearings in St. Louis, Cleveland, Philadelphia, and Baltimore. Prodded by Milton Webster, it set January 25, 1943, for a hearing on the discriminatory practices of the southern railroads and their unions. To begin preparing the case, Henry Epstein, former solicitor of New York State, was named special counsel. Black NAACP attorney Charles Houston was appointed to assist in the case. The committee also discussed cases of discrimination in Texas (a Baytown refinery and a Houston shipyard), in Virginia (the Newport News Shipbuilding Company and the Norfolk Navy Yard), and the Vultee Aircraft plant in Nashville, the Gulf Shipbuilding Company of Mobile, and the Alabama defense training program.[20]

The committee also began taking a look at discrimination in the federal government. FEPC staff members conducted three administrative hearings, one involving the Library of Congress, another the CS. A third hearing aired charges by a resident alien interpreter against the State Department and the Board of Economic Warfare. But the FEPC's greatest challenge was the District of Columbia's public transportation system, which was understaffed, with trolleys standing idle, yet blacks could not get jobs there as platform workers and motor-

19. Verbatim transcript, committee meeting, October 26, 1942, pp. 79–80, R63HR, RG 228.
20. Verbatim transcript, committee meeting, October 26, 1942, pp. 50–86, R63HR, press releases "E," Henry Epstein file, R36HR, summary of committee actions, September 11, 1942, R1HR, Lawrence Cramer to R. J. Thomas, December 2, 1942, in Public Relations 5, T file, R44HR, all in RG 228; Meier and Rudwick, *Black Detroit and the Rise of the UAW,* 156–57; Alexa B. Henderson, "FEPC and the Southern Railway Case: An Investigation into the Discriminatory Practices of Railroads During World War II," *Journal of Negro History,* LXI (1976), 173–87.

men. The Capital Transit Company refused to hire and train them because members of its white AFL union threatened to walk out. In a lengthy conference, company and union representatives were evasive and uncooperative. When the company failed to respond to a November 28 directive, the committee voted to hold a hearing.[21]

All of this FEPC activity did not go unnoticed. According to one Washington, D.C., insider, the Capital Transit case became "a pretty hot issue." He wondered if there was "any way in which releases on dynamite subjects like this about manpower could come to the attention" of administration officials "before they [were] released." In Atlanta early in 1943, the president of the Georgia Power Company, operator of the city's public transportation system, worried about the FEPC order to Capital Transit. "If they try to force similar things here in Georgia," he wrote Senator Richard B. Russell, "they will produce the worst race riots that have ever occurred." Russell responded that he had "been able to temporarily block these hearings," but he did not know how long they would stay that way. On the other side, blacks were elated. "FEPC seems to mean business issuing announcements thick and fast ordering this and that company to cease and desist with plans for major hearings in six cities," observed columnist Harry McAlpin.[22]

By the beginning of 1943, committee activities touched a South already seething over the Birmingham hearing and New Deal policies in general. Southern conservatives were heartened when the November elections went badly for the administration. Conservatives made gains throughout the nation, and southern anti–New Dealers returned to Washington, D.C., with confidence and political clout. Governor Frank Dixon of Alabama, after reading the FEPC's findings and directives on the Birmingham hearing, attacked the administration in

21. Verbatim transcript, committee meeting, A.M., November 23, 1942, pp. 23–69, and hearing, November 27, 1942, both in R64HR, Seth Major Case, Reports 2, Library of Congress, R16HR, CSC hearing, December 14, 1942, R15HR, FDR to the Chairman, August 20, 1942, in Public Relations 5, FDR file, R45HR, R45HR, all in RG 228.

22. Memorandum, Robert J. Blakely to Robert Huse, December 12, 1942, in Philleo Nash file, General Correspondence, FEPC file, Miscellaneous Truman Papers; Richard Russell to Preston S. Arkwright, February 3, 1943, in Series X, Negro 1942–43 file, Russell Papers; Pittsburgh *Courier*, November 21, 1942, p. 1, December 5, 1942, p. 1; Chicago *Defender*, December 5, 1942, p. 1; Harry McAlpin, "Silver Lining," Chicago *Defender*, December 12, 1942, p. 15; Philadelphia *Tribune*, December 12, 1942, p. 20.

a New York speech for undermining the southern social structure. He also threatened to form an independent southern Democratic party. The FEPC's order to "upgrade and promote workers without regard to race" simply meant that the USES would "send negro stenographers, clerical help, office managers and employees . . . from common laborer up through executive positions," he informed Senator Russell. These people would be "fed into the already-existing body of white employees," violating "the principle of segregation of which all Southern social and economic life" had rested for generations. The FEPC was "operating as a kangaroo court obviously dedicated to the abolition of segregation in the South."[23]

Pressures were building up from other quarters. In mid-December, 1942, union leaders from Capital Transit appeared before the District Committee of the House of Representatives to complain about FEPC orders to hire black motormen and platform workers. In response, Congressman John Rankin of Mississippi "yelled bloody murder against the employment of any Negroes" and called for a congressional investigation. When the FEPC cited Vultee Aircraft of Nashville and three Alabama companies, the Smith Committee of the House announced it would conduct a full investigation. Southern congressman planned a caucus to develop a strategy for combat. The whole world was talking about a second front in the European war, the Pittsburgh *Courier* had editorialized earlier, but at home the South had opened up its own second front against blacks. This domestic war involved attacks against "colored soldiers" in southern army camps, with "beatings, murder, mayhem," and the refusal of the Alabama governor to sign defense contracts with antidiscrimination clauses. By January, 1943, the *Courier* could have added numerous other southern campaigns aimed at African-Americans. The Chicago *Defender* expected the Dies Committee would come back to life and use its "red smear" tactics. Tremendous pressures there were, and the White House responded in January by ordering Paul McNutt to cancel the southern railroad hearing. Following McNutt's announcement of an indefinite postponement of the hearing, both special coun-

23. Frank Dixon to Richard Russell, November 25, 1942, in Series X, Negro 1942 file, Russell Papers; Chicago *Defender*, December 12, 1942, p. 3, January 9, 1943, p. 1; Philadelphia *Tribune*, December 19, 1942, p. 20; Pittsburgh *Courier*, December 19, 1942, p. 6; Richard N. Chapman, *Contours of Public Policy, 1939–1945* (New York, 1941), 205.

sels, Epstein and Houston, resigned. George Q. Flynn's account of the cancellation is ambiguous. On the one hand, FDR was "responsible" for the decision that was conveyed to McNutt by Attorney General Biddle. On the other hand, McNutt, failing to persuade Lawrence Cramer to order the cancellation, "acted on his own." McNutt publicly assumed full responsibility for canceling the railroad hearing, though the press remained skeptical.[24]

Following the Birmingham hearing, the FEPC, usually involved in activity that was politically sensitive, probably was never completely out of the White House consciousness. Then, for nearly a month before the cancellation of the railroad hearing on January 11, the FEPC received even closer administration scrutiny. Following a cabinet meeting on December 11, Attorney General Francis Biddle suggested that the president order him to study "the Negro situation" and explore more competent methods of handling it.[25]

Biddle's and the administration's concerns about the black press and Afro-American morale had not changed from the previous May, when the cabinet discussed "the Negro situation." By the end of 1942, several prominent publications, including the *Saturday Review of Literature*, the *Atlantic Monthly*, the *Virginia Quarterly Review*, and *Reader's Digest*, were criticizing radical blacks in the North and their newspapers for stirring up white southern racists. Worried about the tension, Virginius Dabney in December published another article on the racial issue because he feared violent explosions by whites and blacks. Dabney also criticized the black press. Additional fuel was added by a black scholar and associate at the Council for Democracy, Warren H. Brown, whose article entitled "A Negro Looks at the Negro Press," published in the *Saturday Review* and reprinted in *Read-*

---

24. Verbatim transcripts, committee meetings, January 22, 1943, pp. 1–10, and February 8, 1943, pp. 66–77, both in R64HR, RG 228; Pittsburgh *Courier*, September 12, 1942, p. 6, December 19, 1942, p. 6; Chicago *Defender*, December 12, 1942, p. 3, December 19, 1942, p. 6, January 9, 1943, p. 1, January 30, 1943, p. 15; Philadelphia *Tribune*, December 19, 1942, p. 20; James A. Wechsler, "Pigeonhole for Negro Equality," *Nation*, January 23, 1943, pp. 121–22; Charles Houston to the President, January 18, 1943, in Official File 4245-G, Box 5, 1943, FDRL; Pittsburgh *Courier*, January 23, 1943, p. 6; Flynn, *Mess in Washington*, 159–61; Chapman, *Contours of Public Policy*, 205; Chicago *Defender*, January 16, 1943, p. 1; Pittsburgh *Courier*, January 16, 1943, p. 1, January 23, 1943, p. 13; Neuchterlein, "Politics of Civil Rights," 179; Wynn, *Afro-American and the Second World War*, 49; Sitkoff, "Racial Militancy and Interracial Violence," 676.

25. Cabinet meeting, December 11, 1942, in Box 1, Biddle Papers, FDRL.

er's *Digest*, stated that the majority of Afro-Americans were satisfied with the system. Black newspapers, a couple of which Brown had served on as journalist or editor and had left under less than amicable circumstances, branded him a traitor. Liberal white publications such as the *Nation* and the *New Republic* rushed to the defense of the black publishers. Negro morale also had been a continuing worry of the administration at least since spring, 1942, when an Office of War Information (OWI) survey of Harlem residents found deep resentment and anger over discrimination, a belief by many that they might be treated better by the Japanese, and a militancy that was potentially explosive. The government's concern led to the issuance of OWI reports on tension areas in the country and to the creation of tension files in agencies such as the FEPC.[26] Later, under the New Committee, the FEPC's office of Review and Analysis kept extensive tension files by region and city—files that included data from the OWI, from the FEPC's own field investigators, and also from other agencies.[27]

In seeking better methods of handling "the Negro situation," Biddle called an interracial meeting of administration insiders for December 31, informing McNutt of his intentions. The embattled WMC chairman, nearly dismissed earlier because of his administrative mistakes, did not attend. The Biddle group was comprised of two prominent blacks, Ralph Bunche and Judge William Hastie, and several whites, including Frank Graham, Malcolm Ross, and Victor Rotnem, soon to be appointed head of the Civil Rights Section in the Justice Department. Bunche, in the State Department, and Hastie, civilian aide in the War Department, were part of the Black Cabinet. Graham, president of the University of North Carolina, served on the National War Labor Board. Ross was public relations director of the NLRB on loan to the OWI. Other participants included Keith Kane, Donald Young, Adlai Stevenson, and Walter Berge. The conferees were scarcely of one mind, but the majority, including Bunche, who was close to Robert Weaver, reacted negatively to the FEPC. Most believed that race relations could best be handled through education and negotiations instead of public hearings and publicity. This was also the

26. Finkle, *Forum for Protest*, 69, 74–78, 102; John Temple Graves, "The Southern Negro and the War Crisis," *Virginia Quarterly Review*, XVIII (1942), 500–17.

27. See, for example, Central Files, Tension Area Reports, Region V & Region IX, R63HR, RG 228. Sociologist Charles Johnson was also concerned about tension in the Afro-American community. See Johnson *et al.*, *To Stem This Tide*, 2–31.

approach of white southern liberals. Bunche, particularly, stressed the damaging effects of too much public notoriety, but he believed along with Biddle that the FEPC, while being coordinated with the program of the WMC, should remain independent. The group came to no consensus on a location for the FEPC or on the kind of enforcement powers it should have. Graham and Hastie stressed the positive aspects of the FEPC's activities, and both men were critical of Mark Ethridge's Birmingham speech. Hastie supported the FEPC's use of strong sanctions.[28]

Presidential Assistant Jonathan Daniels was also becoming increasingly involved. One of several southern liberals, Daniels, like Mark Ethridge and Will Alexander, gave the administration advice on racial issues. White southerners were experts on race, the curious reasoning went, because most African-Americans lived in the South. Undoubtedly, the advice of these white southerners tipped administration policies toward conservatism. The liberal southerners' counsel generally reflected their judgment on what would pass politically, or at least be tolerated, in the solid, segregated, Democratic South. In the past, being liberal in Daniels' case had meant an abhorrence of lynching, the acceptance of segregation with equality, the absence of discrimination, and noblesse oblige paternalism. In the progressive spirit, he opposed black voting because of alleged poverty, ignorance, and susceptibility to manipulation. He was devoted to states' rights and opposed federal involvement in race relations, including federal legislation outlawing lynching and the poll tax. To say the least, the southern liberal bore little resemblance to the national breed carrying that label. When Daniels arrived in Washington, D.C., in February, 1942, to join the two other southerners near the president, Stephen Early and Marvin McIntyre, he apparently felt at ease with the administration's racial policies.[29]

Daniels had contacts with the FEPC soon after his arrival, but he participated increasingly in racial matters after the Birmingham hearing. By mid-August, more "disturbed about the state of Negro-white

28. Francis Biddle to Malcolm Ross and Victor Rotnem, June 2, 1943, and memorandum on conference, December 31, 1942, both in Box 44, FEPC, Haas Papers; Larry Berman, *Office of Management and Budget*, 26.

29. Helen Fuller, "The Ring Around the President," *New Republic*, October 25, 1943, p. 565; Charles W. Eagles, *Jonathan Daniels and Race Relations: The Evolution of a Southern Liberal* (Knoxville, 1982), 23–93.

relationships" than he could ever remember being, Daniels prepared a personal letter to Lester Granger of the National Urban League, which inexplicably he did not send. In this missive, Daniels recounted numerous messages recently received "from white men in the South . . . interested in the advance[ment] of the Negro." They described the situation between the races as "loaded with dynamite." Two emotional movements were colliding, Daniels thought, the "rising insistence of Negroes on their rights now" and the "rising tide of white feeling against the Negroes in the South and other sections." Some solution had to be found "short of bloodshed at home and the creation of material for dangerous anti-American propaganda abroad." [30]

Daniels believed the Negro position was "logically strong." A people fighting for democracy and freedom in the world would insist on those values at home as well. The "logical cure" would be "the removal of discriminations against which Negroes complain," but this remedy "supposes that there is no majority problem as well as a minority problem." In thinking about a solution, Daniels was frightened at the possibilities. The country could be "so divided in home angers that we would lack the strength for victory over our Fascist enemies," or "we might easily resort to Fascist methods in the creation of a ruthless unity." If fascism came to the United States, it "would not involve the Negro alone . . . but all those who have spoken for justice for the Negro," though "Negroes would suffer worst." Daniels had no solution, but apparently he never considered the possibility that his native South, where legally enforced segregation embittered racial relations, might itself eventually have to change. The unmailed letter to Granger reveals the thinking of the man who shortly would become an important advisor to FDR on racial matters until the president's death. [31]

By late November, Daniels communicated his concerns directly to FDR. In the wake of the election reverses, his message was political in tone. He was quite sure that "this Negro question is one of the hottest, most difficult problems in the world." In fact, as one suspected of being "radical in the South" but "too conservative" for many blacks in the North, he was affected personally. What disturbed him most was first, "the lack of any apparent clear authority anywhere for dealing with this question" and second, "the apparent fail-

30. Jonathan Daniels to Lester B. Granger, August 14, 1942, in Daniels Papers.
31. *Ibid.*

ure" of the FEPC "to exercise all [the] judgment and tact required in its efforts to effectuate justice in employment." As an example, Daniels cited the FEPC's "announcement on the final day of the poll tax fight" in Congress that it would move against the Capital Transit Company. The action may have been justified, he said, but it could also "create Southern fears that the government" may be using the war effort to end jim-crow laws in the southern transportation system. The action "may also lift Negro hopes only to drop them again."[32]

Daniels was concerned, too, about the southern railroad case. Although the FEPC had retained Henry Epstein as special counsel, Daniels heard that others had been approached, including Morris Ernst and Arthur Garfield Hays of the American Civil Liberties Union. "Under any of them, the case could become a civil rights *cause celebre*," which "might result in making more Negroes and more Whites hostile toward the administration" without advancing the Negro's cause. Daniels suggested that Roosevelt create "some kind of supervisory responsibility . . . in some official close to you and in whom you have confidence" to deal with these matters. Otherwise, "the Negro and the white Southerner . . . can do a lot of damage unless the problems in which both are furiously concerned" could be approached with "more wisdom and tact."[33]

Among Daniels' contacts in early December as he brooded over "the Negro question" was Will Alexander, whose Minorities Group in the WMC's Labor Division had been abolished by the October 26 agreement with the FEPC. Alexander then became a consultant to the WMC chief of operations until he left in what was described as disgust. As one of the losers, he had few words of praise for the FEPC, and he told Daniels at a luncheon meeting that "Cramer is doing a very bad job as the executive [secretary]." According to Alexander, "McNutt got very angry when the Committee undertook to hold him up on the basis of the Negro vote," and finally, Fowler Harper "persuaded him that he would have to give in." Alexander attributed MacLean's behavior in the FEPC-WMC negotiations to his "precarious position" at Hampton Institute, where "his faculty and trustees and now the alumni are turning on him." According to Walter White,

32. Memorandum, Jonathan Daniels to the President, November 24, 1942, in Daniels Papers.

33. *Ibid.*; Eagles, *Jonathan Daniels*, 101–102.

MacLean had "rubbed a lot of people [at Hampton] the wrong way" by revamping the curriculum, forcing "wholesale retirements of teachers too feeble to function," ending the "color line at Mansion House," and abolishing the all-white school for faculty children. In the negotiations with McNutt, MacLean had clearly been seeking "the support of Randolph and White." Daniels reported that Alexander particularly opposed the FEPC's "publicity policy . . . [which] is always telling what they are going to do and not what they have done." None of the FEPC's hearings had been followed up, and in Alexander's final analysis, the FEPC had become "largely a publicity agency for the doctrines of Walter White and Randolph." He believed that White, while "pushing the administration[,] had become increasingly closer" to the Republicans.[34]

Alexander's bitterness was perhaps understandable, but his sniping tactics seemed to diminish the stature of a man with sound credentials in southern race relations from an earlier era.[35] Concern over the black vote probably had led the administration to give in to the FEPC before the November election, as Alexander claimed. Weaver's Negro Branch and Alexander's Minorities Group, unlike the FEPC, had never attracted wide popular support. Perhaps the charge that they were ineffective was not so far from the mark. An in-house study of the then–Negro Manpower Service and the Minorities Group Service, after their transfer to the WMC in spring, 1942, described a "gradual deterioration of the staff," a lack of coordination between headquarters activity and the field, and an absence of communication among the regional offices. Whether the Labor Division achieved solid accomplishments equal to the claims of its cheerleaders is still to be documented. Nevertheless, Alexander's opinions in the upcoming months had considerable influence on Daniels, who stood next to the seat of power and rendered influential judgments on racial matters.[36]

By the middle of December, Daniels had produced an analysis of

34. Diary, December 2, 1942, Daniels Papers; Flynn, *Mess in Washington*, 159; Walter White, "Why MacLean Resigned," Chicago *Defender*, January 23, 1943, p. 1; Eagles, *Jonathan Daniels*, 101–102; Jonathan Daniels, *White House Witness*, 116.

35. For details on Alexander's considerable role in southern race relations during the 1920s and 1930s, see Ann Wells Ellis, "The Commission on Interracial Cooperation, 1919–1944: Its Activities and Results" (Ph.D. dissertation, Georgia State University, 1976).

36. "Minority Groups Service–War Manpower Commission" (Typescript, n.d., in Box 21, Philleo Nash files, Truman Papers).

the racial situation that crystallized much of his thinking during the previous weeks. He had also become more bitingly critical of some of the race leaders. Although addressed to Marvin McIntyre, the analysis was surely meant for the eyes of the president. In it, reflecting on a recent letter from Walter White that had informed FDR of an NAACP Board resolution calling for the complete independence of the FEPC, Daniels thought it was time "we began to realize that those who are undertaking to dictate the policies of this Administration with regard to the Negro have also become [its] sharp critics." He also distrusted A. Philip Randolph, who shared "the leadership of the more radical Negro group." When Randolph had recently spoken to a Cleveland meeting of the Federal Council of Churches, Will Alexander reported, his speech had been "straight anti-administration and anti-Roosevelt." Randolph had told the church leaders that FDR "did not create the [President's] Committee until the Negroes forced him to and that he has done nothing to support it since." Ignoring the fact that Randolph's statement was close to the truth, Alexander suspected "some sort of political deal" had been made "by these more radical Negroes, probably with Willkie."[37]

Daniels believed that Randolph and White, through their representatives, dominated the FEPC. There was evidence that the committee's "action in many cases follow[ed] lines laid down by" them "for their own causes and purposes," making the FEPC their political instrument. "Somebody must watch this business or it will injure both the administration and also the great mass of Negroes," Daniels warned. "Many thoughtful Negroes" were disturbed about both the direction they were being taken in and "the noisy demagoguery" of the radical black leaders. Daniels saw a clear threat for the elections in 1944. He wished that someone like Alexander could "have some supervision of what goes on" and also have access to the president, because the situation threatened the war effort, "peaceful race relations," the administration, and "the advance of Negroes themselves." Marvin McIntyre, whose job was made no easier because of the FEPC, certainly concurred. After the southern railroad hearing was canceled,

37. Memorandum, Jonathan Daniels to Marvin McIntyre, December 14, 1942, in Official File 4245-G, Justice Department folder, FDRL: Walter White to the President, December 8, 1942, Marvin McIntyre to Walter White, December 14, 1942, both in General Office File, FEPC–Transfer and Railroad Hearings, 1941–43, NAACP Records.

he told Lawrence Cramer that the FEPC had exceeded its authority. Even if the committee had the right to hold hearings, it was unwise to do so, he admonished, for such hearings encouraged "extremists who were demanding 100 per cent enforcement of the executive order by six o'clock the next morning." McIntyre also believed the FEPC should not issue directives even when discrimination existed.[38]

Francis Biddle's Justice Department was also intimately involved with racial relations. In the Civil Rights Section, Victor Rotnem and his staff expressed greater anger at the FEPC than did the White House. They were also more vicious. In a seven-page, undated, unsigned document from Rotnem's desk, the FEPC was written off as a "political mistake from its inception." This agency, "instead of reassuring the Negro of the administration's interests," gave "widespread new publicity to economic, political and social injustices" by "spotlighting areas" of discrimination "which had never been revealed before and these injustices were invariably blamed on the administration." The committee's structure itself contained "political dynamite liable to explode at any moment" and do "infinite harm to the political interests of the administration." Immediately before the November elections, the document went on, Walter White and Lawrence Cramer were able to force "large concessions" from Paul McNutt as to the committee's "independence and scope of operations" by "using the threat of [the] resignation of certain Committee members to be followed by bitter recriminations against the administration." Armed with these concessions, the committee began "ill-considered activity in the Capital Transit case" and set the stage for "a 'super Scottsboro' hearing of the southern railroad case," that is, "a case where all conceivable issues are tried except the legal ones involved." The latter was to be held amid great publicity in Washington, D.C., under the tutelage of Henry Epstein, a bitter administration foe. "Tensions aroused by this indiscreet program . . . were so acute that it became necessary for McNutt to immobilize the Committee."[39]

38. Memorandum, Daniels to McIntyre, December 14, 1942, in Official File 4245-G, Justice Department folder, FDRL; verbatim transcript, committee meeting, January 22, 1943, pp. 10–11, R64HR, RG 228; Sosna, *In Search of the Silent South*, 108.

39. "Fair Employment Practice Committee" (Typescript, n.d., in Box 45, FEPC, Haas Papers). The document was routed to Monsignor Francis Haas from Rotnem. Other materials in the same folder, which Rotnem also sent to Haas, bore the routing date of January 8, 1943, but this document, which refers to the cancellation of the southern railroad hearing, must have been sent after January 11 unless the writer

Rotnem's document warned that reconstituting the FEPC "would be inviting serious trouble for the 1944 elections." Since the "professional Negro" usually seeks to play the major political parties against each other, it continued, the FEPC's "two Negro members . . . would be a rich capture [in 1944] for the Republicans," who would willingly pay a high price "for their apostasy." Earl Dickerson had just suffered defeat at the hands of Mayor Edward Kelly's Democratic organization in a race for his Chicago aldermanic seat, and Milton Webster "would definitely follow the dictation of Randolph." Furthermore, if Dickerson and Webster were reappointed to a newly constituted committee, "all [its] deliberations . . . [would] leak to the Negro press . . . creating *new sore spots* for the administration in its Negro relations." Such inside information would not otherwise be available to blacks, because they would lack "intelligence on operations *within* the government." Even the "appointment of loyal administration men" to the FEPC would not safeguard against new leaks, with "each new leak *opening new points* of conflict" with black interests.[40]

The FEPC had "failed miserably," the writer believed, in attempting to improve the economic situation of blacks. Indeed, the agency functioned "with the characteristic technique of the professional Negro," who kept "burning issues alive by continual use of the bellows of sensational publicity" in order to improve his own position. In contrast, the methods of handling "Negro cases" used by the Civil Rights Section "would offer an excellent guide" for the committee to follow. The Justice Department used "all possible tact" in avoiding "irrelevant issues which tend to inflame the local community" and usually employed a local lawyer of high repute as a special assistant, whereas the FEPC raised "totally irrelevant issues" and created "needless new frictions." In Birmingham, the writer continued, the FEPC "violated deep seated mores" by allowing the two black committee members to sit in the federal courtroom. It justified its existence with "violent publicity" that impeded or stopped "the orderly integration of Negroes into industry" and aroused racial tensions. As a consequence, "the worst

---

had inside knowledge that the cancellation had been ordered. Victor Rotnem had previously served in several New Deal legal offices; in February, 1935, Rotnem, along with his boss, Jerome Frank, was purged from the Legal Division of the Agricultural Adjustment Administration (Irons, *New Deal Lawyers,* 117, 179–80).

40. "Fair Employment Practice Committee." The writer's fear of Milton Webster's "apostasy" is amusing in view of the fact that Webster was a Republican.

demagogic elements of the South," like the Talmadges, Rankins, and Dixons, had gained "new life and ammunition."[41]

The document envisioned a bleak future for the FEPC. For one thing, the author judged, the agency was greatly overrated. Its activities were unknown to most black citizens, and thus the administration had "greatly overestimated [its] importance." For another, it was "inconceivable" that the FEPC would be allowed to function again "without due regard to the current status of the 'Southern rebellion.'" Reactivating the committee would make "political sense" only if done "in the knowledge that Congress would kill its budget and thus automatically end its life." Until that happened, however, the FEPC should shun publicity and concentrate on playing up the economic gains made by blacks during the war. Any other committee work, particularly involving businesses, should be undertaken behind the scenes and should stress "education rather than intimidation."[42]

Rotnem's document contained some kernels of truth, along with extraordinary hyperbole. Although accurate about the significance of the "Southern rebellion," it underestimated the moral force behind the FEPC. What is interesting, this highly politicized, hostile, and unsympathetic missive came from the section of the Justice Department charged with enforcing civil rights. What is not surprising, it recommended Will Alexander to be the new committee chairman because he was "a middle-of-the-roader . . . [who could] be depended on for a safe and sane approach." Others mentioned for committee positions were the black sociologist Charles Johnson and Malcolm Ross.[43]

The committee and staff as a group were the last to find out about administration plotting, though four white committee members were informed individually about the reorganization: Sarnoff, MacLean, Ethridge, and Brophy. David Sarnoff heard about it when he resigned to take an assignment in the War Department. Chairman Malcolm MacLean, whom the administration rescued from his difficulties at Hampton Institute, resigned and went to the Department of the Navy as a race relations advisor. On January 4, he and Mark Ethridge were told separately by Marvin McIntyre at the White House. Afterward,

41. *Ibid.*
42. *Ibid.*
43. *Ibid.*

MacLean remained in the capital for two days conferring about the FEPC's future. Predictably, he proposed a plan that would diminish the agency into a review board without an investigative staff or contact with the field. This "back-room" dealing by the administration did not go unchallenged. In protesting the cancellation of the southern railroad hearings, Walter White charged that "important matters relating to the Committee" had been decided "in 'off the record' conferences involving the President's Executive Assistant, other high-ranking government officials . . . and, on occasion, some . . . white members of the Committee." [44]

Ethridge resigned when the railroad hearing was canceled, but not in protest. He wanted to give McNutt a free hand in the reorganization. He had also heard that the administration was unhappy over the FEPC's Capital Transit and El Paso activities. It appears that the administration would have been pleased, indeed probably hoped, that the remaining committee members would, like "gentlemen," follow Ethridge's example and resign. Shortly thereafter, on January 11, Attorney General Biddle telephoned Ethridge to state that reorganization of the committee was necessitated by the MacLean and Sarnoff resignations. Biddle asked Ethridge to reassure the committee of the attorney general's intention not to interfere. Thus Biddle, through the former FEPC chairman, seemed to be sending the message that the remaining committee members were still in charge when in fact they were not. Others were writing the scenario. Perfunctorily, it would seem, he also asked Ethridge for advice, as he had MacLean. In response, Ethridge mentioned the three plans that the FEPC had offered to McNutt the previous September, that is, to abolish the committee, to reestablish it under the president, or to create a board of review and appeals. Biddle apparently heard only what pleased him. In obvious confusion, he recorded in a personal memorandum that "Marvin [sic] Etheridge [sic]" suggested that the "Fair Trade [sic] Practices Committee be abolished." In its place, Ethridge allegedly proposed a "Policy Committee . . . directly under the President" to "hear Negro complaints." Federal agencies, when so directed, would be persuaded rather than pressured to stop discrimination. The new

44. Verbatim transcript, committee meeting, January, 22, 1943, pp. 23, 103, R64HR, RG 228; Chicago *Defender*, January 23, 1943, p. 1; memorandum, Walter White to the President, January 22, 1943, in Official File–General, 1943, NAACP Records.

body would hold "secret public hearings [sic]" when relaxation of discriminatory practices could not be obtained otherwise. Biddle thought such a committee would be a good "buffer . . . for the President's relief," but he doubted that blacks would be satisfied.[45]

Ethridge's attitude toward the FEPC's work had been in continuous evolution throughout his tenure. He saw few problems at the beginning and overreacted at Birmingham, but he later defended the committee and argued persuasively for its independence from the WMC. He had opposed both the southern railroad hearing and the Capital Transit action because he thought the FEPC was going too far. Yet after his resignation he urged upon Biddle "the vital importance of the railroad hearing" because it had "really become a matter of good faith between the Administration and the Negroes."[46]

On January 9, John Brophy, the last to be approached by the administration, spent an hour and a half with Jonathan Daniels at CIO headquarters discussing the FEPC. Thus before the southern railroad hearing was canceled on January 11, the White House had unofficially contacted all of the committee members about reorganization except the two blacks and a new member, Boris Shishkin of the AFL, the recent replacement for Frank Fenton, who had stepped down earlier for reasons unrelated to the reorganization. Lawrence Cramer, who also was told nothing, apparently kept himself informed through the grapevine, but he shared no secrets with the staff.[47]

Cramer reported the cancellation of the railroad hearing to committee members by telephone, but two weeks passed before they met. During that time, Earl Dickerson heard nothing from anyone in authority except the outgoing chairman, who instructed them all to refrain from making public statements before the January 22 meeting. Revelations about the reorganization from Ethridge, Cramer, and Brophy were news to Dickerson, who was justifiably outraged that he and Webster had been kept completely in the dark. This attack went to the heart of the FEPC's enforcement policies, Dickerson thought. For the administration to discuss reorganization "behind the[ir]

45. Verbatim transcript, committee meeting, A.M., January 22, 1943, pp. 1–6, R64HR, RG 228; memorandum, January 11, 1943, in Box 2, Biddle Papers.
46. Verbatim transcript, committee meeting, A.M., January 22, 1943, pp. 1–6, R64HR, RG 228; Memorandum, January 11, 1943, in Box 2, Biddle Papers.
47. Verbatim transcripts, committee meetings, A.M., January 22, 1943, pp. 23–27, a.m., February 8, 1943, p. 2, both in R64HR, Mark Ethridge to Francis Biddle, January 25, 1943, in Public Relations 5, Ethridge file, R45HR, all in RG 228.

backs" was an "affront" and an "insult" to the "personal dignity" of men "who served the government without pay for a year and a half" and now were "cast aside" when vital matters were taken up. It was really, he believed, an effort to end the FEPC's usefulness. Those in power who created the committee under pressure from blacks saw it as an appeasement mechanism that would not accomplish anything. "When we proceeded to act like human beings . . . [and tried] to achieve something . . . those who are opposed to Negro improvement" became concerned and tried to halt the committee's aggressiveness. But there was little time for anger. The FEPC was again under attack, and its surviving members wanted to have some influence on the decisions about its future.[48]

With the Justice Department and the White House preparing reorganization proposals, Lawrence Cramer, without consultation, rushed his own suggestions to Marvin McIntyre, warning that any attempt to modify Executive Order 8802 in any significant way would "encourage extremist agitation" and in the end provide no solution at all. Cramer seemed set upon an impossible task. On the one hand, minority groups had to be dissuaded from believing themselves "victims of a plot to 'sell them down the river.'" On the other, the "causes of concern" to the FEPC's opponents should be removed. To achieve this agenda, Cramer proposed an independent agency attached to the OEM and supervised by a full-time, paid committee. Without the power to impose sanctions, the new body inevitably would seek even closer cooperation with the bureaucracy. Public hearings would be held as a last resort and then only with the concurrence of the investigating agency. In case of disagreement, the final decision on holding a hearing would be made by a specially appointed presidential assistant.[49]

A plan from Attorney General Biddle reflected his political concerns. He worried about the "emotional alarm" in the South, the revival of the Ku Klux Klan, congressional threats to investigate the FEPC, and "widespread dissent among the Negroes." All of these translated into a loss of support for the administration. He wrote vaguely about a committee attached to McNutt's manpower agency

48. Verbatim transcript, committee meeting, January 22, 1943, pp. 1–3, 23–24, R64HR, RG 228.
49. Lawrence Cramer to Marvin McIntyre, personal and confidential, January 15, 1943, in Official File 4245-G, WMC, FDRL.

with five full-time, paid members of national standing. Although required to use the WMC field staff, the FEPC would have "very broad powers." Biddle believed that discrimination was basically a manpower problem and that the committee in its operations should emphasize the "need for full employment" in wartime. It should engage primarily in "negotiations and persuasion locally, through men of local standing." Public hearings or the use of sanctions would seldom occur. The FEPC's five members should include a nationally known black "independent of any group . . . one outstanding industrialist . . . one labor man" chosen by organized labor, "a prominent Catholic," and a first-rate chairman, such as Frank Graham. Biddle's plan seemed to provide the FEPC with a prescription for oblivion. Although promising power and prestige, it gave neither. Biddle's committee would negotiate with employers in the manner of Weaver and Alexander without a field staff.[50]

From the White House, Jonathan Daniels saw no possible retreat from the executive order because the FEPC had become a moral issue to minority groups. Since white southerners also viewed the issue in moralistic terms, the FEPC and job discrimination had developed into one of the most explosive and emotional questions on the home front. No matter what was done, Daniels warned, the "continuance of agitation and friction" was unavoidable, and no reorganization plan would completely solve the problem. Because the topic was the administration's sorest political spot, victory at the polls in 1944 was very much at stake. Nevertheless, "whether the South likes it or not," he averred, the president "must reiterate his opposition to discrimination [and] his rejection of any theories of racial superiority." Daniels wanted the committee to be more representative while narrowing its field of operation to defense industries only. Its program must stress the "limitations of the use of all manpower" rather than "the general advance of the Negro race." At the end of April, however, Daniels suddenly changed his mind. Now he thought the president should "let the whole business be centered [in McIntyre's office] rather than have several people around town fooling with it." According to historian Charles Eagles, this shift reflected pure opportunism. With McIntyre's duties inevitably expanding, Daniels possibly hoped

50. Memorandum, Francis Biddle to the President, January 29, 1943, in Official File 4345-G, FDRL; Harry McAlpin, "Biddle Plan to Kill FEP Given to FDR," Chicago *Defender*, February 6, 1943, p. 1, March 13, 1943, p. 3.

to assume some of those tasks. In an earlier memorandum to the president, he had suggested the appointment of a single individual with "some kind of supervisory responsibility" over "this Negro question," though with great modesty he had refrained from directly nominating himself for that position.[51]

The White House considered these various proposals during much of January as telegrams and letters from unions, civil rights advocates, and church and professional organizations protested the cancellation of the railroad hearing and the reorganization of the committee. A letter from Tennessee was signed "All White Southerners." Another group reportedly consulted with Wendell Willkie in New York. Meanwhile, Fowler Harper and McNutt met on January 15 with about forty representatives of civil rights organizations in what became a public relations disaster. Harper, who arrived twenty-five minutes late, talked to the group interminably until they realized he was "stalling in hope that we would one by one leave without seeing McNutt." Later that afternoon, McNutt finally entered and "made a very pretty speech . . . [about] *economic* equality for the Negro," but he asked the group "not to tie his hands." While he took "absolute responsibility for calling off the [railroad] hearings," he refused "absolutely" to discuss the "factors which entered into his decision." Some of the newspaper correspondents began referring to him as "Adolph McNutt" because of his "non-committal and dictatorial attitude." The meeting eventually "broke up in considerable disorder" after McNutt, who "remained stoic and unbending . . . failed to answer a single question."[52]

On February 4, the cabinet devoted a full session to the FEPC's reorganization, but Roosevelt rejected Biddle's advice that he promise to reschedule the "postponed hearings" after the agency's status was settled. Unwilling to make such a pledge, the White House announced

51. Memorandum, Jonathan Daniels to Marvin McIntyre, January 26, 1943, in Official File 4345-G, FDRL; memorandum, Jonathan Daniels to the President, November 24, 1942, in Daniels Papers; Jonathan Daniels, *White House Witness*, 165; Eagles, *Jonathan Daniels*, 102–103.

52. Memorandum, Mr. Perry to Walter White, January 15, 1943, FEPC–Transfer and Railroad Hearings, 1941–43, NAACP Records; Public Relations, Unions, Churches, Miscellaneous Organizations file, Henry Goldstein to the President, January 21, 1943, in G–K, William Donnell to the President, January 19, 1943, in D–F, R46HR, all in RG 228; Pittsburgh *Courier*, January 23, 1943, p. 1; Chicago *Defender*, January 30, 1943, p. 6; Flynn, *Mess in Washington*, 160.

a conference of minority group leaders to be convened on February 19 by McNutt. A wide variety of interracial groups representing twenty-four organizations attended, but nothing was accomplished because the administration refused to make any commitments about the FEPC's future. In the press release of February 4, the White House did compliment the FEPC for opening up job opportunities, but it suggested that the committee members were overworked because they served on a part-time basis. The statement infuriated Dickerson and Webster, for it seemed to put the onus of failure on the committee members themselves. Dickerson's assessment of the real causes for the committee's problems was close to the mark: WMC obstruction, budget restraints, insufficient staff, and lack of support from the administration. In response to the press release, the committee sent the White House a strongly worded resolution, introduced by Milton Webster, that called for the continuation of the committee with seven part-time members.[53]

Roosevelt procrastinated on an answer for nearly four months. The committee's four remaining members, with Earl Dickerson as acting chairman, could do little except hold meetings. McNutt ignored them, even refusing to answer their letters. The October operating agreement remained in limbo. On March 1, Dickerson described the committee's unhappiness in a letter to the president. He exonerated the part-time members of any shortcomings and blamed McNutt's "failure, refusal, and neglect" for the FEPC's problems. The experience of the past seven months under WMC tutelage, he wrote, proved conclusively that there would be no effective enforcement of the executive order until the FEPC received independent status and became directly responsible to the White House.[54]

53. Verbatim transcript, committee meeting, A.M., February 8, 1943, pp. 44–48, 66, R64HR, and verbatim transcript, Conference on the Scope and Powers of COFEP, February 19, 1943, in Predocketed Cases, F22FR, both in RG 228; cabinet meetings, in Box 1, and memorandum of conference with the President and Paul McNutt today, February 4, 1943, in Box 3, Biddle Papers, FDRL; Pittsburgh *Courier,* February 13, 1943, p. 1, February 20, 1943, p. 1; Chicago *Defender,* February 27, 1943, p. 1, March 6, 1943, p. 1.

54. Verbatim transcript, committee meeting, March 1, 1943, p. 17, R64HR, Lawrence Cramer to Paul McNutt, February 16, 1943, in Office Memoranda, L file, R1HR, Ethridge to Biddle, January 25, 1943, Proposed Plan for Reorganization, office files of George M. Johnson, R4HR, and Earl Dickerson to the President, March 1, 1943, in Public Relations 5, White House Correspondence, General, R45HR, all in RG 228. Roosevelt's procrastination over creating the New Committee was not un-

Nevertheless, for a time Roosevelt seriously considered abolishing the FEPC, but James F. Byrnes, soon to become FDR's alter ego in the Office of War Mobilization, advised against it. Despite serious congressional opposition to the agency, Byrnes wrote, abolishing the FEPC would not solve the problem. "The negroes now want the Committee," even if only as a symbol, and permitting the manpower commission chairman to appoint its members would not satisfy them. Too, without the FEPC as a buffer, Byrnes feared, black appeals and complaints would go directly to the White House. To his mind, the important thing was finding a suitable chairman, but appointing a southerner was not necessarily a good idea, for such a chairman would be vulnerable to the charge of race prejudice if "their demands" were refused. Frank Graham should not be chairman, Byrnes wrote, because he was too valuable on the WLB. At any rate, Graham was not interested, nor was elderly former senator George Norris of Nebraska, whom the committee unanimously recommended and whom FDR seemed inclined to consider. Will Alexander told Jonathan Daniels confidentially that Fowler Harper, McNutt's deputy in the WMC, was interested in the chairmanship. Many blacks liked Harper and believed his liberalism made him unpopular with the president's southern advisers. Assistant Secretary of the Interior Oscar Chapman, another possibility, had a sound race record, having secured the Lincoln Memorial in 1939 for black contralto Marian Anderson's concert after the Daughters of the American Revolution refused her the use of Constitution Hall. At the FEPC, however, Cramer and the staff were "very enthusiastic about Oscar and his point of view but unenthusiastic about his spine," which Cramer thought was "very, very feeble." Nevertheless, McNutt offered Chapman the job. When he turned it down, Marvin McIntyre also had a name for him: "gutless wonder." There were many other refusals, which led a Washington wit to suggest that a chairman of the FEPC might be found if the job were raffled off on a currently popular giveaway program.[55]

---

typical, as the OWI's experience a year earlier had indicated; see Allan M. Winkler, *The Politics of Propaganda: The Office of War Information, 1942–1945* (New Haven, 1978), 31.

55. Chicago *Defender*, May 15, 1943, p. 15; Jonathan Daniels to Marvin McIntyre, April 19, 1943, memorandum, James Byrnes to the President, March 15, 1943, both in Official File 4245-G, Box 5, 1943, FDRL; Lawrence Cramer to Mark Ethridge, March 31, 1943, in Public Relations 5, Ethridge file, R45HR, RG 228;

The president's men told Cramer and the committee absolutely nothing about reorganization. "My office is kept severely in the dark," Cramer confided to Mark Ethridge, so that he had to "work out arrangements with newspaper people who attend press conferences to find out what action" had been taken. At times, the committee members were tempted to follow the advice of the Chicago *Defender* and resign, but they wisely refrained, believing such a move would please the FEPC's detractors and forfeit what little standing the committee still retained. Lawrence Cramer, however, was preparing to leave. Having passed a physical examination, he had received a commission from the War Department. Before departing, he suddenly came to life. At the April 19 meeting, he presented a confidential, factual account of the FEPC's work since its beginning. With the appointment of a new committee rumored, he feared that much of the record might be lost or suppressed, and he and his colleagues wanted recognition for their nearly two years of labor. The ninety-three-page typescript, entitled "Report of the President's Committee on Fair Employment Practice," also vindicated the FEPC in its struggle with McNutt and the WMC. The committee voted to publish the entire document.[56]

Cramer had concluded there was little to lose and something to be gained by taking bold initiatives. Positive evidence that the FEPC was trying to do its job might bring pressure on the White House for action. He also wanted to establish a public agenda that would bind a new committee to the work of the old one. Dates should be set for the Capital Transit and Detroit hearings, for example, and investigations should begin in preparation for other hearings in St. Louis, Provo, Los Angeles, and Houston. The committee approved this agenda and then decided to go even further. Following a suggestion from Mark Ethridge, they authorized Acting Chairman Dickerson to seek an interview with Roosevelt to tell him that the present situation was intolerable. Milton Webster urged the group to try to persuade FDR to

---

cabinet meeting, May 6, 1943, in Box 1, 1943, Biddle Papers, FDRL; Jonathan Daniels, *White House Witness*, 159; Perrett, *Days of Sadness*, 316.

56. Lawrence Cramer to Mark Ethridge, April 15, 1943, in Public Relations 5, Ethridge file, R45HR, and verbatim transcript, committee meeting, April 19, 1943, pp. 10, 14, R64HR, "Report of the President's Committee on Fair Employment Practice," confidential, Washington, D.C., May, 1943, office files of Frank Reeves, R48HR, all in RG 228; Chicago *Defender*, January 30, 1943, p. 14. The report was never published.

reschedule the railroad hearing. But it was three weeks before the White House would receive them, and they met on May 5 only with McIntyre, not with the president.[57]

Before adjourning, the committee decided to make another bold move. Although all press releases had to be approved by McNutt, they decided to announce the hearings without his permission. Each one should be directed by his own conscience in explaining to the press what had transpired at the meeting, Boris Shishkin suggested. As Earl Dickerson adjourned the meeting, he was jubilant. "If any of you gentlemen see something in the press . . . you will know I have acted on your suggestion that individual members may do as they please."[58]

After the meeting, the FEPC dutifully sent a news release to McNutt for approval. Then, in defiance of the manpower commission chief, Dickerson held a news conference and announced the press release. His letter to Roosevelt, which mentioned specific dates for the railroad hearing, June 7, 8, and 9, completely bypassed the WMC office. The content of Dickerson's news conference greatly embarrassed McNutt. In addition, when reporters rushed to the OWI, which coordinated agency publicity, to get copies of the FEPC release, they learned that McNutt had suppressed it on the grounds that it would bind any new FEPC chairman to a certain course of action. Meanwhile, Cramer and the staff proceeded with preparations for the Capital Transit hearing and sent out letters of notification requesting the company's presence. Not unexpectedly, the Washington, D.C., area WMC director protested that such a hearing was inadvisable because it would disturb "tranquil waters." According to Charlie Cherokee, staff morale could not have been lower during this period. Staff members "lost faith" in the "uncertain and vacillating" Lawrence Cramer and his brave assurances to the public that "hearings will positively be held" even as he prepared to leave by May 1.[59]

57. Verbatim transcript, committee meeting, April 19, 1943, pp. 18–35, 40–44, R64HR, and Earl Dickerson to the President, April 19, 1943, in Public Relations 5, FDR file, R45HR, both in RG 228; HMH [McIntyre] to the President, May 6, 1943, Official File 4245-G, Box 5, 1943, FDRL.

58. Verbatim transcript, committee meeting, April 19, 1943, pp. 18–35, 40–44, R64HR, and Dickerson to the President, April 19, 1943, in Public Relations 5, FDR file, R45HR, both in RG 228.

59. Verbatim transcript, committee meeting, May 5, 1943, pp. 3, 9, 16, R64HR, and Dickerson to the President, April 19, 1943, in Public Relations 5, FDR file, R45HR both in RG 228; Chicago Defender, April 24, 1943, pp. 1, 4, 15.

Whether the committee's aggressive action had any effect is unknown. Three days after the April 19 committee meeting, however, Biddle sent a memorandum to Roosevelt urging action. Three months had passed since the announcement that the FEPC would be reorganized promptly. Several individuals had turned down the chairmanship, but Biddle now had another candidate, Monsignor Francis J. Haas, who had done excellent work on the NLRB. Biddle believed Haas would accept the appointment if he was given adequate funds and a free hand under the executive order. Haas was a "strong Liberal, entirely loyal to [FDR], and a great admirer of the New Deal." Jonathan Daniels also nudged Roosevelt, sending a list of new names that also included Father Haas. Whoever was chosen, Daniels warned, the job was "one of the most important . . . the administration [had] to fill if it [was] going to avoid a great deal of grief." Two more weeks passed, and neither Roosevelt nor McNutt had found anyone. After a May 6 cabinet meeting, the attorney general belittled McNutt's efforts: "Each man he suggested was worse than the one before," and "his last suggestion . . . was pretty feeble." Fortunately, the man in question had declined. Biddle, worried about a "big Negro mass meeting in Washington" taking place that very evening to protest against discrimination, "urged again with great vigor Father Haas." The president, however, had "a way of sticking to old ideas in new forms" and thought that "George Norris was just the right man." Biddle "did not contradict him knowing that Norris would not accept." [60]

Throughout April and May, several proposals for a new executive order circulated among various administration offices. A Justice Department draft proposed new powers for the FEPC, including sanctions against contractors and subcontractors enforceable in the courts. Biddle recommended this draft because it had "teeth in it," though these new powers should be used "very sparingly." The fact that the power existed would "undoubtedly make the negotiation and mediation activities of the Committee far more effective," Biddle told FDR. Furthermore, "Monsignor Haas is in favor of having such a provision included in the order." But the Justice Department draft was unacceptable to Harold Smith and the Budget Bureau. It "takes a strictly authoritarian approach," Smith complained, and binds "government

60. Memorandum, Francis Biddle to the President, April 23, 1943, and cabinet meeting, May 6, 1943, both in Biddle Papers; Jonathan Daniels to Marvin McIntyre, April 24, 1943, in Official File 4245-G, 1943, FDRL.

contractors and subcontractors by the terms of their contracts to refrain from discrimination." By issuing orders to cease and desist, the
FEPC could even require "affirmative action such as employment,
reinstatement, and payment of back pay." Smith believed it unsound
"to vest quasi-judicial powers in a body partly composed of representatives of the very minority groups which are interested parties to the
proceedings." If the Justice Department's plan were adopted, however,
Smith would reduce the committee's size from seven to three. Basically, he opposed the law enforcement approach to civil rights; instead, he submitted a Budget Bureau plan that emphasized education,
persuasion, and pressure.[61]

When FDR finally acted, the Bureau of the Budget won out over
the Justice Department. On May 27, 1943, Roosevelt issued Executive
Order 9346 creating the New Committee. Monsignor Francis J. Haas,
appointed as full-time chairman on May 19, participated in the draft-
ing of the executive order. The New Committee received what its
predecessor was denied: independent status in the OEM, field offices,
and a half-million-dollar budget. But FDR refused sanctions. In getting organized, Haas went to the NLRB for his top administrators, all
whites with little or no experience in race relations. One of these,
Malcolm "Mike" Ross, a personal friend and confidant of the attorney
general, became the FEPC's deputy chairman, downgrading the status
of George Johnson. Thus the FEPC's top leadership posts went to capable, though not outstanding, white men whom the administration
could trust. Haas also had authority to pick the members of the committee. Only three from the Old Committee stayed on, the two labor
representatives and Milton Webster. The sharp, combative Earl Dickerson was replaced by an elderly, conservative black southerner, P. B.
Young, editor of the Norfolk *Journal and Guide*. One of the new
white appointees was Sarah Southall, employment supervisor for the
International Harvester Company. A liberal Republican, Southall had
philanthropic connections with Hull House, founded by Jane Addams

61. Paul McNutt to Harold Smith, April 13, 1943, Memorandum, Marvin Mc-
Intyre to the Attorney General, April 15, 1943, Memorandum, OSC [Oscar Cox] to
the Attorney General, April 15, 1943, Memoranda, Oscar Cox to Marvin McIntyre,
May 17, 18, 1943, Victor Rotnem to Francis Biddle, May 19, 1943, Oscar Cox to the
Attorney General, May 21, 1943, Francis Biddle to Harold Smith, May 22, 1943,
Memorandum, Harold Smith to the President, May 22, 1943, Francis Biddle to Har-
old Smith, May 25, 1943, Memorandum, Francis Biddle to the President, May 25,
1943, all in DJ-FOI; Neuchterlein, "Politics of Civil Rights," 179.

in the 1880s to improve the lives of Chicago's slum dwellers. She also worked with the Chicago Urban League and served on the staff of the Rosenwald Fund under Will Alexander, who sponsored her. Although Marvin McIntyre preferred "one of our own" for the position, he did not want to interfere too much with Haas's committee choices. Finally, Samuel Zemurray of New Orleans, head of the United Fruit Company, completed the FEPC's new membership. Most of the middle-echelon staff stayed on. These and the three holdover committee members, along with George Johnson, provided the chief continuity in personnel from the Old Committee to the new one.[62]

For Earl Dickerson, who ardently coveted a place on the New Committee, the reorganization was a bitter disappointment, and he mounted a campaign with letters and telegrams from loyal supporters. But the man who had fashioned many of the policies and programs so feared by the administration was out. To Francis Biddle, Dickerson was "an extremist" who "should be taken off the Committee" because "he is bitter and tends to make decisions of the Committee often too extreme." More than any other committee member, he had pushed for hearings, had helped shape their character, and had made the language of the findings and directives forceful. Direct in approach, Dickerson, who later referred to himself in those days as being "like a wild jackass," could be abrasive. He used bad judgment as acting chairman by visiting the Detroit regional office and meeting with complainants, for later, as a committee member, he might have to judge their complaints. His moralistic rhetoric sometimes annoyed committee colleagues, but his goals were realistic within the limits of the executive order. In hearings, his lawyerly emphasis on the cross-examination sometimes led to time-consuming and tedious repetition that Boris Shishkin thought "muddled" the record and detracted "from the effectiveness of the hearing." Shishkin was making an anonymous reference to Dickerson, a member "no longer with us," as the New Committee prepared for the railroad hearing in September,

62. FDR to Francis Haas, May 27, 1943, in DJ-FOI; OWI release, July 2, 1943, in office files of M. Ross, Committee Members folder, R1HR, RG 228; Marvin McIntyre to Francis Haas, July 1, 1943, in Box 45, FEPC, Haas Papers; Marvin McIntyre to the President, June 26, 1943, in Official File 4245-G, 1943, FDRL; Chicago Defender, June 5, 1943, p. 4, July 3, 1943, p. 1, July 10, 1943, p. 1; Pittsburgh Courier, June 5, 1943, p. 1; Dykeman and Stokely, Seeds of Southern Change, 258; Thomas E. Blantz, A Priest in Public Service: Francis J. Haas and the New Deal (Notre Dame, 1982), 208.

1943. He thought Dickerson had "interfered with the order of the procedure of the hearings by taking so much time" in "long speech-making" and in asking "long tiring questions." Shishkin proposed the adoption of a rule that any member could speak at a hearing only through the chairman.[63]

During much of this period Dickerson was also under FBI surveillance. On June 3, 1943, J. Edgar Hoover reported to the attorney general about "a maneuver on the part of . . . Dickerson to have pressure exerted for his reappointment" to the FEPC. According to a "highly confidential and reliable source," Dickerson had "contacted William L. Peterson, Negro member of the National Committee of the Communist Party," to request support by contacting "labor unions and organizations." In another FBI report in 1942, Dickerson was allegedly "affiliated with the National Negro Congress and had engaged in activities sponsored by the Communist Party." FEPC Chairman Malcolm MacLean, when informed of these charges over a year earlier, in March, 1942, stated that they should be dismissed and, in Hoover's words, "that the President should not be bothered with the Bureau's report."[64]

With all these difficulties, Dickerson yet served as a racial conscience in a way no white member ever could. With the solid support of Milton Webster and the sympathy of John Brophy, he, more than any other member, set the agenda for the Old Committee, and he did so without the kind of White House connections and support commonly enjoyed by an Ethridge, a MacLean, or a Sarnoff. In the final analysis, Dickerson was a maverick whose presence at the FEPC made the administration uncomfortable.

Lawrence Cramer was the other major influence on the Old Committee. A dedicated believer, he accepted the FEPC appointment out of conviction at a time when he was also being considered by the State Department for the head of its Caribbean division. His role as shaper of FEPC policies sometimes seemed compromised by his duties as an administration officer, yet he never wavered in pursuit of the cause.

63. Memorandum, January 11, 1943, in Box 2, Biddle Papers; verbatim transcript, committee meeting, September 14, 1943, p. 40, R64HR; interview with Earl Dickerson; interview with John A. Davis, New Rochelle, N.Y., August 30, 1978; Chicago *Defender*, July 3, 1943, p. 14.

64. Memorandum, J. Edgar Hoover to the Attorney General, June 3, 1943, in Box 45, FEPC, Haas Papers.

Cramer firmly believed that the FEPC's goal involved a moral issue so powerful that opponents did not dare challenge it in the open. Although the butt of David Sarnoff's barbs, Cramer laid down foundations in the bureaucracy that became fundamental for the operations of both committees. Weak itself, the FEPC used the power of other agencies to carry out the executive order. These sometimes unwilling confederates often failed the FEPC, but associating them with the committee's objectives was significant, and it confounded and frustrated the FEPC's enemies. Late in 1942, when Senator Russell of Georgia attacked "the [racial] policies being adopted by the War Manpower Commission and the other emergency agencies," he probably suspected that the FEPC was the source of their actions. Indeed, Russell called the FEPC "the most dangerous force in existence in the United States today," according to one report. The Atlanta *Journal* later in 1944 fumed: "So adroit are its maneuvers that it is usually out of the picture when any trouble it has started is full-blown. It calls on other governmental agencies to enforce its decrees and whip dissenters into line." In addition to browbeating other agencies to support the executive order, Cramer also organized the central office and set up the embryonic field organization. Although his administrative skills failed to measure up to the standards of a Sarnoff, most of the structure he created survived under the New Committee.[65]

Besides Dickerson and Cramer, other able men served on the Old Committee. The FEPC's first two chairmen held views close to those of the administration. Mark Ethridge's southern liberal beliefs differed little from those of a Will Alexander, though at Birmingham Ethridge probably went further rhetorically to appease the South than would other racial liberals from that region. While he failed to comprehend the magnitude of the problems facing the FEPC, he was yet his own man. Malcolm MacLean also seemed to have convictions, but in his eagerness to please and his willingness to "obey orders," he compromised himself as well as the committee. There were cynical critics. Crystal Bird Fauset, the black Washington, D.C., Democratic politician, thought both MacLean and Cramer were "anxious to use

65. Verbatim transcript, committee meeting, March 1, 1943, pp. 10–13, R64HR, and Atlanta *Journal*, August 6, 1944, Newspaper Clippings file, both in RG 228; Mark Ethridge to Milton Webster (telegram), August 3, 1941, in Box 18, BSCP Papers; Richard Russell to H. S. Gates, December 28, 1942, in Series X, Negro 1942–43, Russell Papers; Ross, *All Manner of Men*, 55.

the Negro as a means of getting closer to the President and to power." [66]

With either Ethridge or MacLean as chairman, the administration had, for different reasons, men it could trust. Yet the administration did not, probably could not, control a committee that almost from the beginning had an independent life, agenda, and constituency. Perhaps it was a tribute to Cramer's organizing skills, and to his and Dickerson's moral imperatives, that the FEPC survived conservative onslaughts that weakened or wiped out several liberal New Deal agencies, including the Works Progress, National Youth, and Farm Security administrations. Southern conservatives also crippled the Federal Housing Administration and the OWI, the latter because of its domestic propaganda program stressing cooperation and brotherhood. Despite the administration's countenancing of these attacks, the FEPC survived the onslaughts of 1942 and 1943, in the final analysis, because work as a civil right had become a moral issue too powerful to ignore. [67]

66. Jonathan Daniels, *White House Witness*, 94.
67. Pittsburgh *Courier*, July 10, 1943, p. 1; Philadelphia *Tribune*, July 10, 1943, p. 4; "The Jim Crow Bloc," *New Republic*, February 22, 1943, pp. 240–41; Patricia A. Sullivan, "Gideon's Southern Soldiers: New Deal Politics and Civil Rights Reform, 1933–1948" (Ph.D. dissertation, Emory University, 1983), 70, 75.

4 / The New Committee Begins

The Old Committee's work did not go on in a vacuum. While it struggled with the manpower agency, Allied forces began the campaign for North Africa that brought victory by May, 1943. The Battle of the Atlantic was also turning in favor of the Allies. In the Pacific, the navy began the task of clearing out the Japanese by "leapfroging" through various island chains, while Americans and Australians pushed northward into New Guinea. But a final victory was not yet in sight in either theater of war, and months of effort and sacrifice to meet war production and manpower goals lay ahead.

While the administration put the finishing touches on Executive Order 9346 and prepared an announcement for May 27, 1943, a crisis in the Mobile shipyards illustrated how discrimination and racism could impede war production. It also seriously challenged Chairman Francis Haas's judgment and leadership. Prodded for months to upgrade blacks and employ them at their highest skill levels, the Alabama Dry Dock and Shipbuilding Company (ADDSC) suddenly, on the night of May 24, brought in twelve skilled black workers and created a racially mixed welding crew. The action, taken without warning or preparation, precipitated a riot the following morning that injured over fifty people as the shifts changed. Evidence indicates that management, bitterly opposed to the FEPC and the New Deal, anticipated trouble and may have welcomed it to embarrass the administration. White rioting continued for a second day as blacks vacated the yards. Federal troops moved in when company guards and state militiamen failed to maintain order. The FEPC's Clarence Mitchell, a black, and Ernest Trimble, on arriving in Mobile, insisted that the troops remain. The FEPC representatives, along with others from the Maritime Commission and the Department of the Navy, with White House support negotiated an agreement with the company establishing four segregated ways. Only the WMC's area director opposed the settlement, arguing that blacks wanted too much. He insisted, unsuccessfully, that whites wishing to quit their jobs be issued certificates of eligibility. Haas approved the ADDSC agreement on June 2, but he acted alone. The Old Committee was not consulted, and New Committee appointments had not yet been made.[1]

The settlement aroused controversy inside the agency and produced a storm of public protest. To the black press it seemed that Haas had given federal approval to segregation. The action took on "frightening proportions" to columnist John P. Davis, who predicted "that every industry all over the country will seize on the formula of a segregated section or plant . . . and after the war the Negro will be driven out of industry completely." There were also other complaints. Although the four jim-crow ways gave employment to thousands of blacks denied defense work because of state segregation laws, they provided no jobs in the highest skills, including machine operations, pipefitting, and electrical installation. To the Pittsburgh *Courier*, it was proof that segregation caused, rather than alleviated, discrimination. The NAACP's Walter White agreed and went further: the plan also surrendered to "lawlessness," inviting white workers elsewhere to engage in violence. Responding to criticism, Haas claimed that the ADDSC settlement did not set a precedent. He had approved it only in order to end a crisis.[2]

Meanwhile, George Johnson sought the reactions of FEPC field examiners. Four of the five replies were laudatory. Jack Burke in Detroit admired Clarence Mitchell's "fortitude in permitting himself to be

1. Verbatim transcript, committee meeting, July 6, 1943, p. 26, R64HR, RG 228; Merl Reed, "FEPC, Black Worker, and Southern Shipyards," 456–57.
2. Walter White to Francis Haas, June 28, 1943, in Public Relations 5, White file, R45HR, RG 228; Pittsburgh *Courier*, June 12, 1943, p. 4, June 19, 1943, p. 6, July 24, 1943, p. 8, August 21, 1943, p. 3; Chicago *Defender*, July 17, 1943, p. 3; Philadelphia *Tribune*, August 21, 1943, p. 3; Adam Clayton Powell, Jr., *Marching Blacks: An Interpretive History of the Rise of the Black Common Man* (New York, 1945), 166.

seen in Mobile, much less to be active, so short a time after the riot." Under the circumstances, Burke thought, it was difficult to make any other kind of adjustment. From Los Angeles, black examiner Clarence R. Johnson, who formerly had worked in the OPM's regional minority branch, branded press reports as "overstated." Nothing in the settlement suggested "that the Committee had started on an errand of retreat" except one that could "be designated as strategic." Certainly, "the factor of geography had to be reckoned with." Clarence Johnson was "unable to work [himself] into a psychological frenzy over the . . . temporary establishment of 'work islands' for Negroes and Whites until saneness prevails in the company yards." Furthermore, he doubted that the "FEPC or any other agency has authority to decree that" segregated work crews could not be created. If blacks assigned to them suffered disabilities in pay, promotion, or benefits, however, the FEPC had full jurisdiction. Only Edward Lawson, a black field examiner in New York, faulted the Mobile action. Because the committee, lacking new appointees, did not legally exist, he said, Mitchell and Trimble should have been sent as representatives of the White House or the president. While recognizing the extenuating circumstances, Lawson judged the Mobile agreement as illegal because it failed to enforce the executive order.[3]

Chairman Haas, already faulted in the press for his tardiness in rescheduling hearings on the Capital Transit Company and on the southern railroads, took considerable personal criticism. Harry McAlpin acknowledged Haas's long record of effective participation in labor conciliation but noted that the new FEPC chairman, by his own admission, lacked experience in race relations. By introducing labor conciliation techniques, Haas "was getting into a hopeless muddle," and by applying to problems of human rights solutions suitable for property rights, he was jeopardizing public support for the FEPC. Although a black FEPC "staff member . . . participated in the [Mobile] conference, Negroes have no more privilege to bargain away human rights" than they do to waive certain constitutional rights. It was a dangerous precedent.[4]

On July 6, when Haas brought the Mobile agreement to the New

3. Reports, ADDSC, R48HR, RG 228.
4. Morris Milgram *et al.*, to Walter White, June 19, 1943, in General Office File, FEPC-Gen., 1943, NAACP Records; Pittsburgh *Courier*, June 12, 1943, p. 1; Chicago *Defender*, June 19, 1943, p. 1.

Committee, he faced additional criticism. Since it had already been approved in the committee's name, Milton Webster asked why Haas even bothered to submit it. Boris Shishkin suggested that Haas could have consulted the Old Committee since in theory, according to legalist George Johnson, it still existed. P. B. Young, a black conservative, believed the plan to be an "extraordinary arrangement." It set a precedent for all shipyards and industries and undoubtedly delighted the Deep South, which would welcome government approval of segregated industries. In the shipyards at Newport News, Young noted, one-third of the force was black, and they worked all over the place.[5]

Clarence Mitchell made several points as he defended the Mobile action. For one thing, he emphasized, the situation was so explosive that a settlement required the presence of U.S. troops. For another, the ADDSC was not the first southern defense contractor to establish a segregated work place. Mitchell mentioned a previous experience with the Coca Cola–owned Brecon Bag Loading Corporation. Cited to appear at the Birmingham hearing, Coca Cola worked out a settlement beforehand, agreeing to employ Negro women at power sewing machines in a room totally separate from the other employees. All of the remaining companies summoned to Birmingham had ignored the FEPC directives to upgrade black employees. Mitchell thought segregation was stupid, but when "facing a situation . . . [and] either doing something about it or leaving it alone . . . I don't agree that this sets a precedent." He also cited the rivalry between the AFL's Mobile Metal Trades Council and the CIO's Marine and Shipbuilding Workers for control of the ADDSC yards. Although the CIO had won an election primarily with black support, its insistence that black welders should never work at the yard may have encouraged the rioters. Finally, Mitchell noted the city's extreme overcrowding by people "not accustomed to treating Negroes with any respect," the absence of adequate police protection and recreational facilities, and the vicious rumor that blacks would replace white men in the yard and work there with white women. For example, in 1943, author Seldon Menefee interviewed people around Mobile. They had flocked to the city from the backwoods, illiterate and full of anti-Negro prejudice because "the whiteness of their skins [was] the one thing that [gave]

5. Verbatim transcript, committee meeting, July 6, 1943, pp. 26–34, R64HR, RG 228.

them a degree of social status" for they had "little else to be proud of." All of these factors influenced the final settlement at Mobile.[6]

In discussing segregated work places, Mitchell also could have cited one in the North. In 1942 the Sun Shipbuilding Company of Chester, Pennsylvania, with the encouragement and blessing of the Pittsburgh *Courier,* had built a separate yard for black workers. The Old Committee opposed the introduction of segregation into a northern workplace, but even the militant Earl Dickerson, who found segregation contrary to all the things the FEPC was trying to accomplish, believed that setting up a plant for "all colored workers" did not violate Executive Order 8802. If segregation led to discrimination, however, the FEPC had every right to intervene. Dickerson thought it was hopeless to challenge segregation in the South, but he opposed its spread into the North, where blacks had "gotten along reasonably well working around certain spots." The Old Committee had refrained from interfering with Sun Shipbuilding's experiment because it had lacked authority. The New Committee members faced a similar problem in Mobile. Before the vote on a motion to approve the agreement was taken, Haas advised them: "[Don't] spare the Chairman. . . . Kick him out. . . . I have no such pride in my opinion . . . that I am asking you for mercy." Only Webster and Young voted against the Mobile plan, but it was clear that the committee's approval did not constitute an endorsement of segregated work places. Nevertheless, one historian argues that it was Haas's (and later Malcolm Ross's) moderation and willingness to accommodate the White House that led the New Committee to reject segregation as a cause for action against discrimination.[7]

In the ADDSC dispute, Haas, who had accepted the chairman's job "only because the President of the United States put his finger on me," was a victim of circumstance, but his trial by fire was not over. Although he received high marks for a positive approach that "lashed [the FEPC staff] out of [its] complacency," the hapless monsignor faced weeks of suspicion because of his NLRB background, his connections with the Justice Department, and the months of uncertainty

---

6. *Ibid.,* 26–46; Menefee, *Assignment: U.S.A.* 53–55.

7. Verbatim transcripts, committee meetings, June 9, 1942, pp. 82–89, R63HR, July 6, 1943, p. 46, 64HR, and P. B. Young to Francis Haas, July 10, 1943, in Public Relations 5, Young file, R45HR, all in RG 228; Merl Reed, "Pennsylvania's Black Workers," 366–73; Polenberg, *War and Society,* 120.

preceding his appointment. Where job discrimination existed, blacks wanted moral commitment, not conciliation, and they worried about his background, mainly in labor mediation, and his inexperience with racial matters. Haas allayed none of these concerns by his choice of administrative aides. Inheriting a staff of forty blacks and four whites, he tried to achieve a better ethnic and racial balance. Unfortunately, as he recruited staff, the power at the top became more unbalanced: Haas named whites with labor relations backgrounds as his top administrators. These and his committee appointees were suggested by the Justice Department and the administration. Indeed, in the early weeks of his chairmanship, his official memoranda and correspondence, perhaps for reasons of confidentiality, were prepared at the Justice Department rather than at the agency he headed. In selecting committee members, he apparently made the final decisions, but he had help. New Orleans shipbuilder Andrew Higgins, Marvin McIntyre told Haas, was not the correct type, and Haas refrained from appointing that colorful personality to the committee. By early July, with the committee and staff in place, he wrote Walter White that the personnel, "constituted on a strictly labor management basis," should "command public support in whatever it does." Haas apparently could not comprehend black concerns. "FEPC is up, but not about," commented Charlie Cherokee. "The South watches him [Haas], and an 'arbiter' by inclination, he ponders how to reconcile the terms of the 'bargain' incidental to his appointment, with the job to be done."[8]

As Haas plotted his course, it became apparent to black leaders by mid-June that they were having little influence. "We renew our suggestion" that you consult with "those persons who were invited, at the President's instruction," by Paul McNutt and Francis Biddle "to confer on [last] February 19 in the offices of the War Manpower Commission," stated an unsigned NAACP memorandum to Haas. Further, their suggestion "should be considered along with the recommendations which, we understand, have been made to you by what has been termed the 'white cabinet.'" The memorandum also noted "the futil-

8. Verbatim transcript, committee meeting, July 6, 1943, p. 2., R64HR, and Francis Haas to Walter White, July 5, 1943, in Public Relations 5, R45HR, both in RG 228; Marvin McIntyre to the President, June 26, 1943, in Official File 4245-G, Box 5, 1943, FDRL; Francis Haas to Marvin McIntyre, June 23, 1943, and Marvin McIntyre to Francis Haas, July 1, 1943, both in Box 45, FEPC, Haas Papers; Chicago *Defender*, June 19, 1943, pp. 1, 15, July 10, 1943, p. 15; Blantz, *Priest in Public Service*, 210; Ross, *All Manner of Men*, 32.

ity of reliance for field work" on the WMC's regional staff, the importance of having "Negroes at the policy making level" in the FEPC, and the necessity for reconsideration of the ADDSC decision.[9]

By mid-July the press and black leaders, including Lester Granger of the National Urban League, leveled a full-scale attack on the white cabinet and on others around the president who took "unto themselves the responsibility of advising on Negro problems." In the Justice Department, there was Francis Biddle, "the administration's strong man" on black affairs, who had a poor record for investigations and prosecutions of lynchings. Victor Rotnem, the "potent figure" who advised Biddle on civil liberties, investigated, indicted, and prosecuted cases involving "murders of Negro soldiers . . . but [did] not get convictions." Another circle of white advisers included Jonathan Daniels, recently appointed by FDR to handle conflicts involving minority groups. In addition, Haas, Will Alexander, and Frank Graham "were the principal influences on the President on Negro policy." Consequently, except for the influence of Mary Bethune, administration views were shaped by men whose past experience with blacks was spotty.[10]

According to Cherokee, the FEPC had "freed itself from WMC and McNutt" only to be presented by Haas and Deputy Chairman Malcolm Ross, "body and soul to Justice and Biddle." He continued the scenario: "Not a move can be made in the sweltering U street offices [of the FEPC] until liaison tattler Jonathan Daniels has scuddled down to Biddle's air-cooled . . . office and Biddle, Haas, Ross and Daniels have had a huddle." Meanwhile, back at FEPC headquarters, George Johnson, in charge of all internal operations, was "squarely on the spot," handling hearings, planning staff organization and budgets, maintaining morale, preparing "policy for the Biddle-Haas huddle to mull over," and doing "everything but sweep the floor." Cherokee suggested that the FEPC's "'external' operations" had been given to "superfluous Deputy Ross so he would have something to do."[11]

Cherokee may have exaggerated Haas's deference to Biddle and Daniels, but blacks, particularly George Johnson, were isolated during

9. Memorandum, NAACP to Francis Haas, June 15, 1943, in General Office File, FEPC-Gen., 1943, NAACP Records.

10. Pittsburgh *Courier*, July 10, 1943, p. 14, July 25, 1943, p. 14.

11. Frank Knox to Jonathan Daniels, July 30, 1943, in Official File 4245-G, Box 11, Navy file, FDRL; Chicago *Defender*, July 17, 1943, p. 15, August 21, 1943, p. 15.

the New Committee's first few weeks. In the Justice Department, Johnson was regarded as a pariah second only to Earl Dickerson. As Haas assumed his duties, he received vitae from Victor Rotnem's office evaluating the Old Committee's staff. Rotnem's judgment of Johnson was harsh and bitterly partisan. In decision making, Johnson allegedly was inconsistent, jealous of his authority, intimidated, and consequently unable to delegate authority. Because of strong backing from Judge William Hastie and the NAACP, however, he could not be removed despite his lack of "administrative ability." He was an "opportunist," eager to gain favor, endlessly maneuvering behind the scenes, yet he was "industrious" and had "a good mind, and . . . real ability in his special field of law." In the Old Committee, the report went on, Johnson ceaselessly tried to discredit Lawrence Cramer and often threatened to go to the black press if he did not get his way, but he was always cordial and agreeable in direct personal contacts. Rotnem's material also contained the Justice Department's reorganization plan for the FEPC, which demoted Assistant Executive Secretary Johnson to general counsel, a mere department head. Beneath the chairman, two top administrative positions, a deputy chairman and a director of operations, superseded Johnson. Haas accepted this plan, appointing Malcolm Ross as his deputy chairman and Will Maslow, a young attorney at the NLRB, as director of operations. Heated black protest led Haas to back down, and George Johnson was made coequal to Ross, each man receiving the title of assistant chairman and an annual salary of $6,500. Both attended the meetings of the New Committee. The demoted Will Maslow directed the FEPC's field operations.[12]

As the New Committee began operating, the staff immediately initiated a review of the agency's relationships with the bureaucracy. The WMC remained indispensable for enforcement of the executive order, a fact emphasized by John A. Davis, head of the new Review and Analysis division. It was "good policy," Davis wrote, to utilize all the agencies to the fullest possible extent, but the WMC was especially vital because, through the USES, it controlled job placement. In view of past conflicts, Davis counseled caution in referring cases to the

---

12. "Table of Organization and Vitae" (Typescript, n.d.), and Theodore Jones to Francis Haas, August 6, 1943, both in Box 45, FEPC, Haas Papers; OWI Release, August 10, 1943, in office files of George M. Johnson, press releases, R4HR, RG 228; interview with Will Maslow, New York, N.Y., August 29, 1978; Philadelphia *Tribune*, August 14, 1943, p. 16.

manpower commission, yet in many situations the FEPC would have to request cooperation. The WMC, recognizing this interdependency, had already proposed that its regional personnel make most of the contacts with employers, leaving enforcement for the FEPC. Davis opposed such an arrangement. WMC investigations had often been inadequate and had served to educate the employer on "how to cover up his discrimination." Furthermore, the FEPC, as the sole enforcer, would get a reputation for intransigence. Instead, through personal contacts, it should be establishing a good rapport with employers, unions, and the general public. In its operating agreement with the WMC, the FEPC should be responsible both for investigations and for placements resulting therefrom. Any other arrangement would deprive the FEPC of prestige and goodwill, Davis believed.[13]

After three weeks of difficult negotiations with the manpower commission, the staff got an agreement that the committee considered at its first meeting. Upon learning that Robert Weaver's group remained intact in the WMC, however, Milton Webster became alarmed. With a Weaver man investigating discrimination in each regional WMC office, he fretted, the FEPC was "going right back to square one." The Old Committee's experience showed constant interference "by somebody in WMC." People believed the New Committee, with power directly from the president, would be stronger. Now, once again, the manpower agency was "sticking into everything," and "the Negro people [were] tired of being fooled." Others saw it differently. The WMC had pursued hundreds of cases that the FEPC's small staff could not handle. Furthermore, there should not be two agencies contacting employers, so the FEPC ought to delegate some of its investigative powers to the WMC. Whereas the commission had previously been able to hold up discrimination cases for months, and in the recent negotiations it had proposed a waiting period of thirty days before the FEPC assumed jurisdiction, the new agreement required only a ten-day delay. Both Malcolm Ross and George Johnson assured Webster that Labor Division personnel would serve mainly as coordinators of FEPC-WMC efforts, not as investigators. Webster's concern was understandable, but the Labor Division, under Weaver and Alexander, had recruited excellent staff people, including John Beecher, Cy Record, Edward Lawson, and Clarence Johnson. These and many others

13. Memorandum, John Davis to George Johnson, June 16, 1943, in office files of John A. Davis, Agreements with Other Agencies file, R68HR, RG 228.

did commendable work for the Old Committee despite the political interference of their WMC superiors.[14]

Webster was not placated, nor was P. B. Young, who knew first-hand that the manpower agency and the USES administered industry training programs with blatant discrimination. Throughout the South, USES offices headed by local men thwarted Washington's manpower utilization policies. Although the USES was federalized in 1941, Young complained, some southern offices remained so defiant of the national government that they still displayed signs saying "State Employment Office." Previously unaware of the WMC connection, Young found the situation "so foggy" that he "would rather step down off this Committee than start off with it." The agreement with the WMC may have been necessary, but some things had to be changed. A motion by Young for postponement carried. Nevertheless, pressure from the Budget Bureau, which would not countenance two separate agencies and staffs working without coordination, shortly thereafter forced the FEPC to act. The committee's funding waited upon the completion of the WMC agreement, which was finally executed early in August. The FEPC also signed an agreement with the CSC to furnish statistics on all civilian federal employees by race. Whereas Young's description of WMC-USES discrimination was certainly accurate for the South, the manpower agency was helpful in other regions. Edward Lawson, a former Weaver man in the WMC and the Old Committee's examiner-in-charge in New York State, worked out of the WMC regional office for months and reported "complete cooperation" from WMC regional and area directors and the heads of all constituent WMC agencies. Under the New Committee, Lawson would direct the FEPC's Region II.[15]

As Haas struggled with administrative details, he also found time to get a fairly good grasp of the larger picture. Problems he inherited from the Old Committee were readily taken up. Visiting riot-torn

14. Verbatim transcripts, committee meetings, July 6, 1943, p. 12, July 7, 1943, pp. 30–81, both in R64HR, RG 228.

15. Verbatim transcripts, committee meetings, July 7, 1943, pp. 54–70, August 9, 1943, pp. 16–17, both in R64HR, and Malcolm Ross to Sarah Southall, July 21, 1943, in Public Relations 5, Southall file, R45HR, all in RG 228; Chicago *Defender*, July 17, 1943, p. 4; Edward Lawson, "Summary," June 30, 1943, in office files of St. Clair Bourne, R file, R85HR, RG 228; Eleanor F. Straub, "Government Policy Toward Civilian Women During World War II" (Ph.D. dissertation, Emory University, 1973), 32–33.

Detroit late in June, Haas learned that several cases against small Detroit companies were ready for a hearing, though much work remained to be done before major offenders, such as the large automakers, could be challenged. Following the advice of the staff, he wisely resisted local pressures for a hearing. But he wanted to take on the southern railroads as soon as possible. Attorney General Biddle had counseled quick action on the matter and had even offered to supply legal help from the Justice Department. Milton Webster's protest, "Do we have to take it?," was echoed by others. Although Boris Shishkin professed not to be wary of "Biddle bearing gifts," he preferred other counsel. Haas himself laid groundwork for the railroad hearing as a guest columnist in the *American Federationist*, official organ of the AFL. Labor leaders, he wrote, use "endless explanations, excuses . . . [and] 'pass the buck' to their membership which, they insist, will not stand for Negroes" in their unions. It was their duty, he insisted, to fight against discrimination. In conducting the railroad hearing September 15 to 18, Haas probably performed one of his most important roles during his short tenure as FEPC chairman.[16]

The New Committee also reopened the controversial Capital Transit case and reconsidered a Southwest hearing. Appearing before the FEPC on July 7, Capital Transit president E. D. Merrill professed ignorance of how to plan and implement an education program for his white platform workers. Sarah Southall later marveled at his "spinelessness" and "stupidity." Although the committee assigned two staff members to provide advice, Merrill had no intention of cooperating. Shortly after his appearance before the committee, he hired an outside expert to conduct a study of the company's race relations. This delaying tactic succeeded in postponing FEPC moves against Capital Transit for many more months. The proposed Southwest hearing, involving the copper mining industry, presented an equally difficult problem. Once again, the FEPC attempted to overcome State Department opposition. Thus, during its first three months, the New Committee moved into the same politically sensitive areas, railroads, Capital Transit, and later, copper mining, that had previously set in motion a whirlwind of opposition against its predecessor. Yet such continuity must have pleased the departed Larry

16. Verbatim transcripts, committee meetings, July 6, 1943, pp. 59–87, 171–87, July 7, 1943, pp. 3–9, both in R64HR, RG 228; *American Federationist*, quoted in Pittsburgh *Courier*, August 7, 1943, p. 1; Blantz, *Priest in Public Service*, 218–23.

Cramer, who had feared that the work of the Old Committee would be set aside.[17]

There were also new problems. Sarah Southall and Samuel Zemurray, the industry representatives, met with the president of the American Telephone and Telegraph Company (AT&T) on the hiring practices of subsidiaries such as the Chesapeake and Potomac Telephone Company, which refused to employ black operators. On the West Coast, the boilermakers union forced black shipyard workers into discriminatory auxiliary unions. The FEPC scheduled a West Coast hearing for November. Despite complaints from the federal bureaucracy, the FEPC ruled that the nondiscrimination clause had to continue to be part of all contracts and leases connected with the war effort. In short, the New Committee demonstrated a high level of activity. Its first press release, prepared by new public relations expert Malcolm Ross, also announced plans for twelve regional offices. Besides Lawson in New York, the new regional directors were G. James Fleming (Philadelphia), Elmer W. Henderson (Chicago), and Harry L. Kingman (San Francisco). All except Kingman were blacks. The press understood that half of the twelve regional offices would be so headed. As the first four opened in mid-August, complaints came in rapidly. By September, the agency was handling 1,297 active cases, and by October, 1,544. Of the cases, 78 percent involved discrimination against blacks, 7 percent concerned Jews, and 6 percent, aliens.[18]

While Haas was reviving the agency, powerful enemies worked tirelessly to stifle the New Committee. As he prepared for the first committee meeting on July 6, southern congressmen succeeded in re-

17. Verbatim transcripts, committee meetings, July 6, 1943, pp. 131–49, July 7, 1943, pp. 35–53, 84–87, 113, July 26, 1943, p. 96, August 9, 1943, p. 24, and August 28, 1943, p. 2, in R64HR, memorandum, Committee Members to the President, January 31, 1944, Public Relations 5, Roosevelt, Franklin D., President, Roosevelt, Eleanor, Mrs., folder, R45HR, and Ernest Trimble to Francis Haas, July 5, 1943, Reports, A–C, Gen., R47HR, all in RG 228.

18. Verbatim transcripts, committee meetings, July 6, 1943, pp. 98, 114, 166, July 26, 1943, p. 70, August 9, 1943, pp. 123–26, and August 28, 1943, pp. 28, 60–88, 138–40, all in R64HR, Sarah Southall to Francis Haas, September 27, 1943, in Public Relations 5, Southall file, R45HR, OWI Release, August 10, 1943, in office files of George M. Johnson, press releases, R4HR, Maslow to George Johnson, September 22, 1943, Office Memoranda, M file, R1HR, and Will Maslow to George Johnson, October 1, 1943, office files of Malcolm Ross, Materials file, R1HR, all in RG 228; Philadelphia Tribune, July 17, 1943, pp. 1, 19; press releases, A file, in Appointment of Bartley Crum folder, R85HR, RG 228; Pittsburgh Courier, July 24, 1943, p. 8.

stricting the president's emergency fund. Nor had a separate bill been introduced to provide money for the FEPC. With congressional adjournment imminent, the threat was serious. "Board's Demise Visioned," announced one newspaper headline. An alarmed Judge Hastie telephoned NAACP headquarters in New York to warn that the "FEPC literally faces extinction." The emergency funds were restored by a conference committee, but the episode demonstrated again the FEPC's vulnerability to determined and hostile congressional enemies.[19]

Chairman Haas made the best of a difficult situation amid congressional threats, early doubts about his leadership, and his own inadvertent fumbling. Within a few weeks after his appointment, he seemed to have withdrawn from the Justice Department's smothering embrace and to be following a course little different in substance from the course of his predecessors. After the railroad hearing, he held a news conference for black publishers that was well received. "They have exceedingly more confidence" in the FEPC's "work and objectives," noted one editor. Haas overcame their suspicions, especially strong because the militant Earl Dickerson did not survive the reorganization. After a few months, Haas had become a positive asset to the FEPC, but the Vatican had other plans for him. Since March, 1943, he had been under secret consideration for ecclesiastical promotion. The announcement came on October 1 that Haas would become bishop of Grand Rapids. It was a setback that the FEPC did not need. Sarah Southall had scarcely recovered from major surgery, and P. B. Young's health was so poor that he contemplated leaving. Samuel Zemurray was also ailing. Haas resigned immediately, but he delayed his departure until the October 18 meeting, when the southern railroad directives would be completed.[20]

19. Judge Hastie to NAACP (telephone), July 2, 1943, in General Office File, FEPC-Gen., 1943, NAACP Records; Chicago *Defender*, July 3, 1943, p. 3; Philadelphia *Tribune*, July 10, 1943, p. 1.

20. Verbatim transcript, committee meeting, February 11, 1944, p. 2, R65HR, summary of committee actions, October 2, 1943, in R1HR, Sarah Southall to Francis Haas, August 10, 1943, in Public Relations 5, Southall file, R45HR, and Chicago *Defender*, October 16, 1943, p. 15, and Kansas City *Black Dispatch*, September 25, 1943, both in Newspaper Clippings, Box 515, all in RG 228; Malcolm Ross to New York *Times* correspondent W. H. Lawrence, November 5, 1943, in Malcolm Ross Papers, in possession of his son, Sandy Ross, Washington, D.C.; P. B. Young to Walter White, November 12, 1943, General Office File, FEPC-Gen., NAACP Records; Pittsburgh *Courier*, October 9, 1943, p. 1; Blantz, *Priest in Public Service*, 223.

Haas's last committee session was lively like the first, when his Mobile shipyard decision had come under fire. For Milton Webster, who brooded over the injustices suffered by black firemen, the issuance of directives against the railroads was a great triumph, and he wanted no delays or postponements. Samuel Zemurray proposed to withhold a public announcement until the railroads replied. As a courtesy, the FEPC should wait seven days, he thought. Such a procedure would "tie the Committee up in knots," Webster shot back in anger. If Zemurray's proposal were adopted, Webster continued, he would release the story himself. Haas expressed concern. "I simply gave you that as a matter of information, not as a threat," Webster replied. He did not like "to force himself on the Committee so much . . . but it [was] just hard for white people to understand the position of Negroes . . . sympathetic as they might be." Blacks were losing out and being kicked around every day, and conditions were getting worse. Webster was in no mood to be "sitting around the table and patting everybody on the back." When Young noted that only a few days would be lost, Webster was unmoved. It was still a "pussyfooting procedure." He eventually accepted the delay, but the confidential directives appeared practically verbatim in the press. Whether it was he or a staff member who leaked the information is not clear.[21]

As a replacement for Haas, the person mentioned with regularity was Malcolm Ross. The chairmanship, not available to blacks, was a thankless task for whites, having been turned down previously by many individuals. Ross was "expected to win a wide following," commented columnist Harry McAlpin, "because of his strong stand against discrimination." Although he lacked national prominence and stature, a "major criticism," McAlpin thought Ross's prestige had grown since his appointment to the FEPC. Frank Graham gave him an endorsement, but probably the strong recommendation of Haas was crucial. Ross did not pass muster with some black groups, however. "While the appointment . . . would not be a calamity," Walter White informed an Oklahoma City editor, it was "far from the most desirable," because "Mr. Ross is well-known in the Washington scene among our people as a 'Front man' for Attorney General Biddle." White also "felt very strongly" that Ross did not "have the stature

21. Verbatim transcript, committee meeting, October 18, 1943, pp. 2–62, R64HR, RG 228; Ross, *All Manner of Men*, 131.

required for the position." Such an appointment "would be a strong indication" that Roosevelt was "relegating the FEPC to the status of a minor and insignificant activity." He hoped "that certain areas of Negro opinion will make themselves heard at the White House" to protest the "virtual nomination of Mr. Ross by Father Haas." Several of White's correspondents did "make themselves heard," but the effort was futile. Ross's appointment was announced officially on October 15.[22]

The new chairman had scarcely assumed his duties when the FEPC faced a major crisis involving the nondiscrimination clause in defense contracts and leases, which was the linchpin of FEPC activity in the private sector. By violating its provisions, contractors invited FEPC investigations. Recognizing the clause's significance, the Old Committee's Lawrence Cramer had pursued the major procurement agencies, making sure that all defense contracts contained it. The clause was challenged when an AT&T affiliate, Southwestern Bell Telephone Company in Kansas City, Missouri, a supplier of service to federal agencies, refused to sign. When Richard R. Brown, director of the division of Central Administrative Services, requested a decision as to whether the procedure was mandatory, Comptroller General Lindsay C. Warren eagerly responded. In an October 7 ruling sent to James Byrnes, liaison officer of the OEM, Warren construed the nondiscrimination section as not obligatory for government contracting agencies. They could exercise discretion in requiring it. Since "the prime objective is the successful and unimpeded prosecution of the war," Warren wrote, "no useful purpose could possibly be served by a requirement" that a contract could not be negotiated without the clause, "especially if the desired service could not be procured from any other source." The provision of the executive order requiring it was intended only "as a directive" to "the contracting agencies," not as a mandate. Warren's ruling removed the FEPC's authority to enforce the executive order, and if it went unchallenged, the committee would become merely an advisory body. Ross requested the president to obtain an opinion from the attorney general.[23]

22. Walter White to Roscoe Dunjee, October 5, 1943, Roy Wilkins to Lucile H. Bluford, October 5, 1943, in General Office File, FEPC-Gen., 1932, NAACP Records; Frank Graham to the President, October 6, 1943, in Official File 4245-G, Box 7, Appointments file, FDRL; Chicago *Defender*, October 9, 1943, p. 1, October 16, 1943, p. 1; Pittsburgh *Courier*, October 9, 1943, p. 1.

23. Comptroller General to James F. Byrnes, October 7, 1943, Memorandum,

The press and the emerging network of civil rights advocates were "stunned" by the notion that the FEPC could be so cavalierly disposed of by a former congressman, Warren of North Carolina, with the apparent complicity of another southerner, Byrnes of South Carolina. In a telegram to FDR, the NAACP branded Warren "unfit and prejudiced." Walter White noted that between 1936 and 1940, the association "protested five times against Warren's appointment to his present post." During his career as congressman and chairman of the House Committee on Accounts, Warren "bluntly refused and boasted of refusing to permit American citizens, because of their color, to patronize the public restaurant in the House of Representatives." Congressman Oscar DePriest of Illinois "was among those barred from the restaurant." Roosevelt should thus "do whatever is necessary to clarify [the] intentions expressed in" the executive order and, above all, rebuke the comptroller general. Columnist Harry McAlpin called it a "slick maneuver." At the request of Byrnes, "'white hope' of the South for the Presidency," the FEPC was "clipped of all power through the ruling by an obscure Carolina" former congressman, who earlier in the DePriest episode and presently with FEPC, made "a logical choice to do the 'dirty work' which the Southern block might insist upon being done as further appeasement." Individuals from New York to California protested the decision. In addition, appeals to revoke the Warren ruling were sent by the following: National Catholic Welfare Conference; Synagogue Council of America; National Federation for Constitutional Rights; Workers Defense League; Fulton County (New York) United Labor Unions; Social Service Employees Union; American Labor Party, Local 203; United Federal Workers of America, Local 1114; United Electrical Radio and Machine Workers (CIO); United Office and Professional Workers (CIO); New Jersey Metropolitan Council and Kansas City Metropolitan Council of the National Council of Negro Women; Rabbi Morris Adler of Chicago; Progressive Woman's Educational Club (California); Greater New York Industrial Union Council (CIO); AFL; and Coordinating Committee of

---

Charles Fahy, solicitor general, to the Attorney General, November 4, 1943, both in DJ-FOI; Malcolm Ross to the President, November 1, 1943, in Public Relations 5, FDR file, R45HR, George Johnson to Malcolm Ross, November 5, 1943, Office Memoranda, J file, R1HR, and Chicago *Sun*, October 31, 1943, in Newspaper Clippings, Box 516, all in RG 228; Pittsburgh *Courier*, November 6, 1943, p. 1. See Ruchames, *Race, Jobs, and Politics*, 64–65.

Jewish Organizations Dealing with Employment Discrimination in War Industries.[24]

The administration was also displeased. One insider proposed amending the executive order "to make it clear that 'shall' means 'must.'" At the FEPC, Will Maslow believed the Warren ruling could be overcome by amending Executive Order 9346 to give the committee subpoena power. He noted, however, that a "search of the Federal Register reveals no instance" of such a grant by executive order. Nevertheless, Maslow, in a well-conceived legal opinion, concluded that under administrative law "the President can lawfully confer the power of subpoena upon the Committee," and he prepared an amendment that granted the subpoena, along with power to administer not-too-drastic sanctions. As Maslow's proposal circulated among administration legal experts, Judge N. A. Townsend advised against it, because "the authority to exercise" the subpoena power was "quite doubtful." He thought that "the work of the Committee was important" and that the FEPC was "doing a good job." But the agency was controversial, and "any attempt to exercise unauthorized power well might raise such a storm of protest as to prejudice the good already done."[25]

A solution finally came from Solicitor General Charles Fahy, who doubted that "the erroneous interpretation of the Comptroller General should be corrected by an opinion of the Attorney General." Rather than the administration's having to deal with "the conflicting opinions" of Biddle and Warren, the problem could better be resolved by "a Presidential statement indicating" FDR's intention regarding the antidiscrimination clause. As for Richard Brown, the official who sparked the controversy, Fahy advised Biddle not to protest "his having written the Comptroller General for the opinion," for this action seemed "wholly inappropriate" to Biddle. If anything were done

24. "Warren Called 'Unfit,'" (Typescript, October 29, 1943), NAACP to the President (telegram), November 5, 1943, both in General Office File, FEPC, Protest of Warren Statement, 1943, NAACP Records; Chicago *Defender*, November 6, 1943, pp. 1–2; Pittsburgh *Courier*, November 6, 1943, p. 1; DJ-FOI; *PM*, November 4, 1943, and Indianapolis *Recorder*, n.d. [November, 1943?], in Newspaper Clippings, RG 228.

25. Memorandum, Will Maslow to Malcolm Ross, October 11, 1943, Memorandum, N. A. Townsend to Oscar Cox, October 15, 1943, N. A. Townsend to Will Maslow, November 1, 1943, and office memorandum, Alfred E. Davidson to Oscar S. Cox, November 2, 1943, all in DJ-FOI.

about Brown, "I suggest that Mr. Justice Byrnes should speak to . . . [him] about it, suggesting" that requests for opinions should be cleared through proper channels. On November 5, Roosevelt issued a short statement reiterating "the fundamental principles underlying the promulgation of the Executive Order." He wanted "to make it perfectly clear that these [nondiscrimination] provisions [were] mandatory and should be incorporated in all Government contracts." In the wake of FDR's statement, Harry Gerrity, general counsel for the National Association of Building Managers and Owners, announced that he would seek congressional legislation upholding Warren's ruling and would advise the members to refuse to sign leases containing the nondiscrimination clause.[26]

James Byrnes, along with Lindsay Warren, received considerable press condemnation. In response, the administration went to some lengths to assure blacks that no responsible person around the White House, including Byrnes, had anything to do with Warren. In sending the directive to Byrnes, Warren undoubtedly sought to please, but Byrnes did not get personally involved, probably because he was too politically astute to make such a move. He disliked the FEPC, but as a realist he knew the agency was useful to assuage black concerns and channel protest away from the White House. After the Warren episode, the FEPC had neither more nor less power, and internal administration documents reveal a continuing reluctance to change the committee's status by amending the executive order. In securing another statement of support from the president, however, the agency was able to bolster its prestige just as important hearings on the West Coast involving the shipyards and the boilermakers union were about to begin. The struggle over Warren's ruling certainly energized the FEPC's network of supporters and aroused public opinion. In the final analysis, according to Judge Townsend, this support was more important than additional grants of power to the agency.[27]

The West Coast hearings in November went well and brought ad-

26. Memoranda, Fahy to the Attorney General, November 3, 4, 1943, and FDR to the Attorney General, November 5, 1943, all in DJ-FOI; Will Maslow to files, November 11, 1943, in Central Files, Rulings I, R63HR, RG 228.

27. Memorandum, N. A. Townsend to Oscar Cox, October 15, 1943, DJ-FOI; James Byrnes to the President, March 15, 1943, in Official File 4245-G, Box 5, 1943, FDRL; interview with Clarence Mitchell; Pittsburgh *Courier*, November 6, 13, 1943, p. 1; Chicago *Defender*, November 13, 1943, p. 1. See also Ruchames, *Race, Jobs, and Politics*, 65–66.

ditional public support in the wake of the Warren ruling. Internally, however, columnist Charley Cherokee noted, the "FEPC has hiccups which keep shaking staff morale." Nevertheless, "with a slight question mark, Negroes believe Chairman Malcolm Ross is a right guy." They disapproved of Will Maslow, who "appears efficient enough . . . but lacks grounding in all-important race relations." Cherokee also reported concern over the top administration of the agency. Although George Johnson was deputy chairman, Frank Coleman from the Justice Department was rumored to be joining the FEPC. When that happened, "white Maslow will control field, and white Coleman operations, with colored Johnson relegated to something equivalent to a secretary." Cherokee believed that "Ross has to play ball with the White House adviser gang and this is the way they want it." They would "sabotage him with FDR" if he defied them. Cherokee's inside tips and gossip about black discontent over Ross's deference to the White House appear to have been solidly based. With the West Coast hearings over, Ross faced serious challenges to his leadership from within the committee itself.[28]

Initially, Ross's principal antagonist was P. B. Young, the black Virginian who in December began criticizing the staff structure and functions. He also challenged Ross's authority to conduct staff affairs. Since the committee was ultimately responsible to the public, Young thought "someone made a blunder" in delegating so much power to the chairman. The reason for his displeasure was the disorganized state of the office: "People don't know what their functions are" and are "running around in circles." Some did the work of three people and others did nothing. Young moved that the administrative officer, Theodore Jones, a young black accountant from Chicago and a recognized expert on organization, prepare a structural chart indicating the functions of each person, including the chairman. In response, Ross professed "infinite faith" in Jones, but he found Young's motion "shocking" since it concerned a "staff function which lies with the Chairman." Furthermore, if some did the work of three people, "we ought to investigate any such charges." Young persisted. The committee, not the chairman, had ultimate responsibility, and Jones should report without Ross's approval. "You don't trust the chairman's judgment?" Ross asked. That was clearly the case. Young had ad-

28. Chicago *Defender*, November 27, 1943, p. 15.

dressed three letters to Ross since joining the committee and had received a written reply to none of them. "I am not certain that the Chairman is communicative" was his reply. Ross blamed the lapse on the sloppy staff work of his assistant, St. Clair "Sinky" Bourne, but the unpleasant episode provided insight into Malcolm Ross's future performance as chairman of the FEPC. In one respect Young was wrong. Ross was an excellent communicator. He did prove to be weak in organization and administration, however. Young eventually amended his motion, instructing the chairman, not Jones, to have the report prepared. It passed unanimously.[29]

Early in 1944, Ross's performance came under more serious attack from Milton Webster. The chairman had carried on certain functions and had taken action in reference to committee policy without its knowledge or approval until after the fact. Specifically, Ross discussed "policy matters" in the attorney general's office with only two other committee members invited to participate; he sent communications to the president involving policy about which the committee at the time knew nothing; in connection with the railroad cases, Ross issued a public statement, without the committee's knowledge or approval, that among other things implied he did not expect blacks to be promoted to engineers and firemen on southern railroads (Ross was also attacked by Editor Virginius Dabney of the Richmond *Times-Dispatch* on this point because his statement seemed to conflict with the FEPC's earlier directives to the railroads); and finally, Ross recommended to Roosevelt the names of three individuals for a special committee to adjudicate the railroad cases. Webster believed the chairman's actions made it useless for committee members to function.[30]

To "conserve the prerogatives of all the members," Webster offered several motions. First, the chairman should make no public statements on matters of policy without approval. Ross agreed, and the motion passed. Second, when the chairman had to confer with other agencies, a subcommittee to work with him should be selected by the members at a meeting where all were available for appointment. This motion brought considerable discussion. The meeting with Biddle

29. Verbatim transcripts, committee meetings, October 18, 1943, p. 145, December 4, 1943, pp. 39–57, in R64HR, RG 228.
30. Verbatim transcript, committee meeting, January 15, 1943, pp. 65–70, R65HR, and "Railroads and FEPC-II" (Typescript of Richmond *Times Dispatch* editorial, in Public Relations 5, Young file, R45HR, both in RG 228.

took place in an emergency, Ross explained. Boris Shishkin and John Brophy attended because they were available. Webster wondered what constituted an emergency; it seemed to be a matter of opinion. Ross insisted that some judgment had to be left to the chairman. Nevertheless, the members approved the appointment of a subcommittee to deal with emergencies and agreed that every effort should be made to contact the members by telephone. Webster voted nay. Third, Webster proposed that a black should serve on all subcommittees since most FEPC problems involved discrimination against members of that race. Shishkin thought the motion "perfectly proper" but believed it was unfortunate to set down a fixed rule. Although Ross favored the motion, it lost for want of a second.[31]

Webster was angriest over FDR's January 3 appointment, on Ross's recommendation, of a three-man body headed by North Carolina Supreme Court chief justice Walter P. Stacy to deal with the southern railroads and their white unionists. Following the September hearing, the railroads and the unions ignored FEPC directives to stop discriminating against black machinists and firemen, and the committee certified the case to the president, who responded by appointing the Stacy Committee. Webster's fourth motion proposed that all recommendations to the president and government agencies involving policy and programs must first be submitted to the committee. Ross vowed that he had acted within the spirit of Webster's motion and voiced no objection. In his opinion, the motion would help protect the chairman. Brophy and Shishkin knew about the Stacy Committee, Ross explained, and attempts had been made to telephone Webster, but he had not been available. Webster wondered again why the matter was so important that immediate action had been required. No committee member whom he had consulted knew who had recommended the appointment of Judge Stacy. This motion was also adopted. Years later, Ross described the Stacy Committee as "an irretrievable mistake and it was largely my doing." At the time, his action raised questions about his judgment and shattered committee confidence in him. Earlier during the meeting, the group had passed a motion by Webster authorizing Shishkin and Brophy, instead of Ross, to prepare a letter to Roosevelt outlining the FEPC's position on

31. Verbatim transcript, committee meeting, January 15, 1943, pp. 65–70, R65HR, RG 228.

the Stacy Committee. Its easy passage seemed to signal the fact that the whole committee was dissatisfied with Ross's handling of the southern railroad matter.[32]

Ross let the action on the Stacy Committee pass without comment, but later, upon discovering that the members in his absence had selected a two-person subcommittee to draft a letter to Congresswoman Mary Norton (D–New Jersey), chairman of the House Labor Committee, he protested strongly. Norton's committee was writing important legislation for a permanent FEPC. Ross, unquestionably a gifted writer, thought any official correspondence should go out over his signature as chairman. He approached Shishkin, one of the subcommittee members, saying, "It has been a matter of concern to me, Boris, and I want to explore the possibilities of what kind of letter you can write." Ross knew of "involvements" that might require a different approach. When John Brophy moved that Ross serve on the subcommittee, Shishkin refused. "You raise a question as to whether or not you are going to be on; whether you are going to have your way; whether you are going to jam it down the committee's throat. You apparently didn't trust us with the action." Shishkin intended to submit the letter to the full committee for final approval. Ross said he would not accept a place on the subcommittee in view of Shishkin's attitude. Friction between the two men, sometimes bitter and divisive, went on as long as the FEPC existed. Carried on through correspondence and memoranda, it sometimes erupted into personal confrontations during committee meetings. In this and in previous disagreements, the chairman's leadership had been questioned and his authority successfully challenged and diminished.[33]

Although Ross and Shishkin clashed frequently, the complaints about Ross grew mainly out of black dissatisfaction, as had those leveled at Francis Haas during his sometimes-stormy baptism as chairman. Both men, with their Justice Department and NLRB connections, aroused suspicion and distrust. Haas, it seemed, took the criticism philosophically. At times, apologetically, he deferred to the wisdom of the members, and when appropriate, he overcame their

32. *Ibid.* For Ross's account of how the Stacy Committee came into being, see his *All Manner of Men*, 132–33.

33. Verbatim transcript, committee meeting, February 12, 1944, pp. 41–44, R65HR, RG 28.

misgivings with alternate displays of humility and forcefulness, as well as genuine concern. Ross, like Haas, was thoroughly committed to the cause, but he was distrusted more, perhaps because he was perceived as being weaker than Haas and because his Justice Department contacts were personal, through Biddle. In addition, Ross conducted his chairmanship in a more direct and confrontational manner, and at the beginning, at least, he made and executed policy without committee consultation. Lacking the stature of Haas, Ross did not possess the monsignor's humility even though he did often defer to others. Thus, his problems with the committee were more serious, and some of the members were unforgiving. Creating the Stacy Committee was a serious blunder, though no doubt it pleased the White House to send a politically volatile issue to a safe committee graveyard. The Stacy group met over several months with spokesmen for the southern railroads and unions and then did nothing.

The attacks on the chairman came during trying times. As 1943 drew to a close, the FEPC's hearings and directives against the southern railroads and Capital Transit Company rubbed all the raw Washington nerves that the Old Committee had irritated previously. The New Committee, in addition, took on the west coast boilermakers. By the middle of December, with the agency attracting attention from the national press as well as in the black weeklies, the central office put into effect its own internal news-clipping program. Central handled the big eastern papers and certain black weeklies. These were clipped and placed on Ross's desk immediately upon their arrival. The regional offices clipped targeted newspapers in their areas and forwarded the material every week to Washington, D.C. The conservative Washington, D.C., *Star*, pleased to see labor unions called to task, congratulated the FEPC for tackling the difficult problem of racial discrimination with boldness and determination and for trying to set up fair and reasonable standards for the employment of blacks. In the Washington, D.C., *News*, however, columnist Raymond Clapper saw "only mischief, disunity and [the] further irritation of race relations." According to him, the committee and its chairman, Malcolm Ross, one of the early dynamic forces in the NLRB, wanted the "overnight attainment of a goal, regardless of the deep complex of human emotions" involved. The southern railroads, "engaged with all their energy in the most vital war work," had achieved harmonious relations with railway labor as well as the shipping and traveling public. They were more realistic than the FEPC, Clapper thought.[34]

In Congress, attacking the FEPC was seemingly becoming an annual December rite, this time with Mississippi Congressman John Rankin as the key critic. On the anniversary of the Bill of Rights, Rankin accused the FEPC of violating the rights of private enterprise and the railroad brotherhoods. Trying to force businesses in the South to "employ Negroes and promote them" was a dangerous act "of communist nonsense." Telling the white brotherhoods, "who have been good to the Negroes of this country," to accept them "on terms of social equality" was insulting. The FEPC would "bring race trouble" to the South "just as it did in Detroit . . . and Harlem." This "rump organization" should therefore be abolished at once. Meanwhile, white platform workers from the Philadelphia Transit Company Employees Union were appearing before the House's Smith Committee to complain about the FEPC's orders and directives. The House committee also received a letter from the boilermakers union charging communism in the FEPC and warning that its directives, if carried out, would result in race mixing in housing, schools, and social activities. Chairman Howard Smith of Virginia, in the absence of other committee members, had reportedly decided on his own to hold the hearing. The FEPC found out about it from the newspapers.[35]

In this new battle, the black press prepared for the worst. Although the president had made the FEPC's orders mandatory, "the railroad executives and union heads flout them," editorialized the *Courier*, but FDR, unlike Woodrow Wilson, was not likely to take over the railroads. The paper predicted that blacks would be abandoned again. The FEPC's spirit was commendable, but it could not "prevail against such forces with no more than presidential prestige and moral force behind it." Only a federal statute could remedy the situation, and the *Courier* preferred "this attempt even if it is filibustered to death in the Senate." More would be gained "than by [keeping the] FEPC as it is."

34. Washington, D.C., *News* and Washington, D.C., *Star*, December 15, 1943, in Box 516, Newspaper Clippings, and St. Clair Bourne to Malcolm Ross, December 29, 1943, in office files of George Johnson, Memoranda file, R3HR, both in RG 228.

35. Excerpt from Congressional Record, December 3, 1943, p. 10,400, in office files of Emanuel H. Bloch, Rankin folder, R6HR, RG 228; Chicago *Defender*, January 15, 1944, p. 2; Pittsburgh *Courier*, January 15, 1944, p. 10.

While other voices were rallying support for a "real showdown," the Washington *Post* reported on December 28 that Smith Committee agents had seized an FEPC file as the members were meeting to certify the railroad cases to the president. The newspaper report was misleading, Will Maslow telegraphed a concerned regional director. Smith's men had not seized any records. They had merely been given a transcript of the boilermaker hearing. There was no cause for alarm.[36]

Smith Committee investigators were ruthless. Immediately, they began leaking interpretations of the evidence they had gathered, equaling in viciousness the red smear tactics of the defunct Dies Committee. "FEPC Head's Red Leaning Bared in House Probe" screamed a headline in the conservative Chicago *Tribune*. Blaming Ross for the recent racial unrest, columnist Willard Edwards noted that "centering attention on Negro employment practices was in line with the Communist Party practice of inciting Negroes to unrest." Ross's book, *Death of a Yale Man*, published in 1931, was "studded with expressions of sympathy for the Communist cause." In the NLRB, Ross had a close association with Edwin S. Smith, a board member later dropped because of his alleged pro-Communist ideas. The article blamed Ross for issuing the FEPC's "edict" on the southern railroads and observed that the Communist party organ, the *Daily Worker*, supported the FEPC's attempts to wipe out discrimination.[37]

Ross issued a strong denial: "I was never attacked as a communist until I began to head [the FEPC]. . . . It was just a regular liar's business. . . . I have never joined the Communist party, I have no Communist sympathies, and I think the whole thing was designed to discredit the FEPC." The smear campaign aroused sympathy and acclaim that the embattled chairman had scarcely known before. The FEPC's "strongest chairman" was also hailed as "one of the nation's most fearless leaders," who "meets his troubles in big doses with much the same gusto as he sets out to solve" the many problems of the FEPC. Ross's name was entered on the Chicago *Defender's* "Honor Roll" of

36. Will Maslow to Harry Kingman, (telegram), December 28, 1943, Administrative files, Unarranged Correspondence, Maslow file, F104FR, Pittsburgh *Courier*, December 18, 25, 1943, pp. 5, 1, and Washington *Post*, December 28, 1943, both in Newspaper Clippings, all in RG 228; Philadelphia *Tribune*, December 25, 1943, pp. 2, 4, 19.

37. Chicago *Tribune*, December 30, 1943, in Newspaper Clippings, RG 228. The story also appeared in the Washington, D.C., *Times Herald*.

those who had contributed most during 1943 to interracial good will and understanding.[38]

Subsequent FEPC queries established that the Smith Committee would look at only three cases, the southern railroads, the boilermakers union, and the Philadelphia Transit Company (PTC), and the legality of the FEPC's activity therein. Pursuant to the investigation, the Smith Committee took practically all the records in those areas, and it requested from Undersecretary of War Patterson copies of Ross's correspondence. Ross convinced Chairman Smith that the FEPC could not be compelled to surrender the verbatim transcripts of its meetings. The Smith Committee heard the PTC case on January 11. Joseph Sharfsin, former Philadelphia city solicitor and public member of the PTC, volunteered to testify, prepared a legal brief supporting the FEPC's jurisdiction, and told the mostly hostile congressmen that the FEPC was not an idle body without power to act. The president, who possessed the inherent right to preserve the nation's safety, had delegated some of his wartime powers to the FEPC. Only Smith Committee members Jerry Voorhis (D-California) and John Delaney (D-New York) expressed sympathy for the FEPC and its objectives. Besides Delaney and Voorhis, the seven-member committee included Clare Hoffman (R-Michigan), Fred A. Hartley (R–New Jersey), Hugh Peterson (D-Georgia), John Jennings (R-Tennessee), and Smith (D-Virginia).[39]

Four days prior to the January 11 hearing, Ross formally requested to appear and make a statement. Smith refused, but during the hearing, Ross later told his committee, the congressmen grilled him for over an hour and a half. Ross, who had only a few notes, "was not in a position to speak on a lot of things the witnesses put on." A more

38. Malcolm Ross to T. P. Lochard, January 11, 1944, in Public Relations 5, L file, R43HR, Baltimore *Afro-American*, January 8, 1944, Chicago *Defender*, January 8, 1944, Houston *Informer*, January 8, 1944, and Atlanta *Daily World*, January 9, 1944, in Newspaper Clippings, all in RG 228.

39. Verbatim transcript, committee meeting, January 15, 1944, p. 18, R65HR, Will Maslow to Regional Directors (telegrams), January 12, 1944, Teletype folder II, F3FR, Malcolm Ross to John Brophy, January 7, 1944, Public Relations 5, Brophy file, R54HR, Chicago *Defender*, January 8, 1944, p. 5, January 22, 1944, p. 1, Philadelphia *Tribune*, January 15, 1944, p. 1, January 22, 1944, p. 14, in Newspaper Clippings, all in RG 228; Robert Patterson to Harold Smith, March 23, 1944, in Series IIIA, Box 66, 1943–44, Russell Papers. For a more detailed account of the Smith Committee's activity, see Ruchames, *Race, Jobs, and Politics*, 73–86; see also Neuchterlein, "Politics of Civil Rights," 180.

objective account pictured Ross as "enraged by the number of questions . . . missed and left unanswered to the detriment of FEPC." His request for "the chance to 'clear up a few'" was granted, "but before he had concluded, he found that he had been subjected to a withering attack for which he was, at the moment at least, totally unprepared." Ross did so poorly that Chairman Smith several times declared he wanted to be "fair" and not have Ross "leave himself 'in a bad light.'" Even Ross's supporters admitted that his testimony lost much of its effectiveness because of his rambling manner.[40]

In the ensuing weeks, the Smith Committee listened to spokesmen from the southern railroads and added to its agenda the complaints of the Seafarers' International Union. Smith failed to find any illegality in the FEPC's activities and never issued a report. Nevertheless, in the wake of Comptroller Warren's ruling and subsequent congressional attacks, his actions damaged the FEPC and encouraged resistance from government agencies and nose-thumbing by defense contractors who resented its intrusions. Yet as Ross and the committee, sometimes in conflict among themselves, prepared for the grueling weeks ahead, they could take some comfort in the growing and solid ranks of civil rights supporters, still a national minority, that had been activated. Blacks might also have been reassured that the New Committee, despite attempts by the Justice Department and the White House to mute its voice, had spoken out clearly. The increasing clamor of its bitter and dangerous enemies confirmed it.

40. Verbatim transcript, committee meeting, January 15, 1944, p. 18, R65HR, Malcolm Ross to Francis Haas, February 28, 1944, in Public Relations 5, Haas file, R45HR, Chicago *Defender*, January 22, 1944, p. 4, Columbus *Ohio State News*, January 29, 1944, Los Angeles *Sentinel*, January 20, 1944, New Orleans *Sentinel and Informer*, January 15, 1944, in Newspaper Clippings, all in RG 228; Neuchterlein, "Politics of Civil Rights," 180.

5 / The Politics of Job Discrimination

As the New Committee dealt with its detractors, the global war was turning in favor of the Allies. Sicily was occupied, Benito Mussolini had fallen, and Allied troops pressed the invasion of Italy. To the north, Hitler's Reich was pounded relentlessly by saturation bombing. The Pacific offensive had yielded New Guinea and had outflanked the Japanese in the Solomon Islands, where a force of 100,000 remained cut off. Although production for war would continue as the nation's top priority, some cutbacks were possible later in 1944. It was also time to begin planning for reconversion. But the FEPC's enemies became even more relentless and determined as the war against the agency shifted to the Congress.

While the Smith Committee pressed its attack, the FEPC's staff and its harried chairman carried on their routine tasks. When time permitted, Ross worked at what he did best, public relations and negotiation. In enforcing the executive order, wrote columnist Ralph W. Page, the FEPC chairman used "tact, persuasion, good will, and a spirit of compromise and accommodation in settling these issues as they arose." He was "peculiarly fitted for this role" and had been "very successful in working out a practical and acceptable rather than a strictly legal or enforced solution in the great preponderance of cases." Typical was a speech to the Chicago Civil Liberties Committee early in 1944. In a frantic search for labor, he noted, America was importing Mexicans, using prisoners, and working school boys at harvest time, and it was engaging 30 percent of its women in manufacturing. Yet "millions of minority group Americans who comprise our largest pool of unutilized labor" remained on the economic fringe because of "prejudice and custom." The FEPC would strike down the barriers, Ross promised, by using specific evidence that "here stands a worker whom his country needs." The FEPC was not concerned with social relationships, only with equality of opportunity, which was the foundation of the American dream. To the labor unions Ross disclaimed any intention of dictating how unions should conduct their internal affairs or establish membership rules. He insisted, however, that if union practices resulted in discrimination in war employment, they must be corrected "by whatever means the unions chose."[1]

Ross's efforts produced diminishing returns in the South, where he inadvertently got involved in disputes with a newspaper editor and a governor. In Texas, Ross was caught up in a wrangle with the irascible E. M. Dealy, president of the Dallas *Morning News*, because of the fumbling of the FEPC's regional director over a discriminatory newspaper advertisement. Dealy announced that he was "declaring war on the FEPC and would do everything possible to run it out of Dallas and then out of Texas." A conciliatory letter from Ross, who had worked for Dealy as a cub reporter, proved fruitless. Dealy responded curtly, pronouncing the FEPC "indefensible." Then he noted that "one of your efficient secretaries doesn't know" that air mail postage rates increased from six to eight cents. He enclosed the envelope as proof.[2]

Perhaps at Dealy's instigation, Texas governor Coke Stevenson, at a press conference, demanded a statement from the FEPC regarding the Texas segregation laws. All fifteen had been upheld by the United States Supreme Court, and Stevenson wanted to know if the FEPC's purposes violated Texas law. Ross replied that no Texas statute required or countenanced discrimination in employment. Instead, the laws concerned intermarriage, separate railroad coaches and schools, and other matters over which the FEPC had no jurisdiction. He also

---

1. Philadelphia *Evening Bulletin*, March 10, 1944, in Newspaper Clippings, RG 228. See also Pittsburgh *Courier*, January 3, 1944, p. 6, for an account of a Ross interview in New York City.

2. Will Maslow to Malcolm Ross, May 19, 1944, in Office Memoranda, M file, Malcolm Ross to E. M. Dealy, May 31, 1944, in Documents file, R1HR, E. M. Dealy to Malcolm Ross, June 5, 1944, in Public Relations 5, Ross file, R45HR, all in RG 228.

noted, however, that Texas industries reportedly barred blacks from jobs they had traditionally performed, paid blacks and whites different wages for the same work, and refused jobs to skilled blacks who had been trained at government expense. These were the problems that concerned the FEPC. Ross dealt with the issues with gentlemanly restraint and politeness, but his reply did not please W. Don Ellinger, a former labor leader recently appointed as the FEPC's Texas field examiner. The issue in Texas was the FEPC as a federal bureau "operating without regard to local conditions," Ellinger noted. Releasing the letter from Washington, D.C., signed by the chairman instead of the regional director, was a mistake. "After a bitter attack and strenuous accusations, a mild rejoinder is looked upon in this area as weakness rather than restraint." Compounding the error was the delay of a week in the FEPC's response, which detracted from the answer's value. Nevertheless, it is doubtful that a rejoinder, handled Ellinger's way, would have made any difference to the FEPC's southern opponents.[3]

Most of Ross's public relations activity was less heated. Although he responded to an editorial in the Atlanta *Journal* that contained false charges, Ross usually searched for other ways to draw attention to the FEPC's work. There was good cooperation from the black press, but almost none elsewhere, except from a few of the large eastern dailies. The Kansas City *Star* rebuffed the FEPC's regional director on two occasions and never used his press releases. Thus the FEPC and Ross himself took whatever publicity they could get. In July, 1945, Ross appeared on the Mutual Radio Network's "Forum of the Air," a coast-to-coast broadcast that pitted two southern congressman against Ross and the Indiana Republican Charles LaFollette, a racial liberal. On this occasion Ross submitted ten questions highlighting points he wanted discussed.[4]

---

3. Verbatim transcript, committee meeting, June 13, 1944, p. 2, R65HR, Malcolm Ross to Coke Stevenson, June 14, 1944, and W. Don Ellinger to Will Maslow, June 16, 1944, both in Public Relations 5, Ross file, R45HR, and Malcolm Ross to W. Don Ellinger, July 6, 1944, in Committee Office Memoranda, E file, R1HR, all in RG 228.

4. Malcolm Ross to Editor, Atlanta *Journal*, July 21, 1944, A. Bruce Hunt to Mrs. Paul Arrington, July 31, 1944, both in Newspaper Clippings, St. Clair Bourne to Malcolm Ross, George Johnson, and Theodore Jones, April 26, 1945, in office files of George Johnson, St. Clair Bourne file, R3HR, and Malcolm Ross to Ralph McGill, July 4, 1945, in Central Files, Public Relations 6, General Correspondence file, R47HR, all in RG 228.

Early in 1944, Ross suggested a way for the president to help black children who were victims of polio myelitis. Enthusiastically, Ross wrote Eleanor Roosevelt that there was no place at Warm Springs, Georgia, for black infantile paralysis victims, though that health spa enjoyed considerable race support. Ross wanted the president to "consider establishing such facilities, of course, separate from the present buildings." When the first lady forwarded the suggestion to FDR, he said to "tell Mr. Malcolm Ross that Tuskegee has a white unit devoted to the care of negro children" suffering from the malady. Eleanor Roosevelt, who had seen the Tuskegee facility, defended Ross's proposal. There had been "continued pressure to have a unit at Warm Springs because of the prestige and because it would mean an adjustment of the nonsegregation policy which is the point of their demand." FDR replied that it would be difficult, but he would consider it. Jonathan Daniels, with his usual delicacy, advised the president to acknowledge Ross's letter without mentioning Warm Springs. Daniels personally believed Tuskegee was adequate.[5]

In addition to his regular obligations, Ross had other problems. In January, 1944, P. B. Young and Samuel Zemurray both resigned from the committee because of poor health. To replace Young, Roosevelt appointed the black Washington, D.C., attorney, Charles Hamilton Houston. FDR chose Houston instead of Virginius Dabney, white editor of the Richmond *Times-Dispatch*, "in order to have one negro on the Board." That he overlooked or forgot about Milton Webster was undoubtedly another indication of FDR's ambivalence toward this troublesome agency. To replace Zemurray, Charles L. Horn, a Minneapolis arms manufacturer, was tapped.[6]

Both new members came with strong support from the black com-

5. Malcolm Ross to Eleanor Roosevelt, January 25, 1944, Eleanor Roosevelt to the President, February 1, 1944, and Jonathan Daniels to the President, February 8, 1944, all in Box 31, Daniels Papers.

6. Verbatim transcript, committee meeting, January 15, 1944, p. 2, R65HR, Malcolm Ross to Jonathan Daniels, February 12, 1944, Committee Office Memoranda, D file, R1HR, P. B. Young to Malcolm Ross, December 30, 1943, February 15, 1944, Malcolm Ross to P. B. Young, February 19, 1944, Public Relations 5, Young file, R45HR, all in RG 228; FDR to Jonathan Daniels, February 22, 1944, in Official File 4245-G, FDRL; Charles Horn to Francis Haas, July 9, 1945, office files of Cornelius Golightly, History file, R72HR, and Los Angeles *Sentinel*, March 2, 1944, Chicago *Defender*, March 4, 1944, New York *Evening Post*, March 6, 1944, in Newspaper Clippings, all in RG 228; memoranda, Jonathan Daniels to the President, January 15, February 28, 1944, both in Box 31, Daniels Papers.

munity. Charles Houston, with a Phi Beta Kappa key from his under-graduate days at Amherst and a Harvard law degree, was described by Felix Frankfurter as one of the best doctoral students he had taught. A man of great idealism, Houston had entered the law in order to influence government and protect Afro-American citizens. As instructor and dean at the Howard University Law School, he instituted curriculum reforms in the belief that teaching law was important to the struggle for civil rights. If practitioners were of high quality, he believed, the law would become more than just precedent. In 1935, Houston joined the staff of the NAACP as special counsel to fight legalized racial discrimination. His emphasis on issues such as discriminatory teacher salaries in the public schools and unequal graduate facilities in state institutions of higher education helped chart the course that the NAACP would follow for several decades. In 1939, he began concentrating on black workers and racism in railway labor. Before joining the committee, he served as a special counsel in the southern railroad hearings. Charles Horn was also an attorney. As president of the Federal Cartridge Company, he introduced over 1,200 black workers into all levels of his plant, including management, and set a new pattern for the employment of blacks in the Minneapolis area. A member of the national committee of the National Urban League, Horn had strong support from Milton Webster.[7]

Although the FEPC had new blood, old feuds and frictions did not disappear. Boris Shishkin, a brilliant intellectual, shared few personal traits with Frank Fenton, his AFL predecessor on the committee. He was unquestionably and personally committed to the FEPC's goals, but he seemed continually irritated, over petty matters as well as over issues of significance. He disliked the publicity material that the FEPC furnished to the OWI. The statement of purpose "distorts and misleads anyone wishing to learn FEPC objectives," he wrote Ross, but what really bothered him was the description of the committee members. "I was not appointed as a member representing labor nor was Miss Southall" for industry. The membership was drawn from labor and management, with the chairman as a public member.[8]

7. FEPC-OWI press release, n.d., in Press Releases, R, Resignation file, R86HR, RG 228; Genna Rae McNeil, *Groundwork: Charles Hamilton Houston and the Struggle for Civil Rights* (Philadelphia, 1983), 4, 33, 65–75, 83, 131–67.
8. Boris Shishkin to Malcolm Ross, February 7, 1944, Committee Office Memoranda, R file, R1HR, RG 228.

Yet when AFL interests were involved, Shishkin vigorously represented the AFL unions. In the Capital Transit case, he tried unsuccessfully to extend the time period for a company reply in order to remove pressure from the AFL's Amalgamated Association, which was also charged with discrimination. In January, 1944, he got the committee to refrain from certifying the boilermaker case to the president by saying he would try to persuade the union to stop causing the discharge of blacks who refused to pay dues to jim-crow auxiliaries in the west coast shipyards. Shishkin undoubtedly knew he would fail, but he successfully delayed committee action. In subsequent committee meetings he developed elaborate arguments defending the boilermakers, the Seamen's International Union, and other AFL affiliates charged with discrimination. At no time did Milton Webster or John Brophy, also good union men, attempt to influence committee actions so that unions guilty of discrimination would be shielded. However, unlike most of the AFL affiliates, the BSCP and the CIO unions were seldom accused of discrimination.[9]

There was also friction on the staff. Will Maslow, the director of field operations, remained a constant irritant to many blacks in the agency. According to his detractors, Maslow came to the FEPC with such limited racial experience that he spent weeks reading books on the subject, but his close relationship with the chairman undoubtedly rankled. "Mr. Maslow is having the time of his life playing Chairman," George Johnson's secretary, Jeanne Clifton, reported to her boss, who with Ross was attending the boilermaker hearings on the West Coast. At one time Maslow requested verbatim transcripts that Clifton could not locate. She asked if Johnson knew where they were, "not that I am going to give them to him." She implored Johnson to "get back here as soon as humanly possible," because Maslow was "really running away with the show." Giving her judgment of Maslow's leadership qualities, she wrote that "right now a conference with War Department officials is going on, [and Theodore] Jones and [Clar-

9. Verbatim transcript, committee meetings, January 15, 1944, p. 51, February 11, 1944, p. 54, R65HR, Malcolm Ross to All Committee Members, January 26, 1944, in office files of Malcolm Ross, Committee Office Memoranda, R file, R1HR, George Johnson to Boris Shishkin, March 26, 1945, "Minority Statement of Member Shishkin," April 3, 1945, Boris Shishkin to Milton Webster, John Brophy, Sarah Southall, Charles Horn, Charles Houston, April 4, 1945, George Johnson to Boris Shishkin, April 28, 1945, Records of George M. Johnson, Boris Shishkin file, R5HR, all in RG 228.

ence] Mitchell are in it, thank God." Maslow and John Davis, head of the FEPC's division of Review and Analysis, also crossed swords. "After seven months negotiation with the NWLB your recent operating agreement results in absolutely nothing," Davis informed Maslow after a trip south. The National War Labor Board had merely promised to notify the FEPC of any cases involving discrimination and to receive the FEPC's findings and determination in any case pending before it. Davis had wanted the FEPC to refer cases of wage discrimination to this board, because most southern unions were not going to bring up such charges.[10]

Staff problems also arose because of the administrative style and practices of Ross himself. There was a tendency to hold small meetings with various staff members from time to time, Associate Director of Field Operations Clarence Mitchell noted in a March, 1944, memorandum. "I have been in on a few of these myself," but more often "they are gatherings one stumbles into." Mitchell suspected that "some of the policies which affect the entire staff" were decided in this manner. "I, personally, could accept some of the decisions with more enthusiasm if I felt that all points of view had been properly aired." Mitchell used the personal pronoun because he had not talked with other staff people. "I have conviction about the worth of what we are doing . . . [but] I must confess my esprit de corps suffers when I must unearth rather than observe our policy making." Two weeks later, his memorandum apparently unanswered, Mitchell again noted the "limited meeting of division heads from which persons . . . are excluded," and he formally requested admission to those gatherings. George Johnson also complained about staff procedures. "At the risk of appearing to be motivated primarily by the fact that the Deputy Chairman [had] been 'by-passed' in . . . the question of the establishment of a northwest office" in Portland or Seattle, Johnson offered several arguments in support of Regional Director Harry Kingman's request for such an office. Sometimes staff members were delinquent.

10. "Official and unofficial business," Jeanne Clifton to George Johnson, November 10, 1943, "Mostly UNOFFICIAL business," Jeanne Clifton to George Johnson, November 13, 1943, in Records of George M. Johnson, Personal & Confidential file, R5HR, John Davis to Will Maslow, March 14, 15, 1944, in office files of John A. Davis, Mr. Maslow file, R68HR, memorandum, George Johnson to Staff, March 4, 1944, Confidential Memoranda, Administrative Files, V, F49FR, and Chicago *Defender*, March 25, 1944, in Newspaper Clippings, all in RG 228.

"Do you remember those files that I lovingly packed for you?" Virginia Seymour, an FEPC secretary in San Francisco, asked Attorney Frank D. Reeves of the Legal Division. "I don't think that keeping them almost a month [instead of a week] is anything at all—but Mr. [Edward] Rutledge [the west coast examiner-in-charge]! He has it all mixed up with your integrity. . . . Maybe you should return them." [11]

By the fall of 1944, rumors and press reports of dissension among the staff became embarrassing. The Washington, D.C., *Tribune*, reporting an "FEPC split into pro-Ross and anti-Ross factions," thought the bickering was dangerous. Charley Cherokee also observed staff unrest. "FEPC has a swell civil war on," with "Ross' lieutenants . . . fighting for power, and Mike, nice fellow that he is, is world's worst administrator." In addition, Ross, "like many whites who get fame (as well as hell)" from their interest in minorities, "has let being a 'celeb[rity]' throw him." Ross was giving the black Theodore "Ted" Jones "'life and death' power over the rest of the staff," leaving division heads and Deputy Chairman Johnson "suspended in mid-air." Cherokee thought "the Ted-Mike combine" was trying to replace black St. Clair Bourne, a former sports reporter for the Amsterdam *Star News*, as the FEPC's public relations chief. Another black, Marjorie Lawson, from Review and Analysis, would take Bourne's place. Cherokee obviously favored Bourne. The central office resembled "an army with about 60 generals and 15 privates," Cherokee continued, "everybody sitting around on their fat laurels doing 'research,' birthing ideas, and giving orders, and practically nobody carrying out orders." He suspected, for example, that the black John Davis' 10-person staff in the division of Review and Analysis was excessive. Meanwhile, he reported, the newest committee member, Charles Houston, had stepped into the breach and was introducing staff reforms for hiring, firing, and budget arrangements. [12]

11. Clarence Mitchell to Malcolm Ross and Will Maslow, March 30, 1944, and Clarence Mitchell to George Johnson, April 12, 1944, both in office files of George Johnson, C. M. Mitchell file, R3HR, Virginia Seymour to Frank Reeves, May 13, 1944, Administrative Files, Unarranged Correspondence, Frank Reeves file, F104FR, and George Johnson to Malcolm Ross, September 18, 1944, in Office Memoranda, J file, R1HR, all in RG 228.

12. Chicago *Defender*, September 30, October 7, 14, November 11, 25, 1944, and Washington *Tribune*, October 14, 1944, all in Newspaper Clippings, RG 228.

The publicity was generally disconcerting, but committee members became outraged at a piece by Harry McAlpin in the Atlanta *Daily World* under the heading "Ross Gets Wings Clipped by FEPC." McAlpin thought that Ross had "enjoyed almost absolute freedom from criticism . . . because of fear it might hurt FEPC," which already had enough enemies in Congress and in the business community. "Riding on the wave of popularity the agency enjoys among Negroes," Ross had "assumed the stature of an expert on Negro affairs" and had apparently concluded that "he could dispense with the advice and counsel of the exceptionally qualified Negro members of his staff." Ignoring the organizational chart and, McAlpin might have added, Deputy Director George Johnson, Ross took Will Maslow, another white, into his confidence as adviser. Together they recommended changes in the bill for a permanent FEPC that would have weakened the agency's enforcement powers. McAlpin also reported that many committee members were disappointed with Ross's showing as chairman at the hearings in St. Louis and Los Angeles.[13]

At the October, 1944, committee meeting, Charles Houston, who had earlier praised Ross because he was "a great big value to us as a hard hitting functioning Chairman," led the attack on McAlpin. At its previous meeting the committee had spent considerable time discussing staff reorganization, Houston noted. McAlpin's article seemed to interpret reorganization as an attack by the committee on Ross. Further, McAlpin erroneously stated that the committee had adopted certain policies in regard to proposed legislation. Houston's motion ordered the preparation of a letter of protest to the National Negro Press Association, which McAlpin represented, asking cooperation against the appearance of irresponsible articles about the FEPC. In responding, Harry McAlpin took great pride in the accuracy of his reporting, and he seemed to expect the FEPC's gratitude for withholding additional information allegedly "of a far more damaging character." He assured the committee of his "interest in the affairs of the FEPC."[14]

13. Atlanta *Daily World*, October 4, 1944, reproduced in verbatim transcript, committee meeting, October 11, 1944, p. 13, R65HR, RG 228.

14. Verbatim transcripts, committee meetings, September 30, 1944, pp. 132–35, October 11, pp. 13–15, R65HR, Harry McAlpin to FEPC, October 16, 1944, in Records of George Johnson, Committee Material file, R5HR, and Los Angeles *Sentinel*, October 26, 1944, in Newspaper Clippings, all in RG 228.

What McAlpin, as well as Charley Cherokee, wrote hit the mark fairly accurately. Ross had an administrative style that exasperated even the affable and mild-mannered Clarence Mitchell. Ross and Haas each in the beginning had shut out blacks on the staff, and Ross consulted, perhaps too frequently, with the intense and capable Will Maslow, who sometimes aroused the antagonism of committee members as well as of staff. Middle-echelon administrators did spar over power. The committee in the past had justifiably curbed Ross and his staff. Much of the information, though, was very old stuff that some columnists, through leaks, had apparently known about for months. Yet, by one report, the committee had called in the FBI in an attempt to stop the leaks. For some reason, such gossip began pouring out in October, 1944, as the committee worked placidly on staff reorganization. The staff was "plunged into gloom," Charley Cherokee reported, upon learning "how new member Charley Houston" was introducing reforms. There was, however, little hard evidence that directly linked the introduction of reforms to damaging press leaks by the staff except the fact that both occurred in the same time span.[15]

One staff member in particularly deep trouble was the black public relations chief, St. Clair Bourne, who had left the journalism brotherhood to join the FEPC. Ross had been "thoroughly dissatisfied" with Bourne's information section for a long time, he told the committee. Bourne was "a good leg work reporter," but he lacked the "imagination to see what the Committee needs." He was also "pretty lazy," and when Ross assigned him "chores," he got no response. Bourne had never completed "an intelligent digest of what the Negro press is thinking," nor had he maintained contacts with the people in Review and Analysis. Ross wanted to move in Marjorie Lawson from that division and put Bourne in the field. Charles Horn and Charles Houston both suggested firing Bourne. "Could you run a business if you had a man that was lazy?" Horn asked. Ross demurred, because government service did not turn a man away unless he was an "absolute failure." If there were deficiencies, a record had to be built up with a series of demerits before action could be taken. Bourne should, however, be supplanted. It was just this proposed demotion of Bourne

15. Chicago *Defender*, October 14, 1944, and Los Angeles *Sentinel*, October 26, 1944, both in Newspaper Clippings, RG 228.

that Charley Cherokee had found out about, obviously through press leaks, and opposed in the column critical of Ross. Then he warned "all and sundry in FEPC" to "straighten up and fly right, or that 'think piece' Mike [Ross] is always wanting done is going to be a stink piece, and we do mean pfui!"[16]

Internal problems aside, the FEPC's political position remained precarious from the beginning of the Smith Committee investigation until the agency finally expired. Shortly after Smith's first hearing, the FEPC, in a letter to the president carrying the individual signatures of the committee members, requested a "brief personal meeting" with FDR, because "our task has not been easy," the "enforcement sanctions are extremely inadequate," and the FEPC's authority has been openly challenged. The committee's effectiveness depended, the letter went on to say, "in a large measure upon the prestige derived from its designation as the President's Committee." Yet the public was aware that "the Committee has maintained no direct contact with you for some time." The members wanted to discuss the FEPC's authority under the wartime powers, the status of Special Assistant Jonathan Daniels and his relationship with the FEPC, the lack of compliance by the railroads, and discrimination in the Southwest against Mexican-Americans. They suggested February 12, Lincoln's birthday, as a fitting time for the meeting. Their request was denied.[17]

Despite congressional investigations and the lack of presidential support, the FEPC's case load continued to soar. Beginning in 1944, the agency had a larger flow of cases than it could adjust. For the previous six months, new cases averaged over 300 per month, with nearly 1,957 left over at the beginning of the new year. Then, during the first four weeks of January, 355 additional cases were docketed, the largest increase since the docketing system began. By March the number of new cases peaked at 439. Of 5,000 cases received yearly, about 3,500 could be closed, including 1,500 satisfactorily adjusted. While complaints increased, however, a *Fortune* magazine national survey showed general employer satisfaction with black workers. Of the 102 industrial firms responding to the survey, 5 found black work-

16. Verbatim transcript, committee meeting, September 30, 1944, pp. 127–31, R65HR, RG 228; Chicago *Defender*, November 25, 1944, p. 11.
17. FEPC to the President, January 31, 1944, Public Relations 5, FDR file, R45HR, RG 228.

ers superior and 80 believed they equaled white employees in productivity. Only 12 respondents expressed dissatisfaction with blacks.[18]

Although the vast majority of the FEPC's cases involved complaints made directly to the agency by individuals, about 20 percent were referred by the WMC under the agreement signed in the summer of 1943. The FEPC-WMC relationship worked relatively well in the North and West but poorly in the South. In two of the southern regions (IV and X), Ross complained to Paul McNutt, not a single USES 510 report of discriminatory practices was received from the WMC during the twelve months ending November 30, 1944. This performance contrasted sharply with New York (Region II), which issued 150 during the same period, California (Region XII) 166, and Ohio (Region V) 160. Many local USES offices in the South, Ross charged, "to this day do not even know what a 510 report is and do not have copies of the forms." He also complained that the segregated, black USES offices did not receive placement orders as soon as white offices did, failed to use Negro interviewers, and provided no special services for war veterans. A few southern area and state WMC directors sometimes helped the FEPC, but most remained uncooperative and hostile. Ross's complaints about the South to the WMC's Washington, D.C., office brought only limited relief.[19]

As the FEPC tried to carry out its mandate, a more fundamental struggle went on in Congress over funding and over its future when the war emergency ended. Since its creation, the committee had been financed through the president's emergency fund. Early in 1944, the Budget Bureau had approved the FEPC's request for $585,000 and sent it to the president. In a well-planned assault, Senator Richard Russell moved to abolish all agencies in existence for more than a year unless Congress specifically granted the funds. The Russell Amendment, coming on the heels of the Smith Committee hearings, which had portrayed the FEPC as a troublemaker, was passed by the Senate Appropriations Subcommittee toward the end of February; shortly thereafter it was approved by the full Senate. The Montgomery *Ad-*

18. Will Maslow to Malcolm Ross, March 4, 1944, in Office Memoranda, M file, and Budget Request, December, 1943, to November, 1944, Documents file, March 31, 1944, both in R1HR, *Christian Science Monitor*, February 14, 1944, and Chicago *Defender*, March 25, 1944, both in Newspaper Clippings, all in RG 228.

19. Malcolm Ross to Paul McNutt, February 9, 1945, in Central File, U.S. Govt., WMC, R67HR, RG 228; Merl Reed, "FEPC and Federal Agencies," 43–56.

vertiser, reporting gleefully but inaccurately that "this meddlesome committee" had been put to death, rejoiced that the FEPC could no longer be used to further the ideas of Eleanor Roosevelt and others who would force racial equality on the people of the South. The FEPC had support, though, among many northern dailies, including the New York *Post* and *PM,* the Pittsburgh *Post Gazette,* the Minneapolis *Spokesman,* the Washington *News,* and the St. Paul *Recorder.* The Washington *Post* supported the FEPC, but it also endorsed the Russell Amendment. Preparing for the battle in the House, Congressman Malcolm Tarver of Georgia charged the FEPC with trying to force government agencies to hire a greater proportion of blacks. Even from New York, the conservative Republican congressman John Tabor thought the FEPC's reputation was bad.[20]

The Russell Amendment was an astute political move. By associating the FEPC in the public mind with the greatly enlarged federal bureaucracy and by ignoring its wartime origin and mission, Russell appealed to northern conservatives, who according to one Indiana newspaper were "tired of the New Deal encroachments on their rights." An Oregon editor also applauded. He wondered how many agencies, similar to the FEPC, that no one had taken the trouble to count had been established by a New Deal executive order over the past twelve years. Although the Senate at first exempted the FEPC from the amendment, Russell, in a stirring speech, changed enough votes to get the agency included in the amendment. House and Senate conferees approved the Russell Amendment to the Independent Offices Appropriations Bill on May 26. The FEPC for the first time began preparing a budget request of $585,000 for the House Appropriations Committee.[21]

The debate in the House was brief but dramatic and highlighted the charges of several southern congressmen that the FEPC had stirred

20. Philadelphia *Inquirer,* February 27, 1944, Montgomery *Advertiser,* March 27, 1944, Washington, D.C., *News,* March 31, 1944, all in Newspaper Clippings, RG 228; Philadelphia *Tribune,* March 4, 1944, p. 1, March 18, 1944, pp. 1, 8; Pittsburgh *Courier,* March 18, 1944, p. 1; Baltimore *Sun,* May 25, 1944, in Series III, 1943–44, Russell Papers.

21. Norfolk *Journal and Guide,* March 11, 1944, Chicago *Sunday Bee,* March 19, 1944, Richmond (Ind.) *Palladium Item,* May 5, 1944, Salem (Ore.) *Journal,* May 26, 1944, New York *Times,* May 26, 1944, all in Newspaper Clippings, RG 228; Ruchames, *Race, Jobs, and Politics,* 87–90; Neuchterlein, "Politics of Civil Rights," 181–82.

up racial trouble. On the first vote, according to Harry McAlpin, the southerners carried the day. Many FEPC staff members watched in the gallery as the appropriation was defeated, 141 to 103. A number of the women wept, and Malcolm Ross was "crestfallen and bewildered," because an easy victory had been expected. Believing the agency to be dead, they left. In a later vote, however, nearly all of the FEPC appropriation passed, but only by a majority of 4 votes, 123 to 119. Now the southerners were "crestfallen and amazed at the final result." The House authorized $500,000 for the next fiscal year, only $85,000 less than the Budget Bureau's recommendation. "FEPC for the first time since its creation can come out of the shadows and proclaim it exists," observed the New York *Post*. When "Congressional reactionaries" tried to wipe it out by denying funds, the "FEPC took up the challenge" and asked to become legitimate. It was "a responsible federal agency doing an important job." Although the black press praised Chicago's Afro-American congressman William L. Dawson for getting the bill passed, the *Post* more accurately gave credit for the victory to Congressman Vito Marcantonio (I–New York), "a favorite of the Communists." That should be reproof enough for the congressional liberals who failed to fight hard for the FEPC and thus forfeited progressive leadership to the left wing, said the *Post*.[22]

For Senator Russell, to whom white supremacy and segregation were obsessions, burdens from which only death relieved him, the House vote must have been a bitter disappointment, and it came only a short time after the United States Supreme Court, by a vote of 8 to 1, outlawed the Deep South's system of white Democratic primaries. "Powerful forces . . . are at work to force social equality and miscegenation of the races upon our country," Russell wrote an Atlanta constituent four days after the House action. With eastern and western Democrats bidding for black support in the 1944 election, the South was "sadly outnumbered," but Russell promised to do his "best to combat these forces of evil." As the bill with the FEPC's appropria-

22. Will Maslow to Regional Directors and Examiners-in-charge, May 27, 1944, in Administrative Files, Unarranged Correspondence, Maslow-policy file, F104HR, Will Maslow to Malcolm Ross, May 27, 1944, in office files of Will Maslow, Congressional Record References file, R76HR, Philadelphia *Tribune*, June 3, 1944, p. 9, New York *Post*, May 31, 1944, and Atlanta *Daily World*, May 28, 1944, both in Newspaper Clippings, all in RG 228; Philadelphia *Tribune*, June 3, 1944, p. 9; Pittsburgh *Courier*, June 3, 1944, pp. 1, 4; Ruchames, *Race, Jobs, and Politics*, 90–96; Neuchterlein, "Politics of Civil Rights," 182–83.

tion made its way through the Senate, his forces defeated it 3 to 2 in the appropriations subcommittee on June 10, but later they lost in the full committee by a decisive vote of 14 to 6. The agency that, according to Russell, gave a "group of Negro politicians authority to cite employers and harass them in time of war" so far had survived.[23]

On June 15, following a southern strategy session, Russell began a last-ditch fight against the "forces of evil." First, he introduced an amendment stipulating that not more than 25 percent of the FEPC's funds could be used for salaries of persons belonging to any race "comprising less than 15 percent of the total population of the United States." Although this attempt to limit the number of blacks in the agency was rejected, he had better success with other amendments. One, an attempt to trivialize the FEPC's right to certify difficult cases to the White House, gave parties charged with discrimination the same right of appeal to the president as the committee had. Another amendment limited the use of FEPC funds "only for those functions lawfully vested in the Committee," a vague statement that opened up the possibility of court attacks. A third stated that the FEPC could not undertake actions with a view to seizing a plant that failed to obey an FEPC order. These amendments, approved by the Senate, were viewed as "conniving and subtle" but generally not debilitating. The Senate bill also reduced the chairman's salary from $10,000, as provided in the executive order, to $8,000, "not for economy," according to one report, "but to turn FEPC into a second class agency."[24]

The Senate debate of the Russell amendments sank to a new low in the eyes of FEPC supporters, but it reached Olympian heights according to some accounts from the South. To Harry McAlpin, Senators Theodore Bilbo and James Eastland (Mississippi), Russell and Walter

23. Will Maslow to Regional Directors, June 10, 12, 1944, in Teletype folder, II, F3FR, and Baltimore *Sun*, April 4, 1944, in Newspaper Clippings, both in RG 228; Richard Russell to Marvin Mobley, May 31, 1944, in Series X, FEPC 1944–45, Russell Papers; Philadelphia *Tribune*, June 10, 1944, p. 9.

24. George Johnson to Malcolm Ross, June 24, 1944, office files of Maceo Hubbard, Miscellaneous file, R7HR, Malcolm Ross to Francis Haas, June 26, 1944, in Public Relations 5, Haas file, R45HR, New York *Evening Post*, June 23, 1944, and Washington *Post*, June 15, 1944, in Newspaper Clippings, all in RG 228; Philadelphia *Tribune*, June 17, 1944, p. 1, June 24, 1944, p. 1; Pittsburgh *Courier*, June 17, 1944, p. 1; David D. Potenziani, "Look to the Past: Richard B. Russell and the Defense of Southern White Supremacy" (Ph.D. dissertation, University of Georgia, 1981), 41–45. See also Ruchames, *Race, Jobs, and Politics*, 96–99, and Neuchterlein, "Politics of Civil Rights," 183–84.

George (Georgia), Lister Hill (Alabama), and John McClellan (Arkansas) could easily have qualified as advance agents of Hitler in their arguments for white supremacy. These men were worried about the rise of social equality and interracial marriages. Bilbo, as usual traveling the low road, warned his Senate colleagues that passage of the bill might bring "one of those mulattos or high-brown or yellow girls as their stenographers," and when that happened "all the B.O. powders on earth will not dissipate the odoriferous aroma they will find permeating their offices day by day." McClellan deplored government agencies in which white and black girls ate in the same restaurants, worked next to each other, and used the same rest rooms. Then Eastland "jumped to his feet and literally screamed: 'The conditions [just described] . . . are obnoxious to white people, but is it not worse that white girls should be forced to take dictation from a group of burrheaded "Niggers" and "Nigger" supervisors in the departments?'" The *Congressional Record* reported that Eastland said "Negro," McAlpin noted, "but he didn't." To the Jackson (Mississippi) *Clarion Ledger,* Eastland was a hero who had lost a gallant and brilliant fight to kill the "vicious, iniquitous, illegal and communistic" FEPC. In this battle he enhanced his own prestige in the Senate and his national reputation as a statesman.[25]

Polarization around the FEPC issue was inevitable. In the South, however, not everyone applauded the efforts of the region's statesmen in the United States Senate. The Miami *Herald* attacked Senator George for claiming that approval of the FEPC would be like "converting our economic system into a communistic or national socialistic system." His claim was, the paper said, a "measure of the Georgian's capacity" for recklessness. But the debate over the FEPC had wider implications. For an agency previously newsworthy primarily to the black press, the battles waged by Smith and Russell brought extensive coverage for the first time from the nation's dailies, including those in towns and small cities. Whereas many commentators were influenced by Russell's rhetoric and saw the FEPC as just another New Deal agency that should be wiped out, others favored it and provided it with unprecedented publicity.[26]

25. Chicago *Defender,* July 1, 1944, p. 1; Jackson *Clarion Ledger,* June 23, 1944, in Unfavorable Editorials file, Box 513, RG 228.
26. Miami *Herald,* June 26, 1944, and Atlanta *Journal,* August 6, 1944, both in Newspaper Clippings, RG 228.

The FEPC's survival during that difficult spring and summer owed much to its growing constituency of civil rights groups, and within the limits of the law the agency sought their aid. "Two to three weeks remain to do a total job of obtaining support of friendly organizations at the budget Committee hearings," stated an in-house memorandum from Marjorie Lawson. Although the FEPC had to avoid official approaches, it could, if requested, furnish organizations with information. A pamphlet entitled "What FEPC Is" and a statement about the budget had already been prepared by Theodore Jones for distribution. Promotion should be done on a regional basis, Lawson wrote, through personal contact. Organizations should be requested to send telegrams and letters to members of the House Appropriations Committee and to their own congressmen. Supporters also should try to stimulate similar activity from others and, where possible, obtain radio time to make direct appeals. The FEPC's network of supporters became active in March when southern congressional opponents first attacked the budget. After the FEPC's half-million-dollar appropriation was approved, the Los Angeles *Sentinel* gave full credit to the NAACP, the CIO, the AFL, and similar organizations that had helped keep congressmen and senators in line. Additionally, Lawson stressed contacts with groups such as the National Council of Negro Women, the National Council of Jewish Women, the International Brotherhood of Post Office Employees, the Association of Colleges and Secondary Schools for Negroes, and the National Urban League. There were also thousands of individuals who reportedly wrote or wired messages of support.[27]

With the FEPC safely funded for another year, its champions turned their attention once again to a longer-range goal, the establishment of a permanent committee. Vito Marcantonio had introduced such a bill in summer, 1943, but it never cleared the House committee. The following year, as the civil rights movement began building coalitions with religious, civil libertarian, and labor groups, supporters began to focus on the National Council for a Permanent FEPC, founded through the efforts of A. Philip Randolph, who cochaired the organization with the Reverend Alan Knight Chalmers, a

27. Marjorie Lawson to Malcolm Ross and Theodore Jones, March 1, 1944, Office Memoranda, K file, R1HR, and Los Angeles *Sentinel*, June 29, 1944, in Newspaper Clippings, both in RG 228.

prominent white theologian. According to author Lerone Bennett, Jr., when black religious groups began identifying with the FEPC, many churches were stimulated to social activism, and their leaders became more politicized. Early in 1944, as southerners focused their attacks through the Smith Committee, over one hundred leaders of black, religious, and labor organizations met in Washington, D.C., and vowed to keep the discrimination issue alive by endorsing a permanent FEPC. A "mass march" to impress Congress, organized by the BSCP, was allegedly in an advanced planning stage. Meanwhile, three congressmen, Indiana's LaFollette, Illinois' Dawson, and Thomas A. Scanlon (D–New Jersey), had introduced bills to make the FEPC a permanent agency, and hearings were being held before a House education and labor subcommittee.[28]

Toward the end of May, 1944, after the House had approved funds for the FEPC, Congresswoman Mary Norton, chairman of the House Labor Subcommittee, held additional hearings on the three bills. Fearing a divided party after the upcoming Democratic National Convention, however, Roosevelt saw to it that the House hearings were postponed until after the 1944 elections. What was surprising, Jonathan Daniels protested "that the postponement was a mistake." The "whole Negro group is disturbed," he wrote Presidential Assistant Edwin Watson. Worse, the Republicans were circulating rumors "that the postponement was directed from the White House," and Governor Thomas E. Dewey, the leading Republican opponent, "will endorse this permanent" FEPC. Although the legislation "as now drawn" seemed to him "impossible of enforcement" and without a "chance of passage in the near future," Daniels believed FDR should "reiterate . . . his support," for "it would be more effective than anything else he could do to insure the full Negro vote." In addition, Daniels urged Roosevelt to meet with a group of blacks headed by White and Randolph, though he changed his mind "after talking with Congressman Dawson . . . vice chairman of the Democratic National Committee in charge of Negro matters" and the only black in the House. Thus did

---

28. San Francisco *News*, January 20, 1944, and New York *World Telegram*, January 21, 1944, both in Newspaper Clippings, RG 228; Philadelphia *Tribune*, January 29, 1944, p. 1, February 12, 1944, p. 20; Pittsburgh *Courier*, January 29, 1944, p. 1; Bennett, *Confrontation*, 190; Ruchames, *Race, Jobs, and Politics*, 199.

the administration and the president, prior to the election, chart a slippery course between antagonistic southern and Negro supporters as well as between divided black leaders.[29]

Blacks were not pleased with FDR's handling of the FEPC bill. A delegation of ministers prayed silently in a Senate subcommittee room for approval of a permanent committee before election day. Although Congressman LaFollette issued a statement of regret and accused the Democrats of evading the civil rights issue, some blacks blamed both parties for stalling. Whereas the administration feared the "wild men from the South, Republicans [were] courting the white supremacy block . . . with a view to using it to stop important labor legislation." There were sufficient votes in both houses to pass a bill if Roosevelt "would only lend his powerful support." Several newspapers called for blacks to begin mobilizing their forces. According to columnist Raymond Moley, Walter White castigated both House and Senate committees for claiming that action on the bill had been delayed until more witnesses could be heard: "We submit [that] the facts of racial discrimination are well known. . . . Delay is bad faith." Late in September Senator Dennis Chavez's (D–New Mexico) subcommittee on education reported favorably on its FEPC legislation, and the full Senate committee was believed to be willing to give immediate approval. The Kansas City *Call* was not placated, however, and in a blistering editorial entitled "Democrats Let the South Rule the Party," it endorsed Governor Dewey and the Republicans. Roosevelt had once been a friend but was no more; "he puts us at the mercy of our enemies like the Christians and the lions." The editorial noted that though the Democratic convention promised to deal fairly with minorities, neither the president nor the national committee had pushed for a permanent FEPC, and the matter had been postponed until after the election. "It will be killed . . . because the South is in the saddle in the Democratic party," charged the *Call*. "A Negro has to be a double dyed dunce to trust himself and his race to the 'white

29. Memoranda, Jonathan Daniels to Edwin Watson, September 6, 11, 1944, in Daniels Papers; Chicago *Sun*, June 2, 1944, Washington, D.C., *Star*, September 1, 1944, and Washington *Post*, September 2, 1944, all in Newspaper Clippings, RG 228; *Christian Science Monitor*, June 17, 1944, in FEPC 1943–44, Russell Papers; Philadelphia *Tribune*, May 27, 1944, p. 19; Pittsburgh *Courier*, September 2, 1944, p. 1; Neuchterlein, "Politics of Civil Rights," 181.

supremacy' southern politicians who call the tunes for the President."[30]

Apparently stung by the criticism, the administration by October began looking for ways to repair the damage. Roosevelt, who earlier had been too busy to see black leaders, spent fifty minutes with Walter White, Channing Tobias of the YMCA, and Mary Bethune, his first conference with black leaders since June, 1941. Escorted to the White House in an army car after a meeting at the Pentagon, the three talked with the president about the jim-crow army. When asked about the FEPC, Roosevelt quipped, "Didn't I invent it? Of course I'm for it." As usual, it was a masterful performance, but the magic was wearing off. Why did the president do things by indirection, whispering his support to Walter White behind closed doors? asked the Philadelphia *Tribune*. Why did White have to announce FDR's endorsement when the president made nationwide political speeches and said nothing about the agency? Governor Dewey made his position known on the radio, reminded the paper. Finally, nine days before the election, Roosevelt publicly said he favored a permanent FEPC. By this time, however, national council co-chairmen Randolph and Chalmers were warning of a letdown after the election that could be fatal, and civil rights leaders were beginning to realize that the postponement of the House hearings was the kiss of death. If the bill had reached the House and Senate floors before the congressional recess in August, there was little doubt, they believed, that it would have passed despite southern opposition.[31]

Although hearings resumed in the House after the election, there were more setbacks. The AFL, citing its traditional but shopworn principle of voluntarism, refused during an earlier Senate committee

30. Washington, D.C., *Star*, September 1, 1944, Los Angeles *Sentinel*, September 7, 1944, Pittsburgh *Courier*, September 9, 16, 1944, Raymond Moley, Chicago *Journal of Commerce*, September 13, 1944, Houston *Informer*, September 16, 1944, Chicago *Defender*, September 30, 1944, Amsterdam *Star News*, September 30, 1944, Los Angeles *Times*, October 1, 1944, and Kansas City *Call*, October 6, 1944, all in Newspaper Clippings, RG 228; Pittsburgh *Courier*, September 30, 1944, pp. 1, 6.

31. Mary Bethune, Channing Tobias, and Walter White to FDR, September 28, 1944, in Daniels Papers; Chicago *Defender*, October 7, 1944, and Philadelphia *Tribune*, October 21, 1944, both in Newspaper Clippings, RG 228; Philadelphia *Tribune*, October 7, 1944, pp. 1, 3, October 21, 1944, p. 4, November 4, 1944, pp. 1, 2; Pittsburgh *Courier*, November 4, 1944, p. 1.

hearing to endorse a permanent FEPC. While opposing racial discrimination, the AFL decried any governmental control of freely constituted associations of workers. Reinforcing the point, Boris Shishkin
at a Howard University conference warned that the AFL would oppose
any regulation of unions, even to prevent discrimination. Another
discouraging statement came from the national board of the League
of Women Voters. Endorsing the principle of equal economic opportunity for minorities and approving the objectives of the FEPC, the
league, nevertheless, could not support a permanent agency because
legislation against discrimination could not be enforced, which might
cause repercussions damaging to the cause of racial understanding.
Meanwhile, Mary Norton's House Labor Subcommittee moved the
legislation forward. Her hearing concluded without a dissenting witness. The chairman declared that "the right to work is the right to
live" and called for a permanent FEPC. Without it, she predicted,
there would be a rise in racial tension and an absence of job safe-
guards. Yet when Congress adjourned on December 23, no action had
been taken.[32]

As the new Congress convened, the National Council for a Permanent FEPC was still hopeful. A spokesman listed the names of forty
favorable senators and eighty-one representatives, a cross-section indicating strong bipartisan support. Shortly thereafter, thirteen bills
were introduced in the House. Of the various pieces of legislation, the
black press was most interested in those introduced by seven congressmen, LaFollette, Norton, Dawson, Charles Cason (R–Massachusetts), Everett Dirksen (R–Illinois), Joseph Baldwin (R–New York),
and Frank Hook (D–Michigan), who had earlier served as an FEPC
regional director. The President, who had publicly endorsed the FEPC
before the election, remained silent, however. In his state of the union
message, he made no mention of the FEPC, an omission regarded by
some as fatal to the agency. Then, as Congressman Baldwin's bill was
voted out of the House Labor Subcommittee, Robert Taft (R–Ohio),

32. *PM*, October 29, 1944, OWI Press Digest, in office files of Wilfred C. Leland,
Jr., Mobile file, R71HR, FEPC Statement, November 17, 1944, in office files of Marjorie Lawson, League of Women Voters file, R69HR, Washington, D.C., *Star*, November 16, 1944, and Baltimore *Afro-American*, November 25, December 23, 1944,
in Newspaper Clippings, all in RG 228; Pittsburgh *Courier*, November 4, 1944, p.
15, December 16, 1944, p. 1, December 23, 1944, p. 2.

minority leader of the Senate, reversed a preelection pledge and announced his opposition to all the FEPC bills because of their compulsory features. The "colored people are making a mistake," he told a group of black constituents. "I think you are pushing too fast. The colored people are much better off than they were ten years ago." In the meantime, Taft introduced his own bill, which denied the FEPC power even to issue orders or enforce its recommendations. Taft's FEPC would be weaker than the existing one. His bill joined a stronger Senate measure already introduced by Senator Chavez. Despite this show of congressional activity, many supporters remained pessimistic. To the *Courier*, the prospects for passage seemed no better than in the last Congress.[33]

As the time for the House hearings approached, emotions erupted, and fists substituted for argument. Congressman Rankin verbally attacked FEPC supporter Frank Hook, labeling him a communist. By one account, Hook called Rankin "a dirty liar (or goddamn liar)." Rankin swung and pulled hair before Hook clinched, trying to avoid hurting Rankin. After House members separated them, Georgia's Eugene Cox called for Hook's expulsion, while Adam Clayton Powell (D–New York) left the House and made a public statement, calling Rankin "a disgrace to the white race, a buffoon, a fascist, a vicious liar, and a son of a fascist." Besides arousing personal emotions, the issue was laden with political dynamite, reported the Baltimore *Sun*. It represented trouble for southern Democrats, but even Republicans shied away from definite commitments. House minority leader Joseph Martin favored the bill's principles but refused to support it until messages, calls, and visits from Republicans around the country changed his mind. In June, Martin announced he would vote for a permanent FEPC, but he said he could not lead the fight without authorization from the Republican conference. Meanwhile, the bill had gone to the House Rules Committee in late February where it remained for

33. Pittsburgh *Courier*, January 13, 1945, pp. 1, 5; analysis of the Taft bill, in office files of George Johnson, 1945, House Bills for Permanent FEPC file, R3HR, Washington, D.C., *Tribune*, January 6, 1945, in Capital Transit folder, Box 513, Baltimore *Afro-American*, January 14, 1945, and Chicago *Defender*, March 3, 1945, in Newspaper Clippings, all in RG 228; Pittsburgh *Courier*, February 10, 1945, pp. 1, 4, March 3, 1945, p. 2; Philadelphia *Tribune*, January 13, 1945, p. 1, February 10, 1945, pp. 1, 10; Will Maslow, "FEPC—A Case History in Parliamentary Maneuver," *University of Chicago Law Review*, XII (1946), 409–10, cited in Ruchames, *Race, Jobs, and Politics*, 200–202, 239.

months without action. At the same time, the Senate committee on labor began hearings on the Chavez bill.[34]

Civil rights supporters participated in the various House and Senate hearings. Those who testified for the bill came from the Catholic Inter-Racial Council, the United Council of Church Women, the American Jewish Congress, the CIO, the NAACP, and the Federal Council of Churches. Opponents were also active, including, besides the southern white supremacists, the Chamber of Commerce. Its representatives were particularly exercised over proposals to give the FEPC power to subpoena witnesses and evidence, with fines and imprisonment for violations. Even more outrageous, they charged, was the provision that witnesses who lied could be charged with perjury. That provision, according to one chamber spokesman, was the "most damnable" of all. Not all opponents were southern segregationists or businessmen worried about running afoul of the law. Merlo Pusey, in the Washington *Post*, deplored discrimination but thought the FEPC had been assigned an impossible task. The agency would have to take control over hiring, which would amount to the government telling employers whom to hire, promote, and discharge. Yet the *Post* editorially supported the FEPC, as did increasing numbers of dailies both in metropolitan areas and in smaller cities. In addition to the papers mentioned earlier as supporters of the committee, the St. Paul *Pioneer Press*, the Grand Rapids *Press*, the Newark *News*, and the Hartford *Courant* also endorsed the FEPC.[35]

With the House bill stalled in the rules committee and the Senate bill undergoing debate, new leadership came to the White House with Roosevelt's death on April 12. Toward the end of May, President Harry Truman, in a conference with Walter White, brought up the FEPC. He was optimistic about Senate passage but viewed the House as a serious stumbling block. In response to appeals from White and Mary Norton, Truman on June 5 informed House Rules Committee chairman Adolph J. Sabbath (D–Illinois) that the FEPC was of "paramount importance." The president expressed his strong support for a permanent agency and then released the letter to the press. He also wrote Sabbath that he deplored the deletion of FEPC funds from the

34. Baltimore *Sun*, March 11, June 26, 1945, in Newspaper Clippings, RG 228; Pittsburgh *Courier*, March 3, 1945, p. 5, March 24, 1945, p. 5.
35. Washington *Post*, March 12, 1945, in Education folder, Box 513, and Tucson *Star*, June 22, 1954, in Newspaper Clippings, Box 514, both in RG 228.

War Agencies Appropriations Bill and sent a copy of the letter to Senator Chavez. "As soon as it becomes appropriate in the Senate, let me know and I shall send a similar letter," he told Chavez. "*PM* takes off its hat to Truman for the bold stand in behalf of FEPC," proclaimed that New York evening paper. "Legislation for a permanent FEPC would have been enacted if FDR had written" Sabbath in a similar vein, opined the Washington *Tribune*, not mentioning that Roosevelt had attempted to purge Sabbath in 1938. The *Courier* contrasted Truman's forthright position with Roosevelt's "doubletalk, weasel words and glittering generalities." Nevertheless, Truman could not move the House Rules Committee. Ironically, it was the congressman from Truman's home town, Roger C. Slaughter (D–Missouri), who on June 12 produced the committee tie that would kill the bill. Slaughter voted against the FEPC because "the communists had a hand in it." Although Mary Norton circulated a discharge petition among House members, she could not get the necessary 218 signatures.[36]

As the contest continued, the House Appropriations Committee early in June quietly laid aside the FEPC's budget estimate of $585,000 pending passage of the legislation for a permanent agency. News of this deletion from the War Agencies Appropriations Bill hit like a bombshell since FEPC officials thought they had made a favorable impression at subcommittee hearings a few weeks earlier. Chairman Clarence Cannon (D–Missouri) had given assurances that the funding was secure, but the rules committee members vowed that no war agency appropriations would pass as long as funds for the FEPC were included, and Cannon complied. The FEPC would expire unless money was forthcoming by June 30. Meanwhile, Cannon's committee approved $125,000 to liquidate the agency within three months after July 1. John Brophy called the turn of events "a great social tragedy."

36. "Manuscript, A Washington News Letter," supervised by Charley Cherokee and Harry McAlpin, May 28, 1945, office files of Malcolm Ross, Manuscript folder, R2HR, *PM*, June 7, 25, 1945, Washington, D.C., *Tribune*, June 9, 1945, in Newspaper Clippings, Box 531, and St. Louis *Star Times*, June 13, 1945, in A–C, Appropriations Clippings, 1945 file, Box 513, all in RG 228; memorandum for the files (*re*: White letter of June 1, 1945), n.d., memorandum for the files (*re*: Norton letter of June 1, 1945), n.d., Harry Truman to Adolf Sabbath, June 5, 1944, and Harry Truman to Dudley G. Roe, June 8, 1945, both in office file, 37 miscl–40 miscl (June, 1945) Folder 2, Box 210, Truman Papers; Pittsburgh *Courier*, June 16, 1945, p. 6, June 23, 1945, pp. 2, 6; Neuchterlein, "Politics of Civil Rights," 184–85.

Milton Webster vowed that "Negroes would not take it lying down," and there was talk of a demonstration "more dramatic than a march on Washington."[37]

Senator Chavez took up Truman's offer for aid. "[Chavez] does not think that you ought to do anything publicly about it at this time," stated a memorandum to Truman, "but requests that you make three phone calls," to Senator Kenneth McKellar (D–Tennessee), who was unfavorable, to Senator Carl Hayden (D–Arizona), "who is probably for it, but would take your phone call as a 'shot in the arm,'" and to Senate Majority Leader Alben W. Barkley (D–Kentucky), "who is for it, but who is so busy with other things that a call from you would direct some of his activity toward this measure." Shortly after the memorandum, Chavez succeeded in suspending the rules so that the appropriation committee's $446,200 in funding for the FEPC could be considered by the full Senate as part of the war agencies package. McKellar, as Senate president pro tempore, was in parliamentary command and maneuvered for the opposition. According to *PM*, he delayed bringing up the bill until the FEPC's arch-enemies, Richard Russell and Burnet Maybank (D-South Carolina), returned from a European trip. Then he appointed mostly FEPC supporters to the funeral committee of a deceased Nevada senator so they would miss the vote.[38]

Opposition speakers, led by Senators Bilbo and Eastland, "droolymouthed Mississippians" according to the *Courier*, began a filibuster to delay approval until the June 30 deadline passed. To the St. Louis *Post-Dispatch*, it was a "petty battle," because "the merits of FEPC are not in question." Under Malcolm Ross's leadership, the FEPC "has done quietly brilliant work throughout the war . . . by persuasion, not coercion." Majorities in both houses believed the "FEPC should be continued at least until Japan is beaten." It was a disgrace, the

37. Manuscript, June 4, 1945, in office files of Malcolm Ross, MS file, R2HR, James Marlow, typescript, copy, Baltimore *Sun*, June 4, 1945, in Newspaper Clippings, Box 530, *PM*, June 18, 1945, Washington *Post*, June 17, 1945, Baltimore *Sun*, June 26, 1945, in A–C, Appropriations folder, 1945, all in RG 228; Pittsburgh *Courier*, June 9, 1945, pp. 1, 6, June 23, 1945, p. 6; Neuchterlein, "Politics of Civil Rights," 185.

38. Memorandum for the President, June 15, 1945, in Box 310–40, 1945, Truman Papers; *PM*, June 27, 1945, in A–C, Appropriations Clippings, 1945 file, Box 513, RG 228; Neuchterlein, "Politics of Civil Rights," 185.

paper warned, when democratic government was made a "foolish fiction." The *Courier* was less restrained: "The South is in the Saddle. Dr. Goebbels Rides Again." But a cloture petition was circulating in the Senate, and southern fears of its success made a compromise possible. The filibuster ended, and the Senate passed an appropriation of $250,000, less than half of the amount previously approved by the Budget Bureau. It was not an all-out liquidation of the FEPC after all, but the committee would have to curtail its activities drastically.[39]

In the House, the FEPC remained a hostage in the rules committee, where the southern Democrats held sway. As the stalemate continued, southerners caucused and chose Frank W. Boykin (D-Alabama) to appeal to the president on June 29 for a conference. The group, allegedly comprising 177 congressmen, wanted to give "our view of this terrible thing that is . . . tearing *our Party* to pieces," so that both sides would have "an opportunity to *present their case before you take action.*" Although "the entire group [wanted] to be present," Boykin assured Truman that there would be only one speaker. The president, avoiding such an encounter, could not fit it into his busy schedule. Southern congressmen continued their opposition until fear of a discharge petition led to compromise. The final measure, with its quarter-million-dollar appropriation, passed on July 13. There were "sound arguments against FEPC," noted the Columbia *South Carolina Record* after the measure passed, but the Southern opponents made themselves ridiculous in describing it as a "front for the Communists . . . communistic to the core . . . rotten" or by attacking "the record of Negro soldiers in the war," and "such arguments may have helped its proponents."[40]

By omitting a liquidation clause, Congress extended the FEPC for another year. "While this is a victory for democracy and fair play," commented the *Courier*, "it is only a Pyrrhic victory." From the "political jockeying" that went on, the *Courier* believed Congress would eventually kill the agency. It was a mistake to assume that the FEPC's

39. New York *Times*, June 28, 1945, and St. Louis *Post-Dispatch*, June 29, 1945, both in Newspaper Clippings, RG 228; Pittsburgh *Courier*, July 7, 1945, p. 1; Neuchterlein, "Politics of Civil Rights," 185.

40. Frank Boykin to the President, June 29, 1945, in Box 310–40, 1945, Truman Papers; Will Maslow to Regional Directors (teletype), July 2, 11, 1945, Teletype folder, II, F3FR, and Columbia *South Carolina Record*, July 13, 1945, in Unfavorable Editorials file, Box 513, both in RG 228; Neuchterlein, "Politics of Civil Rights," 185–86.

only enemies were southerners, because the debates "showed the enemy forces consisted of representatives from many sections of both major parties." The *Courier's* assessment was close to the mark. Although the FEPC's existence was assured until June 30, 1946, what happened after that time would depend largely on the efforts of its network of supporters and civil rights advocates.[41]

The struggle for funding and the effort to create a permanent FEPC, though disappointing, had also produced positive results. Metropolitan dailies as well as newspapers in small cities and towns, particularly in the North and West, began reacting to the FEPC whereas previously only the black weeklies, a few liberal daily papers, and southern white supremacist presses had carried news about the agency. Possibly some had never before taken a stand on a civil rights issue such as this. Many favored both funding and the creation of a permanent body, others one without the other, many neither. The FEPC's press support had also breached the Mason-Dixon Line, invading the border states of Missouri, Kentucky, and Tennessee, while the excesses of the southern congressional opposition disgusted some of the FEPC's most bitter critics in the South.

As the national press became more involved in the issue, so did individual citizens and many organizations previously not so openly committed to civil rights. For example, a group of white Atlantans braved local disapproval and censure to support the embattled agency. During the short filibuster, Senator Bilbo received a petition from Atlanta deploring his tactics and supporting the FEPC. Editor Ralph McGill of the Atlanta *Constitution* was hostile to the FEPC, but several of the city's white citizens and their organizations favored it, including Rabbi David Marx, Dr. Edward G. Mackay (Glenn Memorial Chapel, Emory University), Professor Glenn W. Rainey (Georgia Institute of Technology), Lucy Randolph Mason (well-known CIO organizer), the American Association of University Women, the American Jewish Congress, the American Unitarian Association, the CIO, the International Ladies Garment Workers Union, and the Upholsterers International Union of North America (AFL). Another petition contained the names of many prominent blacks, including Armand May, the Reverend William Holmes Borders, and M. Ashby Jones. In a characteristic reply, Bilbo referred to "the great majority of these

41. Pittsburgh *Courier*, July 21, 1945, in Newspaper Clippings, RG 228.

petitioners, [as] representing Negroes, Quislings of the white race, and other racial minorities hailing from the city of Atlanta, the hotbed of the Southern Negro intelligentsia, Communists, pinks, Reds, and other offbrands of American citizenship in the South." Thus it appears that though the FEPC lost ground in the summer of 1945, the civil rights movement may have been strengthened.[42]

42. Atlanta *Constitution*, June 15, 1945, and *Statesman*, June 28, 1945, both in Newspaper Clippings, RG 228.

PART II

Fighting Discrimination in the Field, 1941–1945

6 / The Runaround in Defense Training

As the Old Committee geared up for action in the fall of 1941, it discovered widespread discrimination in the defense training program. In the North and West, where public education facilities were not legally segregated, defense training courses were sometimes denied to blacks and ethnics on the grounds that industry would not hire them. By exposing such practices and threatening other action, the FEPC generally succeeded in effecting change. In the segregated South, however, the lion's share of federal funds had already been funneled into training programs for whites only, and USOE, in charge of administering the funds, benignly sanctioned discrimination and sometimes promoted it. Although the FEPC succeeded in making some changes, southern resistance to training for its black citizens persisted throughout the war.

The federal effort to train workers began in May, 1940, in response to shortages of skilled labor. Handled by the NDAC, it stressed training-within-industry (TWI). By July, an NDAC Labor Policy Advisory Committee, headed by Sidney Hillman, got industry and labor to agree that unemployed skilled workers should be trained. Registration of workers began locally through the state employment services, with help from the CSC, the Social Security Board, the Works Progress Administration, and labor unions, which surveyed their own membership. They registered 6,000,000 workers. TWI programs, run by local labor management councils, had trained over 1,500,000 for defense work by the time the United States entered the war.[1]

In addition to TWI, the patchwork of vocational training programs already in existence was expanded under the auspices of the USOE. In June, 1940, Congress appropriated $15 million for state and local vocational training below the college level, and in the fall another $8 million was earmarked for additional equipment and space. Also authorized was $10 million to train out-of-school rural youth in less specialized programs such as auto mechanics, tractor repair, metal and electrical work, and woodworking. Finally, the NYA and the Civilian Conservation Corps (CCC), holdover New Deal agencies, offered training valuable to national defense.[2]

Although the National Defense Training Act, which created TWI, had an antidiscrimination clause, blacks were usually excluded from industrial jobs and derived little benefit from the program. At NDAC urging, the education office, between July and November, 1940, issued warnings that federal money had to be used without discrimination. All applicants should be considered on the basis of ability, it further stipulated, and where there was insufficient or unusable equipment, local school boundaries should be ignored, training centers consolidated, and shifts set up to operate on a twenty-four-hour basis if necessary. Where segregated schools were mandated, equitable provision should be made for minority groups. USOE policies and statements, perfunctory and unenforced, were generally ignored.[3]

In June, 1940, Hillman brought in Robert Weaver to work on discrimination in defense training. When the NDAC was replaced by the OPM the following March, Hillman's Labor Division included Weaver's Negro Employment and Training Branch and Will Alexander's Minorities Group Service. At the time, there were 175,000 TWI

1. Address by Robert C. Weaver, October 9, 1941, in General Correspondence, Public Relations, D–L, R47HR, RG 228; *Program and Administration* (New York, 1969), 163–64, Vol. I of *Industrial Mobilization for War: History of the War Production Board and Predecessor Agencies, 1940–1945*, 3 vols. projected; Kesselman, "Fair Employment Practice Movement," 36–37; Flynn, *Mess in Washington*, 7–8.

2. Testimony of L. S. Hawkins, USOE, April 13, 1942, Hearing on Discrimination in Defense Training, in R15HR, RG 228.

3. "Statement Relating to Equalization of Opportunity in Training," USOE, August 15, 1940, in office files of Frank D. Reeves, Defense Training Program file, R7HR, Bulletin, U.S. Commissioner of Education, November 20, 1940, in office files of George M. Johnson, Office of Education file, R4HR, both in RG 228; Fairchild and Grossman, *Army and Industrial Manpower*, 157.

trainees, only 4,600 of whom were black. Shortly thereafter, the OPM sent a special letter to all defense contractors warning that competent and available workers were being barred from training and jobs. Weaver believed that this and other OPM activity achieved significant results, including the training and employment of about 2,000 blacks in one large aircraft installation. Nevertheless, the OPM seemed to make only limited progress, and blacks in the spring of 1941 began demanding more heroic action from the administration.[4]

The FEPC first discovered bias in defense training during the Los Angeles hearing in October, 1941, when the local NAACP attacked the Santa Monica school system for practicing discrimination. According to the charges, the NYA, the technical school, the superintendent, and four aircraft companies had plotted to deny training to Jews, Mexican-Americans, and blacks. School officials denied conspiracy, but they admitted that those groups were refused training because the companies would not employ them. The local NYA, under NAACP pressure, began admitting all youth, irrespective of race. The NYA state administrator, Robert W. Burns, claimed that a variety of races and ethnic groups were enrolled in the California program, including Americans of African, Chinese, Japanese, and Mexican descent and native American Indians. Blacks, comprising only 2 percent of California's population, made up 10 percent of the NYA enrollment.[5]

The NYA's record was generally good throughout the nation, but it was hardly typical of most training programs. The problem was twofold. Industrial leaders, often prejudiced and fearful of adverse reactions from white workers, usually rejected minorities. Whites, especially skilled unionists, refused to work with minorities regardless of their experience and training. The system caused hopelessness among the trainees and frustration for the training institutions. Although California's Alhambra Vocational School did not discriminate on admissions, its superintendent admitted he advised minority applicants to train only for jobs open to them. With opportunities closed, Negro youths usually gave up. Los Angeles' Jefferson High School, in a mixed neighborhood where the majority were black, established a ma-

4. Address by Robert C. Weaver, October 9, 1941, in General Correspondence, Public Relations, D–L, R47HR, RG 228; Kesselman, "Fair Employment Practice Movement," 36–37.

5. Proceedings, Los Angeles hearing, October 21, 1941, pp. 591, 619, R19HR, RG 228.

chine shop in cooperation with the Los Angeles Urban League. Of 39 black referrals, only 19 showed up for training; at the time of the Los Angeles hearing 16 were enrolled. The apathy drove some Afro-American leaders to despair. "Negro youths in Los Angeles, Oakland, Kansas City . . . and Long Island will not take advantage of training opportunities opened up in industry at great pains by OPM," complained Charley Cherokee in his weekly column. He knew that "industry [would] not accept eager Negro youths for training" in many cities. "Southern youth holler for a chance, but two CCC camps in New Jersey," with a capacity for 500 trainees, "will close" because "only fifty-seven have applied." Mary Bethune of the NYA and Weaver, according to Cherokee, were "biting their nails."[6]

Training practices at the Patterson Vocational School in New Jersey illustrated the problems faced by minority groups. Irving Abramson, state president of the New Jersey CIO, testified in February, 1942, that Patterson Vocational, financed almost wholly with federal funds, was dominated by the Wright Aeronautical Corporation, a branch of the Curtiss-Wright Corporation. In the over two years since its founding in January, 1940, the school had trained no blacks. Fannie Curtis, president of the NAACP-Patterson, described how the system operated. Candidates for training, on applying at the state employment office, were referred to Wright Aeronautical. The company did not hire blacks except for unskilled foundry work, and it approved none for training. The difficulty was compounded, for Patterson's principal believed that blacks should not be trained when they had no chance for employment. An OPM report confirmed the NAACP charges. Wright Aeronautical employed over 17,000, of which only 121 were Negroes. It accepted trainees from Patterson, but as of November, 1941, all African-Americans had "failed" the school's entrance test. Jews and Italians also showed a high incidence of failure, but most applicants with Anglo-Saxon backgrounds passed. The Patterson situation was corrected, but the patterns of discrimination discovered in both New Jersey and California were symptomatic of a national problem. In Wichita, Kansas, for example, the Labor Supply Committee made plans to recruit 315,000 defense workers and urged industry to accept women, blacks, and men outside the draft age. Despite a refer-

6. *Ibid.*, 572, 585; Chicago *Defender*, October 11, 1941, p. 15.

ral from USES–Kansas City, however, several young Afro-American women were refused admittance to the National Defense Training School. Subsequently, the USES was ordered not to qualify and send any more blacks; the school was "not going to train them . . . [because] plants would not hire them."[7]

In the South, as defense contracts brought new economic life to the region, blacks were quick to grasp the implications. The Associated Press had stated that the two shipyards in Mobile had been awarded $49 million to build cargo vessels, J. L. LeFlore, chairman of the NAACP-Mobile, wrote Weaver in September, 1941. LeFlore wanted to know what steps had been taken to ensure that the president's proclamation would be respected. By November, black workers were growing impatient over the lack of information about job training in the defense plants. The ADDSC restricted Afro-Americans to common labor, and the Gulf Shipbuilding Company refused to hire them altogether. The OPM was looking into the matter, Weaver assured LeFlore. Weaver also contacted the FEPC. Early in 1942, John Beecher began an FEPC investigation of defense and vocational training in the South, with special emphasis on Alabama and Georgia.[8]

Alabama education officials took a hard line on training for blacks. Adopting a "requirement that local placement of . . . workers be assured before setting up training," they were unenthusiastic about a November OPM request for a course in ship welding at Mobile for a minimum of 30 blacks. At the same time, they denied that discrimination existed. Half the trainees taken from the WPA rolls in the city of Selma were Negroes, who were then placed at a nearby government aviation plant, Alabama superintendent of education A. H. Collins informed LeFlore. Training for blacks would continue, he said, "when we have reason to believe that there will be a place for them in industry." State Supervisor of Trade and Industrial Education Eldridge R. Plowden was more blunt. "The taxpayers' money should not be wasted on training persons for occupations which they could not ex-

7. Ida Marshall to Glenn E. Brockway, 9th Regional Labor Committee, March 14, 1942, USES–Kansas City, R35HR, proceedings, New York hearing, February 16, 1942, pp. 119–27, 157–59, 172–79, R63HR, and verbatim transcript, committee meeting, May 11, 1942, pp. 11–13, R63HR, all in RG 228.

8. J. L. LeFlore to Robert Weaver, September 1, November 5, 1941, Robert Weaver to J. L. LeFlore, November 13, 1941, in Administrative Division, Complaints Against Particular Companies, Region VII, RG 228.

pect to pursue," he told representatives of the Commission on Interracial Cooperation.[9]

A visit to the Mobile shipyards by Will Alexander in December, 1941, failed to effect any change. At the time, both facilities were expanding rapidly. Alexander saw cars "by the thousands . . . with tags from all parts of the country" from which white workers had migrated. Mobile was asking for 5,000 new houses to accommodate these people, at a cost of $4,000 per house. Meanwhile, the USES had estimated that at least 3,000 local race workers, already housed, were available. Alexander had "every possible argument" for using these workers in shipbuilding and went to the local Labor Supply Committee with the facts, insisting that black labor be utilized. He "met adamant opposition" from the state vocational education people. State Supervisor Plowden demanded to know who was stirring things up, and Alexander "very modestly informed him that it was the Commander-in-Chief of the Army and Navy, and the President of the United States." Plowden vowed they would not train blacks, and if they were required to do so, there would be no training for anyone. Alexander found similar attitudes among educational officials in Birmingham. Having used blacks in almost all the plants, Birmingham business leaders requested that the estimated 2,500 unemployed be trained at once. The only people in flat disagreement were the education authorities.[10]

By January, 1942, Alabama education officials seemed to have changed course. "The time has arrived to begin training for all classes of persons . . . whites and negroes" not subject to induction into the armed forces, the state advisory committee announced. Only one member, a representative from organized labor, requested that the training not be initiated on too wide a front. He needed time to prepare his members so that training for blacks would not draw too much criticism. The advisory committee decided to begin classes not in the industrial centers, where jobs and workers converged, but at black colleges and technical institutions isolated in rural Alabama. Classes

9. L. S. Hawkins to J. B. Hobdy, November 26, 1941, in Vocational Training file, R35HR, A. H. Collins to J. L. LeFlore, n.d., in office files of Ernest G. Trimble, Unarranged Correspondence file, and Field Report, March 6, 1942, in office files of John Beecher, Mobile file, all in RG 228; Pittsburgh *Courier*, December 13, 1941, p. 3.

10. Testimony of Will Alexander, verbatim transcript, Hearing on Discrimination in Defense Training, April 13, 1942, R15HR, RG 228.

in the larger cities would come later. In reporting this momentous decision to the USOE, State Supervisor Plowden thought the advisory committee, voting unanimously, had "dealt very fairly with the matter of training for negroes," approaching "the problem in a very objective manner." Training women, however, was another matter. Because of AFL and CIO opposition, the advisory committee voted against it. Both labor groups believed serious postwar consequences could result if women tried to compete for jobs and if employers took advantage of the situation.[11]

As John Beecher's Alabama investigation got under way, local education officials showed little inclination to pursue even the weak recommendation of the state advisory committee. In Mobile, Cecil M. Ward, director of trade and industrial education, told Beecher that the local council of administrators, which Ward apparently dominated, thought it unwise to proceed. Ward personally believed that blacks with training would not find skilled jobs, and if they did, whites would resort to violence. Three white welders had already called him to threaten that the first black who showed up at the yards "would be properly taken care of." Pressure from education officials at the state and national levels had so far been just verbal, Ward claimed. He wanted instructions in writing "so it would be clear" who was responsible for starting training for blacks.[12]

Beecher also discovered that defense training had become a pawn in the rivalry between Mobile's two labor organizations. Uncharacteristically, the Mobile Metal Trades Council (AFL), whose member unions had organized the Gulf Shipbuilding Company, passed a resolution endorsing the training of blacks for defense work. If serious, Beecher informed Lawrence Cramer, the resolution was revolutionary in light of previous metal trades attitudes in Mobile. Actually, however, the resolution was a political maneuver to attract black support in an exceedingly bitter struggle between the AFL and the CIO for control of Mobile's other shipyard, Alabama Dry Dock. At an evening meeting of the Mobile Metal Trades Council, Beecher congratulated the group for opposing discrimination. When he asked if their resolution was directed solely at ADDSC or if it applied equally to Gulf

11. Eldridge Plowden to C. E. Rakestraw, January 28, 1942, in Vocational Training file, R35HR, RG 228.
12. John Beecher to Lawrence Cramer, February 15, 1942, in office files of John Beecher, Mobile file, RG 228.

Shipbuilding, from which blacks were at that time entirely excluded, the "question provoked a terrific explosion." It was "the one question not to be asked," and it left them "boiling over with indignation." Beecher's conviction was "strengthened that the resolution meant less than it" said and was really a bargaining gambit. No blacks would be admitted to Gulf Shipbuilding "until *all* renounce the CIO." It was only after "that heresy was stamped out" that "there might be some openings." Beecher's activity also infuriated Frank Fenton, the AFL's representative on the FEPC, who demanded an explanation from Lawrence Cramer and who later tried to belittle Beecher as he gave testimony at the Birmingham hearing.[13]

Opposition from southern education administrators and the AFL could be expected, but Beecher soon learned that USOE officials were also sabotaging the program. "I have made contact with Ben Harris" of the USOE "on two occasions," Beecher wrote Will Alexander. "Both times he gave unmistakable indications of his antagonistic attitude toward Negro training . . . [and] freely aired his doubts concerning the southern Negro's interest . . . as well as capability of absorbing it." Only "a few self-styled leaders like LeFlore of Mobile" agitated the question. Beecher found "Harris's expressions of scorn" and his "pessimism regarding employment opportunities . . . characteristic of the most unenlightened southern viewpoint." When Beecher had used the word *discrimination* in describing defense training classes he had visited, "Harris heatedly objected, warning me not to employ that word with respect to" southern employment practices. "These, he said, were not 'discriminatory,' but simply 'traditional'— it was not a matter of correcting 'discrimination' down here but of attempting to modify 'traditions.'" At the end of the conference, Harris expressed the personal opinion "that 'Hitler' and 'the Nazis' were back of 'all this agitation'" to train blacks. When Beecher asked for evidence, Harris "related a story a friend had told him about how somebody's cook . . . had said that 'when Mr. Hitler gets over here, niggers won't have to work any more.'" Beecher's criticism to OPM officials got Harris a USOE reprimand.[14]

13. John Beecher to Lawrence Cramer, February 12, 1942, in office files of John Beecher, Mobile file, Patrick Ryan to Frank Fenton, February 13, 1942, Frank Fenton to Lawrence Cramer, February 20, 1942, both in Public Relations 5, Fenton file, R45HR, all in RG 228.

14. John Beecher to Will Alexander, February 27, 1942, in office files of John Beecher, Cramer, Confidential file, R77HR, RG 228.

After two months of investigating, Beecher produced a report on Alabama that was devastating. Through the middle of March, a total of 205 black Alabamians attended training classes. Over three-fourths of these were held at two nonmetropolitan points, Tuskegee Institute, which offered areo mechanics and arc welding, and Alabama Agricultural and Mechanical College at Huntsville, where a government chemical warfare arsenal was located. At Selma and Luverne, both small towns, 45 blacks took auto mechanics and sheet metal work. In the Birmingham metropolitan area, which according to Beecher contained one of the greatest concentrations of blacks in the country and the largest reservoir of experienced potential trainees in the South, a total of 7 structural steel worker helpers were learning blueprint reading. Nothing else was available to Birmingham's 150,000 blacks except a small NYA facility on the outskirts of the city. At Mobile, "one of the greatest defense centers in the entire South," no defense training for blacks was offered. The same applied to Montgomery, Gadsden, Anniston, Decatur, and Muscle Shoals. Yet courses were scheduled to start in two nonindustrial areas, Cullman and Opelika. In effect, Beecher concluded, Alabama's 1,000,000 Afro-Americans were receiving no defense training of any consequence, and the situation in Georgia was even more depressing.[15]

For whites, there were active training programs in all the southern states, with thousands of trainees and brand-new, superbly equipped trade schools and other shop centers. For blacks, at the Georgia State Industrial College in Savannah, for example, the courses taught "represented a pretense at national defense training." Blacks from the WPA rolls were "herded into classrooms devoid of equipment to study dreary lists of ship nomenclature." The classroom was "decorated with ship pictures cut from Life magazine and a toy store battleship." When one considered "the WPA group enrolled, uneducated, unfamiliar with ships, the course was a pathetic farce." The total value of the equipment at the industrial college was $11,000, matched against a new $100,000 facility with $400,000 in equipment for white trainees in downtown Savannah. Unless comprehensive training was offered to blacks, Beecher warned, southern defense plants would not meet production schedules. At a large aircraft plant located in the Dallas–Fort Worth area, few resident blacks had received training. The Delta

15. John Beecher to Lawrence Cramer, April 11, 1942, in office files of Frank D. Reeves, Defense Training Program file, R7HR, RG 228.

Shipyard in New Orleans had already been publicly reprimanded by the Maritime Commission for falling behind in production. Delta claimed its lagging performance resulted from insufficient local labor, yet the shipyard employed no blacks in a city with one-third of its population from that racial group.[16]

Aggregate statistics on southern defense training were even more revealing. As of January 31, 1942, in eighteen selected border and Deep South states and the District of Columbia, 5,630 segregated training courses were offered, with only 194 for blacks. In the segregated courses, 83,933 trainees were enrolled, of which 3,215 were black. The 1940 census showed Afro-Americans comprising 22.0 percent of the population of the area, but only 3.8 percent of the trainees came from that racial group. Training in six of the Deep South states followed the same pattern. In Mississippi, with a race population of 49.9 percent, just 3.3 percent of its defense trainees were black. Louisiana, Alabama, Georgia, and South Carolina did only slightly better, but Florida, whose black citizens comprised 27 percent of the population, almost totally excluded them; just 0.17 percent of its trainees were Afro-Americans.[17]

By mid-March, the FEPC had enough evidence to charge the USOE with failure to administer the defense training program without discrimination. The legal foundation for the FEPC's case, laid out by George Johnson, rested first on Executive Order 8802, which admonished all departments and agencies involved with training programs for defense production to administer them without discrimination. Under Public Law 146, Johnson wrote, funds for defense training were paid to state educational agencies and to colleges or universities upon approval of the United States commissioner of education, and where segregated schools were required, equitable facilities and training had to be provided. In fulfilling these requirements, the commissioner, on July 23, 1941, had issued regulations that set up a master plan involving budgetary and reporting procedures for the states to follow. Particularly, the regulations informed state and federal officials of the

16. *Ibid.*; Summary, n.d., in office files of Frank D. Reeves, Defense Training Program file, R7HR, and verbatim transcript, Hearing on Discrimination in Defense Training, April 13, 1942, R15HR, both in RG 228.

17. Verbatim transcript, Hearing on Discrimination in Defense Training, April 13, 1942, R15HR, RG 228.

requirements of the executive order. Johnson's memorandum implied that the USOE had failed to follow its own regulations.[18]

With evidence of discrimination in defense training throughout the nation and with knowledge of the South's almost complete refusal to train blacks, the FEPC scheduled a hearing in Washington, D.C., on April 13. Previous hearings in Los Angeles, Chicago, and New York, held in public with wide publicity, had focused attention on bias in the private sector. Defense training, however, primarily involved a federal agency, its administration of the program, the dispersal of funds, and the politically sensitive issue of state and local education policies, particularly in the South. Sensing trouble, the administration ordered the FEPC to hold secret hearings when federal agencies were charged.[19]

As Commissioner of Education John W. Studebaker prepared to testify at the hearing, he was unaware that he would shortly also be under fire from the administration. Dismayed by the education chief's general "lack of leadership," though apparently not concerned over his failure to enforce Executive Order 8802, Roosevelt by May, 1943, was willing to lose Studebaker's services if a position in New Jersey was approved by that state's senate or if any other job outside the federal government came up. None did, and Studebaker's services as education chief continued into the Truman administration until 1948. In his testimony, Studebaker criticized those who "cling slavishly to the idea that all of the people to be employed in a factory" should come from the local community. It speeded up production, he thought, when the employment service negotiated the migration of skilled workers to areas with defense jobs. Studebaker was unaware "of a single case of discrimination or alleged discrimination" in the programs he administered. Not one had been brought to his attention, he averred. John Brophy remained unconvinced. "On the face of this record as to Negro trainees," he charged, "there is toleration of a widespread system of discrimination." Under close questioning, Studebaker admitted that the USOE had used economic leverage to effect

18. Memorandum by George M. Johnson, March 18, 1942, Malcolm MacLean to John Studebaker, March 18, 1942, and verbatim transcript, Hearing on Discrimination in Defense Training, April 13, 1842, all in R15HR, RG 228.

19. Verbatim transcript, Hearing on Discrimination in Defense Training, April 13, 1942, R15HR, RG 228.

certain results in the defense training program, but it had never employed this power to enforce the executive order. "Funds had been withheld, withdrawn and returned by force" from states and local governments in the past, "but none on the basis of discrimination." Brophy was incensed. Executive Order 8802 would be nothing more than a "pious wish" unless government departments enforced it. "It is perfectly despicable . . . [for] private employers to indulge in discrimination . . . [but] it is positively vile when Governmental bodies wink" at such practices or "don't apply themselves." Discrimination had "become a vested interest" that too many agencies were guilty of protecting.[20]

Collis Stocking, chief of the division of Research and Statistics, explained how the USOE established training priorities. His staff had interviewed over 12,000 employers to find out their hiring plans so that training needs could be determined. Only on a few occasions, however, were contracts withheld because an employer refused to accept minority workers. In reference to the FEPC investigation, Stocking was "not too impressed by these eleventh hour converts" who made it appear that "the Office of Education had been delinquent" in performing its functions. "You are not going to solve this problem solely by needling" the USOE, he warned. Under "the Federal-state relationships . . . we have a great deal of difficulty" controlling the action of local officials. On one point, Stocking was adamant: it was wasteful to train blacks for employers unwilling to hire them. Lawrence Cramer strongly disagreed. Perhaps it had been wasteful before the issuance of Executive Order 8802, but it was not so any longer.[21]

The FEPC's investigation and hearing exposed the USOE's total lack of concern about discrimination. Its commissioner had never heard the word mentioned, and his staff, if they recognized bias, did not bother to report it. Some regional USOE officials, like Ben Harris, would not even utter the word *discrimination* in connection with southern practices they regarded as traditional. Nevertheless, the hearing brought out what was probably the most important revela-

20. Testimony of Dr. John W. Studebaker, Hearing on Discrimination in Defense Training, April 13, 1942, R15HR, RG 228; conference, May 8, 1943, in Conferences with the President file, 1943, Harold D. Smith Papers, FDRL; New York *Times*, July 28, 1989, Obituary, 12.

21. Testimony of Collis Stocking, verbatim transcript, April 13, 1942, Hearing on Discrimination in Defense Training, R15HR, RG 228.

tion, the fact that the USOE had clout and could force local and state educational officials to comply with its rulings. For the FEPC's purposes, however, the USOE seemed hopeless. Its layers of bureaucracy, overlapping those of state and local education establishments, usually produced studied evasion and inertia. Its so-called democratic methods of determining priorities, starting at the local level, added to its ineffectiveness when discrimination was involved. The FEPC's hearing on the USOE, as far as achieving results were concerned, seemed an exercise in futility.

The FEPC continued to monitor defense training, and time would show how little the USOE was willing to change its ways. Two weeks after the hearing, Earl Dickerson, on a visit to Atlanta, discovered that despite instructions from Commissioner Studebaker "nothing constructive [had] developed in enrolling Negroes in defense courses" for jobs at the new Bell Bomber plant in Marietta, Georgia. Lawrence Cramer, optimistic that the USOE hearing would produce results, counseled patience. A number of other agencies had to be dealt with in carrying out the program Studebaker had agreed to put in motion. Meanwhile, the commissioner submitted a glowing report on progress the USOE had made in Florida. In St. Augustine, training for blacks was scheduled to precede programs for whites. FEPC chairman Malcolm MacLean, like Dickerson, was in the field, and what he found in North Carolina and Georgia did not please him. MacLean had evidence, he wired Studebaker, "that your USOE office agents, local superintendents and state vocational chiefs are giving you the run around [sic] on your intention to give equitable training to Negroes." J. Warren Smith, training chief in Raleigh, and M. D. Mobley, head of training in Atlanta, were "obviously the centers" of opposition. MacLean believed that "the only effect" Studebaker's directive had on "state agents has been to make them more cagey." These training officers were "obviously using lying and delaying devices" to hamstring the program by claiming there was "difficulty in securing equipment and [in] training Negro instructors." MacLean warned Studebaker to "put plenty of steam" behind the effort "at once or we shall have to air [the] whole program at Birmingham hearings in mid-June."[22]

22. Earl Dickerson to Lawrence Cramer, May 7, 1942, Lawrence Cramer to Earl Dickerson, May 18, 1942, in Public Relations 5, Dickerson file, R45HR, John Studebaker to Lawrence Cramer, May 26, 1942, Vocational Education file, R35HR, Mal-

When the committee met on June 8, Malcolm MacLean, despite his earlier displeasure, endorsed a mildly worded FEPC summary of the April USOE hearing prepared by Cramer and the staff. However, Earl Dickerson, arriving late, was incensed that the "weakest findings" he had ever seen had been approved. "We deal with the Federal agencies with gloves" but "crack down on defense industries." Studebaker was left "to say that he will conform to the law . . . [that] he hasn't known of any case" of discrimination, yet all around him "is the most glaring evidence" that was ever "perpetrated against the people." Dickerson could not understand "how anybody could write such findings." It was "the most weak sister-like set-up of findings and directions" he had ever seen. Through "a recital of the facts," the FEPC should instead show how little in defense training had been provided to blacks, and its directives should be specific. He had evidence from Atlanta that Studebaker was still interpreting training in terms of demand for workers. "Mr. Mobley will be ready to provide training for negroes any time labor data is made available" by the employment service, which "is the primary agency for determining labor needs," Studebaker notified Bell Bomber after the hearing. "Now that shows clearly that this man Studebaker was perpetrating a fraud on this Committee," Dickerson charged. He continued his condemnation of the commissioner: "He did not intend to do anything. This shows he did not, leaving it up to Mobley, a man down in the South, living up to tradition, southern oligarchy . . . to determine when . . . to put these Negroes in." MacLean agreed. In both North Carolina and Georgia the directors of training were playing "a nice, cagey stalling game."[23]

After Dickerson's protest, the committee adopted stronger language, but the administration made certain that few would ever read the findings. In July, when Lawrence Cramer sent a copy of the FEPC's summary of the USOE hearing to the White House and suggested that a useful purpose would be served by publishing it, the reaction was negative. Asked his opinion by FDR, Assistant Secretary of War Robert Patterson thought such a publication was unnecessary. "In the case of a federal agency, to supplement such directions by the pressure of publicity," he wrote, might make it more difficult to get cooperation

colm MacLean to John Studebaker (telegram), June 2, 1942, in office files of John Beecher, Bell Aircraft, Atlanta file, R78HR, all in RG 228.

23. Verbatim transcript, committee meeting, A.M., June 8, 1942, pp. 2–8, R63HR, RG 228.

from state agencies in the areas involved. Subsequently, Roosevelt ordered Marvin McIntyre to get the word to Cramer that "we all feel it would be inadvisable" to publish the summary.[24]

Committee members, frustrated and disappointed, hoped that some progress could be made at the Birmingham hearing, held from June 18 to 20, but testimony there confused the issue even more and failed to establish who was responsible for planning, implementing, and overseeing the program. According to Vernon J. Douglass, director of vocational training for the Birmingham public schools, state and local education officials had agreed in July, 1940, to find jobs for which blacks could be trained. Birmingham employers, in response, said they wanted "healthy, honest individuals" but then refused to use these individuals in the skilled trades. Indeed, no training would be necessary, for employers would teach them what they needed to know. In September, 1941, Birmingham education officials again discussed training, this time for black molders, but an employment survey showed no need. Some forty were already unemployed.[25]

By March, jobs were opening up in the Alabama shipyards, and Birmingham civic and business leaders, allegedly more concerned about winning the war than training labor just for the local area, sent Douglass to Mobile to survey the employment needs. Finding that Alabama Dry Dock was hiring blacks as rivet heaters, buckers, and catchers, the Birmingham group voted unanimously to open up two classes and applied to education officials in Montgomery for equipment, but Washington, D.C., officials did not respond immediately. In the meantime, the state education office had requested training for black welders to work in Mobile. Additional equipment was procured, and classes ran twenty-four hours a day, but the Mobile shipyards refused to hire the black welders. When they could not find jobs, that "about finished the [training] school." Despite this activity for black employment, most of the money utilized in the Birmingham program, Douglass testified, had been spent on facilities for whites: federal funds, $203,181 for whites and $17,916 for blacks; the local

24. Lawrence Cramer to the President, July 3, 1942, Robert Patterson to FDR, July 9, 1942, FDR to MAC, July 17, 1942, all in Official File 4245-G, Box 4, January–July, 1942, FDRL; Marvin McIntyre to Lawrence Cramer, July 21, 1942, in Personal and Confidential file, Box 20, BSCP Papers.

25. Testimony of Vernon J. Douglass, June 20, 1942, Birmingham hearing, R17HR, RG 228.

board of education contribution, $116,100 for whites and $2,650 for blacks.[26]

Although Birmingham's performance in defense training for blacks could scarcely be described as enthusiastic and unbiased, Douglass' straightforward testimony contrasted sharply with the testimony of Eldridge Plowden. Like other state officials criticized by Malcolm MacLean, Plowden was "cagey." For the past twenty-four years, Alabama as a matter of policy had "always looked for every opportunity for the training of Negroes," Plowdon stated. "The training facilities in Mobile are adequate . . . for training Negroes in occupations where the Employment Service or others will assure us they will be employed." David Sarnoff found "quite a lot of qualifications there" and could not "follow all of that being true." If the employment service determined need, Sarnoff concluded, that made the United States government a party to discrimination. Plowden kept insisting, however, that USES directions called for training only where need was determined. When Earl Dickerson reminded Plowden of Commissioner Studebaker's assurances that this interpretation was wrong and that state education departments would be directed to make training facilities available, Plowden claimed that Studebaker's order had not been received. As his testimony ended, Plowden asserted again that "we do all that we can to promote training of Negroes in defense industry where they can be used in Alabama."[27]

The committee heard testimony from one other state training official, M. D. Mobley, of Georgia. As of June 1, his state had spent $1,434,000 to train whites in defense work and $149,406 for blacks. In the Atlanta area, where the Atlanta Urban League had agitated to get blacks into the new Bell Bomber plant, $9,983 had been approved for equipment in the Booker T. Washington High School, but about $175,000 had already been spent in white schools. Since the equipment was owned by the state, however, it could be moved from one training center to another. Mobley claimed that the "same identical training" was offered to both races, and he complained bitterly about "some of the activities" of Atlanta blacks who demanded training facilities. They had hampered "our effort to really do what we honestly wish to do to serve the Negro people." Earl Dickerson was not im-

26. Ibid.
27. Testimony of E. R. Plowden, June 20, 1942, Birmingham hearing, R17HR, RG 228.

pressed. He wondered if Mobley interpreted the law "as giving him the right to provide accommodations for white schools first" and then "for Negroes if equipment could be found." Mobley denied it. Dickerson pointed out that the law provided for "equitable participation." Mobley countered that it was geared to the actual need, which was determined by the local advisory committee and the council of administrators. The matter "never reaches my office," he said. "It is cut off by the local school forces before it gets there." Dickerson was incredulous. He asked if the local schools could carry on any program without recourse to any official. Mobley replied that the state did not operate the secondary schools. His task was to administer a program and set up certain general policies.[28]

David Sarnoff was also baffled by the conflicting testimony and could not "get his teeth into a single fundamental." After numerous hearings about training, he believed he understood less than he did at the beginning: "It is either [as] a fine game of buck passing as I have ever seen or it is as difficult as squaring a circle. We can't get a simple answer to a single question." Sarnoff doubted that the difficulty lay with the local situation. "We ought to be able to get a statement in Washington as to how these grants are made, how these rules are made, and why." If Sarnoff had trouble understanding the hours of confusing testimony, Milton Webster knew exactly what was going on. It was "just a method of shutting the Negro out from this training."[29]

Whereas the administration kept the lid of secrecy on the FEPC's USOE hearing in April, it could not control the news from Birmingham, where public testimony charging the USOE with failure to enforce the antidiscrimination laws must have shaken that agency. In the ensuing months, the USOE made some progress that elicited grudging and guarded praise even from the FEPC's George Johnson. Never admitting error, the USOE blamed its problems on the South's social and cultural organization, with its separate schools. The argument, inadequate in explaining all of the USOE's failures, had some merit. Few, if any, black urban high schools, when they existed, had shops adequate for defense training. Instead, most facilities were located at the black land-grant institutions. Before training could be

28. Testimony of M. D. Mobley, June 20, 1942, Birmingham hearing, R17HR, RG 228.
29. Verbatim transcript, June 20, 1942, Birmingham hearing, R17HR, RG 228.

offered in the populated industrial centers, the USOE explained in a somewhat self-serving document prepared in January, 1943, "proper community attitudes" had to be developed, "suitable shop space and equipment" secured, "competent teachers" trained and hired, cooperation with other government agencies obtained, and "placement in war industries" assured. In many ways, the USOE's explanation of its problems in the segregated states was an unintended indictment of decades of regional neglect in education.[30]

USOE representatives were developing "proper community attitudes," its report stated, and there was "concrete evidence of change." In some states, blacks were "now admitted to [white] war production shops" when these facilities were "not in use." The NYA center in Charleston, South Carolina, admitted "negroes to any of the shifts"; in every southern state the agency could see "some evidence of changed attitudes." But there were problems. "Securing suitable shop space" was complicated by the need for "adaptations relative to housing heavy equipment . . . proper health conditions," the installation of electric lines, and equipment and instruction materials. "Competent teachers" were being drawn from the fields of engineering, industrial arts, and "industry itself," and white instructors, "particularly in aircraft sheet metal, welding, and machine shop practice [were] now being employed in several southern states."[31]

The USOE offered statistical evidence to document the progress it claimed. In June, at the time of the Birmingham hearing, 3,768 black trainees were enrolled in twelve southern states, with an expenditure of $439,839 for equipment and rental space. By November, enrollments had increased to 4,702. In Maryland, Virginia, and West Virginia, the numbers of blacks in training compared favorably with their percentage of the total population. Both the types and the numbers of courses were up, and the participation of black women trainees had increased dramatically. In several urban areas from which complaints of discrimination had originated, including Nashville, Memphis, Atlanta, Macon, and Savannah, special USOE representatives were inspecting the courses and the upgrading activities. Full-time black supervisors of war production training were hired in Nashville and

30. "War Production Training for Negroes in the Southern Region," memorandum, L. S. Hawkins to John Studebaker, January 23, 1943, in Division of Field Operations, office files of John Beecher, RG 228.
31. *Ibid.*

Memphis. In the Atlanta area, the Bell Bomber training program had been pressed with vigor. USOE representatives got the proper teaching materials from Baltimore and other areas and arranged for four Atlantans to take teacher training at Freeport, Long Island, with salaries and all expenses paid. Aircraft training for 47 black Atlantans, 43 of whom were women, began on November 15. Although the attrition rate was quite high (by January, only 13 trainees remained, including 2 males), 50 more were requisitioned in December. Interest in training was expected to pick up when the Bell Bomber plant began hiring. Other areas, however, had not made much progress. Three Georgia communities had run into trouble. The USOE had held up all appropriations for equipment to Macon and Brunswick until "satisfactory plans" for training blacks were developed. It was also dissatisfied with the programs being offered in Savannah. In Alabama, though training had spread to over thirteen major and minor industrial areas, the USOE pronounced the situation as "not encouraging."[32]

In his analysis of the USOE report, George Johnson admitted that it represented progress, but he added qualifications. If training officials had begun black and white programs simultaneously and filed priority requests for funds and equipment for both races under a single clearance, he noted, there undoubtedly would have been less delay in implementing training for both groups. Johnson was also concerned about the slack in Negro enrollment. While admitting that some vacancies resulted because of unavailable trainees, he thought enrollments could be boosted by offering a greater variety of programs in locations more accessible to large numbers of blacks and by choosing times more convenient for people who had jobs. Certainly, offering courses at land-grant colleges had greatly limited the number of trainees.[33]

Johnson was elated at the success achieved in Baltimore. There, large numbers of Afro-American women, comprising 80 percent of the enrollees, were involved. Baltimore also proved that recruitment was very important. When they halted the drive for trainees because the rolls were filled, the number of applicants rapidly fell off, leading local authorities quickly to claim that blacks were not taking full ad-

32. *Ibid.*
33. Memorandum, George Johnson to Lawrence Cramer, February 5, 1943, in office files of George M. Johnson, Office of Education file, R4HR, RG 228.

vantage of the opportunities offered. Recruiters proved, however, that they could produce an adequate number of trainees. Contrasted with Baltimore, Memphis offered some courses listed as war training (blacksmithing, mill work, and wood work) that should have been discontinued because they did not prepare trainees for jobs in war industries. The USOE's rejection of applications from Macon and Brunswick until blacks were included in the programs was heartening. Overall, Johnson thought the USOE had made progress, though its approach still lacked the vigor "which is necessary in this problem." The USOE should seek out discrimination, he believed, not wait for matters to be brought to its attention.[34]

The FEPC's work in defense training produced important results. Although the USOE denied that it had failed to take "every step possible to induce the States to provide adequate training facilities" for blacks, its own report of the progress made during 1942, after the FEPC's hearings, confirmed its previous delinquency. Before the April hearing, 4,446, or 96 percent, of the training courses in the seventeen segregated states and the district were open to whites only, with 194, or 4 percent, for blacks. By July 1, there were 29,011 training stations for whites and 2,958 for blacks. By the end of 1942, blacks had 6,340 training stations whereas the number of white stations remained at the June level.[35]

Expediting defense training for blacks became even more significant in light of the issuance of the WMC's work-or-fight order early in 1943. To the *Afro-American*, the order had terrible implications for blacks classified as nonessential to the war effort, including waiters, chauffeurs, bus boys, bartenders, bootblacks, porters, gardeners, elevator operators, and messengers. These were the jobs to which Afro-Americans ordinarily had access; in most cases, these were the only jobs open to blacks. "All the opportunities in which we have a chance to eke out a bare existence, have been classified as 'not jobs', and we must get a war job or grab a gun." Yet, decried the paper, all of the alleged "essential jobs" in war plants "are barred to us."[36]

34. *Ibid.*
35. Clarence Mitchell to Lawrence Cramer, April 16, 1943, in Office Memoranda, M file, R1HR, RG 228.
36. Washington, D.C., *Afro-American*, February 20, 1943, *People's Voice*, February 20, 1943, both in Publications 3, Weekly Releases on Negro Newspapers file, R47HR, RG 228.

As the FEPC opened up defense training in the South, progress was made primarily in the larger urban areas. Smaller, more isolated communities abandoned the old ways more slowly, if at all. In the fall of 1942 at New Iberia, a town of 14,000 about a hundred miles west of New Orleans in the bayou country of Louisiana, hostile local sentiment from the mayor, the sheriff, the Chamber of Commerce, and others forced a black manpower agency representative out of the area for trying to establish a training school. In spring, 1944, following an announcement that a WMC welding school for whites would be set up, several black citizens, led by J. Leo Hardy, a retired businessman and president of the NAACP–New Iberia, requested a similar facility for race members. He was opposed by the sheriff and the parish school board. According to the Chicago *Defender*, New Iberia whites insisted "that Negroes' vocational efforts should be confined to farm work." Nevertheless, with the support of many of the town's black elite, Hardy complained to the FEPC's regional office in Dallas. Accused of organizing "the Negroes to overthrow the whites," he was warned by the sheriff to stop sending letters to the FEPC and the WMC.[37]

When the white welding school opened on May 15, Hardy enrolled. That afternoon, two deputies took him to the office of Sheriff Gilbert Ozenno, where he was accused of insulting the sheriff in his letter about the establishment of the school and then released. The next evening, however, Hardy, who had two sons serving in the South Pacific, was again taken to the sheriff's office, this time beaten severely, and then driven after dark to a gravel road on the edge of town. Told to walk "and walk fast," Hardy fled under fire. After walking five miles, he telephoned Howard C. Scoggins, a New Iberia druggist, who found Hardy bleeding copiously about the head and face. Scoggins, for his part, left for New Orleans, never to return to New Iberia. His wife remained to liquidate the business. Herman J. Faulk, treasurer of the federal credit union for blacks and a teacher with the Louisiana Extension Service, received a worse beating than Hardy. Picked up at his home about 10:30 P.M. on May 17 by Deputy Sheriff Gus Walker and Abraham Ray, a storekeeper, Faulk was handcuffed, threatened with death, and brutally assaulted "for being one of them smart niggers . . . who kept writing to Washington about the welding school

37. "For Mr. Ross" (Typescript, confidential, n.d., in office files of Malcolm Ross, WILL folder, R3HR, RG 228); *PM*, June 18, 1944, Chicago *Defender*, May 27, 1944, in Newspaper Clippings, Chronological file, RG 228.

you forced us to open." Faulk's tormentors also accused him of "going around telling the other niggers they will be voting soon." Walker then knocked Faulk to the ground and stomped on his face. Driven five miles out of town, he was released on U.S. Highway 90 and told that if he ever returned to New Iberia he would be killed. A physician, Dr. Luins H. Williams, and a dentist, Dr. Ima G. Pierson, were also attacked, as were the remaining blacks involved with the school petition: Octave Lilly, Jr., an insurance salesman; Dr. E. L. Dorsey, owner of the hospital; and Franzella Volter, a teacher in the Iberia Parish school system. All were forced to leave town.[38]

Expulsion of the two doctors left the black community without medical service, and two hospital patients who needed attention died. All the men who left had property and families. Some had businesses of considerable value; Dr. Dorsey, for example, owned hospital and medical equipment worth about $65,000. Some white citizens, appalled at the violence, appealed to Louisiana governor Jimmie Davis and to the United States Public Health Service. There was an FBI investigation. But New Iberia's blacks never received a defense training facility, and a federal government that chose to ignore lynchings could scarcely mete out justice in the case of lesser local offences against black citizens.[39]

Afro-Americans in a small Georgia community also found that challenging the white establishment could be risky. Early in 1942, as word spread in the Macon area that a naval ordinance plant would soon be opened, a citizens' committee of black leaders in Milledgeville, thirty miles east of Macon, began asking about defense training. The Citizens Committee included Dr. J. F. Boddie, J. M. Reeves, A. R. Lewis, R. P. Slater, George Harper, and D. P. Steele. They were initially under the impression that a second plant would be built in their town. Wherever it was located, they were told by officials in USES-Milledgeville, that 800 to 1,000 white workers would be employed, and "only White ladies [would] be trained." With considerable fortitude, they complained to the FEPC. As citizens "living in a true Democracy, fighting for Freedom," they thought, "an equal ratio

38. "Statement of Herman Joseph Faulk" (Typescript, May 27, 1944, in Tension file, Division of Review and Analysis, R75HR, RG 228); PM, June 18, 1944, in Newspaper Clippings, Chronological file, RG 228.

39. PM, June 18, 1942, and Chicago Defender, May 27, 1942, in Newspaper Clippings, Chronological file, RG 228.

of defense work should be given the Negro." The citizens cited as authorities the United States Constitution and "The Bill of Equal Rights." Having heard of FEPC investigations elsewhere, they wanted something done "about the South." The group needed to know "what branch of metal work is needed," because it was their "plan to have Negroes trained by the time the plant [was] completed." Their complaint was turned over to John Beecher, who at the time was gathering evidence for the Birmingham hearing.[40]

On May 5, Beecher and Cy Record met with officials of the F. P. Reynolds Corporation, operator of the new plant to be known as Reynolds Fuse. Also present was the director of vocational training in Macon's Bibb County. The group discussed training for blacks, especially "colored women," and reviewed local "racial restrictions" that might be "detrimental to rapid productions" of an important defense item. Company spokesmen denied that Reynolds, by recognizing "existing conditions," discriminated. Nevertheless, the FEPC representatives warned, Executive Order 8802 must be honored. They requested that Reynolds take up immediately the "matter of vocational training for all persons qualified" and that employment practices be changed to include "all persons irrespective of race."[41]

On May 23 the committee, whose name had been changed to the Civic Committee, wrote to J. R. Wommack, assistant supervisor of trade and industrial education, and asked about plans for training Milledgeville blacks. They wanted to know if Wommack would kindly exert influence with "key individuals" to secure such facilities. "We have available seven men who can teach any branch of machine shop work." Five days later, another letter went to Reynolds Fuse about employment for black men and women. Reynolds was "getting a little better in their attitude to-wards [sic] Negro labor," Reeves wrote Beecher on June 1, and "APPARENTLY [they] are trying to get a training school for us." Reeves had also written M. D. Mobley and E. A. Adams, state director of the USES, but had received no answers.[42]

40. Citizens Committee to Dr. Frank S. Horne, March 6, 1942, Civic Committee to Malcolm McLean [sic], April 20, 1942, both in office files of John Beecher, Macon Naval Ordnance Plant file, R77HR, RG 228.

41. Report on conference with Reynolds Corporation officials, May 5, 1942, in office files of John Beecher, Macon Naval Ordnance Plant file, R77HR, RG 228.

42. Civic Committee to J. R. Wommack, May 23, 1942, in office files of Ernest G. Trimble, Unarranged Correspondence file, R77HR, J. F. Boddie and J. M. Reeves

Those letters would be the last. News of the Civic Committee's activity caused a furor in Milledgeville. Apparently under intense local pressure the members sent a retraction. Their letter of May 23 had been misconstrued, they said: "We did not intend to try to have vocational training for Negroes taken out of the hands of local and state department officials. . . . The best people of Baldwin County are entirely willing to work with the leaders of the Negro race for the best interest of both races." Any outside interference "would only aggravate race relations and might possibly lead to serious consequences" for war production. These citizens had discovered that "true Democracy," the Constitution, and "The Bill of Equal Rights" did not yet apply to blacks.[43]

The forces that generated the Civic Committee's retraction were formidable for blacks in a small southern community to go up against. Alerted by education officials in Atlanta, the Baldwin County school superintendent, P. N. Bivins, "investigated the matter." What was said to the committee, and by whom, is unknown, but apparently in return for their retraction, Bivins "concluded" that "these Negroes, some of our best Negro citizens, did not wilfully and intentionally on their part take any steps or do anything that would bring about racial troubles in this County." Indeed, he continued, in writing to Atlanta training officials, the citizens "were trying to help the Negroes through the proper channel." The complaints to the FEPC were stirred up by some outside agents "for a purpose not to the interest either of the Negro race, white race, or the good of this country." Bivins bitterly attacked Cy Record, who had investigated the Macon situation and had made a highly unfavorable report to Robert Weaver. Record did "a grave injustice to the leading and law abiding Negro citizens" of Milledgeville, Bivins charged.[44]

The USOE in summer, 1942, began enforcing Executive Order 8802, but Macon's request for $95,000 in training funds was held up

---

to C. O. Pickard, Reynolds Corporation, May 28, 1942, and Civic Committee to John Beecher, June 1, 10, 1942, in office files of John Beecher, Macon Naval Ordnance Plant file, R77HR, all in RG 228.

43. Civic Committee to J. R. Wommack, June 15, 1942, in office files of Ernest G. Trimble, Unarranged Correspondence file, R77HR, RG 228.

44. P. N. Bivins to M. D. Mobley, June 16, 1942, in office files of Ernest G. Trimble, Unarranged Correspondence file, R77HR, Cy Record to Robert Weaver, June 1, 1942, in office files of John Beecher, Macon Naval Ordnance Plant file, R77HR, both in RG 228.

until 1943 because of discriminatory practices. By February, 1942, the Macon media had begun appealing for applicants, especially women, to sign up for defense training. The largest employer in the area, Reynolds Fuse, would need a work force of over 5,000. In addition, the Macon area had attracted several federal installations besides Reynolds Fuse, including Camp Wheeler (infantry) and three airfields, Herbert Smart, Cochran, and Warner-Robbins. The area's wartime population was 165,000. Despite the need for workers, when Marie Sharpe, a housewife, applied to the USES, she was refused because of her race. Her complaint to the Old Committee, then in the process of disintegration, was referred to the WMC, which ignored it. The USOE and the state and local education bureaucracies in the meantime apparently reverted to doing business as usual. The Macon defense training facility went into operation without equal opportunities for blacks. The USES-Macon also discriminated. Orders from Reynolds Fuse for production workers went only to the white USES office; the "colored" office received requests for service jobs. With the issue of training for blacks still unsettled, the FEPC again got involved with Reynolds Fuse in January, 1944, when the new FEPC regional director in Atlanta, A. Bruce Hunt, requested WMC intervention. After an investigation, the manpower agency concluded that the USES-Macon was "clearly out of line with the instructions" in the various WMC field manuals.[45]

Macon's blacks, led by A. L. Thomas of the MOWM, began pressing for defense training. The Chamber of Commerce was recruiting 2,000 women workers for Reynolds Fuse. Thomas' group approached the chamber's manager, Lee S. Trimble, on February 15, 1944, and learned the group intended that "white and Negro women [would] not work together." But the blacks persisted, and in May, they submitted the names and addresses of 100 black women who had been refused referrals to Reynolds by the USES. In Atlanta, the FEPC's Bruce Hunt put pressure on the manpower agency's regional chief of training, J. E. McDaniel, who remained reluctant. "To put Negroes on [a segregated] night shift would require 1,000 to 1,500" but "no

45. Memorandum to L. S. Hawkins, January 23, 1942, in office files of Frank D. Reeves, Form Letters file, R7HR, Progress Report on Macon, Georgia, Federal Security Administration, September 9, 1944, A. Bruce Hunt to Frank Constangy, January 4, 1944, R. E. Haines to Frank Constangy, January 18, 1944, Frank Constangy to Haines, February 25, 1944, Case 7GR43 file, F85FR, all in RG 228.

more than 500 additional employees are needed." McDaniel saw no point in establishing a school for blacks unless Reynolds would employ them. Nevertheless, in June, he agreed by telephone to begin training for Macon blacks within three weeks.[46]

Three months passed without further WMC action. Macon officials continued to claim there were too few blacks to train for the one complete shift that would be required to maintain segregated work facilities at the plant. State manpower director Thomas Quigley vacillated, refusing to reply to inquiries even from the Atlanta regional office. Finally, at the end of September, he ordered a "fresh approach to the study of reported discrimination at Reynolds." He directed the USES-Macon to abolish existing discrimination. In effect, his order meant that requests from Reynolds Fuse for production workers would be sent to both USES offices and that blacks who applied for training would be referred. If Reynolds turned them away, the company could now officially be charged with discrimination in a USES 510 report. Nevertheless, it took Hunt and WMC officials two months to persuade the USES-Macon to issue a satisfactory 510 form charging Reynolds Fuse.[47]

By then it was November, 1944, over two years since the plant had begun production, and black employees at Reynolds still served food, pushed brooms, cleaned toilets, and earned service-level wages. Both the FEPC-Atlanta and the central office became deeply involved in the Reynolds Fuse case. In Washington, D.C., Clarence Mitchell requested action from the U.S. Navy, the USOE, and the WMC. The navy cooperated. On December 22, Mitchell learned that the Navy-FEPC operating agreement, in effect since 1942, would be honored. The USOE, however, was hostile. L. S. Hawkins responded in anger, leading Mitchell to conclude that the federal and state education bureaucracies ultimately were responsible for the difficulties in Macon. Hunt and his successor in Atlanta, Witherspoon Dodge, continued to nag the regional WMC office. At a conference on December 1, man-

---

46. Summary of Reynolds Fuse Situation, n.d., A. L. Thomas to James H. Tipton, March 3, 1944, Final Disposition Report, USES-Macon, memorandum, A. Bruce Hunt to Self, n.d., A. Bruce Hunt to Frank Constangy, July 22, 1944, all in Case 7GR43 file, F85FR, RG 228.

47. Frank Constangy to Thomas Quigley, September 7, 22, 1944, Thomas Quigley to J. F. Nesmith, September 28, 1944, report of conference between A. Bruce Hunt and William Klugh, October 17, 1944, and USES 510, November 8, 1944, all in Case 7GR43 file, F85FR, RG 228.

power agency regional director Dillard B. Lasseter assured Dodge that a Macon training school would be established if 10 blacks applied. Within a week, Dodge sent the names of 18 applicants.[48]

Lasseter's pledge did not settle the matter. The WMC's McDaniel, still defiant, was astonished that Lasseter had made such a commitment, for McDaniel would initiate the training only after Reynolds Fuse agreed to hire the black women. Having experienced many previous frustrations in dealing with Lasseter, the FEPC-Atlanta was scarcely surprised at his behavior. He should participate in preparing a joint news release, Dodge told Will Maslow in a telephone call from Macon. If Lasseter refused, he should be asked to approve the FEPC's news release, the purpose being "to assure Mr. Lasseter's cooperation or to make it as difficult as possible for him to retreat from his previous committments [sic]." In addition to Lasseter and McDaniel, there were other obstacles. In a conference involving all of the participating agencies held in Macon on December 12, unexpected opposition came from Captain Roy Pfaff, the navy's resident officer at the ordnance plant. "Let us remember, now, this is Georgia," he told the group. Both Pfaff and Reynolds' general manager R. J. Anderson anticipated unpleasant consequences if blacks were employed in production. The executive order outlawed not segregation, they pointed out, only discrimination. Nevertheless, somehow, finally, agreement came. McDaniel would set up the school, Bibb County school superintendent Mark Smith would seek Board of Education approval, and Anderson promised to hire the trainees on the third shift if 75 or more were available.[49]

Early in January, 1945, Macon's blacks held a mass meeting in support of defense training. John Hope II, the black FEPC examiner in the Atlanta office, addressed the group and reported the attendance at over 4,000. As a result of these efforts, a sufficient number of blacks applied for training. Over 100 registered, and the USES turned away

48. Clarence Mitchell to Rear Admiral F. G. Crisp, November 17, 1944, December 16, 1944, G. S. Hussey to Clarence Mitchell, December 22, 1944, Clarence Mitchell to L. S. Hawkins, November 27, 1944, L. S. Hawkins to Clarence Mitchell, November 29, 1944, memorandum, Clarence Mitchell to Witherspoon Dodge, November 27, December 16, 1944, meeting of Witherspoon Dodge, Dillard Lasseter, et al., December 1, 1944, Witherspoon Dodge to William Klugh, December 7, 1944, all in Case 7GR43 file, F85FR, RG 228.

49. John Hope II to Will Maslow, December 12, 1944, and John Hope to Witherspoon Dodge, December 12, 1944, both in Case 7GR43 file, F85FR, RG 228.

116 others on the grounds that the quota was filled. From Atlanta, Dillard Lasseter, who may have been concerned over future problems with the FEPC, was perturbed. The USES-Macon gave the applicants bad advice, he wrote Thomas Quigley, who was in charge of the Macon office. "Some provision should be made for taking some type of registration so that . . . women can be called for referral." With classes ready to begin, someone discovered there were no power sewing machines. More delay followed as Dodge and Hope frantically worked through the central office to get a "triple A" priority.[50]

By early March, classes still had not begun. Witherspoon Dodge spent two days of repeated telephoning to Washington, D.C., and Macon trying to unsnarl the administrative tangles. The school's opening was delayed because "the requests for priorities were not handled efficiently and probably not in good faith," Dodge noted in his weekly report. "Efforts of the Macon Vocational School, the Georgia State Department of Education, and/or the Regional WPB to obtain the necessary equipment was [sic] lackadaisical . . . if not obstructionist." Certain data necessary for a top priority were sloppily and improperly presented by local representatives. As a result, the priority request for lathes and drill presses was canceled, and the sewing machines received a lower priority. Shortly after the school finally opened on March 19 with over 100 students, another problem cropped up. The machines arrived without motors. Again the FEPC, not the local officials, found a solution. Motors were procured on loan from the white school.[51]

The previous December, as the rumors spread that black women might get defense training, many white Maconites became alarmed, according to Larkin Marshall, a local Negro leader. A white minister who belonged to the Interracial Committee of Macon hoped "that if Negro women" were given training, "the 'domestics would not be disturbed'" because it would "no longer be possible to obtain domestic help if a large number of colored women were given work." Marshall's civil rights activities were under local scrutiny. The Macon chief of police threatened to investigate him, a matter watched closely

50. Dillard Lasseter to Thomas Quigley, January 11, 1945, John Hope to Witherspoon Dodge, January 22, 1945, and weekly report, March 5, 1945, all in Case 7GR43 file, F85FR, RG 228.
51. Weekly report, March 5, 1945, WMC memorandum, May 2, 1945, and Final Disposition Report, May 31, 1945, all in Case 7GR43 file, F85FR, RG 228.

by the newly formed Southern Regional Council. After the school opened, more objections came from laundries and housewives. Macon's leading laundry operator claimed that he lost over $800 in one month as a result of his black labor force going to the naval ordnance class. Three other launderers, who WMC area director G. Roy Bethune believed were trying to put pressure on his agency, said they might close because the Office of Price Administration refused price and wage increases. White housewives complained about the loss of domestic servants. "The labor situation in Macon is tighter than it has ever been," Bethune reported.[52]

Defense training for blacks in Macon, so laboriously implemented by the FEPC, lasted only ten weeks. On May 31, the WMC ended all training programs. The FEPC's efforts to overcome the inertia, obstruction, and outright hostility of local, state, and federal officials provided insight into the difficulty of its task and the dedication of its personnel. That a previously excluded minority could acquire skills, jobs, and pay equal to whites in this southern community, though it took place within the framework of the segregated society, was nonetheless revolutionary. About 200 blacks were put to work by Reynolds Fuse in a separate work area with their own cafeteria and other facilities. Much of the credit for effecting such a change belonged to blacks themselves as well as to the FEPC. As a result of their success, all over the South, black expectations, whether in Macon, Milledgeville, or New Iberia, had received a tremendous charge, leading some to take action and protest in ways never before deemed possible. Its significance for the future could only be conjectured.[53]

On a regional and national basis, the FEPC's efforts to end discrimination in defense training had the potential to be a significant accomplishment for the Old Committee, but the effort was stunted and turned back. Begun early in 1942, the FEPC's attack on bias in defense training for a time turned the policies of the powerful education bureaucracy around. The full impact of this change has not been documented, but aircraft training for Atlanta's black community, for ex-

52. Memorandum, Clarence Mitchell to Witherspoon Dodge, December 5, 1944, and John Hope to Witherspoon Dodge, December 11, 1944, both in Case 7GR43 file, F85FR, and field report, John Hope to Witherspoon Dodge, May 5, 1945, all in RG 228.

53. Memorandum, John Studebaker to State Executive Officers and Directors of War Training Programs, May 5, 1945, in Case 7GR43 file, F85FR, RG 228.

ample, might have been delayed longer or postponed indefinitely if the FEPC had not intervened. The FEPC's struggle with McNutt and the manpower commission during the fall of 1942, the attacks by southerners and the administration, the cancellation of hearings, and the resignations from the committee all left the FEPC isolated and impotent. The momentum for reform in the defense training program was also halted as the various federal and state agencies involved with training, particularly in the segregated states, reverted to their old ways. The timing was crucial because the war effort was still accelerating. Nearly a year would pass before the New Committee could focus again on discrimination in defense training. Yet its perseverance provided civil rights advocates with an important example: even a weak federal presence, if it was determined, could accomplish change.

7 / The Regional Offices

After the creation of the President's Committee in June, 1941, Chairman Mark Ethridge believed that most of the work could be handled through correspondence from the central office. This air of innocence and naiveté soon disappeared as defense contractors and unions neither quaked nor even blinked when communications arrived from the obscure Washington, D.C., agency. Even units of the federal bureaucracy virtually ignored the FEPC until ordered by the president to do otherwise. By fall, after the committee's decision to hold hearings, field investigations became imperative. Understaffed and poorly funded, the Old Committee had to rely heavily on other agencies, especially the staffs of Robert Weaver and Will Alexander at the OPM. Two of these investigators, Cy Record and John Beecher, worked in the South preparing for the Birmingham hearing in June, 1942. Among their accomplishments was the documentation of the USO's acquiescence in discrimination in defense training. After Birmingham, Beecher joined the FEPC and briefly headed its New York office. When he resigned from the agency, he joined the merchant marine and served on the *Booker T. Washington*, a ship with a black skipper and a racially integrated crew. Elsewhere, two blacks from Weaver's branch also worked for the FEPC, Edward Lawson in New York and New England, and G. James Fleming III in Detroit. Fleming previously had been in El Paso investigating discrimination against Mexican- and African-Americans in the copper mines. The FEPC's field staff became indispensable in implementing policy. After the transfer to the WMC in July, 1942, members of the Old Committee fought a heated but ultimately fruitless battle with Paul McNutt over the power to appoint field personnel.[1]

The FEPC finally got control of its field operations after Roosevelt created the New Committee by issuing Executive Order 9346 in May, 1943. Initially, the committee planned twelve regional offices in cities and regions paralleling those of the WMC. Region I covered the New England area, but an office in Boston never functioned, nor did offices planned for Minneapolis (Region VIII) or Denver (Region XI). Region II included New York and northern New Jersey; Region III, Pennsylvania and southern New Jersey; Region IV, Virginia, Maryland, Delaware, West Virginia, and North Carolina; Region V, Ohio, Michigan, and Kentucky; Region VI, Illinois, Indiana, and Wisconsin; Region VII, South Carolina, Georgia, Florida, Alabama, Tennessee, and Mississippi (which later became part of Region XIII); Region IX, Kansas, Missouri, Arkansas, and Oklahoma; Region X, Louisiana (also later part of Region XIII), Texas, and New Mexico; Region XII, California, Arizona, Nevada, Oregon, and Washington; and Region XIII, Louisiana and Mississippi. A white attorney from the NLRB, New Yorker Will Maslow, became director of the Division of Field Operations (DFO). The committee agreed that half of the regional directors would be blacks. The field offices, like the central office, would operate with mixed ethnic and racial staffs. Thus, the FEPC became the first federal agency in history not only to have blacks in policy-making positions but to have black staff appointees in Washington, D.C., and in the field often directing whites and other blacks.[2]

With defense contractors and federal agencies concentrated in the industrialized Northeast and Midwest, the committee established a

1. John Beecher, "S.S. Booker T. Washington," New Republic, October 2, 1944, pp. 421–23; Abe L. Savage to John Beecher, November 27, 1942, in Public Relations, A–C, R47HR, G. James Fleming to George M. Johnson, January 19, 1943, in Reports, FEP 2, R48HR, both in RG 228; Chicago Defender, June 19, 1943, p. 5.

2. Will Maslow to Francis Haas, July 16, 27, 1943, in Office Memoranda, M file, R1HR, and OWI Release, August 19, 1943, in Press Releases, A file, R85HR, both in RG 228; Will Maslow to John R. McCusker, October 5, 1943, U.S. Govt., WMC, R67HR, "Report of the Division of Field Operations as of October 21, 1943" (Typescript, carbon, October 21, 1943, in office files of Will Maslow, Monthly Reports file, R76HR), and OWI Release, November 11, 1943, in office files of Emanuel Bloch, Speeches and Releases file, R6HR, all in RG 228.

number of its offices in those regions: New York (II), Philadelphia (III), Cleveland (V), Chicago (VI), and Kansas City (IX). Where the investigative work became unusually heavy, in Pittsburgh, Cincinnati, Detroit, and St. Louis, suboffices were created. The South, with its Atlantic and Gulf shipyards and its emerging aircraft industry, hosted two regional offices, in Washington, D.C. (IV) and Atlanta (VII). The Southwest was served by an FEPC office in Dallas (X), with suboffices in San Antonio and New Orleans, the latter becoming headquarters of Region XIII early in 1945. Finally, the West Coast (XII) had an office in San Francisco and a suboffice in Los Angeles. No black regional directors were appointed in the Deep South or in the Southwest, though a black ultimately headed the FEPC's Region IV in Washington, D.C., which served the upper South, and black field investigators worked out of Atlanta and Dallas. Blacks also took charge of regional and subregional offices in New York, Philadelphia, Pittsburgh, Cleveland, Detroit, Chicago, and St. Louis.[3]

The DFO's Will Maslow, bright, intense, and aggressive, ran a tight operation, laying down strict and unambiguous field instructions for his regional directors and investigators to follow. The directors were to make no public reference to the name of a complainant or to the party charged in a pending case, since a complaint was merely an accusation until the FEPC investigated and took action on it. They also had to refrain from explaining or interpreting controversial committee decisions or policies and avoid public dispute. "Limit yourselves to calm, dispassionate statements of undisputed facts," Maslow counseled. Above all, they were not to issue any formal press releases or make any speeches unless approved by the FEPC's deputy chairman. In emergencies clearance could be requested from the central office by telephone. Factual statements, however, needed no advance approval. Radio speeches, if cleared by central, should avoid any appearance of obligation to a sponsor or to a broadcasting agency. The FEPC's regional representatives should shun public argument or debate with other government agencies. They ought never to solicit complaints or give the impression of doing so. The directors were nonetheless urged, regardless of these "negative admonitions," to speak before industry, labor, church and civic groups, especially those

3. Pittsburgh *Courier,* July 24, 1943, p. 8.

uninformed about the FEPC's work. Finally, they needed to maintain cordial relations with local press reporters and cooperating agencies.[4]

Errant or indiscreet regional directors and field investigators received scoldings and reprimands. "[Your] speech before the Texas State Industrial Union Council . . . gives the impression of talking down to the audience," Maslow wrote Director Leonard Brin. Then, revealing his own insensitivity, Maslow made a further suggestion: "*Even* trade unionists like to be addressed in terms of more than one syllable. . . . Give them more meat" [emphasis added]. Later, the unfortunate Brin got into more serious trouble. He mistakenly ordered the Dallas *Morning News* to stop advertising for a "colored" worker, on the grounds that newspapers were war industries and came under FEPC jurisdiction. A good staff man, he retired shortly thereafter, though later he did part-time investigative work for the FEPC in Florida. In North Carolina, Examiner Alice Kahn publicly criticized that state's WMC office and vowed to file a complaint against it. Her statement was "extremely ill-advised," Maslow scolded. It was "a policy matter [that] should not have been released without clearance." Furthermore, the president had ordered executive agencies to avoid engaging in public controversies. "The remark attributable to you has embarrassed us" with the WMC, he chided her. Kahn's statements supporting a permanent FEPC were "likewise uncalled for and contrary to instructions." In addition to requiring her to submit a written report about the entire incident, Maslow ordered Kahn to "engage in no interviews or conversations of any description with the press . . . until further notice." When Director Elmer W. Henderson in Region VI publicly charged that the boilermakers union was one of the chief discriminators against blacks, Maslow cautioned restraint. So far only a complaint had been lodged, he reminded Henderson, and the FEPC had not yet announced a position on the issue. If the committee found no discrimination, Henderson would be embarrassed. Carlos Castaneda, an assistant to Ross and later director of Region X, also received a reprimand and an order to refrain from making any more statements on a controversial matter in Texas. Such lapses were rare,

4. Will Maslow to All Regional Directors, September 3, 1943, in Field Instructions file, R78HR, RG 228.

though, and few reprimands, in writing at least, were given throughout the term of the FEPC's existence.[5]

The New Committee's field offices opened first in the Northeast. In Region III, the black G. James Fleming III, a Philadelphia native and a Republican, came home from his assignment in Detroit to become regional director.[6] Another black, Edward Lawson, who had served in the New York area as a field employment assistant in the Labor Division since the spring of 1941, headed Region II. Both men had valuable knowledge and contacts, and Lawson also possessed the case files from his previous activities in both the OPM and the WMC. Along with George Johnson, Earl Dickerson, and the NAACP, he championed social equality and viewed legal segregation as a violation of the Constitution. In the Northeast, there was no legal segregation, and New York State had enacted its own antidiscrimination law, the Mahoney Act, yet as Lawson began investigating in 1941, he found that blacks were excluded from national defense industries. On Long Island, Ford Instrument, a subsidiary of the Sperry Gyroscope Corporation, after promising to hire minority machinists and tool and die makers, refused to do so when blacks began applying. Even jobs for general helpers remained closed. While discriminating against youths trained in New York City and Brooklyn, Ford Instrument recruited unskilled white workers from all over the East and South and trained them in single-skill assembly operations. In trying to break down discrimination, Lawson got full cooperation from the New York State Industrial Union Council (CIO), which suspected that defense contractors were trying to ward off unionization by seeking out the cheapest, most docile labor available. He also received support from the WMC's regional director, Anna Rosenberg, and from state officials. By March, 1942, Ford Instrument, exposed by the New York

5. Will Maslow to Leonard Brin, April 1, 1944, in General Correspondence file, Public Relations, A–C, R47HR, Congressman W. R. Poage to Malcolm Ross, June 12, 1944, in Public Relations 5, Ross file, R56HR, Washington *News*, June 16, 1944, in Newspaper Clippings, Box 526, Will Maslow to Alice Kahn, December 11, 1944, in Office Memoranda, K file, R1HR, Will Maslow to Elmer Henderson, October 30, 1943, in Office Memoranda, M file, R1HR, all in RG 228; Dallas *Morning News*, June 1, 1944, in Series III, Box 66, 1943–44, Russell Papers; Malcolm Ross to R. E. Smith, May 15, 1945, in Public Relations 5, S file, R44HR, RG 228.

6. For Fleming's activities as head of FEPC's temporary office in Detroit, see Meier and Rudwick, *Black Detroit and the Rise of the UAW*, 156–62.

hearing and pressured by these labor and government groups and by wartime labor shortages, announced a change in policy. Subtle company resistance, however, continued to keep the ratio of blacks low.[7]

Ford Instrument's discriminatory policies were typical of many employers operating in the region during 1941. Lawson discovered problems at, among others, Colt's Patent Fire Arms Manufacturing Company and the New Departure Manufacturing Company in Connecticut, American Locomotive Company in Schenectady, and the Civilian Technical Corps, associated with the U.S. Army Corps of Engineers. In addition, Winchester Repeating Arms Company in Connecticut, which hired about 1,200 blacks, exhibited a "slight tendency to keep them out of more highly skilled jobs." On the positive side of hiring practices, Lawson later cited Eastman Kodak in Rochester as "one of the best companies in western New York in regard to Executive Order 9346," and he found several hundred companies, large and small, with and without defense contracts, that employed or claimed they were willing to hire blacks at all skill levels. In some cases, however, the controlling AFL unions had blocked black referrals.[8]

With the entrance of the United States into the war, defense contracts proliferated and the labor market tightened. Lawson, still with the Labor Division, increasingly stressed job quality and upgrading, but the ambivalence toward blacks in the work place that Lawson found during 1941, involving both discrimination and acceptance, was typical of Region II throughout the remainder of the war. With more jobs available than ever before, there were also more complaints of discrimination as the New Committee's regional office opened in the summer of 1943. Region II had three fair practice examiners and four clerk stenographers by 1944, though Lawson thought the workload justified his request for eight examiners and ten clerks. Certainly,

7. Theodore Jones to Edward Lawson, February 23, 1943, in 2BC1952, F15FR, Lawson notes, April, 1941, Field Report, August 15, 1941, Edward Lawson to Robert Weaver, September 9, 1941, Edward Lawson to Alexander Davis, Jr., April 26, 1942, in Ford Instrument, Predocketed Cases, F23FR, all in RG 228.

8. Field Trip, July 25, 1941, Edward Lawson to Robert Weaver, August 16, 1941, H. D. Fairweather to Mark Ethridge, September 11, 1941, Edward Lawson to Robert Weaver, September 12, 1941, Field Report, September 13, 1941, Leonard J. Maloney to Edward Lawson, October 6, 1941, D. G. Phelps to Robert Weaver, December 31, 1941, all in F22FR, Field Report, October 4, 1941, in Predocketed Cases, F23FR, and Howard A. Van Dine to Richard Brockway, October 28, 1941, in USES, Predocketed II, F25FR, all in RG 228.

many employers in the New York area continued to challenge both Executive Order 9346 and New York's Mahoney Act, which prohibited discrimination by utilities, labor unions, and defense industries.[9]

In upstate New York, where blacks were far less numerous, FEPC field visits to six cities in 1943 and 1944 revealed similar patterns. An Auburn, New York, employer, when told that writing *colored* on a job application violated the executive order, "became somewhat irate" and thought the FEPC "was too much like the gestapo." In Buffalo, where serious labor shortages existed, Bell Aircraft Corporation hired between 300 and 500 black women for maintenance and production work, but the company was slow to take on skilled blacks. In Jamestown, the Marlin Rockwell Company, which made bearings for aircraft engines, ran a segregated polishing room and advertised for "Negro polishers." The UAW, which had a closed shop agreement with Marlin Rockwell, had been slow to recognize the existence of any racial problems. When the company moved a black polisher into production work, three delegations of white workers visited the company president at both his office and his home and threatened to walk out. A black woman could not get a job in the grinding department because of anticipated opposition from white women. In addition, a few workers of Italian descent complained of discrimination because they were assigned to the same menial jobs that blacks were forced to take. After long negotiations, most of these problems were adjusted. Polishing was desegregated and grinding integrated, but black women never got into the plant except as maids. Generally, however, Region II displayed an ambivalence toward blacks, both accepting and rejecting them in the work place.[10]

In Pennsylvania, G. James Fleming and Field Examiner Milo Manly, also black, found similar attitudes. Negroes were excluded from most white-collar jobs and faced obstacles in both hiring and upgrading in

9. "Mahoney Act" (Typescript, copy, in Records of George M. Johnson, Legal Division, R5HR, press release, Committee on Discrimination in Employment, March 1942, in Reports, FEP 1, R48HR, A. I. Savin Construction Co., in Correspondence II, D–Gi, F5FR, and Region II staff, Budget, Fiscal 1944, F3FR, all in RG 228; Capeci, "Wartime Fair Employment Practices Committees," 47.

10. Field visit, December 29, 1943, in 2BR437, F11FR, WMC Employer Information Unit, February 23, 1943, in Predocketed Cases, F22FR, and Final Disposition Report, October 27, 1944, in 2BR120, F16FR, all in RG 228; Leonard P. Adams, *Wartime Manpower Mobilization: A Study of World War II Experience in the Buffalo-Niagara Area* (Ithaca, 1951), 49.

the skills. Region III, like all FEPC offices, apportioned the staff work on the basis of actual complaints received. Except for a bitter strike in 1944 on the Philadelphia Rapid Transit system to prevent the assignment of blacks to conductor and platform jobs, Region III concentrated mainly on problems in the eastern shipyards and in the steel mills of western Pennsylvania. The Sun Shipbuilding Company, near Philadelphia, established a segregated yard in which black crews worked under white supervisors. In other Sun Shipbuilding yards, whites and blacks, skilled and unskilled, worked side by side. Whether in segregated or nonsegregated work situations, however, there were complaints of discrimination over hiring, upgrading, and promotion. That the situation was complicated by interunion rivalry and obtuseness on the part of management would tend to suggest that worker unrest arose out of the internal dynamics of each work place as well as out of racial problems. In Pittsburgh, the FEPC's Milo Manly, who eventually headed a suboffice in that city, labored diligently and usually successfully in trying to work out managerial and racial problems in the steel mills.[11]

Thus, black workers in the Northeast often faced discrimination when seeking defense jobs despite the scarce supply of labor. Prejudice and racism existed in abundance, but shortages of labor, the militancy of the black community, and the persistent prodding of the FEPC and other agencies brought about change. On January 1, 1944, 475 cases of discrimination were pending in Regions II and III. During the next six months, 645 new cases were docketed. In that period, however, 552 cases were adjusted satisfactorily. Northeastern ambivalence generally meant the absence of the bitter white resistance to blacks that often characterized other regions. The FEPC's special contribution, besides the work of competent and sympathetic field investigators,

11. Merl Reed, "Pennsylvania's Black Workers," 356–84; Dennis C. Dickerson, "Fighting on the Domestic Front: Black Steelworkers in Western Pennsylvania During World War II," in Charles Stephenson and Robert Asher (eds.), Life and Labor: Dimensions of Working-Class History (Albany, N.Y., 1986), 224–36; Dennis C. Dickerson, Out of the Crucible: Black Steelworkers in Western Pennsylvania, 1875–1980 (Albany, N.Y., 1986), 172–75; Winkler, "Philadelphia Transit Strike of 1944," 73–89; August Meier and Elliott Rudwick, "Communist Unions and the Black Community: The Case of the Transport Workers Union, 1934–1944," Labor History, XXIII (1982), 182–97; Ruchames, Race, Jobs, and Politics, 100–20; and Kennard Harry Wright, "Sun Shipyard Number Four—The Story of a Major Negro Homefront Defense Effort During the Second World War" (M.A. thesis, Morgan State College, 1972), 1–13, 15–16, 27.

was its insistence that blacks must be hired at their highest level of competence and receive upgrading and promotions without discrimination.[12]

The Midwest presented more serious challenges. Into this industrial heartland large numbers of white and black southerners, as well as eastern Europeans, had migrated. These groups, often not strangers to poverty, ignorance, and racism, were susceptible to the racist propaganda permeating work places just before World War II. The wartime labor scarcity and the lowering of racial barriers produced some of the worst discrimination and violence in the nation. Throughout 1942 until its race riot the following year, Detroit was a focal point of unrest. In the automobile industry, black workers were concentrated in unskilled, service, and other less desirable jobs. Late in 1941, whites forced 2 blacks, transferred into defense work by the Packard Motor Company, to return to their original stations. That and other similar events had wide symbolic significance for both races. In addition, race morale plummeted as black women found it difficult or impossible to get defense employment in Detroit's 164 and the area's 1,500 industrial establishments. At the end of 1942, there were 32 companies with unfair employment practice complaints against them for their refusal to hire black females and upgrade black males. These businesses also hired black males below their skill levels. In numerous cases, USES 510s had been filed. Many of these offenders bore the names of the largest corporations in the nation. Black citizens began demanding a local FEPC office, an investigation, and a hearing.[13]

When G. James Fleming opened Detroit's temporary FEPC office in January, 1943, he faced a nearly impossible task. In Washington, D.C., his organization, under attack from southerners, the administration, and the WMC, faced possible extinction. In Detroit, when

12. Case load activity by region, in office files of John A. Davis, Miscellaneous file, R69HR, RG 228; Merl Reed, "Pennsylvania's Black Workers," 383–84.

13. "Detroit Employers and Their Employment Practices," (Typescript, January 29, 1943, in Reports, FEP 1, R48HR), M. M. Gilman to Sidney Hillman, January 17, 1941, in office files of John Beecher, Birmingham file, R77HR, Robert Weaver to Lawrence Cramer, February 12, 1942, in Reports, FEP 1, R48HR, Lester A. Walton to Adolph Berle, June 20, 1942, in Reports, A–C, R47HR, R. J. Thomas to Lawrence Cramer, November 27, 1942, in Public Relations 5, T file, R44HR, and memorandum, Industrial Morale in Detroit, December 23, 1942, in U.S. Govt., ND, R67HR, all in RG 228; Chicago *Defender*, January 16, 1943, p. 8; Herbert R. Northrup, *The Negro in the Automobile Industry* (Philadelphia, 1968), 9; Clive, *State of War*, 139; Meier and Rudwick, *Black Detroit and the Rise of the UAW*, 109.

hearings were threatened against the numerous defense firms charged with discrimination, the Navy Department and the WMC blocked them. Nevertheless, Fleming continued shrewdly to push for hearings, and some employers, fearing the publicity, made concessions. Fleming and his staff, with coaching and prodding from Lawrence Cramer, went on with their investigations, satisfactorily adjusting cases where possible. Generally, they provided a federal presence that, though weak, benefited black workers. By the time the FEPC's Region V office opened in Cleveland in summer, 1943, the Detroit employment situation seemed to have stabilized following the riot. The FEPC opened a subregional office in Detroit shortly thereafter.[14]

In Indianapolis, the FEPC faced a different kind of problem when the Chamber of Commerce sought to become the local intermediary between the committee and area businesses. In a conference with Cramer in November, 1942, the chamber's executive vice-president, William H. Book, three times requested that Cramer forward to him complaints against Indianapolis employers. Through "our personal approach method," Book maintained, he could "accomplish the results which the President's Committee" desired, and he was "depending on being consulted and used" whenever it had "a problem affecting this community." More to the point, however, Book thought that Diamond Chain Manufacturing, an accused company, was innocent of wrongdoing, even though it had submitted a discriminatory work order to USES-Indianapolis. A USES 510 report charging discrimination was issued when the company refused to modify the order. Nevertheless, Book pronounced the FEPC's action "disruptive and punitive."[15]

When Cramer failed to cooperate, Book wrote a long confidential letter to Indiana's former governor and Cramer's present boss, WMC director Paul McNutt. Cramer had sent seven communications to prominent Indianapolis employers, Book complained, including Na-

14. Fleming to Johnson, January 19, 1943, in Office Memoranda, F file, R1HR, Fleming to Johnson, February 6, 17, 22, March 4, 5, April 23, 1943, Lawrence Cramer to G. James Fleming, February 26, March 10, 1943, G. James Fleming to Lawrence Cramer, March 25, 26, April 26, May 1, 3, 5, 1943, G. James Fleming to Lawrence Cramer and George Johnson, June 3, 1943, Fleming Reports, March 25, 26, 27, 1943, all in Reports, I, Fleming file, R48HR, and Region V, Report of Active Cases, February 21, 1945, in office files of Clarence M. Mitchell, UAW-CIO, R76HR, all in RG 228; Meier and Rudwick, *Black Detroit and the Rise of the UAW,* 156–74.

15. William Book to Lawrence Cramer, November 23, 1942, in Public Relations 5, R42HR, and Lawrence Cramer to Fowler V. Harper, December 10, 1942, in Reports 1-1, USES 510s, 1942, R58HR, both in RG 228.

tional Malleable & Steel Castings Company, Kingan & Company, and Republic Creosoting Company, "all three with many years of employing large numbers of colored at a wide variety of skills, even up to the grade of foreman," and these companies were "community leaders in such employment." Book was writing McNutt, he said, because the FEPC's "peremptory letters" had caused "disruption and indignation." He accused the FEPC of acting on the basis of "haphazard complaints or insufficient field work," yet he strenuously objected to the committee's reliance on the USES for investigations. For ten years the chamber had sought to improve employer opinion of the USES and get fuller cooperation with it, he noted, but when that agency was put on the spot by having to report alleged violations to the FEPC, businesses lost confidence in it. In a gracious reply to Book's complaints, Cramer pointed out that a promise to forward case files to Book was never given "during our conversations," and Cramer's careful explanation of committee procedures at that time should have made clear why he could not do so. There the controversy ended. What was interesting, intense chamber pressure earlier, in 1941, had led the Indiana Senate to scuttle a House bill, passed overwhelmingly, that would have outlawed discrimination in defense industries. At the least, Book's presumptuous proposal was hypocritical and self-serving to the interests he represented.[16]

Nevertheless, Book could justifiably complain about the absence of FEPC field work, a situation greatly relieved by the establishment of the New Committee's three midwestern offices. Two blacks, William T. McKnight and Elmer Henderson, headed Region V, in Cleveland, and Region VI, in Chicago, respectively, and the white Roy A. Hoglund served Region IX, in Kansas City. McKnight, formerly an Ohio assistant attorney general, had worked with the United States Department of Labor and had also been a member of the NAACP's legal committee before joining the FEPC. Henderson had taught social anthropology at Dillard University in New Orleans. Hoglund, a former Kansas high school principal, directed student work for the state's NYA.[17]

16. William Book to Paul McNutt, December 31, 1942, in Public Relations 5, R42HR, Lawrence Cramer to William Book, January 12, 1943, in office files of Malcolm Ross, Extra Copies file, R1HR, both in RG 228; Cavnes, *Hoosier Community at War*, 112–15.

17. Detroit *Chronicle*, January 22, 1944, in Newspaper Clippings, Box 529, and OWI Release, n.d. [November, 1943], in office files of Emanuel H. Bloch, Speeches

There were enough problems in the Midwest to keep these people fully occupied for the remainder of the war. Outside the work place, the social climate mirrored the segregated South. In Indianapolis, no blacks could patronize the downtown theaters or lunch counters at the five- and ten-cent stores, and many restaurants and drugstores posted signs refusing service. Although the labor shortages forced some establishments to place black women behind the counters, many of these women quit when they were ordered not to serve black customers. In 1943, taxicabs refused service to blacks, a discriminatory practice that had ended during the Great Depression, when money was scarce. These matters did not fall under FEPC jurisdiction, but similar conditions existed in Indiana's war industries. The General Motors Delco Remy plant in Anderson, Indiana, employed black workers, male and female, primarily in service and labor areas, and company officials intended to keep it that way. Several incidents in the cafeteria early in 1944 indicated to management, at least, that "enough dynamite [existed] in the plant to blow the lid off if the situation [was] not handled properly," and that meant resisting change. There was so much tension in Gary over the lack of recreation, education, transportation, and housing facilities for blacks that six federal agencies investigated the situation as a threat to war production. At Akron, 1,500 white workers at the Goodyear Rubber plant walked out over a proposal to train 2 black women preparatory to their assignment to a different shift; white women refused to train them or let them use the machines manned by whites. A black machinist was denied a promotion to his highest skill level, because Goodyear thought his transfer might impair the war effort.[18]

These examples and scores of others like them illustrate the racial tension and the handicaps under which black citizens functioned in the industrial Midwest. The FEPC's regional offices, except for Kansas City, carried heavy workloads. On January 1, 1944, 727 cases were

and Releases file, R6HR, both in RG 228; Chicago *Defender*, November 8, 1941, p. 2.

18. Joy Schultz to Elmer Henderson, February 12, 1944, Tension file, Indianapolis, and "Confidential Report and Recommendations on the Racial Situation in Gary, Ind.," Tension file, Gary, both in R75HR, John A. Davis to Cornelius Golightly, April 25, 1944, Tension file, Akron, in R76HR, Maceo Hubbard to George Johnson, July 6, 1944, in Documents file, 5BR120, R1HR, all in RG 228; Cavnes, *Hoosier Community at War*, 155.

pending, many with multiple complainants, and in the next six months, 514 new cases were docketed. Although 685 of these 1,341 active cases had been satisfactorily adjusted by June 30, the meanness of spirit evident in the white opposition and the stubborn resistance of many midwestern defense contractors produced tension and bitterness in marked contrast, except for the Philadelphia Transit strike, with attitudes in the more ambivalent Northeast. Some problems in the Midwest so challenged FEPC attempts at resolution that the committee found it necessary to hold a hearing in Cincinnati early in 1945.[19]

When Cincinnati's Crosley Radio Corporation advertised in the summer of 1942 for several hundred white women, it revealed a pattern of employment that would not be voluntarily changed at Crosley or at most other war industries in this city of 900,000 residents. A year later, the FEPC's Ernest Trimble reported conditions "as bad as any place I have visited," except Wright Aeronautical Corporation, a private plant under U.S. Air Force tutelage. Black women could find work at these places only in domestic and industrial service, despite the fact that a number of them had acquired training and skills through the NYA. In August, 1943, the WMC estimated that 15,000 workers would be needed within the next two months and that only 2,500 were presently available. Officials at Crosley and at the Baldwin Piano Company were "too busy" to talk to Trimble; Baldwin sent that message by way of a young boy to a waiting Trimble in the reception room. "For the sake of our reputation," he wrote to Malcolm Ross, "I think that we should take vigorous action against a few of these companies here."[20]

Because of Region V's backlog of cases, Cincinnati received little attention for eight months. In March, 1944, when Trimble returned with the Region V director and another FEPC investigator, the three had separate meetings with officials of F. H. Lawson & Company, Rex Dye and Tool, and Crosley, the last for over five hours. USES 510s

---

19. Case load activity by region, January 1–June 30, 1944, in office files of John Davis, Miscellaneous file, R69HR, RG 228. The FEPC also held hearings in St. Louis, Mo., and in Alton, Ill., during this period; see Patricia L. Adams, "Fighting for Democracy in St. Louis: Civil Rights During World War II," *Missouri History Review*, LXXX (1985), 58–75.

20. Ernest Trimble to Malcolm Ross, August 13, 1943, in Reports, N–Z, R48HR, RG 228; Pittsburgh *Courier*, September 5, 1942, p. 5; Chicago *Defender*, January 29, 1944, p. 11.

were issued against all three companies. Crosley, the largest, employed over 4,500, of whom 58 percent were women. F. H. Lawson had 560 workers, and Rex Dye over 200. All three admitted that they refused to hire blacks, but Crosley and F. H. Lawson blamed the unions and the "hillbillies" from Kentucky and Tennessee. Company officials claimed to be sympathetic with the position of black people and would do more except for the unions. Production Workers Local 1089 (IAM), whose international union had a color bar in its constitution, had forced F. H. Lawson to dismiss 7 blacks already working there when the union came in. Company officials were willing to sign a stipulation that these were the facts. At the Crosley meeting, local officers of the International Brotherhood of Electrical Workers (IBEW) were present. Union president Fred Ross was outspoken in his prejudice against both blacks and Jews. White employees would quit, he warned, if blacks were introduced into the plant. The third company, Rex Dye and Tool, announced a change in policy. The company had already hired "one colored girl," and she had promised to bring 6 others when reporting for work in two weeks.[21]

Nevertheless, racial wounds in Cincinnati continued to fester. In June, 1944, hate strikes erupted at Wright Aeronautical as blacks were assigned to the "center," all-white shop. Regional Director McKnight, investigating the incident, reported that the company operation consisted of three buildings. By previous agreement with Wright's black personnel representative, Afro-American workers had been assigned to a segregated area in the north shop. A spokesman for the strikers blamed the trouble on dissension within the UAW. A black union organizer, William Beckham, accused of being arrogant and dictatorial, had been elected chairman of the bargaining committee after the UAW won a victory six months earlier in a bitter contest with the AFL. Since then, the AFL had worked to undermine and weaken the UAW, and it was supported, McKnight learned, by elements in the Cincinnati white community opposed to blacks entering into skills, working beside whites, sharing facilities, and taking responsible positions in labor unions. Beckham, a brilliant organizer and charismatic figure, ran the union through a figurehead white local president. Although he lacked tact, polish, and the ability to deal with people,

21. Memorandum, Ernest Trimble to George Johnson, March 17, 1944, in office files of George M. Johnson, Trimble file, R4HR, RG 228.

Beckham had real power, and he chopped down other black and white unionists who exhibited leadership talent.[22]

At midmorning on June 5, the strike began as 7 blacks were assigned to idle lathes and other tools at the center shop. After 175 white workers protested, the blacks were sent back to their stations, but management decided to remain firm, because no skilled whites were available to operate the machines. A slow exodus of whites began, and by midafternoon the walkout was 100 percent effective. Worse, the strike spread to the south shop as protesters roamed through the plant urging other employees to leave. The 3:30 P.M. shift left, as did the late one at 11:30 P.M. Some white women, reluctant to leave, were manhandled by male workers in full view of plant supervisors. Employees in the north shop, mostly blacks with a few whites, stayed on the job. In this confrontation, management, the army, the UAW, and government representatives put up a solid front. Blacks were needed and would be used at their highest skills levels. The National War Labor Board, receiving the case on referral, agreed. By June 8, the white workers began returning.[23]

The outcome at Wright Aeronautical was not typical of strike settlements in Cincinnati when racial issues were involved. The community and most businesses continued to hold firm against change. Individual employers took positions so similar that McKnight concluded a united front had been organized. At FEPC central, Emanuel Bloch, the trial attorney who was preparing the case, agreed. Employers, by falling back on the argument of white opposition, tried to assume a moral offensive, Bloch thought. The tactic sought to shift responsibility for strikes and work stoppages away from management, which ought to share the responsibility, he argued, because of its failure to provide employee education programs and to fight prejudice. By January, 1945, McKnight and his investigators had carefully laid the groundwork for a hearing against eight Cincinnati defense contractors: Crosley Radio Corporation, Victor Electric Products, United Biscuit Company, F. H. Lawson Company, Baldwin Piano Company, Cambridge Tile Manufacturing Company, Kirk & Blum Manufacturing Company, and Schaible Company. The evidence was impressive, including USES 510s issued by the WMC and complaints that had

22. Memorandum, William McKnight to Will Maslow, June 8, 1944, in Tension file, Ohio, Strikes and Work Stoppages file, R76HR, RG 228.
23. *Ibid.*

been thoroughly investigated and documented. In addition, the FEPC had contacted and held conferences with company and union representatives and had carefully briefed personnel from the armed services and government agencies. Bloch directed McKnight to gather some additional data from the WMC and also to procure the testimony of a distinguished social scientist.[24]

Scheduled for the middle of March, the Cincinnati hearing was based on 60 complaints filed over the refusal to employ or train blacks except in menial pursuits. Employers reportedly were surprised at the charges. According to the Cincinnati *Enquirer*, it was impossible to comply with all of the FEPC's regulations. "We don't want to discriminate," one official stated, but "in a borderline city [with] . . . many Southern workers," companies had to listen to them. Defense contractors undoubtedly were not pleased to learn that an FEPC suboffice would open in Cincinnati in February to assist in preparing for the hearing. Under the direction of Harold James from San Francisco, the office would also handle the backlog of cases in southern Ohio and Kentucky.[25]

With the hearing imminent, three companies satisfactorily adjusted the complaints against them by signing stipulations and agreements not to discriminate in promoting, upgrading, classifying, compensating, or hiring any employee. They also promised to notify the USES and other recruitment services in writing, to instruct hiring and training personnel on policies consistent with Executive Order 9346, and to notify the FEPC within ninety days of the steps taken. The Schaible Company, specifically, agreed to interview black women and

24. Memorandum, William McKnight to Will Maslow, January 4, 1945, in Records of George M. Johnson, FEPC Miscellaneous file, George Johnson to Emanuel Bloch and Frank Reeves, February 14, 1945, in Records of George M. Johnson, Bloch file, R4HR, Victor Electric, December 21, 1944, Request for Further Action, Crosley Corp., January 4, 1944, Victor Electric Products, January 6, 1945, Kirk & Blum, January 6, 1945, Schaible Co., January 12, 1945, Cambridge Tile, January 25, 1945, in Cincinnati hearing, R49HR, Emanuel Bloch to George Johnson, January 24, 1945, in office files of Frank D. Reeves, Opinions—Other Staff Members file, R7HR, and Statement of Charges, Baldwin Piano and United Biscuit Co. of America (Streitman Biscuit Division), both February 21, 1945, in Cincinnati hearing, R22HR, all in RG 228.

25. Eugene Davidson to William McKnight, January 18, 1945, in Administrative Files, V, Cincinnati Office, F49FR, Cincinnati *Post*, January 11, 1945, in Box 514, Cincinnati *Enquirer*, February 28, 1945, in Box 529, both in Newspaper Clippings, all in RG 228.

place the first group on production by March 19. Kirk & Blum and Cambridge Tile were the two other companies to reach agreement before the hearing began. The hearing for the remaining five companies went on as scheduled, with twenty witnesses testifying that they had been discriminated against. All of the accused denied guilt, placing the blame instead on the local unions and the workers. Company spokesmen spent much time explaining the nature of the people working in the plants. The hearing, attended by Ross, Brophy, Houston, Shishkin, Southall, and Johnson, succeeded in publicizing the problem, and the FEPC could then proceed with the issuance of its findings and directives.[26]

Afterward, the Region V office exuded both euphoria and dismay. McKnight was delighted with the interest in race relations that the hearing aroused locally. Examiner James, pressed for time, turned down several invitations to speak. More significant was the scheduling of a meeting of community groups, including churches, labor leaders, university and public school people, public officials and the press, to discuss community responsibility and leadership. Editorial comment after the hearing, however, picked up the theme that had been stressed by the accused companies and blamed labor for the problems. Under particular attack by local columnists were union leaders, who testified they would walk out of the plants if blacks were hired.[27]

In Cincinnati's defense industries, though, there would be little change. FEPC investigators making compliance checks during the week of the hearing turned up a "glaring situation." Of five companies that had signed compliance agreements the previous year, only one, Cincinnati Advertising Products, had instituted any kind of reform. The others had ignored the agreements. "There was an amazing smugness in management's flat statements that they had done nothing," McKnight reported. One steel company had hired 80 blacks,

26. Weekly report, March 17, 1945, in Tension file, Various States, Miscellaneous, R76HR, minutes, April 11, 1945, R1HR, Legal Division, Kirk & Blum Manufacturing Co., Schaible Co., United Biscuit Co. (Streitman Co.), F. H. Lawson Co., Hearing file, R22HR, F. H. Lawson Co., Hearing file, R21HR, Cincinnati cases, summary by Bloch, n.d., in office files of Malcolm Ross, Difficult Cases file, R2HR, Washington Afro-American, March 24, 1945, in Newspaper Clippings, Box 530, all in RG 228; Chicago Defender, March 24, 1945, p. 6.

27. Weekly report, Region V, March 24, 1945, in Tension file, Various States, Miscellaneous, R76HR, RG 228.

assigned them to the heavy labor unit, and gotten rid of them within thirty days, alleging that they would not do the hard work required. The personnel manager indicated, however, that pressure from the boilermakers union had also influenced company behavior.[28]

After the hearing, the Crosley Corporation, rather than pursuing new initiatives, set out to document its assertions that white workers would quit if the company were integrated. A survey conducted for Crosley by the IBEW produced predictable results: 582 union members said they would definitely quit, 2,328 strenuously objected, 828 advised the creation of separate shifts, and only 17 expressed no objections to working with blacks. Despite the indications of the survey, some Cincinnati workers labored in integrated work places. At Stacey Manufacturing Company, a partial defense contractor, the FEPC discovered that white and black skilled men had been working side by side in structural steel, lay-out, welding, and lathe operations since early in the war. They received equal pay and shared restroom facilities. Furthermore, the white skilled, like workers in other Cincinnati plants, were recruited from Kentucky and Tennessee.[29]

The FEPC's work in Cincinnati was only marginally successful. Except for Wright Aeronautical, where the FEPC had some leverage through the armed services, the area's defense contractors and unions, though inconvenienced by the hearing, seemed otherwise unaffected. Less than a month later, a strike over the employment of 2 black youths as porters at Continental Can followed a pattern similar to previous work stoppages. Under intense pressure, the 2 voluntarily resigned, and the company refused to hire more blacks. When threatened with the issuance of USES 510s, Continental Can ceased recruiting workers through the WMC. Meanwhile, the FEPC, under constant attack in Washington, D.C., ran out of time and funds. No Cincinnati findings and directives were issued, and there was little follow-up before the Region V suboffice closed in August, 1945.[30]

Whereas Cincinnati tried to ignore the FEPC, Atlanta declared war

28. *Ibid.*

29. *Ibid.*; W. C. Lambers to G. F. Gamber, April 4, 1945, in Crosley Corp. hearing, R21HR, RG 228.

30. Carle C. Conway to Continental Can Employees, April 13, 1945, biweekly report, Region V, April 14, 1945, in Tension file, Various States, Miscellaneous, R76HR; Harold James to Will Maslow (teletype), April 14, 1945, in office files of George M. Johnson, Miscellaneous file, R3HR, RG 228; Chicago *Defender*, August 18, 1945, p. 4.

even before the Region VII office opened in November, 1943. Initially, the FEPC could not even find office space. In the past, this regional center had welcomed federal agencies and their lucrative payrolls. All of them had procured office space for white employees, usually in the central business district, and shunted their Afro-American personnel to Auburn Avenue in the black business area. The new Region VII director, Virginian A. Bruce Hunt, refused to split his office staff along racial lines, because his agency's mission and its credibility with the black community would be negated. "[We] must have a place where Negroes may work and be interviewed," Malcolm Ross told Secretary of the Treasury Henry Morganthau in an urgent telephone call from the West Coast, where Ross was chairing a hearing. He had heard that there were 1,200 square feet of unused area in the Treasury Department's Atlanta offices. The FEPC got the space, but its troubles were by no means over.[31]

With a mixed racial staff imminent, the next serious problem was toilets. Complaints from employees of the building's owner and from federal workers in the Procurement Division led local Treasury Department officials to demand segregated facilities. Some workers complained to Georgia congressman Robert Ramspeck and to city officials. Ramspeck took the matter to Regional Director Bruce Hunt. For over an hour, he objected to the interracial sharing of the same office, expressed concern that blacks might use all the toilets in the building, and worried about blacks insisting on being served in the first-floor restaurant. Ramspeck was surprised to learn that two small office buildings in downtown Atlanta had mixed personnel who used the same toilet facilities. One, the student YMCA, had a black assistant director, and the other, the United Service Organization, employed two black women, an assistant director and a secretary. A city council resolution calling upon Georgia's congressional delegation to remove the FEPC from Atlanta received no support, but the council on December 6 took note of the FEPC's race mixing: "Local people can best handle the race situation in a spirit of fairness and justice without intervention from Federal agencies." In April, 1944, another city

31. Interview with John Hope II, Washington, D.C., September 7, 1978; Malcolm Ross to Henry Morganthau (telephone), November 18, 1943, in Unarranged Correspondence, Clarence M. Mitchell file, F104FR, and Atlanta *Daily World*, November 24, 1943, in Press Clippings, Administrative Records, Region VII, both in RG 228.

council resolution applauded Senator Richard Russell's attacks on the FEPC.[32]

The complaints of Atlanta's Treasury Department employees were not appreciated in some quarters. Malcolm Ross protested to the department, which launched an investigation. To Bruce Hunt, the local complaints from federal employees were indefensible. What was needed from their supervisors, he thought, was "a little firmness." Even Jonathan Daniels, the White House counselor, was disturbed that federal employees had initiated the complaints and commented, "As we say in North Carolina, 'we are being chewed up by our own dogs.'" In its investigation, the Treasury Department found the rumors and complaints to have originated with employees of the building's owner, and it deplored the reaction to the situation shown by workers in the Procurement Division. Its own three local officials were exonerated, "having acted out of motives they considered in the best interest of their respective services."[33]

In January, more attacks came after Hunt hired a black stenographic secretary, Thelma Horton, a native of Athens, Georgia, and a graduate of Morris Brown College. The Southern Industrial Trades Association sent a letter attacking the "brazen negress" and "carpetbaggers" such as Hunt. But these phrases paled beside the rhetoric of a more accomplished race baiter, former Georgia governor Eugene Talmadge. When Hunt "introduced a flat-nosed mulatto to his office staff," Talmadge wrote in the *Statesman*, "the white girls were stunned at first" but then protested to Governor Ellis Arnall, who said he could do nothing. Then the white women painted a large sign on the rest room door that said "White Only," but this "BRAZEN LITTLE NEGRO" ignored it. Hunt even called her "Miss" and seemed "to be enjoying . . . teaching Georgia white girls a lesson." Talmadge also accused the Atlanta

32. A. Bruce Hunt to Will Maslow, November 29, 1943, Robert Ramspeck to A. Bruce Hunt, December 4, 1943, A. Bruce Hunt to William D. Hearington, December 29, 1943, Atlanta *Journal*, December 7, 1943, in Press Clippings, Administrative Records, Region VII, Chicago *Defender*, December 18, 1943, in Newspaper Clippings, Box 516, Atlanta *Constitution*, April 18, 1944, in Press Clippings, Administrative Records, Region VII, all in RG 228; telephone interview with Edward Rutledge, Croton-on-Hudson, N.Y., January 14, 1987.

33. Hunt to Hearington, December 29, 1943, in Administrative Records, Region VII, RG 228; Edwin M. Watson to Congressman Stephen Pace, December 27, 1943, in Official File 4245-G, 1943, FDRL; Lewis O. Padgett to Elmer L. Irey, January 14, 1944, in U.S. Govt., Gen., N–Z, R67HR, RG 228.

newspapers of suppressing the story. The toilet tempest finally calmed down after the building's owner installed a brand new lavatory for the sole use of the FEPC's black personnel. In the meantime, however, Hunt by one account became so exasperated that he sent to Eleanor Roosevelt memoranda drafted on toilet paper.[34]

As the FEPC's offices began operating below the Mason-Dixon Line, the personnel discovered the existence of two Souths. Region IV in the upper South comprised the Atlantic coastal states from Delaware to North Carolina, plus West Virginia. Here, the FEPC concentrated primarily on the industrialized areas around Chesapeake Bay. By January 1, 1944, 195 cases of discrimination had been pre-docketed, and only 96 more were docketed during the next six months; 160 of these were satisfactorily adjusted by June 30. Region IV's director for most of the time was the black Joseph H. B. Evans, who sported a Phi Beta Kappa key from the University of Michigan and among other New Deal assignments served as Will Alexander's administrative assistant in the Resettlement Administration before joining the FEPC. Although the upper South did not welcome the FEPC with open arms, its industrial race relations were already undergoing change.[35]

Region VII, encompassing the Deep South plus Tennessee, became an extremely difficult assignment for FEPC personnel. Regional Director Bruce Hunt was so concerned about the racial problems in that area that he consulted Atlanta *Constitution* editor Ralph McGill before taking the job. Although McGill feared that opening the Region VII office would cause a riot, Hunt decided nonetheless to accept the Atlanta assignment. A brilliant attorney whom other southerners sometimes considered abrasive, Hunt maintained a legalistic and uncompromising stand against job discrimination. Inevitably, he was in continual conflict with other federal agencies, particularly the WMC's

34. Telephone interview with Edward Rutledge, January 14, 1987; William E. Dunn to A. Bruce Hunt, February 11, 1944, in Administrative Records, Region VII, RG 228; Pittsburgh *Courier,* January 29, 1944, p. 5; *Statesman,* February 3, 1944, in Newspaper Clippings, Box 513, RG 228.

35. Personnel file, Administrative Records, Region VII, RG 228; case load activity by region, January 1–June 10, 1944, in office files of John A. Davis, Miscellaneous file, R69HR, RG 228; Greenville (S.C.) *Observer,* in Civil Rights–FEPC folder, Correspondence, 1944, Series X, Box 131, Russell Papers; Merl Reed, "FEPC and Federal Agencies," 50–54; Raymond Wolters, *Negroes and the Great Depression: The Problem of Economic Recovery* (Westport, Conn., 1970), 72.

regional, state, and area offices, most of which tried to shield defense contractors. On January 1, 1944, there were 143 cases pending in Region VII, 234 others were docketed during the next six months, and only 73 had been satisfactorily adjusted by June 30. Hunt's successor, Witherspoon Dodge, an outgoing Florida native, Congregational minister, and former Textile Workers Union of America (CIO) organizer, came to the FEPC in October, 1944, from the WPB. Dodge operated in a less confrontational manner than had Hunt and became particularly interested in the discriminatory practices of the southern shipyards and the boilermakers union. He pursued the shipyards vigorously and tried to get hearings scheduled in spring, 1945. By that time, however, the FEPC could no longer sustain the effort because of mounting troubles in Washington, D.C.[36]

In the Deep South, FEPC investigators, particularly when they were black, faced unusual problems and challenges. John Hope II, a native Atlantan who served under both Hunt and Dodge, had a complexion light enough to pass for white, and he was sometimes "mistakenly" addressed as "Mr." by whites. Yet, as he went about his tasks, fear never left him. He always traveled by car and never let locals know where he would be staying. After working awhile for the FEPC, Hope stopped calling on friends in the communities he visited for fear of compromising them. Sometimes he was followed, most clearly in "Boss" Edward Crump's Memphis, where he was told city hall watched every place he went. For Hope, his time working for the FEPC was a sobering experience in a world fighting against Nazi supremacy. Despite the hostility of southern segregated society, Hope, Hunt, Dodge, and the other dedicated workers in the Region VII office made some gains in the shipyards, in the aircraft factories of Atlanta and Nashville, and in other smaller industrial establishments. However, as Dodge pointed out in one of his final communications to the central office, "there was not a single industry in the South of which we are aware in which highly skilled Negroes were integrated to work with white laborers." Although some situations approached integra-

---

36. Interview with John Hope II; personnel file, Administrative Records, Region VII, and case load activity by region, January 1–June 10, 1944, in office files of John A. Davis, Miscellaneous file, R69HR, both in RG 228; Greenville (S.C.) *Observer*, in Civil Rights–FEPC folder, Correspondence, 1944, Series X, Box 131, Russell Papers; Merl Reed, "FEPC and Federal Agencies," 50–54; Merl Reed, "FEPC, Black Worker, and Southern Shipyards," 460–61.

tion, "very few Negroes [were] employed" therein. Wherever highly skilled blacks found jobs, the work areas were nearly all still segregated.[37]

Like the Deep South, the Southwest could scarcely be described as territory hospitable to the FEPC's work. Probably no African-Americans and few Mexican-Americans in Texas, New Mexico, and Arizona received the treatment ordinarily due citizens. During July, 1942, in a fact-finding trip to the defense industries along the Gulf Coast of Louisiana and Texas, John Beecher found that blacks were welcome only in unskilled jobs, but he made few comments on the other large minority group, the Mexican-Americans. As the number of complaints mounted, the committee in May decided to hold a July hearing on the copper industry in the Southwest, but pressure from the State Department prevented such a hearing. With the opening of the FEPC's Dallas office in August, 1943, Mexican-American problems passed to Carlos Castaneda, an educator and historian of Mexican descent who joined Region X in October, 1943, as an examiner. The black L. Virgil Williams, a Dallas native, briefly served the region's other large minority group.[38]

If Region X sometimes had faltering leadership under Leonard Brin, his successor, W. Don Ellinger, a former labor leader, was often misguided. Together, they concluded that black examiners could not function in the segregated society of the region because employers did not take these agents seriously. The two men apparently minimized the needs of black workers in eastern Texas who also had to be contacted and interviewed, for when Virgil Williams transferred to the Chicago office, Ellinger did not replace him with another race examiner. Ellinger also opposed pressuring the WMC and the USES to issue 510 reports against employers because the practice was confrontational. Yet USES 510s became a mainstay in every other FEPC re-

37. Interview with John Hope II; FEPC-VII, December 22, 1943, in Press Releases, R file, Regional Office Releases, R86HR, Witherspoon Dodge to Maceo Hubbard, December 3, 1945, in office files of Maceo W. Hubbard, To Deputy Chairman file, R7HR, Clarence Mitchell to George Johnson (telephone), February 5, 1945, in office Memoranda, M file, R1HR. RG 228.

38. Field trip to Houston, July 17–20, 1942, in Reports, 1-1, John Beecher file, R48HR, and Lawrence Cramer to Frank Fenton, June 10, 1942, in Public Relations 5, Fenton file, R45HR, both in RG 228; Lou Ella Jenkins, "The Fair Employment Practice Committee and Mexican-Americans in the Southwest" (M.A. thesis, Georgia State University, 1974), 59, 62–73.

gional office. Finally, until ordered to do otherwise, he pursued a strategy of "segregation by location," which practically gave an FEPC sanction for the establishment of segregated work places. Nevertheless, Ellinger vigorously attacked discrimination against Mexican-Americans in the oil refineries, and he sought to ease conditions for both minority groups in the Texas shipyards.[39]

With Ellinger's transfer to New Orleans' Region XIII early in 1945, Carlos Castaneda took over the Dallas office. Described as an outgoing and garrulous person, Castaneda could also become pugnacious and even intemperate when outraged over the mistreatment of Mexican-Americans. Although he spent several months investigating discrimination in the copper towns in hopes of reopening the Southwest hearing, his evidence proved inadequate and the hearing was canceled. This disappointment did not overshadow his tenure in the Southwest Region, though, for a man with Castaneda's knowledge, background, and reputation was indispensable. The tasks he undertook, successfully or otherwise, were difficult, and the FEPC benefited from his services. The hostility to the FEPC in Texas was evident in that only 89 cases of discrimination were pending on January 1, 1944, just after Castaneda arrived in Dallas. During the next six months, however, 172 were docketed. The Region X staff was able to get 138 satisfactory adjustments by June 30, 1944.[40]

On the West Coast, Region XII spanned distances as vast as the Southwest. Because of burgeoning wartime industrial growth and increases in population, it suffered from understaffing probably more than any other FEPC region. Despite numerous requests, a separate examiner was never provided for the Northwest with its shipyards, aircraft factories, and iron and steel plants. The Region XII office in San Francisco was directed by Harry Kingman, previously the general secretary of the YMCA at the University of California at Berkeley. A tall, rangy man with an outgoing personality, Kingman was a civil libertarian with long experience in minority problems in the Orient

39. Jenkins, "Fair Employment Practice Committee and Mexican-Americans," 62–73; Merl Reed, "FEPC and Federal Agencies," 52–53.
40. Ross to Smith, May 15, 1945, in Public Relations 5, S file, R44HR, and case load activity by region, January 1–June 10, 1944, in office files of John A. Davis, Miscellaneous file, R69HR, both in RG 228; Jenkins, "Fair Employment Practice Committee and Mexican-Americans," 73.

as well as in the United States. He firmly believed that civil liberties should be preserved even during wartime. The "Bill of Rights should not be mothballed, as radio commentator Walter Winchell" and others advocated, Kingman wrote Attorney General Biddle early in 1942.[41]

The West Coast went through difficult wartime racial adjustments similar to those occurring in the Midwest, including a large population influx, black and white, from the South. Racial friction and discrimination existed on the job and in the larger society. Signs proclaiming "We Serve Only White" and "We do not solicit colored Trade" appeared in Seattle area restaurants, lunch rooms, bus stations, and sandwich counters on ferry boats. The Oregon Fruit Growers Association opposed the mixing of the races and refused to let black soldiers work in the canneries. Farther south, the Poultry Producers of Central California turned away two black females who wanted jobs as egg candlers. Other employees would walk out, the association said. On January 1, 1944, 241 cases of discrimination were pending. By June 30, 385 more had been docketed, yet the regional office and its suboffice in Los Angeles were able to get satisfactory adjustments in 330 of those cases during that six-month period. By the fall of 1944, the western region led the nation in the number of discrimination charges. Under Harry Kingman's leadership, Region XII dealt with these and the numerous other problems of Mexican- and African-Americans, and after 1944, Japanese-Americans, in the copper mines, in the aircraft industry, and in government installations. By far the most troublesome and time-consuming task, however, involved the shipyards and the boilermakers union, which put skilled blacks into segregated auxiliaries subordinate to the white locals, charged regular union dues, and gave few benefits. The boilermaker problem alone took up untold hours of investigation and two hearings by the full committee. On the West Coast, as elsewhere, the FEPC worked without real power. Too often, difficult problems could

---

41. Employment of Negroes in the Northwest, n.d., Harry Kingman to Malcolm Ross, December 7, 1943, September 4, 1944, all in Unorganized Correspondence, Clarence M. Mitchell file, F104FR, Clarence R. Johnson to George M. Johnson, August 4, 1943, Memoranda to and from Clarence R. Johnson, R15HR, all in RG 228; Harry Kingman to Francis Biddle, January 15, 1942, in Correspondence, K–P, Box 2, Biddle Papers, FDRL.

not be solved. Many individuals became disillusioned with the agency, though countless others rejoiced that even this federal presence, weak as it was, existed.[42]

The FEPC's field work suffered initially because the committee underestimated the difficulty of its task, failed to recognize its importance, and was forced to rely on other agencies. After 1942, with the opening of temporary offices in New York and El Paso, no committee member doubted the importance of field work. Indeed, they battled with the WMC to retain control over their field investigators. The establishment of the DFO in the summer of 1943 finally gave the FEPC something of the investigative arm that its task required, though the size of the field staff remained small because of inadequate funding. It was a conscientious and dedicated group of people who worked long hours, carried out difficult assignments, and often met with hostility. A few faced real physical danger. Compared with agents of other investigative agencies such as the NLRB, their case load was heavy. For example, by October, 1944, the FEPC had thirty-six full-time field examiners, each with an average load of 60 cases. The case load at the NLRB was 10 to 20 per examiner. Each FEPC field examiner closed out about 10 cases each month. The DFO got about 300 to 350 new cases monthly and closed about 300, one-third being satisfactorily adjusted. The backlog of cases, however, remained relatively constant, with about 900 cases pending over a six-month period. Thus, the field offices provided a major thrust for the committee's work throughout the nation.[43]

42. Final Disposition Report, December 4, 1943, in Closed Cases–San Francisco, 12BR83, F109FR, Joy P. Davis to John A. Davis, May 13, 1944, in Tension file, Washington, Miscellaneous, R76HR, Final Disposition Report, March 23, 1944, in Closed Cases–San Francisco, 12BR291, F112FR, Los Angeles *Sentinel*, November 23, 1944, in Newspaper Clippings, Box 528, Vera Vetter to Harry Kingman, January 12, 1945, in Administrative Files, 1945, Los Angeles file, Ignacio L. Lopez to Harry Kingman, March 1, 1945, in Administrative Files, 1945, Lopez file, F103FR, Dean E. Hart to Bernard Ross, March 22, 1945, in Seattle Transit Co. file, 12BR673, F106FR, Clarence Mitchell to Malcolm Ross, October 22, 1945, in office files of Clarence M. Mitchell, Malcolm Ross file, R76HR, case load activity by region, January 1–June 10, 1944, in office files of John A. Davis, Miscellaneous file, R69HR, all in RG 228; Chicago *Defender*, April 8, 1944, p. 3; Harris, "Federal Intervention in Union Discrimination," 327; Wynn, *Afro-American and the Second World War*, 61.

43. Verbatim transcript, committee meeting, October 11, 1944, pp. 52–55, R65HR, RG 228.

8 / Other Minority Groups

Over four-fifths of the committee's work involved black Americans, but other minority groups also knew about job discrimination during the war years. In the Southwest, Mexican-Americans lived in a segregated system. Texas, for example, had a three-tiered society of Anglos, Latins (Mexicans and Mexican-Americans), and African-Americans. Latin Americans regarded themselves as Caucasians, yet in some Texas localities they had separate school systems. In Laredo, those permitted to attend the public schools with Anglos were forbidden to speak Spanish on the school grounds. On the West Coast, Japanese-Americans, already excluded from jobs, experienced additional humiliation during the hysteria after Pearl Harbor. Eventually, the entire ethnic Japanese population, nearly two-thirds of which comprised citizens, was moved inland to concentration camps. Religion also divided Americans, as Christians discriminated against Jews and Protestants against Roman Catholics. Other Christian minorities, such as Jehovah's Witnesses and Seventh Day Adventists, also ran into problems.

The Mexican-American population was concentrated in the Southwest and West, from Texas and Colorado to California. Although in the 1930s members of this group had begun moving from agricultural into industrial employment, they got the worst jobs in the lowest occupations with little mobility. In Colorado, those in war-essential industries did common labor. The same applied in New Mexico's mining industry, with over 60 percent of its workers from that ethnic group. In Texas, Mexican-Americans labored in copper mines, oil refineries, and shipyards for wages lower than Anglos received for the same work. Many of them had moved to the cities, particularly in southern California, where they also faced job discrimination. Complaints of bias in the war industries were aired at the FEPC's Los Angeles hearing. In a situation similar to the employment situation for Negroes in the South, the state employment service refused to refer Mexican-Americans to employers who did not customarily hire them. The Los Angeles riot in 1943, though less publicized than Detroit's, lasted four days and revolved around Mexican-American dissatisfaction.[1]

Besieged with complaints, the FEPC in May, 1942, voted to hold a July hearing in the Southwest on employment practices in the copper industry. The State Department, in the midst of delicate negotiations with Mexico over the *bracero* program, objected to the hearing, and Roosevelt notified the FEPC on June 23 that "for international reasons [the] public hearing should be stopped." For an explanation, he said, the FEPC could consult Sumner Welles, the assistant secretary of state. Committee members were nonplussed. Since the Southwest hearing had been announced publicly, Cramer told Welles, more harm might result from a postponement or cancellation than from keeping the scheduled date. A request to cancel the hearing came directly from the Mexican government, Welles replied. The State Department feared that disclosures of discrimination against Mexican-Americans would disrupt the Good Neighbor Policy and cause adverse reaction in Mexico. When Chairman MacLean reminded Welles that the FEPC was created as an independent agency and had never been told what to investigate, Welles pointed out that the president was head of both government bodies. Welles admitted that FDR was unaware the

---

1. Office files of George M. Johnson, Press Releases file, R4HR, and Guy T. Nunn to Will Alexander, February 26, 1942, in U.S. Govt., Social Security Board, R66HR, both in RG 228; Douglas Monroy, "Essay on Understanding the Work Experience of Mexicans in Southern California, 1900–1939," *Aztlan*, XII (1981), 60; Luis L. Arroyo, "Chicano Participation in Organized Labor: The CIO in Los Angeles, 1938–1950. An Extended Research Note," *Aztlan*, VI (1975), 279; Wynn, *Afro-American and the Second World War*, 18; Mauricio Mazon, *The Zoot-Suit Riots: The Psychology of Symbolic Annihilation* (Austin, 1984).

Southwest hearing had already been announced, but he doubted that information would have changed the president's decision.[2]

The committee on July 6 postponed the hearing, though lack of preparation would have necessitated such action even without White House interference. Nevertheless, the FEPC continued its investigation, despite complaints from the administration and congressmen. By mid-July, G. James Fleming had arrived in El Paso to open an FEPC office. Meanwhile, Cramer set out to change Roosevelt's mind. Several CIO unions wanted the hearing, field investigations had already started, and the State Department would acquiesce if the FEPC pursued the matter short of holding a hearing. Should cases involving Mexican-Americans, Cramer asked the president, be treated any differently than others?[3]

Within a few days, Fleming had opened the El Paso office in a building that housed several other war agencies, but he ran into serious trouble in the city's white section. Although he was not in charge of the office, whose personnel included two other FEPC staff people and two special consultants, local whites viewed it otherwise. MacLean, fearing somebody would "take a shot at him," was ready to order Fleming out, but Earl Dickerson strongly objected: "We might as well fold up if everything is conceded to the South." Fleming would remain, the committee decided, and Ernest Trimble was sent to head the office. Fleming, a man of distinguished appearance, with a courteous and tactful manner, later experienced other indignities during field investigations of the mining industry. In Silver City, New Mexico, the Hotel Sideplay and the Murray Hotel refused him lodging and dining room service, though he was permitted, along with white investigator Daniel Donovan, to meet with complainants in a hotel conference room.[4]

2. Memorandum, FDR to MAC, June 23, 1942, in Official File 4245-G, January–July, 1942, FDRL; verbatim transcript, committee meeting, P.M., July 6, 1942, p. 54, R63HR, RG 228; Polenberg, War and Society, 118; Jesse H. Stiller, George S. Messersmith: Diplomat of Democracy (Chapel Hill, 1987), 190–92.

3. Lawrence Cramer to the President, July 10, 1942, in Public Relations 5, FDR, R45HR, verbatim transcript, committee meeting, A.M., July 21, 1942, p. 22, R63HR, and G. James Fleming to Lawrence Cramer, July 22, 1942, in office files of Ernest G. Trimble, Unarranged Correspondence, R77HR, all in RG 228.

4. Fleming to Cramer, July 22, 1942, in office files of Ernest G. Trimble, Unarranged Correspondence, R77HR, verbatim transcript, committee meeting, A.M., July

The employment practices of the Nevada Consolidated Copper Company of Silver City, as described by complainants, were typical of the nine or more companies under investigation. Of its 2,000 employees, 60 percent were Mexican-Americans. Seven Anglo craft unions (AFL) had contracts, as did the Mine, Mill, and Smelter Workers (CIO), the last composed mostly of Mexican-Americans. There was also an independent union. Nevada Consolidated paid Mexican-Americans lower wages, refused them promotions, barred them from certain jobs in the open mine pits, such as shovel operator, driver, craftsman, mechanic, locomotive engineer, and fireman, and maintained a pay differential in favor of the Anglos among the common laborers. There was also discrimination in the quality of the segregated company housing and in the company-sponsored recreation clubs.[5]

In the middle of August, Trimble reported that the investigation was nearly complete. The evidence included at least 150 affidavits charging discrimination. Although negotiations with the companies involved went on, concessions seemed unlikely except around El Paso and Douglas, Arizona. Elsewhere, the work had been so dangerous that staff members were advised not to travel alone. Trimble, in a revealing Freudian slip, thought the situation resembled "Harlem [sic] County, Kentucky, transferred to Arizona." What he was most concerned about, though, was the future. When news of the agency's transfer to the WMC arrived at the Southwest office, their "morale dropped almost to zero for a while." Of more immediate importance, however, was the status of the Southwest hearing. An official announcement of its cancellation would have serious effects on negotiations, Trimble warned. At the Phelps-Dodge plants in El Paso and Douglas, the threat of a hearing might help the CIO get a contract that would effectively eliminate discrimination against Mexican-Americans, he continued. Without such leverage, the company would

21, 1942, p. 22, R63HR, G. James Fleming to Ernest Trimble, August 15, 1942, in office files of Ernest G. Trimble, T file, R77HR, Ernest Trimble to Lawrence Cramer, August 15, 1942, in Public Relations 5, R45HR, all in RG 228; Chicago *Defender,* August 22, 1942, p. 5.

5. Statements of Harry Hafner and Leo Ortiz, July 30, 1942, LULACS file, report by Daniel R. Donovan and Barron B. Beshoar, n.d., Unarranged folder, both in office files of Ernest G. Trimble, R77HR, RG 228.

likely make fewer concessions. Trimble suggested the delay of any announcement until his negotiations ended.[6]

While Trimble remained in El Paso, Cramer maneuvered to turn the situation around in Washington, D.C. Heeding Trimble's request for delay, he avoided any public announcement about the Southwest hearing. Meanwhile, Cramer received information that U.S. ambassador to Mexico George S. Messersmith had misinformed the State Department as to that country's attitude. From a Mexican-American, Ernest Galarza, an official in the Pan American Union, Cramer received a copy of a letter from Mexico's minister of foreign affairs, who had written Galarza that he did not oppose steps the FEPC might take to eliminate discrimination. Earlier, Ambassador Messersmith had informed Sumner Welles that the same foreign secretary believed efforts by the United States to combat racial discrimination against Mexicans, if publicized, could be harmful to their mutual relations. Messersmith had claimed not that the Mexican government had submitted any objections in writing but only that it had communicated its fears verbally, Cramer shrewdly noted, implying that the complaint may never have been made. Meanwhile, Sumner Welles, in his June 20 communication to the president, added his own flourish: "In my opinion, the holding of the proposed public hearing [in the Southwest] with testimony by both sides would be certain to result in increased ill feeling and very likely increased discrimination." Ambassador Messersmith certainly had been told by Mexican foreign minister Ezequiel Padilla that the welfare of the Mexican workers must come first. Padilla remembered the breakdown of the *bracero* program during the previous world war and the adverse effects of the jim-crow laws on Mexican workers. He also suspected that avarice, not need, motivated the demands of most American employers for more workers. Thus, there is every indication that the Roosevelt administration had a much greater interest in squelching the FEPC investigation than did the Mexicans. Roosevelt accepted Welles's evaluation and ordered the FEPC to back off. Both Milton Webster and John Brophy were justifiably suspicious. Webster believed that "objections to the hearing really came from the State Department and

6. Trimble to Cramer, August 15, 1942, in office files of Ernest G. Trimble, Unarranged folder, R77HR, and verbatim transcript, committee meeting, October 26, 1942, p. 30, R64HR, both in RG 228.

that some of the people objecting [had] some other interests rather than just offending Mexico." Brophy thought "the Mexican government was not as concerned as [were] American corporations."[7]

With Galarza's letter in hand, Cramer proposed that the committee reopen the question of a public hearing. The mining corporations had headquarters in the East. The FEPC could hold the hearing in Washington, D.C., and bear the greater expense of bringing witnesses "from way out there." The situation was so bad that something had to be done. If the committee agreed, Cramer proposed to get Welles to ascertain if the Mexican government would inform him, as it had others, that it had no objection to the hearing. Then Welles might be forced either to take some action against the companies or to object to the hearing in Washington, D.C. Either way, the FEPC could hand Welles the complaints and say it was his job thereafter, and he would be moved out of his arbitrary position. Cramer's suggestions were adopted, but they accomplished little. In November, the State Department did take up with Phelps-Dodge Refining Corporation the necessity of doing something, and two other mining companies made firm commitments to redress grievances, but the FEPC could not follow through. The administration, highly displeased with the committee, by January, 1943, had canceled practically all of the hearings. Nevertheless, the time and effort invested in preparing for the Southwest hearing was not a total loss.[8]

By July, 1943, when the New Committee took up the Southwest question, the Mexican government was declining to send laborers into the mining areas unless it received assurances that the wage differential would end. At that time, common laborers of Mexican descent received $4.90 per day, compared with the wage spread of $5.85 to $6.25 for Anglos in the same job classification. Negotiations had continued with the mining companies even after the FEPC's El Paso office closed, and Ernest Trimble reported that Phelps-Dodge, the most important mining concern, had agreed to upgrade Mexican-Americans in a particular operation where discrimination had been most blatant.

7. Sumner Welles to the President, June 20, 1942, quoted and discussed in verbatim transcript, committee meeting, October 26, 1942, pp. 30–39, R63HR, RG 228; Stiller, *George S. Messersmith*, 190–92.

8. Verbatim transcripts, committee meetings, October 26, 1942, pp. 32–39, R63HR, and November 23, 1942, p. 9, R64HR, A. Bruce Hunt and Frank Reeves to Maceo Hubbard, May 18, 1945, in office files of Maceo Hubbard, D.C. folder, R7HR, all in RG 228.

According to a WPB investigation, however, two other companies, Miami Copper Company and Inspiration Copper Company, refused to change their practices despite Mexico's threatened labor embargo.[9]

As the complaints continued, Chairman Malcolm Ross in February, 1944, had a two-hour conference with Messersmith. The ambassador renewed his objection to a hearing and indicated he would "ask the President to stop [it]." Messersmith was "still raising the same representations" about Mexican foreign minister Padilla's objections—representations that were "no more valid than . . . earlier." Ross had a plan, however, to get the ambassador overruled. In order formally to approach the State Department, the committee voted to hold a hearing. The chairman himself received a letter from the Mexican ambassador to the United States welcoming public hearings to remedy practices in the Southwest mining industry that were detrimental to Mexican workers. Indeed, he informed Ross, Mexico's secretary of foreign affairs had never opposed such hearings and supported all steps that would eliminate unjust practices. Addressed to Ross, the letter was marked "Informal" and gave the chairman permission to reveal its contents to the State Department. Then, with assurances from that department that clearance would be given, the committee instructed the staff to prepare for a hearing.[10]

Carlos Castaneda, as a special assistant to Malcolm Ross, spent several months in the copper towns during 1944 trying to pick up the pieces of the earlier investigation. Like Ross, he also pushed hard for a hearing, which the committee finally scheduled for December, 1944. A. Bruce Hunt, then an FEPC trial examiner on the West Coast, took charge of the legal preparations. There were some seventy cases against six mining concerns, but as December approached, they had not been sufficiently developed for a hearing, and Hunt recommended a postponement. By May, it was obvious that the evidence gathered by Castaneda was inadequate. Because of manpower shortages, Mexican-Americans had received promotions and upgrading to jobs previously denied them. In some cases the Mine, Mill, and Smelter Workers had successfully raised job ceilings and eliminated wage differentials. Many complainants, having gone into the armed services or taken better jobs on the West Coast, could not be reached. Finally,

9. Verbatim transcript, committee meeting, July 7, 1943, p. 96, R64HR, RG 228.
10. Verbatim transcript, committee meeting, March 4, 1944, pp. 114–22, R65HR, RG 228.

a large number of the complaints lacked merit. Hunt concluded that a hearing was not warranted.[11]

The diligence the FEPC showed in its work in the Southwest's copper mines was matched by its concern over conditions in the Texas oil refineries. An FEPC hearing in December, 1944, aired complaints of discrimination by both the Shell Oil Company and the Oil Workers International Union, charges both parties admitted. As a result, Shell made some modification in its promotion chart. Despite heated opposition from Anglos, some Mexican-Americans were promoted. Although the FEPC never achieved full acceptance of its program in the Southwest, many Mexican-Americans were determined not to return to the conditions of the prewar period. In 1948, New Mexico passed a fair employment law. Partly because of the FEPC, some Mexican-Americans got experience in better jobs and made contacts with the larger Anglo community as equals on the job market. On the West Coast, however, reports indicated that the number of complaints failed to reflect the existing level of discrimination. Apparently, Mexican-Americans, who sometimes were handicapped by language and cultural barriers and who frequently faced problems of citizenship status, were far less aggressive than blacks and did not make comparable advances during the war.[12]

The Japanese-Americans, most of whom resided on the West Coast, were destined for a different fate. Before America's entrance into the war, a few complained to the FEPC about discrimination by craft unions, by the civil service system, and by war contractors, and their problems received a brief airing at the Los Angeles hearing. Susuniu Yenari had graduated in aeronautical engineering from Los Angeles Junior College and had ranked fourth on the civil service exam, but the CSC had not called him. In May, 1941, he had applied at Lockheed Aircraft but had never heard from them either. Later, the California

11. Verbatim transcript, committee meeting, November 11, 1944, pp. 3–6, R65HR, and Hunt and Reeves to Hubbard, May 18, 1945, in office files of Maceo Hubbard, D.C. folder, R7HR, both in RG 228.

12. Clarence Mitchell to Will Maslow, February 2, 1944, in office files of George M. Johnson, C. M. Mitchell file, R3HR, Shell Oil, minutes, May 11, 1945, R1HR, Press Release, FEPC, December 20, 1944, in Press Releases, R, Typewritten Releases file, R86HR, A. Bruce Hunt to Malcolm Ross, April 10, 1946, G. Raymond Booth to Laurance I. Hewes, March 15, 1946, in office files of Malcolm Ross, Difficult Cases file, R2HR, all in RG 228; Pittsburgh *Courier*, December 30, 1944, p. 15; Jenkins, "Fair Employment Practice Committee and Mexican-Americans," 109, 121, 139.

State Employment Service could find no record of his civil service test. Lacking an essential defense job, he faced induction into the armed forces.[13]

After Pearl Harbor, the widespread belief on the West Coast that all Japanese-Americans were disloyal brought disaster to this minority group, which included first generation Issei, who were classified as aliens, and second generation Nisei, who were American-born and therefore citizens. The December 7 attack had a tremendous impact on Caucasian-Americans. The day after in Detroit, complaints from employees and calls from newspapers about Francis T. Nakahara, a Nisei who worked as a supply clerk, flooded the telephone switchboard at the Central Air Corps Procurement District. Nakahara, who had a B.S. degree in mechanical engineering from the University of California, was sent home for his own protection and later dismissed on the grounds that he would be blamed if any act of sabotage occurred. A small group of Japanese workers on the Santa Fe Railroad were evacuated from Clovis, New Mexico, to an isolated ranch. On the West Coast, ethnic Japanese eventually lost more than their jobs. Under Executive Order 9066 they were banished from the coastal areas for reasons of national security, though in Hawaii, where 35 percent of the population was Japanese in origin, such drastic measures were rejected. For a brief period, the group on the West Coast was urged to leave strategic areas voluntarily, but after March 27 the army took charge of the evacuation. By the end of August, 112,000, nearly two-thirds of whom were American citizens, had been moved to concentration camps, which were designated by less forbidding euphemisms such as "internment camps" or "war relocation centers." Italian- and German-Americans, whose ancestors had also migrated from enemy nations, escaped such treatment.[14]

13. Tom C. Clark to Frank [Mark] Ethridge, September 22, 1941, in Closed Cases Referred to Washington Office, A–E, F107FR, Saburo Kido to Lawrence Cramer, November 18, 1941, in FEP Complaints Against Unions, Boilermakers file, R35HR, and verbatim transcript, Los Angeles hearing, pp. 84–85, R18HR, p. 321, R19HR, all in RG 228.

14. Edith V. Alvord to Will Alexander, December 22, 1941, Francis Nakahara to Will Alexander, December 23, 1941, William H. Hastie to Lawrence Cramer, February 28, 1942, all in U.S. Govt., Aliens in Defense, Specific Groups, Japanese, R66HR, RG 228; Raymond Y. Okamura, "American Concentration Camps: A Cover-up Through Euphemistic Terminology," Journal of Ethnic Studies, X (1982), 96; S. Frank Miyamoto, "Forced Evacuation of the Japanese Minority During World War II," Journal of Social Issues, XXIX (1973), 12–13; Gary Y. Okihiro and Julie Sly,

In March, 1942, the CSC began to exclude ethnic Japanese citizens from jobs in the federal government. "Whenever the name of a person of Japanese origin is reached for certification on any register maintained by the Commission," stated Circular Letter 3615, a confidential communication to all district managers, "the name should not be certified . . . for appointment to any position until the case has been thoroughly investigated." For several months these restrictions went largely unnoticed, but in September, 1942, the War Relocation Authority (WRA), convinced that the establishment of normal community life was impossible in the concentration camps, instituted registration for indefinite leaves and began permitting internees, after undergoing rigorous investigations, to seek employment, education, or residence outside. Release brought the restoration of full citizenship, except freedom to return to the West Coast or to take up residence in the East Defense Command, for which a War Department clearance was required. Shortly, some Japanese-Americans began leaving the centers and entering civilian life.[15]

The WRA's indefinite leave policy sought the wide dispersal of Japanese-Americans to localities throughout the nation, except strategic coastal areas, though initially most ended up in the Mountain states near the concentration camps. When the program began in September, 1942, the WRA had already granted successful seasonal leaves to students entering college and to internees willing to perform agricultural labor. Many Japanese-Americans were professionals and businessmen, with little or no experience in farming or mining, yet their access to positions with the federal government, a major employer in the Mountain states, was blocked by the CSC. Other jobs, when available, were in unskilled, low-paying, service areas. The In-

---

"The Press, Japanese-Americans, and the Concentration Camps," *Phylon*, XLIV (1983), 69; John Culley, "World War II and a Western Town: The Internment of the Japanese Railroad Workers of Clovis, New Mexico," *Western Historical Quarterly*, XIII (1982), 51; Roger Daniels, *Concentration Camps USA: Japanese-Americans and World War II* (New York, 1971), 52–53; Harry H. L. Kitano, *Japanese-Americans: The Evolution of a Subculture* (London, 1969), 32–33; Richard Polenberg, *One Nation Divisible: Class, Race and Ethnicity in the United States Since 1938* (New York, 1980), 78–85; Bernstein, "America in War and Peace," 295–96.

15. L. A. Moyer to District Managers, Circular Letter 3615 (Confidential), March 7, 1942, and WRA, Indefinite Leave Policy, n.d., both in U.S. Govt., Aliens in Defense, Specific Groups, Japanese, R66HR, RG 228; Miyamoto, "Forced Evacuation of Japanese Minority," 29–30; Edward Spicer et al., *Impounded People: Japanese-Americans in the Relocation Centers* (Tucson, 1969), 189–95.

terior Department's Geological Survey branch in Denver had to refuse employment to Kazuyoshi Senzaki, a Nisei graduate engineer with a civil service rating. Senzaki survived by wringing clothes in a laundry. Denver's postmaster wanted to hire Thomas Okabe if his civil service status could be cleared up. With examination ratings of eighty-five and ninety, 2 other Nisei were eligible as mechanic learners. The Denver civil service office refused placement.[16]

Although the CSC denied it, the FEPC's Lawrence Cramer believed that artificial delays in conducting investigations had either been "spontaneously generated" in the field or had emanated from Washington, D.C., contributing "to the belief that Japanese-Americans should not be employed in the Civil Service." Field reports from the Denver area seemed to confirm Cramer's suspicions. His complaint on March 1, 1943, to Lawson A. Moyer, CSC executive director, brought no relaxation of the procedures, and Moyer did not schedule an investigation into the situations of the 3 Nisei about whom Cramer inquired. By this time, the CSC was already preparing new guidelines, published on March 27 in Circular Letter 3982, that listed some forty steps necessary before released Japanese-Americans could be placed. Moyer, who waited four weeks before replying to Cramer's letter, explained that the delays were caused by the tremendous wartime workloads, particularly investigations of persons already appointed. His regional directors could not possibly consider Nisei eligibles until the backlog had been reduced.[17]

The War Department, though not opposed to the employment of Japanese-Americans in private industry and in federal agencies unrelated to defense, issued a secret directive banning them from all defense activity. This action was particularly puzzling because, as Lawrence Cramer noted, there were probably a greater number of Japanese-Americans in the War Department, "right in intelligence," than in any other government agency. Yet other agencies, even those

16. Lawrence Cramer to Harold L. Ickes, Lawrence Cramer to Lawson Moyer, and Lawrence Cramer to Barron B. Beshoar, all March 1, 1943, in U.S. Govt., Aliens in Defense, Specific Groups, Japanese, R66HR, and Barron B. Beshoar to Lawrence Cramer, March 31, 1943, in office files of Malcolm Ross, Extra Copies file, R1HR, all in RG 228; Audrie Girdner and Ann Loftis, *The Great Betrayal: The Evacuation of the Japanese-Americans During World War II* (London, 1969), 339–44.

17. Cramer to Beshoar and Cramer to Moyer, both March 1, 1943, CSC Circular Letter 3982, March 27, 1943, Lawson Moyer to Lawrence Cramer, March 30, 1943, all in U.S. Govt., Aliens in Defense, Specific Groups, Japanese, R66HR, RG 228.

under the War Department, "dealing with procurement of gloves, shoes, boots, soap, and whatnot," would not have them. The secret directive often caused the mindless dismissal of useful workers from rather routine jobs far removed from sensitive information. The Fitzsimons General Hospital, a military installation near Denver, fired 6 Japanese-Americans who were citizens. When a contractor constructing the Camp Hale Ski Cantonment in Colorado advertised for "3,000 patriotic workmen," 50 young Japanese-Americans traveled the 125 miles from Denver and offered to go to the mountain site and work in construction and in grubbing the valley floor. Army engineers rejected them, and the next morning the Nisei volunteers were rounded up and placed on a bus. The driver was ordered not to let them out before reaching Denver. Camp Hale would eventually house many Nisei soldiers. An arsenal in Ogden, Utah, also discharged Japanese-Americans on orders from the army.[18]

Although the FEPC complained, the War Department, as the nation's heroic defender in a national emergency, usually was invulnerable to criticism. Instead, the FEPC tried to modify civil service practices. Both Will Maslow and George Johnson believed that the use of separate procedures in appointing Japanese-Americans was contrary to Executive Order 9346. Whereas the CSC investigated other citizens *after* their appointments, Japanese-Americans since March, 1942, had been investigated *prior* to going on duty, with no time limit for such investigations. In response to WRA complaints about this matter, the CSC issued Circular Letter 4056 in July, 1943, which set a three-week deadline on its inquiries. Regardless of the CSC's decision, however, almost any agency appointment officer who persisted in objecting to an eligible on grounds of national origin could prevent certification. Thus, three months after the issuance of 4056, twenty-two WRA cases had been under CSC review from four to six weeks, and there was still no word on the outcomes.[19]

18. Verbatim transcript, committee meeting, P.M., January 6, 1943, p. 55, R64HR, Barron B. Beshoar to Will Alexander, November 24, 1942, William Hastie to George Johnson, December 31, 1942, Beshoar to Cramer, March 31, 1943, in U.S. Govt., Aliens in Defense, Specific Groups, Japanese, R66HR, all in RG 228.

19. Earl Dickerson to Robert Patterson, March 1, 1943, in office files of Malcolm Ross, Committee Members file, R1HR, Lawrence Cramer to Robert Patterson, April 6, 1943, CSC Circular Letter 4056, August 13, 1943, Will Maslow to Stanley D. Metzger, October 16, 1943, Stanley Metzger to Will Maslow, October 23, 1943, in U.S. Govt., Aliens in Defense, Specific Groups, Japanese, R66HR, all in RG 228.

The case of T. Scott Miyakawa illustrates the dilemma that loyal Nisei faced. Born and educated in Los Angeles, he attended Cornell University along with two hometown, Caucasian classmates, and received a degree in mechanical engineering in 1928. While still in high school, Miyakawa had notified the Japanese government of his desire to become an expatriate and had received official acknowledgment of his decision. Rejected after graduation from Cornell by American corporate employers because of his race, he got a job with the New York City YMCA and stayed during the Depression until 1932, when he was hired at the New York office of the Southern Manchurian Railway, owned by Japanese corporations and their government. Until March, 1941, Miyakawa did general office work there, though he applied for federal employment without success. During this period, he earned extra money in New York doing part-time secretarial work and translations for Prince Tokugawa, chairman of the Japanese Red Cross, for a Japanese economic mission, for the Japanese Chamber of Commerce, and for Admiral Yoshida, commander of the Japanese Naval Cadet Squadron and an official guest of the U.S. government. While visiting Japan in 1934, he turned down an offer as assistant to the editor of the English-language Tokyo *Times*, and later he refused to write articles for that paper. Miyakawa did send the *Times*, without reimbursement, clippings from American newspapers and magazines for the purpose, he stated, of countering Nazi propaganda in Japan.[20]

In 1941, Miyakawa, who had begun working on a doctoral degree in sociology at Columbia University, was hired to do contract work for Marketing Analysts, Incorporated, a private firm doing confidential research for the OWI involving the analysis of Japanese political material in order to anticipate and counter Japanese propaganda among other Asiatic peoples. Miyakawa's boss, Sanford Griffith, a former major in military intelligence, was pleased with the work and recommended him to the WPB. The interviewing officer in the Non-Ferrous and Non-Metallic Minerals section approved Miyakawa and assumed he would be hired. When Miyakawa's dossier was routinely flagged at civil service, Carlton Hayward, a WPB superior who was suspicious of all Japanese, did not request a continuance of the CSC investigation, which might have cleared Miyakawa's record. Hayward also re-

20. Verbatim transcript, hearing, T. Scott Miyakawa case, February 17, 1943, R15HR, RG 228.

fused to give reasons for his action and vowed that, even with a CSC clearance, Miyakawa would face a separate loyalty inquiry because the production board handled confidential statistical material on resources. Miyakawa filed a complaint of discrimination with the FEPC, and in January, 1943, he applied for admittance to the civil service register, an action that reopened the investigation of his fitness for service.[21]

At an FEPC hearing in February, 1943, Miyakawa had strong support from two Caucasian friends from his boyhood and college days who vouched for his loyalty. One, C. S. Williams, was a Japanese expert in the OWI, and the other, A. E. Arent, was an attorney in the Department of Justice who privately acted as Miyakawa's counsel. The FEPC was able to get from the CSC an account, given confidentially and verbally, of the allegedly damaging information contained in Miyakawa's file. In addition to his prewar associations, an FBI report had focused disapprovingly on the "ultra-liberal" writings of Miyakawa's sociology professor at Columbia. The FBI had also interviewed two persons who mentioned a speech Miyakawa had made at a New York University extension class four years before Pearl Harbor in which he justified noninterference with Japan and supported that country's invasion of Manchuria. The FEPC hearing ended inconclusively, but apparently Miyakawa, despite strong testimonials in his favor, failed to pass muster at the CSC and the WPB.[22]

Besides War Department intelligence, the government service was not totally devoid of Japanese-Americans. In October, 1943, the WRA reported that 125 citizens of Japanese descent worked in several agencies, including the WMC, the WRA, the Office of Price Administration, the Labor Department, the National War Labor Board, the Central Administrative Services, the OEM, and various divisions of the Public Health Service. The WRA believed that few, however, had been appointed after Pearl Harbor. Privately, WRA officials were furious at the CSC's intrusion into the relocation process. The WRA gave each applicant an examination that required completion of a detailed questionnaire more searching than the form used by the CSC. Applicants also needed letters of recommendation from citizens in their home communities. Such testimonials would obviously have to come from

21. *Ibid.*
22. *Ibid.*

west coast Caucasians familiar with the former residents. In addition, WRA officials knew of and monitored the individuals with whom relocation applicants associated at the center, and they scrutinized work records. Each file was reviewed by the WRA's Washington, D.C., office, which could return it for further investigation. The records were then turned over to a joint board consisting of representatives of the provost marshall general's office, naval intelligence, the FBI, and the WRA. If the applicant wished to move to the Eastern or Western Defense commands, these units conducted additional investigations. After clearance by the joint board, the evacuee was released on indefinite leave. Considering the close scrutiny given Japanese-Americans before they could leave the centers, the WRA labeled the CSC investigations as entirely useless and a waste of money.[23]

Despite its unhappiness with the civil service, the WRA politely rejected an FEPC suggestion for joint action to get the practices changed. Twenty-two WRA cases already submitted to the CSC had to be settled first. Since the WRA's relocation policies were under attack from conservatives, its officials may well have been wary of working with an agency as controversial as the FEPC. By the end of 1943, the CSC's obstructionism had apparently eased, though separate investigations of Japanese-Americans continued. The FEPC received few additional complaints until Japanese-Americans began returning to the West Coast in 1945.[24]

If the WRA's indefinite leave program stiffened the CSC's resistance, it stirred near-apoplectic outbursts from some of the nation's more virulent Japanese-haters. Lieutenant General J. L. DeWitt, who oversaw the evacuation in 1942, vowed that the Japanese would not return to the West Coast. "I got 'em out of the area and into relocation centers and I want to keep them there." He warned a congressional committee against "soft sentimentality" toward them. Whether Japanese- or American-born, "you can't change a Jap by giving him a piece of paper," he testified. "A Jap's a Jap." The testimony had an effect. Read in Provo, Utah, at a union meeting called to consider a proposal to permit Nisei internees to take jobs with the Columbia Steel Company, the statement influenced the majority of the

23. Metzger to Maslow, October 23, 1943, in U.S. Govt., Aliens in Defense, Specific Groups, Japanese, R66HR, RG 228; Girdner and Loftis, *Great Betrayal*, 355–68.

24. Metzger to Maslow, October 23, 1943, U.S. Govt., Aliens in Defense, Specific Groups, Japanese, R66HR, RG 228.

members, some of whom had already opposed hiring Japanese, to vote in the negative. Columbia Steel needed 1,000 men to complete a plant vital to the war effort. The Denver *Post*, one of the region's principal dailies, also took up the crusade, urging that Japanese-Americans not be given jobs or accorded friendly treatment. Efforts by responsible leaders to persuade the *Post's* publisher, W. C. Shepherd, to moderate his attacks proved fruitless. "We are Jap haters here," he announced to government emissaries trying to explain the region's manpower needs. Every Japanese-American was disloyal, he averred, and he was "sick and tired of having them grin audaciously and sneer at him on the streets." [25]

The WRA's excellent advance preparation usually resulted in more friendship than hostility as Japanese-Americans relocated around the nation. Institutional barriers, however, sometimes were a problem. Edward Flore of Buffalo, general president of the Hotel and Restaurant Employees International Alliance and the Bartenders' League, thought that most people of Japanese descent were inclined toward domestic occupations. From this erroneous assumption he concluded that once released from the centers they would seek jobs in hotels and restaurants. Although Japanese immigrants and their offspring had been part of the American market system for several decades, they supposedly had gone through no acculturation and would, according to Flore, compete with free labor without regard to American standards of employment. Flore opposed this "invasion of industry by evacuated Japanese" and warned that his organization would not cooperate in finding job opportunities for them. [26]

In New York, the state's manpower commission at first took a surprisingly negative position toward the evacuees. In July, 1943, Regional Director Anna Rosenberg, without consulting the FEPC, made an exception to Executive Order 9346. Employers who discriminated against minorities ordinarily would be denied USES referrals, but Rosenberg declined to follow this policy when companies refused to hire Japanese-Americans. Objections from the FEPC's Edward Lawson

25. Barron B. Beshoar to Lawrence Cramer (telegram), April 14, 1943, typescript copy of front page, San Francisco *Examiner*, April 14, 1943, Barron B. Beshoar to Lawrence Cramer, July 2, 1943, U.S. Govt., Aliens in Defense, Specific Groups, Japanese, R66HR, RG 228. See also Girdner and Loftis, *Great Betrayal*, 355–68.

26. Edward Flore, editorial in *The Catering Industry Employee*, (Typescript, June, 1943, in U.S. Govt., Aliens in Defense, Specific Groups, Japanese, R66HR, RG 228); Girdner and Loftis, *Great Betrayal*, 335–55.

were futile. New York's USES offices would assist the WRA in placing the Japanese-Americans, Rosenberg promised, but treating them differently was consistent with all existing official actions, which had made them a "special group" in the eyes of employers and the public and which had directed far more drastic measures against them than against other groups.[27]

The FEPC challenged Rosenberg's interpretation of the executive order. Although the agency's field instructions counseled care in handling Japanese-American cases, the committee opposed special procedures that left the impression that group received treatment different from the treatment accorded to others. An outraged Harry Kingman believed the New York directive to be out of line with the position taken by all government agencies. In Hawaii, after the FBI investigated and rounded up those considered dangerous, the remaining Japanese-Americans were treated "just like any other citizens." On September 14, President Roosevelt stated that unless proof existed to the contrary in individual cases, Japanese-Americans should be treated as loyal citizens. The FEPC continued to insist on the right of Japanese descendants to equality of employment, and in November, Rosenberg modified New York's employment procedures manual to conform with Executive Order 9346.[28]

With the apparent acceptance of Japanese-Americans as full citizens by the manpower commission and the CSC, the FEPC could begin challenging other federal agencies. Accordingly, the General Accounting Office, investigated by the FEPC early in 1944, promised to instruct its field agencies to avoid discrimination based on national origins. The Second Service Command of the army service forces, which dismissed five ethnic Japanese, took them back after the provost marshall general's office, at the FEPC's insistence, examined the cases and found the suspensions lacked sufficient cause. By November, the War Department, apparently anticipating adverse rulings from the United States Supreme Court, began modifying its policies: in the future,

27. Edward Lawson to Francis Haas, June 24, 1943, and Anna Rosenberg to Lawrence A. Appley, September 4, 1943, in U.S. Govt., Aliens in Defense, Specific Groups, Japanese, R66HR, Francis Haas to Edward Lawson, August 2, 1943, in Procedures folder, II, F3FR, all in RG 228.

28. Verbatim transcript, committee meeting, October 2, 1943, p. 86, R64HR, Employment Procedures Manual, November 16, 1943, and Edward Lawson to Will Maslow, November 18, 1943, both in U.S. Govt., Aliens in Defense, Specific Groups, Japanese, R66HR, all in RG 228.

approval by the provost marshall general would not be required in most war plants and facilities. Then, on December 19, the Supreme Court, while unanimously upholding the legality of the 1942 evacuation, ruled in the *Endo* case that citizens of Japanese ancestry and of unquestioned loyalty could not be detained in war relocation centers. Hours earlier, the army had issued an order allowing their return, with permission, to the western seaboard.[29]

The Los Angeles *Times* predicted that "as good Americans, the great majority of Pacific Coast residents will accept, with the best grace possible to muster, the Army decree," but the paper strongly opposed it. The decision was a "grave mistake" based on snap judgment in reaction to political pressure, it claimed. The return of the evacuees would be bad for the communities, the Japanese-Americans, and the war effort, no matter how well the returnees were screened. The order was based on the fact that an enemy invasion was no longer possible, but the *Times* doubted that Californians with relatives in the armed services would welcome back these "tens of thousands of Japs with jobs and patronage and the spirit of equality." The issue raised important questions that had to be answered. With housing scarce, where would they find accommodations? Would war workers and service families be denied? "Will the Fair Employment Practices [*sic*] Committee require employers to put Japs on their payrolls, regardless of the opposition of other workers?" If they were not self-supporting, should Californians be taxed to keep them on relief?[30]

In this hostile climate, the FEPC's Region XII expected a flood of new cases. After assurances from the central office that the committee had jurisdiction because of the race matters involved, Harry Kingman in January instructed his Region XII staff to investigate all complaints and if discrimination existed, to do their best under the provisions of the executive order to eliminate it. "Because of the splendid war record of the Japanese-Americans in the armed services," it was "reason-

---

29. Clarence Mitchell to Malcolm Ross, February 4, 1944, in Office Memoranda, M file, R1HR, Final Disposition Report, October 26, 1944, in Army Service Forces, 2GR709, 751, F19FR, WRA, Relocation Division Memorandum 72, November 24, 1944, in U.S. Govt., Aliens in Defense, Specific Groups, Japanese, R66HR, and New York *Times*, December 19, 1944, and Los Angeles *Times*, December 19, 1944, both in Newspaper Clippings, Box 517, all in RG 228.

30. Los Angeles *Times*, December 19, 1944, in Newspaper Clippings, Box 517, RG 228.

able to expect employers and unions . . . [would] give returning workers a fair break." By March, 1945, it was clear, however, that Kingman's hope was not to be realized. Complaints of discrimination were reported daily. At the Production Engineering Company of Berkeley, which earlier had successfully integrated black and white employees, the workers protested when a Nisei was hired. Although the victim agreed to await the completion of an education program for the workers at the plant, the FEPC urged prompt, constructive handling of the matter and consented to a meeting with the employees. At an automobile repair business that serviced McClellan Field near Sacramento, army intelligence would not clear Frank Nagano, a mechanic with twenty-four years of experience, for work on the base. In this case, Nagano gave up and returned to the Topaz Relocation Center in central Utah. Ruby Kobata could not get a temporary appointment as junior clerk with the California State Personnel Board because of her Japanese ancestry. Unlike others, she first had to pass a civil service test. The WRA reported an organized boycott of produce grown by a Japanese-American truck farmer in the Portland area.[31]

Fortunately, the Twelfth Naval District, a large employer on the West Coast, cooperated with the FEPC. The chief of staff, Admiral H. R. Heinz, believed the Nisei were loyal and should not be molested. In April, 1945, the FEPC negotiated an agreement for joint cooperation in investigating charges of discrimination against the navy. At the discretion of the commanding officer, FEPC representatives could be present at navy investigations in order to be assured that all pertinent sources of information were developed and lines of questioning pursued. Cases would be settled by informal conferences where possible. Formal investigations would be carried out only when controversy arose. Above all, every effort would be made locally to

31. Robert Brown to Harry Kingman, December 19, 1944, Harry Kingman to Robert Brown, December 26, 1944, in Administrative Files, Correspondence with Other Offices, Robert E. Brown, Jr., F104FR, Harry Kingman, "FEPC Policy Regarding Workers of Japanese Ancestry on the West Coast," January 10, 1945, in Administrative Files, 1945, Policy, American-Japanese, F130FR, weekly report, Region XII, March 20, 1945, in Tension file, California, San Francisco, R75HR, McClellan Field, 12BR610, in Tension file, California, Sacramento, R75HR, weekly report, Region XII, March 24, 1945, in Tension file, Oregon, Portland, Focal Issues, R76HR, all in RG 228.

resolve difficult cases and avoid forwarding reports to Washington, D.C., on appeal.[32]

Within a short time, the Navy Department scuttled this arrangement and put into effect a new policy rejecting Japanese-American citizens for certification or appointment to navy establishments in the three western coastal states and Hawaii, though later Hawaii was exempted from the order. On the West Coast, instructions went out to the CSC to cease recruiting Japanese-Americans. Harry Kingman was particularly incensed because the policy applied to veterans and nonveterans alike. In view of this "most flagrant discrimination," he requested that the matter be taken up with Navy Department officials in Washington, D.C. Even on naval establishments outside the West Coast, Japanese-Americans were still subject to the investigative procedures of the CSC, a condition not required of citizens of German extraction. While the central office was looking into that problem, Kingman suggested, it might also ask the CSC to explain why, before Japanese-American citizens were appointed to governmental agencies on the West Coast, the agency had to stipulate that the job in question was not of a confidential nature or closely related to the war effort. "Someday the United States is likely to look back with shame upon its treatment of a racial minority many of whose members have proven their loyalty the hard way."[33]

The policy that so outraged Kingman had been put into effect by Admiral Chester Nimitz for "military reasons," Clarence Mitchell discovered. The basic cause went back to the navy's training program, which promoted hatred of the Japanese. Servicemen would fight the enemy better when they hated him, Mitchell was told. After returning from the Pacific war zone, however, they would not be able to distinguish between the enemy and Americans of Japanese descent and seeing Nisei working in various naval yards might lead to violence. Elsewhere, the navy permitted Japanese-Americans in all types of war work. There was no explanation for Nimitz's decision to permit Nisei veterans to work in naval installations in Hawaii, an area much

32. Twelfth Naval District Memorandum 93–45, April 10, 1945, in U.S. Govt., Aliens in Defense, Specific Groups, Japanese, R66HR, and Clarence Mitchell to Will Maslow, May 26, 1945, in Region XII, Administrative Files, 1945, Policy, American-Japanese, F103FR, both in RG 228.

33. Harry Kingman to Clarence Mitchell, May 1, 1945, in U.S. Govt., Aliens in Defense, Specific Groups, Japanese, R66HR, RG 228.

closer to the war zone. When Mitchell mentioned that an unnamed west coast naval commander (Heinz) had been favorably inclined toward Japanese-Americans, he learned that this information, if publicized, "would be rather bad for him." The FEPC failed to get Nimitz's policy reversed before Kingman left the agency in June. Indeed, the order was still in effect after the FEPC ceased doing investigative work.[34]

This saga of navy intransigence and FEPC helplessness illustrates once again how easily the agency could be frustrated. Initially, the position of all Japanese-American internees had been nearly hopeless. Once permitted to leave the camps, they faced discrimination from "patriotic" employers, war workers, and even the government. In defending members of this racial group, the FEPC embraced a cause that in some quarters was even less popular than taking up for blacks in the South. There was no question, however, that staff members did their duty to the fullest extent. Their work was particularly significant because it touched on the fundamental question of the rights of the citizen as well as on the issue of job discrimination.

Discrimination against religious minority groups also went on in every part of the nation and included every class and occupation in the private and public sectors. "[I] should like to ask if you are of Jewish nationality," wrote a medical doctor from Rutland, Vermont, to a New York City woman who in the fall of 1940 applied for a technician's position at the local hospital. "This is a very important point as the situation of a Jewish person in this community would be very unfortunate." At the University of Maryland, a psychology professor in 1944 regretted being unable to encourage a highly recommended candidate from the University of California at Berkeley to apply for a faculty position, for it would be doing the man an "injustice." Because the candidate was a Jew, he said, "the situation here would be unfavorable for his advancement." Such genteel concern, possibly genuine, seldom appeared at other levels of the employment ladder. Jewish NYA youths from the Northeast, like blacks, were flatly turned down by defense contractors, and a Jewish electrician inter-

34. Mitchell to Maslow, May 26, 1945, and Edward Rutledge to Clarence Mitchell, July 15, 1945, in Region XII, Administrative Files, 1945, Policy, American-Japanese, F103FR, and Clarence Mitchell to G. James Fleming, November 5, 1945, in U.S. Govt., Aliens in Defense, Specific Groups, Japanese, R66HR, all in RG 228.

viewing at a New Jersey shipbuilding company lost his chance after stating his name.[35]

Not surprising, Jewish groups took a keen interest in the FEPC, and a network of Jewish societies, like the black civil rights organizations, operated nationwide. To the Old Committee, Jewish leaders wrote letters and sent proposals and criticism; they also conferred with Lawrence Cramer and other staff members. The Jewish Occupational Council, for example referred cases and submitted a proposal for training Jewish youth, who traditionally chose careers outside the mechanical trades, for work in defense plants. Its executive director, Eli E. Cohen, made frequent contact with the FEPC. The council, established in 1939 by Albert Abrahamson of Bowdoin College, claimed several prominent organizations as constituents, including the American Jewish Committee, the American Jewish Congress, B'nai B'rith, the Conference on Jewish Relations, the Hebrew Sheltering & Immigrant Aid Society, the Jewish Agricultural Society, the Jewish Labor Committee, the Jewish Welfare Board, the National Council of Jewish Women, the National Refugee Service, the Union of American Hebrew Congregations, and local Jewish vocational service agencies. The American Jewish Congress, another prominent organization and one of the council's supporters, asked for copies of complaints involving nondefense industries, an area outside the committee's jurisdiction. What was surprising, Cramer agreed, at the same time noting that few such complaints existed.[36]

One of the more interested organizations, the Jewish Coordinating Committee (JCC), in which Eli Cohen was also involved, harbored hopes of becoming a semiofficial arm of the FEPC. The JCC claimed a constituency of seventy national and local organizations concerned

35. B. F. Cook, M.D., to Sarah Axelrod, October 21, 1940, in Vocational Training file, R35HR, Joseph H. B. Evans to Max Levin, October 4, 1944, in Region XII, Administrative Files, Unarranged Correspondence, 4BC373, F104FR, Prof. Weston R. Clark to Prof. Edward C. Tolman, May 23, 1944, in Closed Cases file, University of Maryland, 4BC373, F47FR, Elmer A. Habel, NYA, to Sidney Hillman, October 2, 1941, in U.S. Govt., Gen., N–Z, R67HR, and Federal Shipbuilding & Drydock Co., Predocketed Cases file, F23FR, all in RG 228.

36. Bernard Rosenberg to Lawrence Cramer, October 8, 1941, in Public Relations 5, American Jewish Congress, J. Harold Saks to Abel Berland, February 27, 1942, Eli E. Cohen to Lawrence Cramer, April 15, 1942, "Proposal for the More Effective Utilization of the Jewish Labor Supply in the National War Production Program," n.d. [April, 1942], in Public Relations 5, Jewish Occupational Council file, R45HR, all in RG 228.

with race relations. During the summer of 1942, before the transfer of the President's Committee to the manpower commission, the JCC proposed that specially deputized representatives of private agencies collect information and make follow-up contacts with companies cited by the FEPC for discrimination. It also pushed for the creation of community councils to act as representatives of the committee. All of these proposals for private assistance had to be rejected despite the FEPC's desperate need for a field staff.[37]

The JCC also wanted to stop employers from asking questions about religion and race on job application forms. Lawrence Cramer thought that "ninety percent of the time" such information was gathered for discriminatory purposes, though he cited one company that made a good argument for retaining the question on religion: the information was used for reasons of efficiency, the plant being "so big that they [could] absorb all applicants and [through selected assignment at job stations] . . . avoid isolated trouble spots." A number of companies used questions on religion, they stated, because the FBI wanted the maximum information available on each defense worker. Fairchild Aviation testified at the New York hearing that such information aided in determining character and fitness for the job. Fairchild denied that it discriminated, but USES files showed that up to September, 1941, its orders carried notations for "White Christian" applicants. At the Chicago hearing, as elsewhere, the FEPC took a strong stand against the use of questions regarding race or religion in employment applications. The action got wide publicity, and by 1944, few firms in the Midwest used such questions.[38]

During the summer of 1942, the FEPC's stand was reinforced when the WMC ordered all defense contractors to drop all mention of race and religious affiliation in their employment questionnaires. Some companies, however, continued the practice into 1945. Eastern Air Lines, Inc., and McKesson & Robbins, Inc., persisted in asking a question on religion, as did the S. H. Kress Company (church attended), Athenia Steel Company (childhood religious training), Western

37. Summary of discussion between the JCC and Lawrence Cramer, July 6, 1942, in Public Relations 5, Eli Cohen file, R45HR, RG 228.

38. *Ibid.*; summary of New York hearing, 2BC1252, Fairchild file, F15FR, John Beecher to Complainant, October 30, 1942, in Correspondence file, F4FR, Sarah Southall to Congressman Clarence Cannon, March 23, 1944, in Public Relations 5, Southall file, R45HR, RG 228.

Union Telegraph Company (national origin), Prentice-Hall, Inc. (religion and descent), and the Coca Cola Bottling Company of New York City (religion and race), which operated twenty-seven plants and had army and navy contracts. Coca Cola not only asked questions on these matters, but it placed coded references on each form (W for white, X for Christian, P for Protestant, and PR for Puerto Rican, the last with a written comment: "not too dark and no foreign accent"). There was no coded C or N for colored or Negro because blacks obviously were not even considered for employment by Coca Cola.[39]

When the candidate did not fit the company's preferred religious and ethnic profile, the recruitment process, in many cases, included an investigation. Thus, an interviewer for Grumman Aircraft Engineering Corporation, recruiting specialists in automobile electrical repair, hired a Gentile on the spot, but Carl Weisberg, interviewed at the same time, was investigated. Shortly afterward, a representative of the Retail Credit Company of Atlanta, a private firm with branches nationwide, called Mrs. Weisberg at home and asked if her husband was Jewish. John Beecher, who handled Weisberg's complaint, believed the FEPC had stumbled upon a practice with national ramifications, because several aircraft companies and possibly numerous other defense contractors used the Retail Credit Company; so also did government agencies such as the War and Navy departments, among others. Beecher's suspicions were confirmed upon his discovering that Retail Credit's investigators used standard procedures throughout the country, including queries on racial and ethnic origins and on religious preference, such as "Is he an active church goer?" Retail Credit was not a war industry, however, so there was continuous uncertainty over whether it fell within the committee's jurisdiction.[40]

In the public sector, federal departments and agencies clung to their

39. Ben T. Levin to G. James Fleming, November 17, 1943, and G. James Fleming to Will Maslow, May 25, 1944, both in 3BC225, Athena Steel Co. file, F27FR, Final Disposition Report, February 1, 1945, in 2BC1136, McKesson & Robbins file, F16FR, Final Disposition Report, September 14, 1943, in 2BC83, Eastern Air Lines file, and Final Disposition Report, November 12, 1943, in 2BC113, Coca Cola Bottling Co. file, both in F14FR, Final Disposition Report, May 24, 1945, in 2BC899, Prentice-Hall file, F18FR, and Final Disposition Report, October 1, 1943, in 2BC15, Western Union file, F21FR, all in RG 228.

40. John Beecher to Lawrence Cramer, December 4, 1942, in U.S. Govt., Application Forms, R66HR, and Charles Horn to George Johnson, November 16, 1944, in Public Relations 5, Eli Cohen file, R45HR, both in RG 228.

old questionnaires. The War Department, when approached by the FEPC about its employment applications, refused to change them. It had worked with the civil service to unify subject matter, it insisted, and such statistics were necessary so that the numbers of employees from each of the five races working in the department would be available. A declaration of race was doubly important to the Intelligence Division, the department claimed, and that arm opposed the removal of the question on race. It also professed to be disturbed at the possibility of being unable to respond to requests from "numerous Negro organizations" asking for the number of blacks employed. In July, 1942, when the FEPC again broached the subject, there was another negative reply, though the secretary of war was prepared to require war contractors to eliminate reference to race. Meanwhile, Lawrence Cramer had decided to work through the Council of Personnel Administration and the CSC. Those agencies, he thought, should join with the FEPC in recommending a presidential order to drop the offensive questions. As fall approached, the CSC prepared uniform applications acceptable to the FEPC for use by all government agencies. The War Department agreed to use the form, but it would continue to require an additional personnel history statement identifying an employee by race after a job appointment had been made.[41]

The FEPC also tried to eliminate queries about religion on government job applications. A War Department circular memorandum, for example, instructed applicants to list the church they attended and its pastor. In November, 1942, the Old Committee asked the general counsel of the WMC if these questions properly could be asked under Executive Order 8802. In the reply, the counsel set forth such difficult standards for proving discrimination as to render enforcement nearly impossible. According to his judgment, if there was no indication that the questions on religion were used for the purpose of discrimination, whether asking them constituted a violation of a statute or of the civil service rules was a matter beyond the FEPC's jurisdiction. If there was evidence that discrimination had been practiced on the basis of information obtained in the questionnaire, however, the FEPC could take steps to eliminate the questions. At the time, the War Department's

41. William Hastie to Lawrence Cramer, February 14, 1942, Lawrence Cramer to Malcolm MacLean, February 25, 1942, Lawrence Cramer to William Hastie, September 24, 1942, L. B. Swartz to Civilian Aide to Secretary of War, October 8, 1942, all in U.S. Govt., WD, A–L, R67HR, RG 228.

questionnaire was undergoing revision, and its two queries on religion were eventually eliminated without further action on the committee's part.[42]

Although the JCC must have been pleased with the changes in the employment questionnaires, it was dissatisfied with the FEPC's overall performance. In January, 1943, it submitted a long analysis and critique according to which the FEPC was in trouble because of the agency's newness, size, and small constituency, which constituted "only a portion of our citizenry." The FEPC also handled mostly "critical situations" and usually ended up "on the spot" whenever it took "remedial responsibility." It lacked "well-defined authority" and "its present techniques in some instances simply serve[d] to crystallize hostility against its purpose and its operations." The JCC recommended that the FEPC continue to pursue the goals outlined in Executive Order 8802 but that it take a "basic approach . . . less dependent upon public exposure" and use the older "Federal establishments" to further its efforts. The FEPC needed to carry out its goals with a "definitely established plan" as well. The committee should avoid public hearings as a primary procedure, employing them only to "secure ultimate redress." The JCC's wish list generally included most of the things the FEPC itself had already done or planned to do if it could be funded and independent, including prompt, nationwide investigations with a large staff and "adequate public relations." Finally, the JCC preferred paid committee members instead of volunteers.[43]

This rather pompous and presumptuous document, which reached the FEPC in the midst of hearing cancellations, committee resignations, and attacks from all quarters, must have been less than welcome, particularly because the JCC's opposition to hearings mirrored the thinking of the FEPC's severest administration and southern critics. There is no record of a committee or staff response, but Walter White of the NAACP reacted strongly. In the absence of important sanctions, including the power to assess penalties such as fines and imprisonment, the FEPC used public hearings but only as a last resort, White told the JCC. The President's Committee had held only

42. Office of General Counsel, WMC, to Lawrence Cramer, November 19, 1942, in Rulings I, R63HR, RG 228.

43. Memorandum, Jewish Coordinating Committee to FEPC, January 22, 1943, in Public Relations 5, Eli Cohen file, R45HR, RG 228.

five hearings involving forty-six employers and unions, yet only two hundred of the more than seven thousand complaints received had been aired. In view of the limited staff and budget, White found in this record "a most extraordinary restraint"—a restraint that had led many to believe the committee had been "too timorous in its activities." Working patiently with employers and unions, however, the FEPC had been most successful in a number of instances, one of the reasons for its success being the power of public exposure through hearings. Believing he had to speak frankly, White warned the JCC that "you are treading on very thin ice when on behalf of one of the two minorities which have suffered the most from discrimination you propose that the one sanction the Committee possesses be practically taken away from it." [44]

With the creation of the New Committee in June, 1943, the JCC submitted another list of recommendations. These again stressed the need to clarify the role of private agencies as evidence-gathering bodies. In effect, Jewish leaders sought from the New Committee the kind of semiofficial role for private groups that the Old Committee refused. As to hearings, however, Walter White's message apparently had been heeded. The JCC called for additional hearings in more localities, with better preparation and more conclusive evidence. To this end, it urged the FEPC to delegate the responsibility for preliminary screening of complaints to appropriate private agencies by appointing them as temporary special representatives chosen because of their familiarity with local conditions. Private committees of fair employment practice should also be established to take part in the investigative function. It thought the FEPC should encourage local groups to form metropolitan councils and then give them access to confidential case information. This type of partnership never materialized, though Will Maslow, the director of field operations, apparently met frequently with Jewish leaders. In November, 1943, he prepared a list of organizations affiliated with the JCC and advised the FEPC's regional directors to establish close and friendly relations with them. The JCC's wish for local "FEP Committees" or councils came true in many areas, but these bodies became so numerous that the committee asked them to choose a different name. Although they were "extremely

44. Walter White to Sidney Hollander, January 30, 1943, in Public Relations 5, NAACP file, R45HR, RG 228.

valuable for forming public opinion," the FEPC feared their use of its name would cause confusion.[45]

Jewish groups and organizations, like those of the black community, cooperated enthusiastically with the FEPC, but their hopes for official participation far exceeded anything the blacks proposed. What is curious, whereas Jewish leaders clearly understood the importance of maintaining confidentiality in their own fact-gathering activities, they seemed not to appreciate that a federal agency would have to be even more circumspect with such information. The FEPC had to operate with trained staff members and established procedures to guide their conduct. The JCC somehow failed to understand that government agencies could not take the chance that investigations might be carried out by untutored individuals from private organizations or by private zealots who, under the imprimatur of an official agency, might turn such activities into witch hunts. In view of the superb FEPC investigative work in El Paso and the South in 1942, it is also difficult to understand the JCC's constant criticism of this aspect of the agency's performance, unless the work of Eugene Davidson is taken into account. A Howard University Law School graduate who had failed to pass the bar examination, Davidson came to the FEPC as an investigator in 1941 on the recommendation of Walter White. He did poor staff work in preparing for the hearings both in Los Angeles and in New York and was eventually given a title and an obscure assignment as assistant director of field operations under Will Maslow and Clarence Mitchell. Referenced in some of the correspondence from Jewish leaders, Davidson's performance may have inspired their repeated criticism of FEPC investigations.[46]

45. "Proposal of the Coordinating Committee of Jewish Organizations Dealing with Employment Discrimination in War Industries," June 22, 1943, in Public Relations 5, Eli Cohen file, R45HR, Will Maslow to All Regional Directors, November, 1943, Region XII, Administrative Files, Unarranged Correspondence, Maslow-Policy, F104FR, Will Maslow to Ben F. Levin, December 18, 1943, in Public Relations 5, American Jewish Congress file, R45HR, and verbatim transcript, committee meeting, July 26, 1943, p. 147, R64HR, all in RG 228.

46. Verbatim transcript, committee meeting, July 6, 1942, R63HR, verbatim transcript, Los Angeles hearing, October 21, 1941, p. 479, R19HR, Lawrence Cramer to Eugene Davidson, October 23, 1941, Eugene Davidson to Lawrence Cramer, October 25, 1941, Region XII, Closed Cases, A–E, F107FR, and Rosenberg to Cramer, October 10, 1941, in Public Relations 5, American Jewish Congress file, R45HR, all in RG 228; Lawrence D. Hogan, A Black National News Service: The Associated Negro Press and Claude Barnett, 1919–1945 (London, c. 1984), 93.

The committee throughout its existence handled many complaints about religious prejudice. Nearly four-fifths of these cases were in the Northeast, 57 percent in New York State (Region II). Most involved a company's refusal to hire Jews or the reluctance of private recruiting agencies to refer Jews to employers. A few complainants reported discriminatory working conditions and the denial of upgrading. Occasionally, discrimination against other religious minorities occurred. When the American Jewish Congress investigated a blind advertisement for a "Protestant" bookkeeper or stenographer that appeared in a Riverside, New Jersey, newspaper, it found that the Florence Thread Mill, which had placed the advertisement, discriminated against Catholics. Over a five-month period, about half of the religious cases handled in Region II were satisfactorily adjusted, 20 percent were withdrawn by the complainants or dropped by the FEPC because of insufficient evidence, and the remainder could not be processed for technical reasons or because the FEPC lacked jurisdiction.[47]

Despite the satisfactory adjustment of many religious complaints, the problem of religious discrimination persisted. In May, 1944, the New York *Times*, which had itself earlier had to be persuaded to cease carrying classified advertisements specifying an employer's religious preference, deplored such prejudice. Imprints such as *Jew* or *Hebrew*, stamped or penciled on job applications, set Jews apart as surely as the arm bands that the Nazis compelled them to wear, the *Times* noted. Nevertheless, as the war ended and the manpower shortages eased, religious discrimination in hiring increased, according to the National Community Relations Advisory Council, a Jewish organization. War veterans were affected with the same frequency as nonveterans. In fifteen leading cities with 80 percent of the Jewish population, discriminatory help-wanted advertisements had on the average decreased by March, 1946, compared with the previous March. But in five of those cities, there was a 145 percent rise in such notices, and in seven, complaints to Jewish organizations increased by 37 percent. Private employment agencies, by discouraging Jewish registrations, maintaining separate files for Jews, asking employers for their religious preferences, and refusing to solicit openings for Jews, were a major

47. "Status of Jewish Complaints, July 1 to November 27, 1943" (Typescript, n.d., in office files of Marjorie M. Lawson, Statistical Reports re: Jewish Complaints, R70HR), and Madeline Bachrach to Fleming, n.d. [November, 1943], in 3BC296, Florence Thread Mill file, F27FR, both in RG 228.

source of the problem, according to the council. In New York and New Jersey, however, where state antidiscrimination laws existed, only 2 of the 107 agencies visited were using registration forms with references to religion. Outside New York and New Jersey, 89 percent did so. The council concluded that antibias legislation did succeed in reducing discrimination.[48]

Jewish leaders spent untold hours preparing memoranda and communicating with the FEPC, and their organizations provided research data, complaints, witnesses, and a variety of services. Many of those who worked in the FEPC offices were Jews. Their national network of organizations and groups, like those of the black community, could be relied on to rally behind the FEPC with letters, telegrams, petitions, or other forms of support. The blacks and the Jews, one with numbers and resolve, the other with political influence and resources, both well organized, became the main legs of FEPC support. These relationships greatly benefited both the agency and its clients.

The FEPC also got involved with religious groups whose Sabbatarian faith required the avoidance of work on Saturdays, such as Jews and Seventh Day Adventists. As Congress in the fall of 1941 debated a bill providing for a six-day work week, a Seventh Day Adventist wrote the president that his promotion to inspector in an aircraft plant had been denied because of his creed. His supervisors were reluctant to train anyone who would not work on Saturdays. The FEPC, which made a basic distinction between refusing to employ someone because of creed and refusing to grant a favor because of it, found no discrimination if the worker was employed on the same terms as others. As complaints from Sabbatarians continued, a War Department administrative memorandum in September, 1942, announced a policy that the FEPC labeled "sound and enlightened." It permitted absence from work during certain holy days and suggested scheduling to provide substitute work time. Where such arrangements were impossible, the absence would be charged against accumulated annual leave, if any existed, or otherwise be recorded as leave without pay with no prejudice.[49]

48. Survey of Employment Discrimination, National Community Relations Advisory Council, n.d. [Spring, 1946], in office files of Malcolm Ross, West Coast Material file, R2HR, and New York *Times*, May 3, 1944, in Newspaper Clippings, Editorials, both in RG 228.

49. Evert F. Holcomb to the President, October 9, 1941, Lawrence Cramer to Evert Holcomb, November 15, 1941, both in Region XII, Closed Cases Referred to

But complaints against the government by Sabbatarians continued, partly because some supervisors took an uncompromising stand on Saturday work. In a few cases, agencies required job applicants to disclose religious affiliation and then refused to hire Sabbatarians. One WPB official polled his employees and fired the Seventh Day Adventists. A worker with accumulated annual leave time was still dismissed for refusing to work on Saturdays. So was another, even though the eight hours he missed on Saturday were made up by his working nights. The FEPC maintained that employers who refused to make special arrangements for certain religious groups did not violate Executive Order 8802 as long as all groups were treated the same. Nevertheless, good personnel management, the committee believed, ought to permit the exercise of innocent preferences if the war effort was not hindered thereby.[50]

Particularly troublesome were Navy Department practices. Although paragraph two of the department's statement advised supervisors to make every effort to permit the observance of commemorative and religious holidays, the policy as a whole was much less conciliatory in tone than the policy of the War Department. Individual units executed it, so some Sabbatarians received satisfaction and others did not. The FEPC's appeal to the CSC for a uniform policy was passed on to the White House, which concluded that a formal regulation was not needed.[51]

Meanwhile, the FEPC was bombarded with complaints about the navy by Seventh Day Adventists and by the Religious Liberty League. "If the officials of Naval Establishments outside of Washington were paying attention to paragraph 2 of the instruction . . . we would not be bothering either the Navy Department or you," wrote a furious league official to Lawrence Cramer. Loyal workers, some with considerable longevity, faced penalties and threats of dishonorable discharges for absences on Saturdays from the Brooklyn Navy Yard, and

Washington Office, F–N, F107FR, and Administrative Memorandum 55, September 10, 1942, in U.S. Govt., Policies and Agreements Between Govt. Agencies & FEPC file, R67HR, all in RG 228.

50. Lawrence Cramer to Lawson Moyer, December 12, 1942, in U.S. Govt., Seventh Day Adventists file, R67HR, RG 228.

51. Secretary of the Navy to All Shore Establishments, December 17, 1942, and Harry B. Mitchell to Mark Ethridge, February 12, 1943, both in U.S. Govt., Seventh Day Adventists file, R67HR, RG 228; Davis, "Non-discrimination in the Federal Agencies," 68–69.

there were similar complaints about other navy yards. The official blamed the willfulness of local naval officers, "men with a little authority who are as mean as men can well be and intend evidently to magnify their offices." While the navy harped about absenteeism, he pointed out, "Seventh Day Adventists . . . never [had] a hangover on Monday morning or Sunday morning or any other morning" and were "anxious to serve the Government," except for their greater obligation to God. "Personally I am getting a little tired of . . . fighting for religious freedom and having it denied by some petty executive officers," he wrote.[52]

The Navy Department apparently tired of the controversy and the persistent nagging of the FEPC. In July, 1943, the navy secretary sent a new order to all shore establishments. Although repeating nearly verbatim the existing policy statement, he made his emphasis perfectly clear. "It appears [from the large number of appeals from disciplinary action] that the Navy's intention that such cases should be given sympathetic consideration was not clearly understood by all levels of supervision." The statement that "as a matter of policy every effort should be made to permit the observance of commemorative and religious holidays" was intended to be the navy's policy. The secretary directed management to assure itself of employees' sincere religious scruples and then to find ways and means to satisfy their needs. Shortly thereafter, the committee, somewhat belatedly it would seem, took the position that an employer's failure, even at considerable inconvenience, to arrange work schedules to permit absences on days workers could not perform secular duties was a violation of Executive Order 9346.[53]

Sabbatarian complaints came less frequently after the secretary's directive, but the FEPC had other thorny problems over the Jehovah's Witnesses, many of whom were working in defense plants when the United States entered the war. Inclined toward zealousness, most were eager to discuss publicly their religious beliefs, and a few did so at the work place. After Pearl Harbor, however, a new patriotism in the war

52. Cross Reference Sheets folder, n.d., Secretary of the Navy to All Shore Establishments, December 17, 1942, Herbert H. Votaw to Lawrence Cramer, March 7, 1943, all in U.S. Govt., Seventh Day Adventists file, R67HR, RG 228.

53. Secretary of the Navy to All Shore Establishments, July 6, 1943, in U.S. Govt., Seventh Day Adventists file, R67HR, and summary of committee actions, September 14, 1943, R1HR, both in RG 228.

plants stressed reverence for the flag and for the nation. Rallies and other public observances followed, including pledging allegiance to the flag, standing and singing the national anthem, and buying war bonds. Out of conscience, Jehovah's Witnesses usually refused to participate in one or all of these activities while still insisting on their loyalty as citizens. Such behavior, tolerated or ignored before Pearl Harbor, appeared disloyal afterward. At the Columbus Steel Company plant in Pittsburg, California, most of the twenty-nine men in Foreman Earl M. Hood's department, all members of the Steel Workers Organizing Committee (CIO), signed a petition vowing not to work with him after he skipped a flag-honoring ceremony. Hood, who had fifteen years of continuous service at the Columbus plant, was fired in April, 1942. At the Pittsburgh Plate Glass Company in Clarksburg, West Virginia, the Dow Chemical plant in Midland, Michigan, and the Northwest Mining and Exchange Company of Clearfield, Pennsylvania, Witnesses who committed similar offenses were discharged at the insistence of the other workers.[54]

Earl Hood could not salute the flag, he explained, after praying "Thy Kingdom Come" and believing that the "Kingdom will be established on this earth in a short time." According to the dictionary, he said, "'to salute' means to 'bow down'; and I could not bow down to any flag representing a man-made government, and not the one I was praying for." He had broken no law or company rule and could not understand what all the fuss was about. At Pittsburgh Plate Glass, Clyde Seders was dismissed for refusing to stand during the playing of the national anthem. So were six other Witnesses who stayed away from a flag-raising ceremony to avoid trouble. The company acted at the insistence of their fellow workers and the unions. Although the general superintendent regarded the Witnesses as disloyal, he did not report their conduct to the FBI. The companies, admitting they were productive workers, were willing to take back the Witnesses if the other employees agreed.[55]

Jehovah's Witnesses presented the FEPC with problems of more-

54. Earl M. Hood to Benjamin F. Fairless, May 26, 1942, in Region XII, Closed Cases Referred to Washington Office, A–E, F107FR, and verbatim transcript, committee meeting, P.M., November 23, 1942, R64HR, both in RG 228.

55. Hood to Fairless, May 26, 1942, in Region XII, Closed Cases Referred to Washington Office, F107FR, and summary of hearing, December 21, 1942, in office files of Malcolm Ross, Committee Members file, R1HR, both in RG 228.

than-ordinary difficulty because, as Lawrence Cramer put it, "patriotism [as a motive for discrimination] is a more respectable emotion than race or religious prejudice." In addition, the beliefs of the Witnesses were so individualized that establishing the existence of a uniform religious creed was virtually impossible. All Jehovah's Witnesses, according to the Watchtower Bible and Tract Society, were considered to be duly ordained ministers of the gospel from the standpoint of the Bible. As to buying bonds, objecting conscientiously, saluting the flag, or even participating in war itself, "this Society [did] not tell people what to do," because it did not engage in worldly controversies. Its members, many of whom were in civilian public service camps or in prison over difficulties with their draft boards, tended, however, to be classified by Selective Service as ordained ministers or conscientious objectors.[56]

After considerable study, the staff of the Old Committee concluded that Earl Hood's dismissal violated Executive Order 8802. Columbia Steel agreed to reinstate him at his previous rank in a new plant near Provo, Utah. For the other Jehovah's Witnesses, the FEPC held hearings and found that the companies discriminated because of creed. The discharged men were to be reinstated on the same jobs, with the full seniority rights they would have had had they been employed during the entire period. The wisdom of this judgment was later verified when the United States Supreme Court in 1943 declared that the Jehovah's Witnesses were not seditious.[57]

The New Committee had much less sympathy for the Witnesses, particularly since some complainants themselves were charged with disrupting the work place by arguing and preaching. The FEPC could not be a civil liberties committee, observed Sarah Southall. There was ample testimony in one case that "this bird was around on company time talking to everybody about joining Jehovah Witnesses, and how

56. Watchtower Bible and Tract Society to FEPC, April 2, June 11, 1943, in U.S. Govt., Religious Discrimination file, R67HR, and address by Lawrence Cramer, March 11, 1943, in General Correspondence, Public Relations, A–C, R47HR, all in RG 228.

57. Lawrence Cramer to John A. Stephens, April 23, 1943, Lawrence Cramer to Earl Hood, May 20, June 16, 1943, Earl Hood to Lawrence Cramer, June 12, 1943, in Region XII, Closed Cases Referred to Washington Office, A–E, F107FR, summary of hearings, December 21, 1942, in office files of Malcolm Ross, Committee Members file, R1HR, all in RG 228; M. James Penton, *Apocalypse Delayed: The Story of Jehovah's Witnesses* (Toronto, 1985), 133, 136.

he didn't believe in the war." If the FEPC ordered a Witness rehired, she warned, the finding had to make it clear that religion must be kept out of work relationships. Committee member Charles Horn, the Minneapolis munitions maker, employed Witnesses and thought they were no trouble, but, he indicated, it was "almost impossible to keep plant discipline where they start[ed] preaching." Nothing could be done about it, however, for there was "no way of muzzling them."[58]

For the New Committee, the issue ultimately boiled down to creed. If an employer punished or dismissed a Witness over the refusal to buy bonds, for example, was this discrimination based on creed, considering the fact that the Watchtower Bible and Tract Society had never formalized any position on the issue? Trial Examiner Ernest Trimble believed that such punishment or dismissal was discriminatory. It was general knowledge that most Witnesses, basing their actions on the Bible, did have religious scruples against such purchases, and thus dismissing them from their defense jobs violated Executive Order 9346. Because buying bonds was a voluntary matter, Sarah Southall agreed. So did Charles Houston, but he wondered if the committee should reach out into areas where its jurisdiction became shadowy. The committee finally took the position that the FEPC would decline jurisdiction in cases based on religious grounds unless it was shown that the action taken by an employer violated some established precept of a creed.[59]

The FEPC's efforts to eliminate discrimination against "the other minority groups" aroused almost as much controversy as its activities on behalf of Afro-Americans. Sometimes opposition came from the highest and most powerful in government, including the State, War, and Navy departments, the civil service, and the administration itself. Undoubtedly, the Old Committee's dogged pursuit of a hearing on behalf of Mexican-Americans in the Southwest irritated the administration and some departments almost as much as the FEPC's efforts on behalf of the black railroad firemen upset southerners. The agency

58. Verbatim transcripts, committee meetings, January 15, 1944, p. 49, March 18, 1944, p. 9, R65HR, committee meeting, January 15, 1944, hearing, Midland, Mich., September 26, 1943, hearing, Clearfield, Pa., October 1, 1943, in Documents file, R1HR, all in RG 228.

59. Ernest Trimble to George Johnson, February 15, 1944, in U.S. Govt., Seventh Day Adventists file, R67HR, confidential memorandum, George Johnson to Staff, March 4, 1944, in Administrative Files, Confidential Memoranda, V, F49FR, and minutes, committee meetings, March 4, 18, 1944, R1HR, all in RG 228.

also took up the cause of the despised Japanese-Americans, who throughout much of their ordeal could not get relief even in the courts. The FEPC's moves against religious discrimination seemed to arouse less opposition, yet almost everything the agency did proved to be unpopular, except with the minorities who benefited. All of these matters had deep roots in the nation's heritage: religious persecution or forms thereof, the rights of the citizen in wartime, and second-class citizenship because of ethnic origin. The FEPC's involvement with the problems of the other minority groups, in addition to those of blacks, gave a hitherto unappreciated breadth and depth to its activities.

9 / The Boilermaker Challenge on the West Coast

As the defense program got under way in the late 1930s, the nation's shipyards, some lying dormant since World War I, took on new life. By 1942, a trickle of lucrative defense contracts became a flood as old shipyards reactivated and new ones sprang up on the shores of the two oceans, the Gulf of Mexico, the Great Lakes, and the major rivers. Overseeing this vast expansion were various federal procurement agencies, especially the army, the navy, and the Maritime Commission. The navy was the largest contractor, with 50 percent of the total, followed by the army with 41 percent, and the Maritime Commission and Treasury Department with 9 percent. They built plants for lease to private operators and in some cases ran them outright. At the height of the war, the shipbuilders employed over a million and a half workers, hundreds of thousands on the West Coast alone.[1]

Although the CIO's Industrial Union of Marine and Ship Workers of America made inroads in the east coast shipyards, the AFL's Metal Trades Department and its various regional councils dominated most

---

1. Memorandum, War Manpower Commission to All Regional Representatives, November 14, 1942, in Minutes and Decisions of Regional and Essential Committees, Region VII, RG 211; FEPC, *Final Report* (Washington, D.C., 1947), 122–23; Herbert R. Northrup, "Negroes in a War Industry: The Case of Shipbuilding," *Journal of Business*, XVI (1943), 160–172. Statistics on employment and contracts appear throughout the records of the FEPC (RG 228) and those of the WMC (RG 211), located in the National Archives and its branch at East Point, Ga.

of the industry nationwide, including the west coast shipyards, which were concentrated around the four major population centers, Los Angeles, San Francisco, Portland-Vancouver, and Seattle. All the AFL metal trades, including the boilermakers, machinists, electrical workers, and plumbers and steamfitters, either excluded African-Americans from membership or shunted them into powerless auxiliary unions. Through closed-shop agreements with the shipyards, the metal trades initially kept all blacks out of skilled defense jobs. After FDR intervened in 1941, the machinists began giving out work permits without union membership, and other AFL unions later adopted this practice.[2]

The boilermakers union, chartered by the AFL in 1897 after a merger of two skilled unions, created the Helpers division in 1902. Joining the AFL Metal Trades Department in 1908, the International Brotherhood of Boilermakers, Iron Shipbuilders, and Helpers (IBB) elected as president J. A. Franklin, who served until 1944, when the union had over half a million members. At their 1937 convention, the IBB decided to create auxiliary unions for blacks. These bodies, subservient to the local white lodges, lacked such basic union functions as membership in the international, the right to have independent business agents and grievance committees, the universal transfer of members seeking employment in other cities, and the right to advance in status. Auxiliary members paid full premiums for inferior insurance coverage, could not train apprentices, and might be penalized for such misconduct as intoxication, a punishment not applied to whites. In order to work in the shipyards, blacks had to join the boilermaker auxiliaries and pay dues. By 1943, particularly on the West Coast, union practices brought on black protest and litigation that ultimately undermined the IBB's racist practices and left the status of the master agreement with the shipyards in doubt.[3]

2. Analysis of the discrimination against Negroes in the boilermaker union, in office files of George M. Johnson, Herbert R. Northrup file, R4HR, RG 228; Northrup, "Negroes in War Industry," 164–66.

3. Northrup, "Negroes in War Industry," 164–66; Gary M. Fink (ed.), *Labor Unions* (Westport, Conn., 1977), 35–37. See also Herbert Hill, *Black Labor and the American Legal System: Race, Work, and the Law* (Washington, D.C., 1977), 185–208. Some of the primary material on the boilermakers, the black shipyard workers, and the shipbuilders, particularly the West Coast hearings, was generated in FEPC headquarters and appears in R13HR to R16HR. Other information of great importance appears in the office files of various administrators at the central office (R1HR, R3HR–R5HR, R8HR, R48HR), in the indispensable verbatim transcripts of the com-

Complaints of boilermaker discrimination surfaced before Pearl Harbor. In the fall of 1941 the Portland Urban League reported that blacks could not get training or defense jobs in the shipyards. IBB Local 72 explained that blacks already had jobs as janitors but failed to mention that they earned only $0.77 an hour, whereas skilled white boilermakers received $1.25. The international union staunchly denied discrimination. "Somebody has been misleading" the FEPC, union president Franklin wrote William Green in September, 1941. Blacks could be admitted "through a colored auxiliary lodge." Since twelve of them existed, he said, the charge of discrimination was unjustified. Franklin's assurances seemed to ring true. Oakland Local 39, under his orders, referred Afro-Americans and even instructed one shipbuilder of his duty to employ them. Even Clarence Johnson, the OPM's black investigator on the West Coast, was impressed. Over 50 blacks received permits, many in such skilled occupations as chipper and caulker, Johnson wrote Robert Weaver early in 1942. Although Local 39 anticipated some difficulty in clearing black riggers, the question would be settled at a union meeting, and opposition would not be tolerated. Local 39 would shortly establish an auxiliary union, Johnson reported. Already signed up for membership were 42 men.[4]

This official acceptance of auxiliary unions as late as 1942 pointed up an important difference between Weaver's Negro Training Branch and the FEPC, which sought to match a trained applicant with a skilled job, regardless of race. Clarence Johnson apparently anticipated no problems with the auxiliaries as long as blacks could get work. Weaver was pleased simply that black workers had received clearances, and he immediately issued a press release. But there was another side to the boilermaker operations. In summer, 1942, Welders & Burners Local 681 in Oakland elected a slate of liberal officers and began admitting blacks as regular members. When Franklin refused to recognize the new officers, citing Negro membership as a violation of the

---

mittee meetings (R64HR–R65HR), and in the field records of Region XII (F103FR, F104FR, F107FR, F108FR), all in RG 228. For an account based primarily on the material in R13HR to R16HR, see Harris, "Federal Intervention in Union Discrimination," 325–47.

4. J. A. Franklin to William Green, September 23, 1941, and D. N. Umthank to Mark Ethridge, August 19, 1941, both in Early Complaints file, R15HR, and Clarence R. Johnson to Robert Weaver, January 21, 1942, in Region XII, Closed Cases, IBB Local 6 file, 12UR76, F108FR, all in RG 228.

IBB constitution, Local 681 appealed in vain to the WPB. Since the matter involved internal union affairs, the FEPC lacked jurisdiction. All of Oakland's black shipyard workers had to join the auxiliaries. There were other problems connected to the auxiliaries. By July, 1943, IBB A-26 in Oakland had nearly $51,000 in its treasury, owned $15,031 in real estate, $4,468 in furniture and fixtures, an automobile worth $1,761, and $6,000 in war bonds. In August, Daniel Donovan reported that salaried officers receiving $125 a week opposed the attempts of more militant members to fight the boilermakers' auxiliary system. C. L. Dellums, the prominent vice-president of the BSCP, feared A-26's officers and their opulence would discredit the entire black community.[5]

By 1942 the west coast shipyards faced serious labor shortages. The various Kaiser enterprises, stretching from the Bay Area to Portland and Vancouver, began seeking workers across the country, and New York City, with its light industries, a relative dearth of war contracts, and high unemployment, became a prime recruiting area. In September, 1942, the USES was asked to supply 20,000 laborers and prospective trainees. Initially, Kaiser industries asked for white applicants only, because the AFL metal trades would not accept blacks. According to John Brophy, Kaiser, through a back-door agreement, had signed a closed-shop contract with the machinists and the boilermakers before any manpower arrived on the scene. Since no representation election was ever held, the CIO challenged the agreement. In Portland, IBB Local 72 and its business agent, Tom Ray, refused to certify any more blacks for skilled shipyard work. Ray also insisted on segregated work crews. In response, USES offices in New York City, as well as in Little Rock and Bartlesville, Oklahoma, refused Kaiser's "white only" requests. Tom Ray came under considerable pressure from the shipyards, the government, and the IBB itself, which later tried to remove him. Dr. Richard Steiner, a Unitarian pastor and member of Portland's Selective Service Appeal Board, proposed inducting into the army skilled men who enjoyed occupational deferment: "As long as skilled

5. Daniel Donovan to George M. Johnson, August 5, 1943, in Legal Division, Donovan-Wolfe Investigation file, R15HR, Audit Report, Boilermakers, OPM press release, January 23, 1942, in General file, R14HR, Eugene Davidson to George M. Johnson, August 24, 1942, Rhue Brown to George M. Johnson, October 20, 1942, in Region XII, Closed Cases Referred to Washington Office, A–E, F107FR, all in RG 228; Pittsburgh *Courier*, January 31, 1942, p. 1.

Negroes are not doing skilled work . . . the men now employed in the highly-paid crafts cannot be regarded as 'irreplaceable.' . . . Men who don't want to work with Negroes may have to get out and fight." At Steiner's insistence, some men apparently lost their deferments. When Kaiser promised to work out agreements with the metal trades unions, USES referrals resumed. By October, 1942, a total of 2,893 workers, of whom 192, or 6.5 percent, were black, many with skilled backgrounds, had arrived in the Portland area. But boilermaker opposition continued. A year later, as Kaiser agents recruited in Philadelphia, IBB locals continued to oppose the importation of Afro-Americans, though they were not strangers to the Portland-Vancouver scene. In 1943, a total of 11,316 blacks resided there, 1.7 percent of the total population of 660,583. By July of that year, about 6,000 were employed in the area.[6]

For black workers, the Portland experience was disheartening. On the train west, Kaiser representatives arranged to upgrade many whites, but blacks remained as laborers. One angry man left the train in South Dakota and returned to New York. Many other skilled blacks upon arrival in Portland refused labor assignments. Eventually 18 became welder trainees over Tom Ray's opposition. Nevertheless, by February, 1943, nearly half of the 495 Negro arrivals at Kaiser's Swan Island shipyard in Vancouver had left because of discrimination. Kaiser also had a housing shortage that did not ease until June. At first blacks blamed the company for the discrimination, but the main problem was IBB Local 72, which in May received a USES #510 reprimand for refusing to accept black referrals and clear them for employment.[7]

6. Verbatim transcript, committee meeting, P.M., July 6, 1943, p. 98, R64HR, testimony, November 15, 1943, Portland hearing, R13HR, Portland *Oregonian*, October 10, 1942, in Records of George M. Johnson, Boilermakers file, R5HR, Edward Lawson to Robert Weaver, September 21, 26, 1942, Clarence R. Johnson to Robert Weaver, October 12, 1942, in Legal Division, Boilermakers, General file, R14HR, Edward Lawson to Robert Weaver, September 22, 1942, Clarence R. Johnson to Lawson, October 12, 1942, in Oregon Shipbuilding Co., Predocketed II, F24FR, George M. Johnson to A. L. Nickerson, June 30, 1943, in Region XII, Administrative Files, 1943–44, H file, F103FR, and Will Maslow to George M. Johnson, October 5, 1943, in office files of George M. Johnson, Maslow file, R3HR, testimony, November 15–16, 1943, Portland hearing, Exhibits file, R13HR, all in RG 228; Menefee, *Assignment: U.S.A.*, 25.

7. Malcolm Ross to Francis Haas, July 29, 1943, in Official Memoranda, R file, R1HR, Walter R. Carrington, Chairman, Grievance Committee, to Portland WMC, February 17, 1943, Edgar Kaiser to Lawrence Cramer (telegram), May 22, 1943, in

Boilermaker practices at Kaiser's Richmond yard also created problems. Black shipyard workers, who eventually would comprise 13 percent of the labor force of the Bay Area's four leading shipbuilders, responded by forming the Bay Area Council Against Discrimination in the fall of 1942. But IBB Local 513 refused to cooperate even with the WMC, which then set up an Area Advisory Committee on Discrimination, headed by prominent jurist Sylvan J. Lazarus. By January, 1943, Judge Lazarus, after using every means to discover the facts, reported his complete frustration as union representatives remained inaccessible. His committee charged discrimination. In May, Local 513 committed a new outrage. With 5,000 openings for welders, welder trainees, and helpers at Richmond, the union and its auxiliary, A-36, virtually excluded additional blacks from certification. Business Agent H. E. Patten, with jurisdiction over 60 percent of the shipyard jobs, believed the two unions had already accepted "their fair share of Negroes." If they took any more blacks, Patten claimed, there was a danger of race riots in the yards.[8]

Besides the Bay Area Council, several organizations of black workers were already challenging the boilermakers. The San Francisco Committee Against Segregation and Discrimination, led by Joseph James, president of the NAACP–San Francisco, began distributing handbills addressed "TO ALL DEMOCRATIC WORKERS." They charged IBB Local 6 with being a "dictatorial big shop who [sic] controls your organization," and asked leadingly, "Sounds like a Nazi 'labor front,' doesn't it?" In Los Angeles another protest group, the Shipyard Workers Committee for Equal Participation, became active, picketing Auxiliary 32 of IBB Local 92 and refusing to pay dues. They also complained to the WLB and President Roosevelt. When Local 92 ordered blacks removed from the production lines, the Shipyard Workers Committee switched tactics, called off the picketing, discontinued

Legal Division, Evidentiary Material file, R15HR, Clarence R. Johnson to Robert Weaver, October 12, 1942, and USES 510, May 27, 1943, both in Legal Division, Boilermakers, General file, R14HR, all in RG 228.

8. USES 510, May 22, 1943, in Region XII, Administrative Files, 1943–44, WMC–Sam Kagel file, F103FR, and press release, Bay Area Council Against Discrimination, February, 1943, in office files of George M. Johnson, Press Releases, R4HR, both in RG 228; Albert S. Broussard, "Strange Territory, Familiar Leadership: The Impact of World War II on San Francisco's Black Community," *California History*, LXV (1986), 22.

the no-dues campaign, and urged black workers to pay under written protest registered with the United States government. The dismissals continued, however, and the California Shipbuilding Corporation (Calship) refused to issue termination papers stating that the cause for leaving was union trouble. Without such papers, black workers could be fined and penalized under wartime antistrike legislation. On July 22, Walter E. Williams, president of the Los Angeles group and a member of the CIO Anti-discrimination Committee, telegraphed the FEPC of the "fast approaching" danger of a race riot. Williams' rhetoric and timing in the wake of the recent riots in Detroit seemed astute. He ended his message with a request for an FEPC hearing. In December, 1942, blacks in Portland formed the Shipyard Negro Organization for Victory, challenged the boilermakers in the Oregon courts, and formed a delegation to present their grievances directly to the FEPC in Washington, D.C.[9]

The Old Committee, by then deeply preoccupied with its own survival, kept abreast of the emerging shipyard crisis by correspondence and information provided by Weaver's WMC staff. When the New Committee met on July 6, it ordered an immediate investigation and sent two special representatives, Daniel Donovan, a field investigator, and James H. Wolfe, chief justice of the Utah Supreme Court, to the West Coast. What is curious, the two men spent most of their time in the Los Angeles area, interviewing and gathering statistical material. Their joint report concentrated on background information and slighted current events and analysis, and it seemed to have been pre-

9. Verbatim transcript, committee meeting, July 26, 1943, p. 70, R64HR, Handbill, TO ALL DEMOCRATIC WORKERS, n.d., Handbill, ATTENTION BOILERMAKERS, May 22, 1943, in San Francisco Committee Against Segregation and Discrimination, Region XII, Closed Cases–San Francisco, IBB Local 6 file, 12UR76, F108FR, news sheet, News from the Bay Area Council Against Discrimination, June 1943, and two other news sheets, in office files of George M. Johnson, Press Releases, R4HR; "Petition in Support of Application for Adjustment of Membership Rights in Local #92, Los Angeles, Cal.," June 3, 1943, in Legal Division, Memoranda to & from Clarence R. Johnson, R15HR, Walter Williams to WLB, June 14, 1943, Walter Williams to the President, July 14, 1943, Walter Williams to FEPC (telegrams), July 22, August 30, 1943, Walter Williams to FEPC, August 2, 1943, Reginald Norris to George M. Johnson, August 20, 1943, in Legal Division, Shipyard Workers Committee for Equal Participation file, George M. Johnson to Harry Kingman, August 3, 1943, in Legal Division, Memoranda to & from Harry Kingman, all in R14HR, Ross to Haas, July 29, 1943, in Official Memoranda, R file, R1HR, all in RG 228; Arroyo, "Chicano Participation in Organized Labor," 292.

pared by Wolfe the jurist rather than by Donovan the seasoned investigator. It added little to the committee's grasp of the situation and satisfied neither Monsignor Haas nor John Brophy, both of whom criticized it. More pertinent were Donovan's own written and telephoned messages reporting discrimination by several unions, including the boilermakers, the laborers, the steamfitters, and the painters. An alarming situation was developing. About 8,000 dues-paying blacks belonging to IBB auxiliaries were in rebellion, Donovan warned, and a movement was underway to stop paying dues. The boilermaker reply was "no dues—no job." Such an impasse could seriously hamper war production.[10]

In dealing with the crisis, the FEPC decided on direct negotiations with the boilermakers union and the shipbuilders. When the IBB suggested that Donovan and Wolfe stop at its national headquarters in Kansas City, however, the WMC's Clarence Johnson was opposed. He thought the FEPC would have the psychological edge if it could bring the international leaders to Washington, D.C., rather than go to them. The FEPC eventually did neither, setting up instead an August 20 conference in San Francisco. Assistant Deputy Chairman George Johnson hurried west to represent the committee, while Chairman Haas tried to work out something through the AFL. Several hundred workers had been discharged for refusing to pay dues to the IBB auxiliaries, he wired John P. Frey, president of the Metal Trades Department, and the situation was serious. Haas recognized the AFL's inability to interfere with boilermaker autonomy, but the metal trades unions were parties to the master agreement with the shipbuilders, and the FEPC needed Frey's assistance. Frey gave no encouragement and took offense at the tone of portions of Haas's telegram, which he pronounced "peremptory."[11]

10. Daniel R. Donovan and James H. Wolfe, "Report of the Investigation of the Discharge of Negro Workers for Non-Payment of Dues Because of Segregation into Auxiliaries," July 16–28, 1943, in Legal Division, Extra Copies file, George M. Johnson to Kingman, August 3, 1943, in Legal Division, Memoranda to & from Harry Kingman, R14HR, verbatim transcript, committee meeting, July 26, 1943, p. 70, R64HR, Daniel Donovan to George M. Johnson, July 5, 1943, George Johnson to Francis Haas, July 19, 1943, in Official Memoranda, J file, R1HR, James Wolfe and Daniel Donovan to Francis Haas (telegram), July 25, 1943, in Legal Division, Donovan-Wolfe Investigation, R15HR, all in RG 228; Pittsburgh Courier, July 31, 1943, p. 14; and Harris, "Federal Intervention in Union Discrimination," 331–32.

11. Clarence R. Johnson to George M. Johnson, August 4, 1943, in Legal Division, Memoranda to & from Clarence R. Johnson, R15HR, and Francis Haas to John

The San Francisco conference on August 20 included representatives from several shipbuilders, from the IBB and its locals, and from the WPB and the FEPC. Kaiser attorney Harry M. Morton appeared to dominate the session, spending considerable time arguing that management did not discriminate. Under the master agreement, the shipyards were legally obligated to employ only those union members in good standing and to discharge others. The FEPC lacked authority to order management to stop releasing workers, because such action would abrogate the contract, Morton maintained. If blacks worked without paying dues, white worker morale would be undermined. Management's sole concern, according to their attorney, was getting people to work. It would accept any procedure for reinstatement not in conflict with the master agreement.[12]

Morton's vigorous presentation left labor unhappy and clearly on the defensive. Something had gone wrong at the meeting, wrote Emmett Kelly, an AFL advisor to the WPB. He blamed the FEPC's regional director Harry Kingman, who as chairman of the meeting "did not give a complete picture." The result was a "confused view by all participants." What Kelly labeled as confusion, however, was the clear impression at the conference that labor was the major cause of discrimination. This impression was not true, Kelly insisted. Discharging for nonpayment of dues was a colorblind act that affected workers equally, regardless of race. In their report to IBB headquarters, Kelly and the other union men also attacked the FEPC's George Johnson. He blocked progress at the conference, IBB vice-president Charles MacGowan informed Haas in a telephone conversation. MacGowan insisted that the boilermakers did not discriminate; they had not asked for the discharge of blacks rather than whites. Then Haas explained again the central problem that the IBB refused to acknowledge. It was not the discharge of blacks. The issue was rather the auxiliaries, which deprived them of full union membership.[13]

P. Frey, August 16, 1943, in Legal Division, Extra Copies file, R14HR, both in RG 228.

12. George M. Johnson to Francis Haas, August 24, 1943, in Official Memoranda, J file, R1HR, RG 228.

13. Emmett Kelly to Joseph D. Keenan, August 22, 1943, in Records of George M. Johnson, Boilermakers file, R4HR, and Charles MacGowan to Francis Haas (telephone), August 21, 1943, in office files of George M. Johnson, Father Haas Memoranda file, R3HR, both in RG 228.

Although Haas and Johnson believed further meetings would be futile, they agreed to union demands for another session the following day, this one without management participation. At that meeting, the IBB's Thomas Crowe charged that the FEPC and the other agencies were being misled by Communists, who were stirring up complaints. Crowe expected the FEPC to order disgruntled blacks both to pay their dues without reservation and to accept on faith promises of a satisfactory settlement. George Johnson's insistence that there could be no waiver of the complaints infuriated the union men, who charged that he was "merely protecting" the black workers "and not seeking a definite solution." Kelly wrote, "Were he to recommend the payment of dues and return to work, I am certain that the situation would clear itself." [14]

With nothing settled on the West Coast, the President's Committee on August 28 decided to hold hearings in Portland and Los Angeles on the complaints against the boilermakers union. Harry Kingman and Bay Area blacks took strong exception to the decision to bypass San Francisco, but George Johnson explained that the Bay Area situation was very complex and the complaints could not be processed in time. Some auxiliaries, such as A-26 in Oakland, for example, had wide but undefined autonomy. A hearing later in San Francisco was a possibility, he wrote. Having decided to go after the union, however, Monsignor Haas then changed his mind. It would "be wiser," he thought, if the hearings included the companies that had discharged black workers and were a party to the complaint. George Johnson agreed, even though in previous cases he had advised blacks to direct their grievances against the union alone. Milton Webster understood that the general complaint was against the boilermakers, but Haas was emphatic. It had to be both "the companies and the union," because "the end thing complained about [was] the discharge of Negroes by the company." [15]

14. Charles MacGowan to Francis Haas, George Johnson to Francis Haas, Francis Haas to Joseph Keenen, and Francis Haas to Charles MacGowan (all telephone), August 20, 1943, in office files of George M. Johnson, Father Haas Memoranda, R3HR, Kelly to Keenan, August 22, 1943, in Records of George M. Johnson, Boilermakers file, R4HR, George Johnson to Haas, August 24, 1943, in Official Memoranda, J file, R1HR, all in RG 228.

15. David E. Slevin to FEPC (telegram), October 15, 1943, and George Johnson to Harry Kingman, October 16, 1943, both in Legal Division, San Francisco Bay Area

The committee accepted Haas's view, but the decision to charge both the shipbuilders and the unions, questioned at the time, may have been a serious blunder. As events would show, it infuriated management, particularly the Kaisers, and it created a rift between central and the Region XII office, which had received excellent cooperation from Kaiser industries and had justifiably blamed the boilermakers. The decision also left Haas and his deputy, Malcolm Ross, both veterans of the NLRB, vulnerable to charges of favoritism to organized labor. No doubt Haas and his legal advisers wanted to keep the shipbuilders in the case, hoping that the FEPC, which lacked jurisdiction over internal union affairs, might be able to chip away at boilermaker discrimination through the companies and the master agreement. It was a questionable tactic, despite the fact that management's hands were far from clean. Even Kaiser, more enlightened than most shipbuilders, exhibited serious blind spots in the recruitment and treatment of black workers.[16]

Evidence unavailable to Haas and the committee reveals that Edgar Kaiser made secret deals with the boilermakers that discriminated against black workers. Three days after the San Francisco conference, Emmett Kelly met in Portland with Kaiser and Tom Ray of IBB Local 72 to settle certain matters that Kaiser believed lacked clarity and hampered production. First, Kaiser accepted Ray's decision not to refer black welder trainees to the Oregon Shipbuilding and Swan Island yards. The former, particularly, was an older, permanent facility likely to have peacetime employment. Black workers found jobs primarily in the new Vancouver yard, a temporary structure created during the war emergency. Because of Oregon Shipbuilding's permanence, blacks already suspected that white workers at that yard had the more desirable jobs. Second, Ray, who had refused to establish an auxiliary union in Portland, promised to permit blacks from IBB Auxiliary 32 in Vancouver to take shipyard jobs in his territory, which would pro-

file, R15HR, George M. Johnson to Elizabeth H. Holland, December 16, 1942, in Region XII, Closed Cases Referred to Washington Office, F–N, F107FR, verbatim transcripts, committee meetings, August 28, 1943, pp. 138–40, October 18, 1943, p. 71, R64HR, all in RG 228.

16. Verbatim transcript, committee meeting, August 28, 1943, p. 138, R64HR, RG 228; Herbert Corey, "Portrait of a Man with a Mission," *Nation's Business*, XXXII (February, 1944), 36.

vide Kaiser's Portland yard with more workers. Ray would so inform the state vocational education director of this decision. Opposed to racial mixing, Ray nonetheless accepted an integrated work force. Under this agreement, Kelly believed, the situation at Portland might be "temporarily cleared," though he predicted flareups at any time. Kaiser was pleased and felt the settlement would last. Despite the fact that the secret deal affected black trainees adversely, Kaiser later denied charges filed by the Shipyard Negro Organization for Victory that his company discriminated. It was clear, Kaiser wrote Haas, that the blacks were attacking the company to get at the union.[17]

In preparation for the West Coast hearing on November 15, FEPC investigators worked frantically to document old complaints and a flood of new ones. Special attorneys assisted the FEPC's Legal Division in organizing and briefing the presentation. In addition, chapters of the Lawyers Guild in San Francisco and Los Angeles volunteered assistance. Although not a court of law, the hearing had to follow acceptable procedures, for the shipbuilders employed some of the sharpest legal talent in the nation. Malcolm Ross instructed the FEPC's attorneys to avoid leaving the impression that the committee had any intention of disturbing the master agreement. On the contrary, it sought equal opportunity within whatever framework labor and management chose to operate. Mindful of an upcoming IBB convention at the end of December, Ross believed that charges or rumors of FEPC intrusion into internal union affairs could bring undesirable results. Instead, the committee should concentrate on a public display of the facts, he thought, so there would be real issues for the IBB convention to consider.[18]

At the Portland hearing, the FEPC presented a case that stressed boilermaker discrimination, though the shipbuilders were also charged. The opening statement of Special Counsel Marvin C. Har-

17. Emmett Kelly to Joseph Keenan, August 26, 1943, in Reports, N–Z, R48HR, Edgar Kaiser to Francis Haas, August 28, September 2, 1943, in Kaiser Co. file, Clarence Mitchell to George Johnson, October 23, 1943, in Boilermakers, General file, Legal Division, R14HR, all in RG 228.

18. Verbatim transcript, committee meeting, October 18, 1943, pp. 76, 79, R64HR, Malcolm Ross to Bartley C. Crum, October 13, 1943, in Public Relations 5, R42HR, and Benjamin Dreyfus to George Johnson, October 15, 1943, in Memoranda to & from Benjamin Dreyfus, R15HR, all in RG 228. Letters and memoranda documenting the intense preparation for the hearings appear in various folders throughout R14HR and R15HR, RG 228.

rison recalled the boilermaker union convention of 1908, which had approved a ritual restricting membership to whites, their rejection in 1920 of a proposal to extend union rights and benefits to blacks, and the adoption in 1937 of the auxiliary system presently operating in the shipyards. The boilermakers, however, were not of one mind, Harrison noted. Lodge 204 in Honolulu wanted to remove the word *white* from the ritual, and Lodge 349 in Newport News proposed black membership with full bargaining rights. Herbert Northrup, a labor relations scholar and author of a book on black workers and unions, labeled IBB policies governing boilermaker auxiliary lodges the worst he had ever seen. The testimony of black workers was mixed. Although some faulted the company for its handling and classification of black recruits and for the racism of some of the white supervisors, one black witness cited a welding supervisor named Hunt, who after being reprimanded for saying "as long as I am superintendent . . . you will not work alongside of white men" put his black workers on regular welding. Most black witnesses attacked the boilermakers for blocking welder training and for establishing auxiliaries that denied full union membership.[19]

After company attorneys explained that management could not violate the collective bargaining agreement without committing an unfair labor practice, Edgar Kaiser described his 1942 recruitment efforts and his problems with the boilermakers union. Under close questioning from Milton Webster, Kaiser acknowledged that "ill-founded rumors" of a "terrible influx of large numbers of colored" alarmed whites in the Portland area until he met with civic and business leaders and got their support. He admitted his company did a poor job in classifying the new workers. That there was a large percentage of whites who also came on the train as laborers ameliorated this fault, he believed. He was aware, too, that the actions of the supervisory personnel sometimes appeared discriminatory, but, he explained, whites were not used to working and mixing with blacks. When Milton Webster asked about Way 6, called the "dogwatch," where six crews of black welders worked under white leadmen, Kaiser avoided a direct answer. He denied emphatically, however, the existence of segregated gangs with black foremen and pointed out that 80

19. Testimony, Raymond L. Gee, Robert Rhone, Herbert Northrup, Marvin Harrison, *et al.*, November 15–16, 1943, Portland hearing, R13HR, RG 228.

percent of his black employees labored in nonsegregated situations. Although he described his attempts to work with Tom Ray and Local 72 during the recruitment activities in 1942, he did not mention the secret deal on welder training made with Ray the previous September.[20]

As for Tom Ray, the fortunes of that slippery operator were in decline as he attended the Portland hearing and used that forum to launch an attack against the IBB and its aging president, J. A. Franklin, who had boycotted the proceedings. Ray had accumulated real power as Local 72 grew from a prewar group of 175 to a wartime giant with over 50,000 dues-paying members. By various accounts, he had controlled from 50 to 65 percent of the 92,000 to 95,000 jobs in Kaiser's Portland shipbuilding empire. He had been featured by the Portland *Oregonian* in flattering articles. As defense contracts and well-paying jobs had expanded and enriched the membership, Ray and Local 72 had constructed a "magnificent building," referred to derisively by blacks as the "Boilermakers' Marble Palace." According to the *Boilermaker's Journal*, it housed not only the union's business offices, but a "spacious auditorium . . . and in the downstairs six fine modern bowling allies [sic]" for the enjoyment of the members. In addition, the union had a $200,000 building fund and $645,000 in war bonds. During Kaiser's 1942 labor recruitment drive, Ray had traveled to New York to deal, usually heavy-handedly, with the powerful in government and business. Piqued over an unfriendly article in the New York *PM*, he had abruptly returned to Portland to brood over the threat of an integrated work force, particularly blacks and white women, and to turn down black applicants for union certification, ejecting from his "palace" those who had come in person.[21]

Late in 1942, Ray had ignored an order from the IBB president to set up an auxiliary union for blacks. Franklin responded by chartering a new white lodge in Vancouver, Local 401, which he ran from international headquarters through a former Ray lieutenant, Homer Par-

---

20. Testimony, Edgar Kaiser, November 16, 1943, Portland hearing, R13HR, RG 228.

21. Testimony, Edgar Kaiser, William Johnson, Dr. J. James Clow, Charles W. Robinson, November 15–16, 1943, Portland hearing, R13HR, and Portland *Oregonian*, October 8, 9, 1942, in Records of George M. Johnson, Boilermakers file, R5HR, all in RG 228.

rish. Shortly thereafter, an auxiliary union, A-32, was chartered and placed under Local 401's tutelage. It was blacks from A-32 that Ray had permitted into his jurisdiction during his secret September meeting with Edgar Kaiser. At the time of the Portland hearing, Local 401 still had no elected officers or local governance. Meanwhile, Franklin and the IBB had proceeded against Ray by setting up a "Board of 21" to govern Local 72. Ray, apparently still very much in command, then established his own auxiliary, appointed a black Portland attorney as its business agent, and persuaded the Board of 21 to lend $5,000 as start-up money. The new auxiliary's September application to the IBB for a charter was denied, however. By early November, Ray was in Kansas City defending himself from charges of creating dissension: after having refused to establish an auxiliary and after he knew one was established at Vancouver, he had instigated a campaign to set one up in Portland contrary to an agreement and understanding with the IBB. Ray was ordered to show cause why he should not be stripped of his offices and expelled. During this meeting, conducted by the IBB's executive committee, Ray walked out; he later appealed to the Oregon courts.[22]

At the Portland hearing, Ray, who attended but did not testify, was portrayed as the essence of good will and brotherhood. Through his attorney, he expressed his complete accord with the letter and spirit of the executive order and with the principle of economic opportunity for all. Ray and Lodge 72 had "actually appropriated money and done everything to proceed toward unionization," but the IBB had refused and nullified this action, argued the lawyer. Nevertheless, he continued, Ray was prepared to sponsor for blacks in the area all the rights and economic opportunities possible under the IBB constitution. The FEPC's Boris Shishkin then read into the record excerpts from the *Oregon Journal* that reported an earlier statement Ray had made to the boilermakers' executive committee: "Ray said he also would rekindle the race-discrimination issue when he returned to Portland. He declared that the practice of Henry J. Kaiser in bringing in Negro workers in wholesale lots is leading to a 'serious situation.'" Asked to comment, Ray's attorney, acknowledging the reliability of the reporter

22. Testimony, Leland Tanner, Charles W. Robison, William Johnson, November 15–16, 1943, Portland hearing, R13HR, RG 228.

who wrote the story, responded weakly that he did not hear Ray say anything like that.[23]

The hearing adjourned in Portland and resumed on November 19 in Los Angeles, where the committee heard complaints against both the shipbuilders and the boilermakers union. Introduced into the record at the beginning was a statement from the National Lawyers Guild that called trade unions "bulwarks of democracy when democratically conducted" but charged that their discriminatory activity "imperils democracy, impedes the war effort, and must be eliminated." In line with this theme, Shishkin, the AFL representative on the committee, noted that racial discrimination in America was a major pivot of Japan's propaganda in Southeast Asia and the East Indies. The Japanese used the issue to impress the conquered people there with the righteousness of their cause. Clearly, discrimination had the "inevitable effect of giving aid and comfort to the enemy."[24]

Witnesses accused Western Pipe and Steel Company and the boilermakers union of keeping the work force mostly white for as long as possible. As blacks became more numerous, the company denied upgrading beyond a certain point. Consolidated, another large shipyard, had received several USES 510 citations for discrimination. Both Consolidated Steel Corporation and Western Pipe defended the sanctity of the master contract and denied discrimination. They admitted dismissing workers from both races who were not in good standing with the union but noted a larger percentage of the dismissals involved whites. What was interesting, dismissed blacks generally supported unionization and protested their exclusion from full union activity, whereas white workers, who received most of the benefits, often opposed the union and demanded releases to avoid paying union dues of any kind. The CIO's Walter Williams, president of the Shipyard Workers Committee for Equal Participation, lauded Calship for its mixed work crews and the good relationship between blacks and their supervisors, though he was critical in some instances of the shipbuilder's upgrading policies. Williams charged in his testimony that it was IBB Local 92 that discriminated. When the company called for workers, Local 92 filled the quota first from its white membership and gave

23. Testimony, Charles W. Robison, November 16, 1943, Portland hearing, R13HR, RG 228.

24. Los Angeles National Lawyers Guild to FEPC, and statement by Boris Shishkin, November 19, 1943, both in Los Angeles hearing, R16HR, RG 228.

the jobs left over to blacks in its auxiliary, A-35. Consequently, blacks did not get a fair share of the work.[25]

When the West Coast hearings ended on November 20, the committee and staff hurried back to Washington, D.C., to study the record and issue findings and directives as quickly as possible. In the meantime the tension between angry blacks and the IBB locals mounted. In the San Francisco area, the boilermakers, who for over a year had allowed blacks to work in the shipyards without joining the auxiliary, suddenly, in obvious defiance of the FEPC, began ordering dismissals. Local 6 sent Marinship Corporation a list of 600 who refused to join A-41. Most of those were protesting against the auxiliary, Harry Kingman reported in a telephone call to central on November 23. Attempts to halt the union's action were futile. Local 6's membership, consisting primarily of white southerners, was adamant: blacks could not work without paying union dues. Kingman should advise them to pay their dues under protest, pending further investigation, the central office counseled, and so inform Marinship. On the basis of that action, the men should not be discharged. In response to the IBB dismissals, the San Francisco Committee Against Segregation and Discrimination, following a well-thought-out plan, called a mass meeting on November 24 at the First AME Zion Church. The assembly voted to resist joining a "phony [auxiliary] union that isn't a union." At the shipyard, 31 blacks who reported for work failed to find their time cards. The following morning, 1,500 massed at the company gates in an orderly, dignified demonstration against the jim-crow auxiliary, but Marinship, despite Kingman's appeal, decided to honor the master agreement.[26]

IBB Local 6, having ignored the FEPC, also turned a deaf ear to the WMC, which requested restraint in the face of an acute manpower shortage that already seriously threatened production. The FEPC and

25. Testimony, Walter E. Williams, Antonia Williams, Christopher C. Kemp, Samuel Gill, John Rooney, November 19, 1943, Los Angeles hearing, Western Pipe and Steel, R16HR, RG 228.

26. Will Maslow to Malcolm Ross, November 23, 1943, in office files of George M. Johnson, Will Maslow, R3HR, Harry Kingman to Malcolm Ross (telegram), November 25, 1943, Clarence M. Mitchell, press release, November 29, 1943, quoted in Theodore Jones to Will Maslow, January 11, 1944, in Region XII, Administrative Files, Unarranged Correspondence, F104FR, mass meeting, November 24, 1943, in Region XII, Closed Cases, A–F, IBB Local 6 file, F108FR, San Francisco Committee Against Discrimination, Report on Auxiliary Situation, December 21, 1943, in Legal Division, IBB General file, R14HR, RG 228.

its sister agencies were powerless to alter the practices of either the company or the union. Fortunately, the San Francisco Committee and its president, Joseph James, were pursuing another alternative. Having hired attorneys, they succeeded on November 29 in getting from the federal district court a temporary order restraining company and union from further action. The discharged men had to be rehired pending a hearing. Since Marinship accepted the order, most of the blacks could return directly to the yards. By early December the temporary restraining order was extended to the IBB unions at Bethlehem Steel Company and Moore Dry Dock Company. The Marin County Superior Court applied the injunction to IBB Local 6 and Shipfitters Local 9.[27]

With boilermaker rancor increasing and with the arguments in federal court scheduled for December 13, the committee staff prepared its findings and directives on the West Coast hearings in record time. On December 9, the FEPC labeled the auxiliary system discriminatory and illegal. The IBB, through the policies and practices imposed on the auxiliaries by the supervising white locals, was guilty of discrimination, for the status forced on blacks constituted a denial of union membership. IBB policies aggravated manpower shortages in wartime, impaired morale, and hindered the prosecution of the war. The FEPC ordered the IBB to take steps to eliminate discrimination and to report within forty-five days on the progress it had made.[28]

The shipbuilders also discriminated, and the findings rejected their argument that failure to enforce the master agreement constituted interference with the union's internal affairs and violated the Wagner Act. The FEPC argued that the shipbuilders hired and fired regardless of union preferences and were obligated to eliminate discrimination. The committee cited the nondiscrimination clauses in contracts with the various procurement agencies as evidence of the management's

27. George M. Johnson to Malcolm Ross, December 10, 1943, in Malcolm Ross file, Robert Diggs to Malcolm Ross, November 30, 1943, in Records of George M. Johnson, Boilermakers file, R4HR, W. K. Hopkins, WMC, to Ed Rainbow, November 29, 1943, Region XII, Administrative Files, 1943–44, WMC, F103FR, Harry Kingman to Malcolm Ross (telegram), November 30, 1943, Region XII, Administrative Files, Unarranged Correspondence, Clarence M. Mitchell file, F104FR, *Joseph James et al.* v. *International Brotherhood of Boilermakers*, November 29, 1943, in Region XII, Closed Cases–San Francisco, IBB Local 6 file, F108FR, report on auxiliary situation, December 21, 1943, Legal Division, IBB General file, R14HR, all in RG 228.

28. Summary, findings and directives, December 9, 1943, Portland hearing, Exhibits file, R14HR, RG 228.

responsibilities. In addition, the FEPC noted the Bethlehem–Alameda Shipyard case, in which the NLRB strongly suggested that an employer with a closed-shop contract, far from breaking the law if he ignored a union request for the discharge of blacks, would violate it if he put the request into effect.[29]

Responding angrily, the IBB ordered all west coast locals to ignore the FEPC's "alleged directives" and to insist on strict compliance with the closed-shop contract. Shipbuilders were warned to employ "only workmen who [were] members in good standing of the respective unions . . . regardless of any [FEPC] opinion to the contrary." The directives were, according to the union, an "arrogant attempt to destroy collective bargaining agreements." Company responses varied, but all vowed to uphold the master agreement. Some questioned the FEPC's jurisdiction, which, they claimed, conflicted with the National War Labor Board's "ultimate authority" to settle labor disputes in wartime. The shipbuilders also charged the FEPC with inconsistency in its conduct of the hearings. Before the hearings began, the FEPC's special counsel had allegedly notified the companies that "no evidence [would] be offered or received" on management discrimination. Yet the findings and directives, without presentation of such evidence, so charged the shipbuilders. Kaiser's attorneys petitioned for a rehearing, which the committee ultimately granted. In the interim, the FEPC's Region XII reported continuing instances of discrimination by company and union at Kaiser's Richmond shipyard.[30]

By late December, complex and significant events began interacting, ultimately affecting the participants in this struggle and the decisions they would make. One was the annual convention of the IBB, which opened in Kansas City on December 29. Another was the litigation initiated by the San Francisco Committee Against Segregation and Discrimination, which was progressing through the federal

---

29. *Ibid.*; verbatim transcript, committee meeting, December 4, 1943, p. 97, R64HR, RG 228.

30. Verbatim transcript, committee meeting, February 12, 1944, pp. 76–78, R65HR, George Johnson to Harry Kingman (telegram), December 23, 1943, IBB General file, Charles MacGowan to Western Pipe and Steel, December 15, 1943, Chalmers L. McGaughey to FEPC, December 28, 1943, Extra Copies file, Legal Division, R14HR, Edward Rutledge to Sam Kagel, January 22, 1944, Edward Rutledge to Harry Kingman, January 25, 1944, Region XII, Administrative Files, 1943–44, WMC–Sam Kagel file, F103FR, Final Disposition Report, February 11, 1944, Region XII, Closed Cases–San Francisco, 12BR152, F112FR, all in RG 228.

courts. At a December 13 hearing, at which the FEPC appeared amicus curiae, the boilermakers had challenged the temporary restraining order of November 29 for lack of jurisdiction. This issue was immediately appealed, and a three-judge panel on January 3, 1944, gave the boilermakers a victory six days after their convention had begun—a victory that no doubt reinforced their belief that the master agreement could not be violated even when it discriminated. The euphoria the IBB delegates must have felt would be temporary, however, as the black shipyard workers pursued other legal strategies.[31]

Indeed, the federal restraining order had already affected the boilermaker leadership. Well before the appeals court ruled, Vice-President Charles MacGowan, who faced a hardline opponent in a struggle to replace the ailing Franklin, became more conciliatory. In a December 23 telegram to Malcolm Ross regarding Kaiser's request for a rehearing, MacGowan suggested that he "hold all matters status quo until after our conference," for his cooperation would "materially assist in placating a situation" that MacGowan was convinced was "serious, if not ominous." MacGowan's message seemed to signal a realization that the success of his candidacy partly depended on dampening the rhetoric and controversy over the boilermaker auxiliaries. It was a complicated game that he was playing, however. Many of the locals, with orders over MacGowan's signature, were resuming their campaign against non-dues-paying blacks, and in Los Angeles all the area shipbuilders cooperated with the unions.[32]

At the boilermaker convention, Malcolm Ross spent four hours with MacGowan and left with a highly favorable impression of the IBB vice-president. Ross believed MacGowan would like to see the auxiliaries wiped out. At one point, MacGowan even mentioned giving black business agents in the auxiliaries the same power as business agents in the white lodges, but "then [he] talked himself" out of it. "MacGowan's problem is that he is quite unique in that outfit," Ross told the committee at its meeting on January 15. Around him were very tough people who were uncompromising on the auxiliary issue,

31. Report on the auxiliary situation, Marinship case during January, 1944, Legal Division, IBB General file, R14HR, and Memorandum, Harry Kingman to Malcolm Ross, January 3, 1944, Documents file, R1HR, both in RG 228.

32. Charles MacGowan to Malcolm Ross (telegram), December 23, 1943, in re: Hearings file, R14HR, verbatim transcript, committee meeting, January 15, 1944, p. 31, R65HR, Eugene Davidson to Will Maslow, January 10, 1944, Legal Division, Memoranda to & from Harry Kingman, R14HR, all in RG 228.

including the outgoing president, and MacGowan needed support. He had offered Ross a chance to talk to the Resolutions Committee, but if he came "all out for this thing," Ross warned, his opponent, Jasper Davis, would "win [the presidency] and everybody [would be] lost." Ross thought it would be embarrassing for MacGowan if the forty-five-day limit for responding to the FEPC's findings and directives ended in the middle of the boilermaker convention, so the committee approved an extension.[33]

As the committee members met, they must have known that two days earlier a California superior court in Marin County had issued a temporary restraining order on behalf of 400 black workers who had branded IBB Local 6 a "racket" and "not a bona fide union." The union had waived their membership for over a year, permitting them to work in the shipyard. Then, suddenly, the boilermakers saw an opportunity to make money, Judge Edward I. Butler was told, and demanded back dues of $45,000, plus $3 per man per month in the future. If this suit had any effect on the boilermakers, it was to make them even angrier, as Ross learned when he returned to Kansas City to face the Resolutions Committee. Treating the group and their vice-president with inexplicable indulgence, Ross "took three hours of battering" led by MacGowan himself, a situation that Ross said he "perfectly understood because [MacGowan] was in a position where he didn't want to seem to have any liberal ideas on this issue." Ross told the committee later, "They went at me pretty hard." Their lawyer presented a long analysis of the San Francisco injunction and discussed how weak the FEPC's case was against the boilermakers. Whereas MacGowan was calm, Ross recalled, the other participants were "just plain shouting at me . . . and it may have served some use to have me as a whipping boy."[34]

Boris Shishkin, who also made the convention rounds, brought a rosier report to the committee on February 11, but he spoke mostly in generalities. Shishkin described intense AFL pressure to weaken the color bar as much as possible: William Green himself had taken a

33. Verbatim transcript, committee meeting, January 15, 1943, p. 31, R65HR, RG 228.

34. Verbatim transcript, committee meeting, February 11, 1944, p. 50, R65HR, Report on the Auxiliary Situation, Marinship Case During January, 1944, Legal Division, IBB General file, R14HR, San Francisco *News*, January 14, 1944, San Francisco *People's World*, January 21, 1944, in Newspaper Clippings, Box 517, all in RG 228.

very strong position, and Shishkin had used his contacts with the IBB. In addition, a letter from President Roosevelt, who urged that "every worker capable of serving his country be permitted" to do so regardless of race, also had an effect. The convention took "quite broad" action, and there was hope that the executive board could be persuaded to implement it in a similar way. Getting additional rights for black members in the political atmosphere then existing "was a very notable gain." With major IBB locals in the North willing to pursue FEPC policy much further than the convention had done, the west coast delegations were very much on the defensive, though the main opposition to change came from the South. The issue of segregation also influenced the election of officers. MacGowan, who won the IBB presidency, was very cooperative, but he had "gone as far as he" could. In the end, however, the convention neither abolished the auxiliary system nor took steps to assure full black participation, and Shishkin knew it.[35]

On the following day, Shishkin produced a copy of the convention action. It recommended continuation of the auxiliaries with several changes. Henceforth, auxiliary unions could send voting delegates to the IBB convention, file application for membership in the metal trades council and district lodges, and receive better insurance coverage. Auxiliary members would also have "all rights with respect to participation in the unit," including the right to vote without restriction in elections and the right to have their own business agents, under supervision. The white supervising lodges, however, would be represented at all auxiliary meetings and would control collective bargaining, because the IBB said it could not "face the situation of an auxiliary completely" independent in that area. Although the new policies fell far short of the FEPC directives, Shishkin presented them as a "tremendous step forward."[36]

Milton Webster was not impressed. The boilermakers had already discharged 500 men on the West Coast. He asked sarcastically if on the basis of the convention's performance, the IBB was under the impression that the FEPC should hold its action in abeyance for a few weeks. "They are all wet," he declared. "I think they are stupid."

35. Verbatim transcript, committee meeting, February 11, 1944, pp. 50–67, R65HR, RG 228; Chicago *Defender*, February 12, 1944, p. 1.
36. Verbatim transcript, committee meeting, February 12, 1944, pp. 67–72, R65HR, RG 228.

Shishkin countered that the locals, not the IBB, were discharging blacks. "We are trying to tell them . . . to hold up until" they explore the problem with the IBB executive council. Webster had another harsh judgment: "[The] Council has also been stupid. They want to supervise Negroes for fear they will write a substandard contract. Anybody in the labor union business knows the possibility of a substandard contract was far greater with thousands of men outside the organizations." That was where blacks would be when the shipyards closed down after the war. The IBB was "laying itself wide open to competition." Furthermore, Webster asked, how much influence would "a handful of Negroes have at a convention"? It was a "meaningless gesture." They could elect their own delegates and business agents, but what did that mean? It was "almost an insult to people who know anything about this business . . . simply putting a little sugar over castor oil." Webster was "willing to commend those who tried to straighten" the situation out, but he believed "they [had] failed." Shishkin admitted that instead of making real progress, they had succeeded only in "easing up the situation a bit."[37]

As Webster suggested, the committee had to decide what to do about the IBB reply to the findings and directives from the West Coast hearing, due on February 15. The committee had voted an extension in January. Ross thought the situation was "very real with these 500 [dismissed] people," but if the boilermakers would take some affirmative action to reassure the rank and file in the auxiliaries, the "situation might be saved." Otherwise, more drastic action was called for, and the case might have to be certified to the president. Sarah Southall, weary after earlier experiences of extending time to recalcitrant unions and employers, favored immediate certification. So did John Brophy, who objected to the convention actions "on two major counts": segregation and auxiliaries that were not autonomous. Milton Webster also supported certification but was willing to wait ten days if the boilermakers union would defer the discharges. His motion to that effect passed three to two, but it was not a popular decision among blacks. The Los Angeles Sentinel's headline "FEPC Dodges the Issue" seemed to sum up the negative attitude of the black press. The Chicago Defender was outraged at the AFL's Boris Shishkin, who had allegedly quashed "efforts to crack down on the union through presi-

37. Ibid., pp. 72–76.

dential intervention" by promising FEPC members "he would take further steps to secure integration" in the union. But, as the paper noted, "labor experts [have] pointed out that this is impossible since the union's convention is the top authority." The *Defender* believed that the FEPC, in giving additional time to the IBB, had set a bad precedent.[38]

Another force went practically unnoticed at the boilermaker convention and at the FEPC as superior courts in California and Rhode Island entered the controversy. On February 17, Judge Edward Butler, in *Joseph James v. Marinship*, ruled that black shipworkers had good cause for action against the boilermakers, and he issued a preliminary injunction that restrained Local 6 and Marinship (but not the IBB) from discrimination and from segregating blacks into auxiliaries. Such practices, he said, were contrary to the public policy of California. Butler pronounced the closed-shop provision of the master agreement void as applied to the plaintiffs. Local 6 appealed to the California Supreme Court, while black shipyard workers initiated more cases in other California courts. By July, 1944, three suits had been filed in U.S. district courts and four in various California superior courts. When the *James* decision was handed down, however, the boilermaker convention had already adjourned. Flushed with victory, Joseph James astutely pledged his group's "complete loyalty to the principles of democratic trade unionism" and so notified the officials in Local 6. He offered the "entire facilities of our organization to see that every Negro worker" became a member of Local 6 in good standing.[39]

In Providence, Rhode Island, IBB Local 308 admitted blacks into full membership, an act that violated the IBB constitution. The international responded by chartering an auxiliary union, which the members of Local 308 rejected by unanimous vote on September 1, 1943.

38. *Ibid.*, pp. 67–81; Los Angeles *Sentinel*, February 24, 1944, in Newspaper Clippings, Box 316, RG 228; Chicago *Defender*, February 19, 1944, p. 1, February 26, 1944, p. 4.

39. Frank S. Pestana to Frank Reeves, July 8, 1944, in Recent Memos & Letters in IBB Case, Joseph James to Ed Rainbow and E. Medley, February 26, 1944, in Recent Telegrams & Letters, Kingman file, Legal Division, R14HR, Frank Reeves to George Johnson, May 9, 1944, Legal Division, Records of George M. Johnson, Frank Reeves file, R5HR, *Joseph James v. Marinship*, Superior Court of California, Marin County, February 17, 1944, Case #15371, in office files of Frank D. Reeves, Raymond F. Thompson *et al.* file, R8HR, Harry Kingman to George Johnson, February 17, 1944, in Region XII, Administrative Files, Unarranged Correspondence, George M. Johnson file, F104FR, all in RG 228; Chicago *Defender*, February 26, 1944, p. 1.

Blacks in Local 308 took the IBB to court in December after its officials refused to count black ballots in a local union election. On January 7, in *Hill v. Boilermakers,* a Rhode Island superior court granted a temporary injunction. The complainants had reasonable grounds to believe they were members of Local 308 in good standing, the court rules, and the purpose and effect of the auxiliary was to segregate them in a less favorable position. The court found that the Fourteenth Amendment to the Constitution, a similar amendment in Rhode Island's fundamental law, and a state civil rights statute all evidenced profound public policy in regard to equal treatment of all persons. So also did Executive Order 9346, though as a declaration of public policy its enforceability as a matter of law remained doubtful. In conclusion, the court pronounced, the IBB's conduct was illegal and void.[40]

That these important cases, then moving slowly through two obscure state courts, had any effect on the boilermaker convention's deliberations is doubtful, and their potential effect was uncertain. As the FEPC's attorney Frank Reeves noted, the two decisions had to be "considered in light of their restricted applicability." If upheld by state and United States supreme courts, Reeves believed, their value as legal precedents would be limited to Rhode Island, California, and states having similar constitutional and statutory provisions. Their most significant feature was ordering the union to admit blacks to full and equal membership without regard for any contrary rule or custom. "In this they are unique," Reeves noted. The California decision was also important for its declaration that a closed-shop contract was void as it applied to blacks. Unlike Rhode Island, both the California state courts (and the federal courts as well) refrained from mentioning Executive Order 9346 as a declaration of public policy. Thus, from a national viewpoint Reeves was less sanguine. The earlier federal court decision in California was of primary importance, but the United States Court of Appeals, though sympathetic to the objectives of the plaintiffs, could not find sufficient jurisdictional grounds for federal intervention. Despite the uncertainties, however, the effect of the

40. James N. Williams to Edward Lawson, September 10, October 20, 1943, in Oregon Shipbuilding, Predocketed II, F24FR, Edward Lawson to Will Maslow, October 22, 1943, IBB Local 308 file, R15HR, and Frank Reeves to George Johnson, March 7, 1944, in Legal Division, Analysis of IBB Auxiliary Decisions file, R15HR, all in RG 228.

James decision was salutary. It brought considerable restraint to future IBB behavior and strengthened the hand of the FEPC.[41]

Time would show that the *James* decision was potentially damaging to the boilermakers union on the entire West Coast, but for the present, at least, it applied only to shipbuilders and unions in a few California counties. Thus the boilermaker problem did not disappear, and in some cases it became worse. For the FEPC, difficult days lay ahead. The committee had to understand and interpret the language in various IBB convention resolutions, bylaws changes, and constitutional revisions, deal with tough and often aloof union officials, and try to get compliance with its directives. For several weeks after the convention, Charles MacGowan remained inaccessible, strengthening his position in the union, it was said. The IBB, too, faced a difficult situation. Black workers were twitting whites about paying dues that blacks did not pay. The unions feared that whites might also rebel. The IBB therefore had an interest in getting the matter settled. While MacGowan traveled around the country dealing with internal IBB problems, Joseph Keenan, an official in the Chicago AFL building trades and vice-chairman of the WPB, served as intermediary with the FEPC.[42]

In early March, 1944, Keenan told the President's Committee that several of its differences with the boilermakers could be worked out. "I think MacGowan will take a chance on it," he ventured, but "one basic point [the subserviency of the auxiliary lodges] can't be cleared up now." A "group from one section of the country," the South, would fight on that point, and it had more power in the boilermakers than in any other AFL union. Before the IBB convention began, Keenan twice went before the executive committee urging the abandonment of the auxiliaries. He believed a majority would have done so, but one man, Tom Crowe, the west coast representative, upset things. Elsewhere in the West, even Ed Rainbow and Tom Ray talked of giving blacks full membership, but the southerners, it seemed, would "fight to the very finish against FEPC and their international

41. Reeves to George Johnson, March 7, 1944, in Legal Division, Analysis of IBB Auxiliary Decisions file, R15HR, and Thurgood Marshall, "Negro Status in the Boilermakers Union," *Crisis* (March, 1944), 77–78, in Legal Division, IBB General file, R14HR, both in RG 228.

42. Verbatim transcripts, committee meetings, March 4, 1944, pp. 125–32, March 18, 1944, p. 82, R65HR, RG 228.

union." Keenan wanted to know what the FEPC would accept in the way of autonomy for the auxiliaries in view of the fact that an international union could not have two groups, an auxiliary and its supervisory union, making a collective bargaining agreement.[43]

John Brophy thought if there must be two lodges, some type of joint representation on a committee should be worked out. When organizing the anthracite fields, he recalled, the UMW had a language (ethnic) local besides a native one in the same mine, but it got rid of the two when some stability had been achieved. Two unions usually existed only for organizational purposes. George Johnson thought the IBB was "trying to have their cake and eat it too" by setting up one union with exclusive jurisdiction but leaving out people who were entitled to the full benefits derived from that situation. The IBB should not ask black workers to make concessions at both ends, he argued. If they insisted on separateness, they ought to give the blacks more autonomy. Boris Shishkin seemed to agree, noting that the boilermakers did not have a separate voice because the master agreement was negotiated by the Metal Trades Council.[44]

Keenan became impatient. He asked again if the committee had any proposals he could take back to the boilermakers. Committee members had "to make up [their] minds" about something for him to follow through on. "If there is no give, then it's a waste of time." Keenan was eager to get the matter settled because the present confusion would "hurt the whole trade union movement." In response, Milton Webster threw the blame right back to the union presidents, who, he said, "haven't got the common sense to see how stupid they are [for] insisting" on segregating workers along color lines. They were the disloyal ones, "gumming up the whole labor movement and all the good things labor has fought for in the last fifty years." International union presidents could do pretty much what they wanted to, Webster challenged, and MacGowan and others "must make up their minds" to proceed on broad trade union principles. "Negroes ought not to compromise on principles." Keenan agreed it was a big issue, but he thought Webster, who knew "the makeup of some of these unions," could be more sympathetic. Keenan wished Webster could

43. Verbatim transcripts, committee meetings, March 4, 1944, pp. 125–40, April 1, 1944, pp. 53–57, R65HR, RG 228.
44. *Ibid.*

have been with him for the past four years, "talking with these fellows . . . where your whole country was at stake, and have them turn
their backs." To Webster, that was more evidence of stupidity. Union
"bosses who believe in the right thing must [exercise leadership and]
hammer on these fellows." At this point, Keenan became angry. "You
and I had an understanding but it is all off," he told Webster. "I don't
think you can do anything if you keep giving them shots in the arm
to make them madder. . . . [and] everything you have done today has
only agitated the thing." Furthermore, he continued, if the FEPC directive "that went out to Los Angeles" had not been issued, some
progress could have been made, but the boilermakers "took the position all the way through they were acting with a gun in their back."
In a flight of whimsy, Boris Shishkin demurred. He did not think the
FEPC had that much power: "It wasn't a gun . . . only a shoe horn,
but they took their shoes off." [45]

The discussion with Keenan was carried on almost exclusively by
the seasoned labor men on the committee. Keenan and MacGowan
were dealing with knowledgeable labor insiders. So guided, committee
members asked Keenan to do what he could to narrow the issues sepa-
rating the FEPC and the boilermakers. Two weeks passed, and Keenan
still had not been able to contact MacGowan. He requested another
two weeks and asked for postponement of the West Coast rehearing,
scheduled for April 1 in Chicago. With considerable reservation, the
committee once again consented to a delay. "With this goes an agreement by MacGowan that there will be no more firings," Ross warned,
and shortly he telegraphed Region XII's Harry Kingman that such a
pledge had been given. [46]

But the agreement fell through. MacGowan claimed he was not
under any such commitment. Instead, the new IBB president initiated
a program of token discharges of black auxiliary members who had
refused to pay dues. At the Richmond shipyard, 20 were called in and
warned. Protest leaders being singled out as examples reportedly happened at other yards, too. The boilermakers adopted another tactic,
one that FEPC attorney Frank Reeves labeled a "conspiracy." At the

45. Verbatim transcript, committee meeting, March 4, 1944, pp. 125–32, R65HR,
RG 228.

46. *Ibid.*; Malcolm Ross to Harry Kingman or Edward Rutledge (telegram),
March 29, 1944, in Region XII, Administrative Files, Unarranged Correspondence,
Clarence M. Mitchell file, F104FR, RG 228.

shipyards operating under the court injunction preventing discharges, IBB locals stopped accepting "new Negro hires" because the injunction did not cover prospective employees. Reeves believed the number rejected to be very high and cited examples of newly arrived black families being forced to leave when shipyard jobs did not materialize.[47]

The refusal of blacks to pay dues deeply troubled the IBB, particularly since the infection was spreading to the white membership. Although IBB officials blamed black defections for the problem, John Brophy thought the internal struggle for control of the international to be a factor. There were other considerations also, according to Malcolm Ross. The war had brought in thousands of workers, with and without union backgrounds, from all over the country. They had to join the burgeoning local lodges, but there was no real union discipline in any of the yards, and local union meetings were not held consistently. Almost anything could have inspired the refusal to pay dues. In one yard about 9,000 whites were reportedly dismissed on the grounds that they did not pay their dues. At the same time, blacks got a "free ride" for a year and more. Ross's greatest fear was that this issue would cause a strike, which in turn would hurt the war effort.[48]

The FEPC, though still a significant moral force, was pathetically helpless in dealing with the IBB. Having issued directives to perpetrators of discrimination, it benignly granted extensions of time when deadlines were ignored. The committee had to approach difficult and inaccessible union leaders through intermediaries because the principals refused to meet or even communicate with the FEPC. After a hearing failed to bring compliance, certification to the president was the FEPC's chief remaining leverage. Most blacks apparently believed such action could produce results against the IBB, but it was risky business to defer to an extremely political president who viewed the FEPC as useful when it kept minority problems away from the White House and a nuisance otherwise. Roosevelt had already avoided taking punitive action against the southern railroads and their unions,

47. Verbatim transcript, committee meeting, April 1, 1944, pp. 48–53, R65HR, and Reeves to George Johnson, May 9, 1944, in Legal Division, Records of George M. Johnson, Frank D. Reeves file, R5HR, both in RG 228.

48. Verbatim transcript, committee meeting, April 1, 1944, pp. 48–53, April 20, 1944, pp. 132–34, R65HR, RG 228.

both brazen discriminators that the FEPC had certified to him in 1944.[49]

Under the circumstances, the committee had to work, as it had from the beginning, through other agencies. Joseph Keenan, vice-chairman of the WPB, was a loyal AFL partisan. The California injunctions, which struck at union contracts, alarmed him, and he feared possible action in Congress. The boilermaker issue had to be settled. Keenan, in this case pursuing labor's self-interest, could be far more useful than the president if the FEPC could work with him and not compromise its principles. Keenan's position on the boilermaker auxiliaries was very simple. Discrimination, as distinguished from the separate question of segregation, came from the auxiliary system itself and could be eliminated by doing away with the supervisory arrangement, he believed. The auxiliaries should have their own business agents who would work in cooperation with, rather than under, white business agents. The auxiliaries would be separate but not subordinate. The same arrangement would apply to the shop stewards. At some point, though, the white local would have to be the contracting party because having two competing units violated all trade union principles. This difficulty could be gotten around, however, since master agreements were negotiated higher up, and local lodges generally did not bargain. Even George Johnson was impressed with the argument. Keenan wanted "one more chance to get hold of" MacGowan, who during his west coast tour apparently had fallen under the influence of the uncompromising Tom Crowe. He would have an opportunity to see MacGowan in the middle of April in Chicago. The committee was willing to wait until then. It believed blacks could make gains within the auxiliaries because MacGowan, as Milton Webster stated, had the power to satisfy the FEPC directives.[50]

By April 20, Keenan described to committee members his meeting with MacGowan, but his report on the substance of their talks consisted mostly of vague proposals apparently put out by the boilermakers to gauge FEPC reaction. Auxiliaries could elect their own officers, and their business agents would have the same power as other business agents working under a "chief," a term not familiar to committee members and staff. In white lodges, however, there were elected busi-

49. Alexa Henderson, "FEPC and the Southern Railway Case," 186.

50. Verbatim transcript, committee meeting, April 1, 1944, pp. 57–60, R65HR, RG 228.

ness agents and appointed assistant ones who took orders from the "chief" business agent. The IBB would now consider assistant agents in auxiliaries as equal to those in the white lodges, but any chief could overrule an assistant, with appeal only to the international. In other words, auxiliary agents, whether elected or appointed, would still be subject to the orders of the white lodge, whose business agent was now vested with the title of chief. An appeal over the chief to the international, for what it was worth, seemed to be the only new feature introduced into this relationship. The problem of seniority was yet to be worked out. George Johnson wondered if these arrangements would be put in writing in the constitutions of the auxiliaries. Keenan thought that ultimately there would be no auxiliaries, though such action could be taken only by the next convention, and a struggle within the IBB was still going on between southerners, who had the most influence, and the northern bloc. For the time being the FEPC would have to be satisfied with indirect negotiations through Keenan, who reported that MacGowan was under orders from his attorney and the IBB executive committee not to appear before the FEPC, even though personally he was ready for a meeting.[51]

As the pressure mounted on both the FEPC and the boilermakers, Keenan received written proposals from MacGowan in language that conveyed a "vast change of viewpoint" from the "brusque, almost insulting exchange of telegrams previously." The IBB president expressed a hope to be able to meet with the FEPC toward the end of May. As the committee discussed the upcoming session, Ross warned that the "nub of it" was still the "amount of subserviency" the auxiliaries would have to endure until the next IBB convention. "If the Committee thinks that is totally wrong and has power to move against it, it ought to." He suggested that if the IBB was willing to make concessions, "perhaps more good [could] come out of pressing them on that line than to certify it to the President." Ross favored negotiations, but Webster was "fed up." The directives stated that auxiliary membership under a closed-shop agreement was discriminatory: "It is or it isn't." Yet the IBB, "despite what the Committee said," had decided at their convention to keep the auxiliaries. MacGowan's attitude had not changed "one iota." Webster was ready to

51. Verbatim transcript, committee meeting, April 20, 1944, pp. 126–131, R65HR, RG 228.

certify and then wait to see what happened. Having waited for months already, however, the rest of the committee wanted to hear MacGowan's proposals.[52]

The IBB response to the directives became the focal point of a two-hour meeting on May 23 among Ross, Shishkin, and Charles Houston, representing the FEPC, and MacGowan, his vice-president, and Joe Keenan. Unfortunately, Ross failed to have the proceedings recorded. If unintentional, as he claimed, the lapse was inconceivable in view of the session's importance. MacGowan, in his letter, had stated that auxiliaries would elect their own officers, including a business agent "where they had sufficient members to maintain one." In May, 1944, thirty-six IBB auxiliaries, with 12,685 members, existed on paper, at least; twenty-seven of them were in the South, seven on the West Coast, and two in the Midwest. MacGowan frankly admitted that only one auxiliary, A-26 in Oakland, was financially able to support a business agent on full salary, a revelation that, in effect, constituted an unintended indictment of the whole IBB auxiliary arrangement. Auxiliary meetings had to follow the standard ritual, but since most members were unfamiliar with IBB laws and policies, the meetings followed the stipulation that the business agent or president of the sponsoring local "shall attend to give advice and direct the deliberations." The 1944 convention had already authorized the auxiliaries to be represented in the international's deliberations and to vote therein. To handle grievances, the auxiliary would appoint a shop steward who was to hold regular meetings to sort out the complaints by merit. Unadjusted grievances would be turned over to the auxiliary's business agent or, if none existed, the supervisory union's business agent. Grievances from the auxiliary would receive the same attention as any others.[53]

Auxiliary members had the right to change classifications and to transfer membership to other auxiliaries. If none existed, they could deposit their clearance cards with the IBB secretary and pay dues directly to him. The 1944 convention corrected the complaint on insur-

52. Verbatim transcript, committee meeting, May 13, 1944, pp. 91–99, R65HR, RG 228.

53. "Membership of Auxiliary Lodges" (Typescript, May 18, 1944, in Legal Division, Auxiliary Bylaws & Analysis file, R14HR), Charles MacGowan to Malcolm Ross, May 23, 1944, in Documents file, May 27, 1944, R1HR, and verbatim transcript, committee meeting, May 27, 1944, pp. 72–88, R65HR, all in RG 228.

ance, extending to blacks the same premium rates and benefits enjoyed by the members of the subordinate lodges. The contract with
the insurance company was revised even though the general membership might have to absorb additional costs because of higher death
rates among auxiliary members. As to the apprenticeship system,
none existed in the shipyards. If one were to be established, however,
auxiliaries would get the same privileges as subordinate lodges. In the
meantime, the existing training programs would operate evenhand-
edly, so both types of members could be classified fairly. There would
be no difference in the treatment of auxiliary and subordinate lodge
members for misconduct such as drinking at lodge meetings. Finally,
the alien clause was removed from the IBB constitution.[54]

MacGowan refused to "put into clear words a forecast" that the
next convention would eliminate the auxiliaries and establish "equal
status for Negroes." He could not commit the executive committee to
that extent, but he believed he had "squeezed all he could out of the
1944 convention platform." Ross, after reporting on the meeting, told
the committee members that he himself favored compromising with
the IBB, but he sympathized with those who would hold to strict
principle. By compromise, Ross obviously meant a continuation of
negotiations rather than certification to the president. He viewed
MacGowan's letter as a platform from which the FEPC could guard
the situation, processing any complaints that involved a violation of
those pledges. He warned the committee: "The whole situation is
going to go down hill very fast and we are going to find ourselves
with no compliance at all, with no chance to get back at them, and
with a lot of trouble out there on the West Coast. I feel this very
deeply."[55]

Did MacGowan's reply constitute compliance with the December
directives? The black FEPC attorney Frank Reeves was unusually sanguine. To begin with, he wrote, the IBB convention eliminated or
directed the elimination of three of the ten discriminatory features
cited by the FEPC. As to grievance machinery, MacGowan's answer

54. MacGowan to Ross, May 23, 1944, in Documents file, May 27, 1944, R1HR,
verbatim transcript, committee meeting, May 27, 1944, pp. 72–88, R65HR, San
Francisco *People's World*, May 22, 1944, Baltimore *Afro-American*, June 6, 1944, in
Newspaper Clippings, Boilermaker folder, Box 513, all in RG 228.
55. Charles MacGowan to Joe Keenan, May 3, 1944, in Legal Division, IBB General file, R14HR, and verbatim transcript, committee meeting, May 27, 1944, pp. 72–
88, R65HR, both in RG 228.

seemed "to indicate that there [could] be no valid practical criticism of the present policy." In regard to the universal transfer of membership, Reeves found "substantial compliance in the absence of facts which may belie this equality of privilege." He had difficulty, however, appraising MacGowan's statement regarding the subservience of the auxiliary unions, and he concluded that a business agent elected by an auxiliary would not "operate autonomously or on a plane of equality" with the agent of a supervising lodge. That the auxiliaries allegedly chose their own officers, conducted their meetings according to standard union ritual, and engaged in other activities did not, consequently, answer the directive's fundamental criticism, which was that they totally lacked autonomy. In a practical sense, they were subservient.[56]

Nevertheless, in the letter from MacGowan Reeves found "specific or substantial compliance in nine of the ten particulars" in the FEPC directive. Since the union's answer indicated 90 percent compliance, Reeves argued, consideration should be given to MacGowan's statements "as to the official position" of the IBB: that there would be no discrimination in hiring, in length or tenure of employment, or against any workers enjoying the full benefits of the collective bargaining arrangements, including wages, seniority, upgrading, vacations with pay, handling grievances, and all other matters within the agreement, regardless of race, creed, color, or national origin. Reeves found MacGowan's statement to be salutary and predicted that "if forcefully and practically implemented, it should serve as the basis upon which many of the complaints from the Auxiliary system can be satisfactorily adjusted."[57]

From the West Coast, however, came a different analysis. The San Francisco Committee pointed out wide variances between MacGowan's words and the actual practices of the boilermakers union in the shipyards. Where two locals, a parent and an auxiliary, operated in an area, the one being supervised was virtually denied representation. Sending black delegates to an IBB convention as representatives of their auxiliaries was interpreted by the IBB as equal treatment, but in practice it created a small convention faction, despised by southern delegates and totally without power. An auxiliary could elect its own

56. Frank Reeves to George Johnson, May 27, 1944, in Region XII, Unarranged Correspondence, Clarence M. Mitchell file, R104HR, RG 228.
57. *Ibid.*

business agent if it had sufficient funds, but this action still would not end the supervisory function of the parent lodge. In regard to the grievance procedures, the San Francisco Committee found no such machinery operating in the Bay Area. MacGowan guaranteed an appeal if a change in classification was denied a member of an auxiliary, yet this concession was also useless. Approval had to come from the sponsoring local, and appeal to the IBB was tantamount to denial because of the months and years involved in the process. Finally, the guarantee of transferability was meaningless. No black auxiliary member could go to a shipyard in the South and get equality of opportunity or the equal right to have his grievance presented.[58]

The President's Committee discussed the boilermaker issue at every meeting for the remainder of the summer. Boris Shishkin, like Ross, favored compromise instead of certification. Production was being curtailed in many of the shipyards as contracts were completed, he observed, and the demand for labor was declining. Workers, particularly middle-class whites, were taking their savings and returning to the farms and cities of their origin. John Brophy also leaned toward compromise. Everyone on the committee opposed segregation in the unions, he noted, but the president had ordered the FEPC to deal with discrimination, not segregation. The boilermakers had come "quite a ways" from their original position. If segregation resulted in the denial of equal employment opportunities, which Milton Webster insisted was inevitable, then, Brophy thought, the committee would have to act when such discrimination became apparent.[59]

Still, the FEPC was unwilling to state that the IBB was in compliance. A letter answering MacGowan was drafted after the June 13 committee meeting but was never sent. In a summary of committee actions following the June meeting, George Johnson wrote Harry Kingman that the "minor concessions" made by MacGowan were unacceptable. Kingman, who adamantly opposed any compromise, was elated. He suspected that the boilermakers were trying to secure a committee whitewash to be used in their upcoming appeal of the *James* case to the California Supreme Court. Although the majority

58. Frank Pestana to Harry Kingman, June 10, 1944, in Legal Division, Telegrams & Letters, Kingman file, R14HR, and Ray Thompson to Harry Kingman, July 24, 1944, Documents file, R1HR, all in RG 228.

59. Verbatim transcripts, committee meetings, May 27, 1944, pp. 90–96, June 13, 1944, pp. 29–82, R65HR, RG 228.

of the committee apparently were willing to continue negotiations with MacGowan, both Webster and George Johnson in September pressed for certification. Charles Houston held back because a considerable amount of time had elapsed since the directives had been issued, and he wanted fresher evidence of discrimination from the regional offices. On September 11, the committee finally responded formally to MacGowan's letter. The boilermaker policies, when effective, it said, would satisfy seven of the FEPC complaints. The three remaining issues, two having to do with the subserviency of the auxiliaries and the third with the handling of grievances, had not been resolved. Because these matters were "so fundamental," the committee informed MacGowan that the "Boilermakers [were] not in conformity" and requested a report indicating what further steps had been taken. At the same time, the FEPC waited for the California Supreme Court's decision in the *James* case.[60]

While the committee dealt with the boilermakers, the shipbuilders pressed the FEPC over their own complaints. Stung by the findings and directives and convinced of their innocence, Kaiser and several others appealed for a rehearing to challenge the finding that they discriminated or had anything to do with the denial of membership in the IBB. They rejected the directives in their entirety for lack of evidence. If the boilermakers union had not discriminated, then there would certainly be no case against the shipbuilders, for they had merely enforced the provisions of the closed-shop agreement. The complaints against them should have been dismissed, because they were not responsible for the policies of the union. The FEPC granted a rehearing and acknowledged that union practices were fundamental, but it rejected management's claim of being absolved from responsibility. The FEPC cited *Wallace v. NLRB*, handed down by the United States Supreme Court in 1944, which imposed an affirmative

---

60. Malcolm Ross to Charles MacGowan, September 11, 1944, in Legal Division, Boilermakers file, R14HR, draft of letter to Charles MacGowan, Documents file, July 1, 1944, Minutes, committee meeting, June 13, 1944, R1HR, verbatim transcripts, committee meetings, May 27, 1944, pp. 90–96, June 13, 1944, pp. 29–82, September 7, 1944, p. 42, R65HR, Pestana to Kingman, June 10, 1944, Harry Kingman to George Johnson, June 28, 1944, in Legal Division, Recent Telegrams & Letters, Kingman file, R14HR, Harry Kingman to Malcolm Ross and George Johnson, June 9, 1944, in Region XII, Administrative Files, Unarranged Correspondence, Clarence M. Mitchell file, F104FR, all in RG 228.

duty on the employer not to use a closed-shop contract to discriminate.[61]

The depth of the shipbuilders' anger became apparent at the Los Angeles rehearing on August 7, attended by committee members Ross, Houston, Shishkin, Brophy, Webster, and George Johnson, when Gordon Johnson, an attorney for Calship and Kaiser, frustrated and embarrassed the FEPC in every way possible. He demanded that the events and agreements from the boilermaker convention and other materials about the union, including Herbert Northrup's testimony, become part of the record. The committee's situation had changed since the original 1943 hearing, Johnson claimed, because the 1944 congressional appropriation permitted an appeal to the president by an employer. Consequently, companies were entitled to all the records, complete with all the facts. His actions implied the shipbuilders would appeal any unfavorable committee decision to FDR, a move that would embarrass the FEPC. Then Gordon Johnson demanded a copy of an FEPC–Maritime Commission agreement on the processing of complaints of discrimination. This document, similar to those arranged between the FEPC and other government agencies, specified that complaints to the FEPC would be sent to the field offices of the Maritime Commission. Gordon Johnson alleged that the FEPC failed to follow these procedures. His tactics so disrupted the hearing that Ross declared a recess. On resuming, Ross announced that the FEPC–Maritime Commission agreement would be provided later. Committee attorneys did not have a copy with them. Gordon Johnson immediately moved for dismissal of the action, which was denied. He then demanded that the FEPC's George Johnson be placed on the stand and sworn in so he could be examined on the content of the missing document. "Of course," the Calship attorney noted, "I can't examine him on something I have not got, so how can I proceed?"[62]

In presenting his arguments, Gordon Johnson charged that the committee findings against the shipyards were based just on one short

61. Frank Reeves to George Johnson, May 30, 1944, in Legal Division, Records of George M. Johnson, Boilermakers file, R4HR, transcript, Los Angeles rehearing, August 7, 1944, in Western Pipe and Steel file, R16HR, decision on rehearing, n.d., in Documents file, February 12, 1944, R1HR, all in RG 228.

62. Transcript, Los Angeles rehearing, August 7, 1944, Western Pipe and Steel file, R16HR, RG 228.

paragraph, which said that regardless of union responsibility, the power to hire and fire remained with the companies, and their obligation to eliminate discrimination was primary and fundamental. Then the attorney for the huge shipbuilding companies fretted that the FEPC's program would destroy the gains made by organized labor. The committee, he argued, should never place any employer in a position of overruling a union notice to dismiss members who were not in good standing. Yet the FEPC had made the shipbuilders' reluctance to overstep their bounds a company failure. The FEPC's position was thus illogical and unreasonable, he continued. The committee feared that the boilermakers would not obey its orders and directives, so "as a matter of convenience" it sought to find the employers guilty of discrimination in order to get at the union. "FEPC should find some way or other to see that labor organizations guilty of discrimination are stopped." It should not concede, as it did when it blamed the shipbuilders, that "it is powerless to get at a party causing discrimination." [63]

Charles Houston, who sparred continually with Gordon Johnson throughout the hearing, presented the FEPC's case mostly through leading questions he put to the Calship attorney. First, he established that through the contract the companies were parties to the process of discrimination. When the union carried discrimination into the execution of the contract, the FEPC could seek to stop it at the point of its end product, the act of discrimination, by forbidding the carrying out of the contract while discrimination was present. The courts could enjoin the union for discriminating or the company for carrying out that policy. Both men agreed that if the closed-shop agreement itself was "infected with discrimination," the FEPC had the authority to remove it. If the company and the union were in collusion outside the written agreement and conspired not to hire blacks, they both could be enjoined. Yet even if on the face of it the contract was fair, it could be stricken, Houston insisted, if it was administered so that the end product was discrimination. The very act of hiring involved the company's continual process of selection, which in turn was ratified by a union guilty of discrimination. It was possible to cut off the process at the point where the company made the selection. Noting

63. *Ibid.*; George Johnson to Harry Kingman, October 14, 1944, in Legal Division, Records of George Johnson, Boilermakers file, R4HR, RG 228.

that the shipyard contracts with the Maritime Commission contained a clause against discrimination, Houston declared that the company, when hiring a man who was not in good standing because the union had violated Executive Order 9346, should ignore the union's request to fire him, because such a request was illegal.[64]

Before the Los Angeles proceedings adjourned, Gordon Johnson requested another rehearing in Portland for the Kaiser interests. Prior to the 1943 hearing in that city, Kaiser had been misled by the FEPC counsel "into a sense of security" that did not exist. As a result, the shipbuilder offered only one witness and failed to present its own case. At a rehearing, several witnesses would be presented, all high officials of the company. On October 18, this rehearing was conducted by Ross and Houston. As the date approached, the Kaiser attorneys began creating new legal stumbling blocks to frustrate the committee. They wanted the FEPC to summon some twenty-two area union leaders so the shipbuilders could develop the full facts about union practices in their defense against the FEPC's charges. Kaiser's attorneys were attempting to enlarge the hearing beyond the testimony of a few company witnesses to a broad discussion of boilermaker discrimination and an examination of the FEPC–Maritime Commission agreement. In an urgent telegram he sent the day the hearing began, George Johnson warned Ross and Houston to "be extremely careful about commitments to any future hearing," because the Kaiser attorneys were trying "to drag the matter on endlessly."[65]

What George Johnson feared did not materialize. Local union leaders did not appear, and Ross succeeded in taking the testimony of Kaiser management personnel within two days. Predictably, all the witnesses praised Kaiser and blamed the boilermakers union for any discriminatory practices. In what appeared to be an attempt to trivial-

64. Transcript, Los Angeles rehearing, August 7, 1944, Western Pipe and Steel file, R16HR, and George Johnson to Harry Kingman, October 14, 1944, in Legal Division, Records of George Johnson, Boilermakers file, R4HR, both in RG 228.

65. Transcript, Los Angeles rehearing, August 7, 1944, Western Pipe and Steel file, R16HR, and George Johnson to Harry Kingman, October 14, 1944, in Legal Division, Records of George Johnson, Boilermakers file, R4HR, Gordon Johnson to FEPC, September 2, 1944, in Documents file, September 7, 1944, R1HR, Gordon Johnson and Harry F. Morton to Malcolm Ross, October 12, 1944, George Johnson to Malcolm Ross (telegram), October 18, 1944, in Legal Division, Petition for Rehearing file, R14HR, George Johnson to Kingman, October 14, 1944, in Legal Division, Records of George M. Johnson, Boilermakers file, R4HR, all in RG 228.

ize black concerns, the company's labor coordinator testified that both whites and blacks complained about discrimination. White workers, when they could not get a certain job, usually claimed the boss disliked them. Blacks also cited discrimination if they thought they were not getting a fair break. J. O. Murray, director of public relations, admitted to cases of top supervisors permitting their personal prejudices to interfere with the company policy of nondiscrimination, but these men had been advised to cease doing so. The company had also resisted several requests from whites for separate work crews and facilities.[66]

There was a general feeling among top management that black women were less well adapted to shipyard work than white women, attitudes that seemed to reflect white stereotyping and folklore. Virginia Lemire, Kaiser's assistant personnel manager, testified that black women were too large to climb, walk around, and get into difficult positions and places. "Size cuts down adaptability," she explained. Lemire also thought black women feared heights, worried about falling into the water, and were afraid to go into dark, closed, and confined places. She then cited their high rate of illiteracy, which prompted Charles Houston to ask if all of these black women came from the South, but there was no clear answer. It was also unclear whether white women ever suffered from these handicaps and fears. Houston was more interested, however, in the work of Kaiser's black assistant personnel manager Clarence Ivey, who was also an assistant head porter at Portland's Union Station. Ivey worked part-time at each job, though in 1942, when the large influx of war workers began arriving in Portland, the railroad let Ivey off for a month to find housing for blacks and get them settled. He also adjusted grievances, advised on transfers, and handled difficult cases passed on to him. Questions from Houston brought out the fact that Ivey exercised little authority, played no role in making policy, and had no jurisdiction over union discrimination. For four hours each day he dealt only with case work when such was referred to him.[67]

The confrontational nature of the two West Coast rehearings greatly alarmed the FEPC's regional personnel in Los Angeles and San

66. Testimony, Volney Martin, J. O. Murray, Elmer L. Hann, October 18–19, 1944, rehearing, Kaiser Portland file, R13HR, RG 228.
67. Testimony, Clarence Ivey, Virginia Lemire, October 18–19, 1944, rehearing, Kaiser Portland file, R13HR, RG 228.

Francisco. From the beginning some questioned the central office's position toward the shipbuilders. With the rehearings over, the dissenters began to speak out. The FEPC was "missing the boat in Portland," Edward Rutledge wrote Kingman, by concentrating its "fire works" on Kaiser rather than by being firm with the boilermakers union. Local 72 still refused "to refer any Negroes to any of the yards or jobs under its jurisdiction." Rutledge complained that the FEPC directives "have boomeranged against the Regional office in that each time it approached" Kaiser with a complaint of discrimination now, the company was suspicious and believed the agency was attempting to build up a stronger case, even though "that has not been . . . our attitude." The FEPC could have accomplished more integrating and upgrading, he lamented, had the company not become so resentful over the directives tying it to the boilermakers. It was clear not only that Kaiser hired over 90 percent of all black war workers, Rutledge wrote, but that Edgar Kaiser himself took a much more progressive position on integration, both on the job and in housing, than did the boilermakers.[68]

Rutledge based his statements partially on a "revealing private session" with Tom Ray, held at Ray's request. The boilermaker agent had quarreled with Edgar Kaiser over segregating blacks in the areas of work and housing. Over Ray's opposition, Kaiser had refused to separate workers along racial lines. Rutledge visited the Kaiser dormitories and confirmed they were completely interracial, with the sharing of community stores and cafeterias. Next, Ray had fought attempts by Kaiser to mix workers on the job. Kaiser opposed separate shifts but compromised where feasible. Rutledge confided, "Frankly, I don't know why Ray told me these things," except he thought perhaps Ray was trying to show Kaiser as a "double crosser." Kaiser's original mistake, Rutledge indicated, was making a deal with the AFL instead of with the CIO. A progressive union could have done an excellent job of integrating workers in the yards and in housing. Even at the present time, he believed, if an agreement could be worked out to cancel the directives against Kaiser in return for cooperation in clearing up the boilermaker situation, the FEPC could make considerable progress in handling the shipyard cases throughout the Pacific Coast.[69]

68. Edward Rutledge to Harry Kingman, November 10, 1944, in Legal Division Office files of Frank D. Reeves, Miscellaneous file, R8HR, RG 228.
69. Ibid.

Harry Kingman forwarded the Rutledge letter to central and added his own pungent comments. He thought the year of deadlock resulting from Kaiser's reaction to the findings and directives should be broken as soon as possible. Because of this impasse, the FEPC's work in processing cases against Kaiser had been "much more difficult," action "against flagrant Boilermaker discrimination" had stalled, the outlook for blacks employed by Kaiser during the cutback and reconversion period was clouded, and the Kaisers had withheld cooperation that might have aided the FEPC's entire agenda of west coast activities. Despite some admitted Kaiser shortcomings, he noted, "they have done better than any other large establishment" and have indicated a willingness to do more if and when the FEPC would dismiss "what they consider an unfair and unrealistic finding" of discrimination. Regardless of the merits of the FEPC's handling of the case, Kingman warned, "Kaiser [intended] to fight the Committee to the bitter end." Company spokesmen had made a grim promise: "Instead of helping you people put #9346 into effect, as we were ready to do a year ago, we are going to trip you up every chance we get."[70]

Kaiser's charge of bad faith could not be documented because most of the allegations involved informal, word-of-mouth exchanges and understandings. Yet Kingman related the charge to the central office and apparently believed it. Prior to the first hearing, Malcolm Ross had gotten word to Kaiser officials through Paul Porter of the WPB that the boilermakers were primarily responsible for discrimination at the shipyards and that the case against the company would not be pressed. At the same time, FEPC special counsel Marvin Harrison, fearful that Henry J. Kaiser would blast the FEPC for holding a hearing when internal boilermaker quarrels complicated matters for the company, promised Edgar Kaiser that the hearing would deal almost exclusively with boilermaker violations of Executive Order 9346. Consequently, the FEPC findings and directives against Kaiser were "entirely unexpected and unacceptable." Believing it had been "persecuted" by the FEPC, the company, henceforth, would provide "little cooperation."[71]

Kingman's advice to break the deadlock was echoed by the Legal Division's Frank Reeves. Visiting the West Coast in November, he

70. Harry Kingman to Malcolm Ross and George Johnson, November 14, 1944, in Legal Division, office files of Frank D. Reeves, Miscellaneous file, R8HR, RG 228.
71. *Ibid.*

suggested that the FEPC request an opinion from the attorney general on whether under Executive Order 9346 the agency might "legally direct and require an employer to hire or retain persons otherwise qualified whose employment [was] opposed by a union with a valid closed shop contract." He also recommended, "in the interest of present and future relations" with Kaiser, that the charges be dropped and company support be enlisted in prosecuting complaints against the unions. The Legal Division, itself divided on the Kaiser issue, was reluctant to throw out the charges against the shipbuilders, but it did recommend modification of the directives. All other committee action, however, it suggested be postponed pending the outcome of the IBB appeal of the *James* case to the California Supreme Court. On December 2, 1944, the committee voted to affirm the findings and directives with modifications from evidence produced at the rehearing, an action not communicated formally to the shipbuilders until February, well after the *James* decision had affirmed the FEPC's legal position.[72]

The committee was thus well advised to wait for the California Supreme Court. On December 30, by a vote of seven to zero, that body upheld Judge Butler's decision against Marinship and IBB Local 6 in the *James* case. The court, in justifying its intervention, noted that states, though forbidden to deprive labor unions of the right of free speech through picketing, retained the power to provide protection against abuses of that right. The fundamental issue was whether a closed union coupled with a closed shop could be a legitimate objective of organized labor. No one questioned that in California the closed shop was lawful, but the union argued that as a private voluntary association it had the right "to limit membership to persons mutually acceptable." The court believed, however, that an "arbitrarily closed union is incompatible with the closed shop," for under such an arrangement, the union could monopolize the supply of labor. Consequently, the union "occupies a quasi-public position similar to a

---

72. *Ibid.*; decision on rehearing, February 12, 1945, in Legal Division, Petition for Rehearing file, R14HR, Frank Reeves to George Johnson, November 21, 1944, in office files of Frank D. Reeves, Miscellaneous file, Evelyn Cooper to George Johnson, December 1, 1944, in office files of Evelyn Cooper, Memos from Johnson file, Legal Division, R8HR, Frank Reeves to Members of the Legal Division, December 11, 1944, in Records of George M. Johnson, Frank Reeves file, R5HR, George Johnson to Frank Reeves, November 15, 1944, in Records of George Johnson, Boilermakers file, R4HR, all in RG 228.

public service business with certain obligations." Although the ship-building industry operated in interstate commerce under the NLRB and the Wagner Act, nothing in that statute gave unions the right to maintain closed membership under a closed-shop agreement. Marinship contended it was bound to enforce the contract, yet in doing so, the company "indirectly assisted the union in its discrimination." The court ruled that a third person involved in the commission of a prohibited act could also be enjoined and so enjoined Marinship. In its conclusion, the court stated that "Negroes must be admitted under the same terms as non-Negroes unless the union and employer refrain from enforcing the closed shop agreement against them." The court also relieved the black shipyard workers of paying union dues pending the outcome of the action.[73]

In the black community, the joy was universal. For the shipyard workers, it was a just reward for years of hard work, real sacrifice, and gnawing uncertainty. To the press, the case represented a "great community victory" that strengthened the democratic process. But it was scarcely "one of the most far-reaching [cases] in labor history," as the Pittsburgh *Courier* claimed, nor would it necessarily, as the Chicago *Defender* stated, "have direct influence on all courts in the United States." At this point, it was still unclear what the longer-range consequences would be. For the FEPC, the outcome provided justification, in a strictly legalistic sense, of its position against the companies, but it fueled the serious questioning of the central office's judgment by the agency's west coast agents, who for over a year had operated in a special purgatory created for them by the shipbuilders. With the *James* decision, however, the hostile and abrasive tone of the shipbuilders' attorneys abruptly changed for the better.[74]

Although additional court appeals remained a possibility for the boilermakers, they realized they would also have to change, and the

73. *Joseph James* v. *Marinship Corporation and Boilermaker Local 6,* Supreme Court of California #17015, in Legal Division, Decisions file, R15HR, RG 228.

74. Harry Kingman to Malcolm Ross and George Johnson (telegram), January 30, 1945, in Legal Division, Petition for Rehearing file, R14HR, and San Francisco *People's World,* January 11, 1945, in Newspaper Clippings, Box 529, both in RG 228, Pittsburgh *Courier,* January 13, 1945, pp. 1, 5; Chicago *Defender,* January 13, 1945, p. 6. For a discussion of another important victory blacks won in December of 1944, this one in the United States Supreme Court, *Thomas Tunstall* v. *Brotherhood of Locomotive Firemen of Norfolk, Virginia,* see Philip Foner, *Organized Labor and the Black Worker, 1619–1973* (New York, 1974), 245–47.

substance of that transformation became the subject of additional weeks of negotiation with the FEPC. That the committee would prevail was by no means certain, but the IBB membership, even in the South where their racist ideology was unchallenged, could be pragmatic when union goals were at stake. At the Brown Shipbuilding Company in Houston, Texas, for example, the boilermakers early in 1945 began championing the rights of black workers. In an NLRB election, the employees had been given a choice between the IBB or no union, but the company had admittedly classified hundreds of blacks who might have supported the union as common laborers to bar them from voting. After losing the election, the boilermakers objected to the exclusion of blacks and were sustained by the regional NLRB.[75]

Whether Charles MacGowan was affected by the Houston situation is unknown, but the California Supreme Court decision must have profoundly shaken the IBB leadership. On February 10, MacGowan proposed policy changes that "should put the Boilermakers in compliance" with all of the FEPC's directives. The union "is a very old organization," he wrote, and the practices that concerned the FEPC "developed over a long period of years": opinions and prejudices "are deep-rooted, so that change . . . cannot be brought about overnight." Nevertheless, IBB leaders explained the FEPC's position to the membership "to get their consent to make the changes necessary to be in compliance," and the executive council in January altered boilermaker laws and practices to eliminate FEPC objections. The auxiliary system would be changed. As to which auxiliaries, however, MacGowan's letter seemed purposely vague. "Auxiliary lodges mentioned in the directives, and other auxiliaries in California, Oregon and Washington, and other Auxiliaries" would be dissolved "as expeditiously as possible . . . and rechartered as regular Subordinate Lodges . . . with full autonomy," but they would be segregated. Boilermaker attorney Clif Langsdale had carefully searched federal and state case law and found no legal bars to such organizations.[76]

When Ross, Johnson, and their legal counsels met with Langsdale

75. Will Maslow to Malcolm Ross, February 2, 1945, in office files of George M. Johnson, Will Maslow file, R3HR, RG 228.

76. Charles MacGowan to Malcolm Ross, February 10, 1945, in Documents file, February 12, 1945, R1HR, and Clif Langsdale to Charles MacGowan, February 15, 1945, in Legal Division, Boilermakers file, R14HR, both in RG 228.

on February 20, they found that MacGowan's carefully crafted letter, couched in generalities, offered much and little, according to the beholder. The FEPC's 1943 directives, Langsdale pointed out, objected to certain bylaws of the auxiliaries that made them subservient to the subordinate lodges. MacGowan would dissolve these auxiliaries and place all members under the same bylaws and form, without distinction. He judged these changes as sufficient to assure compliance. When matters such as jurisdiction, universal transfer, job referral, cutbacks, seniority, and other vital issues were explored, however, it became clear that MacGowan's proposals contained little real substance. One of the most fundamental problems was jurisdiction, which bothered the FEPC staff more than any other issue. If an employer needed a hundred workers, which local would he notify, Frank Reeves asked, and how would they be supplied? "That is a detail on which I cannot commit myself," was the reply. "It will be worked out fairly and without discrimination." Otherwise, the union knew, legal action might result. In California, there had been no discrimination in allocating jobs through the white lodges, Langsdale asserted. George Johnson disagreed. There was substance to complaints that blacks were assigned a quota, he countered, and no auxiliary members were referred even though whites were unavailable. "So long as the situation makes a condition like that possible," the black worker "is at sufferance." Langsdale stated emphatically that such a condition "is not going to be," for the boilermakers were proposing "absolute equal lodges with equal rights." [77]

Another difficult question involved universal transfer of membership, increasingly important during the transition period. According to MacGowan's proposal, a black worker could transfer to another black local or, if none existed, deposit his card with the IBB. If there was no black lodge, Johnson asked, what rights would the worker have in a white subordinate lodge? Langsdale said blacks could not join a white lodge, but there would be black lodges wherever five or more black boilermakers worked. FEPC attorney Evelyn Cooper discovered that MacGowan's proposals on universal transfer initially would be put into effect only in California and Oregon, where the union presently faced FEPC directives. Langsdale responded that "the International could not go down to Birmingham and tell them to do it right

77. Meeting with Clif Langsdale, February 20, 1945, in Legal Division, office files of Evelyn N. Cooper, Miscellaneous file, R8HR, RG 228.

now and not lose membership." The point seemed of little consequence since blacks probably would not want to go to Birmingham to work. MacGowan saw no chance that more could be offered in this area.[78]

Obviously aware of the seriousness of the jurisdiction issue, Langsdale subsequently submitted additional proposals from MacGowan on dispatching members to jobs when two subordinate lodges, white and black, existed in the same plant. Two methods to handle this situation were possible. A district lodge could be created, supervised in good faith by the IBB president. Under this body, the referral and dispatching of men would take place in a "commonsense," practical manner. By "commonsense," MacGowan meant a quota system based on the ratio of the total membership of each subordinate lodge. Or, where no district lodge existed, a joint committee of the two locals could handle the matter.[79]

When the meeting with Langsdale ended, the IBB attorney requested "speedy movement" by the FEPC. In view of the California lawsuit, the course to be taken by the IBB would depend largely upon what the FEPC decided. The shipbuilders were also weighing their options. Even as the meeting with Langsdale went on, west coast newspapers reported that the shipyards would obey the court. By mid-April, most of the California shipbuilders had notified the FEPC of their compliance. So had the Kaiser Company in Oregon, which advised the committee on the procedures it had put into effect. Prospective black employees were referred for clearance to the offices of the IBB subordinate lodges in Portland and Vancouver with instructions to return to the company employment office whether or not they had obtained clearance. Such persons, if qualified, were then hired, and no black worker faced discharge because of failure to maintain membership in the auxiliary. Kaiser intended to pursue this policy until informed by the committee that the IBB was in compliance with its directives.[80]

Achieving accommodation with the IBB, however, was not so easy.

78. *Ibid.*

79. Clif Langsdale to Malcolm Ross, March 13, 1945, in Legal Division, West Coast Hearings–General, R15HR, RG 228.

80. R. E. Brown to Malcolm Ross and Harry Kingman, February 20, 1945, in Recent Telegrams and Letters, Kingman file, Harry F. Morton to FEPC, March 21, 1945, in Kaiser Co., Legal Division, R14HR, and FEPC release, March 28, 1945, in Legal Division, West Coast Hearings–General, R15HR, all in RG 228.

Whether "separate but equal" subordinate lodges established in place of the auxiliaries would satisfy the committee's findings was the basic question. FEPC attorney Evelyn Cooper thought that merely abolishing the auxiliaries was "too simple an answer." Looking at the "formality" of MacGowan's proposal was not enough, she insisted. It had to be examined substantively to determine whether blacks were assured "essential union representation and protection" in tenure, hire, and terms and conditions of employment, including equal bargaining power. Cooper concluded that the assumption of equality between the new black lodges and the white lodges was unwarranted. Unless these issues were clarified, black representation would be by sufferance, as it was under the auxiliary system. Democratic collective bargaining was impossible when there were two bargaining agents within a single unit.[81]

The committee accepted Cooper's analysis almost verbatim. The proposals made by the IBB and the steps to be taken did not, in its judgment, constitute compliance. The suggested division of members into separate lodges denied blacks essential equality in collective bargaining in the day-to-day application of the contract to individual workers. Indeed, the committee wrote, a system of dual representation based on race "is inconsistent with the principle of majority rule" as applied by government agencies administering the labor relations laws. Furthermore, MacGowan's proposal for a "commonsense method" of dispatching workers to jobs contemplated "job referrals based upon racial quotas or percentages," tying individual opportunity to the artificial criterion of race rather than to personal qualifications. In addition, the committee concluded that the system of separate subordinate lodges denied black boilermakers the rights and benefits of universal transfer. Whereas blacks could move their membership to some 40 lodges, a white member had a choice of 560. Consequently, the value of a transfer was substantially less for blacks, who assumed the same obligations to the union as whites did.[82]

The controversy between the FEPC and the IBB was never resolved. With the war winding down and peacetime production resuming, the shipyard boom ended and so did the jobs. The FEPC's jurisdiction as

81. Evelyn Cooper to George Johnson, March 8, 1945, in Legal Division, Records of George M. Johnson, Committee Material, R4HR, RG 228.
82. "Statement of the Basis for Committee's Decision . . . RE Boilermaker's Proposal," in Legal Division, Boilermakers file, R15HR, RG 228.

a wartime agency in industries converting to peacetime production was in doubt. At the same time, the crippling attacks in Congress and the slashing of appropriations added to the agency's impotence. Charles MacGowan's testimony to a congressional committee in the spring of 1945 opposing the establishment of a permanent FEPC was the IBB's final act of defiance. What influence the agency had would soon end.[83]

In the midst of a great national crisis, the IBB clung to its traditional practices with astonishing persistence, despite FEPC attempts to bring about change. The IBB also faced widespread disapproval within the labor movement. During this period of emergency, the boilermakers and the AFL metal trades unions seemed to be pursuing a double agenda. While winning the war may have been important, they fought to preserve certain cherished traditions, such as white-oriented craft exclusion and discrimination, even when such goals hampered the war effort. Although the IBB's auxiliary unions for blacks were totally subservient, even its subordinate white lodges functioned like local fiefdoms, herding in thousands of raw workers and collecting their dues but failing in the vital task of education and unionization. Whether the white boilermakers received the services to which they were entitled in the day-to-day application of the contract to the work place is unknown. Black shipyard workers certainly got little in return for their membership in the IBB auxiliaries except wartime jobs.

Yet blacks, in their anger, turned the shipyard employment situation around on the West Coast. The leaders of the shipyard protest movements came from the three organizations most important to black activism during this period: the Urban League in Portland, the NAACP in San Francisco, and the CIO in Los Angeles. Their action, next to the MOWM and possibly CORE, was probably the most important black protest activity undertaken during the war years. Although they could have preserved lucrative jobs by paying dues to the IBB auxiliaries, they chose to challenge a system degrading to them as citizens and human beings. In taking their grievances to the courts, they forced the boilermakers for the first time to begin negotiating in earnest with the FEPC. Their suits also strengthened that agency's position with the shipbuilders.

83. "Rebuttal Draft to MacGowan's Testimony on HR 2232" (Typescript, carbon, n.d., in Documents file, June 25, 1945, R1HR, RG 228).

The *James* case represented a tremendous victory for black activism, but there were many things that the decision did not do. With the war winding down, its practical application in providing jobs was limited and its effects temporary. Although contemporaries hailed the decision as a landmark and one historian called it a "major new interpretation in U.S. labor law," such claims have never been documented.[84] Indeed, the IBB's plan to substitute segregated subordinate lodges for black auxiliaries set the stage for the subversion of the decision, as the FEPC conference with Clif Langsdale so clearly indicated. When the IBB, at its next quadrennial convention, abolished the auxiliaries and established segregated local lodges, the FEPC, in its *Final Report*, pronounced that action inadequate for removal of the directives. Nor is there evidence of the *James* decision's positive effect on postwar labor union membership prior to affirmative action in the 1960s. However, it did have considerable meaning in the larger context of an emerging civil rights movement because it demonstrated that minority activism, working through federal agencies and the courts, could bring about change.[85]

Boilermaker discrimination and intransigence also affected the shipbuilders, some of whom, like Edgar Kaiser, squirmed uncomfortably when FEPC findings and directives made them bedfellows in discrimination with the recalcitrant union. The shipbuilders' marriage to the AFL was of their own making. In their rush to turn back the more militant, and also more racially liberal, CIO industrial unions, they bound themselves to the AFL metal trades organizations in nearly every west coast shipyard except in the Los Angeles area. It was a brilliant industry coup against the CIO, carried out before most of the shipyard workers arrived, imposed without NLRB elections, and sealed by closed-shop contracts with the AFL metal trades councils. Edgar Kaiser, to his credit, resisted the more outrageous boilermaker demands, but for the sake of harmony, he sometimes compromised black workers' jobs. Most of the shipbuilders, with the possible exception of Moore Dry Dock and Calship, did much less than Kaiser.

84. See Harris, "Federal Intervention in Union Discrimination," 344.

85. FEPC, *Final Report*, June 28, 1946 (Washington, D.C., 1947), 21; Hill, *Black Labor and the American Legal System*, 206–207. For a discussion of black worker protest in Winston-Salem and Detroit during this period, see Robert Korstad and Nelson Lichtenstein, "Opportunities Found and Lost: Labor, Radicals, and the Early Civil Rights Movement," *Journal of American History*, LXXV (1988), 787–801.

None of them curbed completely the racism of supervisors at the shop level, though Kaiser seems to have tried harder than most. Unfortunately, the shipbuilders, in their pique over the directives, apparently fought FEPC attempts to adjust individual complaints of discrimination, regardless of merit.

In the struggle with the boilermakers, the FEPC assumed its accustomed role of weakness. Yet it is difficult to imagine the unfolding of events as they did on the West Coast without this type of federal presence serving as a catalyst for change. The groundwork had been prepared by the OPM and the WMC and by the capable Clarence Johnson, among others. Then, under the New Committee, FEPC regional offices listened to complaints and recorded them, carried out investigations, provided positive encouragement, stirred other federal agencies to action when possible, and used moral suasion against violators. The FEPC hearings and the publicity generated therefrom provided a powerful and hitherto unavailable tool for disseminating information about minority grievances. The FEPC's findings and directives, even when ignored by the likes of the IBB, were fretted over by powerful industrialists like Kaiser. FEPC hearings provided mass publicity for a moral cause and were vitally important to black activists, who appreciated their effectiveness and demanded more of them. The FEPC's experience with the west coast shipbuilders and the IBB illustrated how coalitions of minorities and sympathetic federal agencies could pursue significant civil rights goals with some success.

PART III

The FEPC: Reconversion and Demise

10 / From Reconversion to "Rest in Peace"

While the FEPC's struggle with the boilermakers union dragged on, the war in Europe ended. As industries abandoned war production, they passed out of the FEPC's jurisdiction. The President's Committee believed, however, that its influence over war industries could continue during reconversion if war and nonwar activities were commingled or interdependent or if a plant's facilities were used to maintain and service war industries. Labor unions in such industries would also have to answer to the FEPC. Government agencies would be the last to slip beyond FEPC control. Ultimately, though, the changeover to peacetime activity would narrow committee jurisdiction under the executive order even if congressional funding continued.[1]

Reconversion would leave thousands of minority workers without jobs. In view of prewar employment patterns, their chances for work in the labor market after the war were highly uncertain. Many forecasters, looking back at the depressed reconversion period following World War I, expected a repetition in 1945. Even if the postwar economy performed well, racial bias would wipe out many of the minority wartime gains. Protection from discrimination was still needed. "Peace may bring untold suffering due to industrial displacement and partly to downright discrimination," the Chicago *Defender* warned its readers as early as November, 1943. "By the time the war ends, the

1. Minutes, committee meeting, September 30, 1944, R1HR, RG 228.

moral force of . . . [Executive Order 9346] will have spent itself."
Unemployment insurance and social security would not be enough to
tide over the black unemployed. Negro organizations "should do
something now to prevent the tragic invalidation of the gains made
under the stress of war," it urged.[2]

As the New Committee's division of Review and Analysis began
functioning, its director, John A. Davis, also became concerned about
reconversion. Much of the white resistance to minority employment
stemmed from fears of competition after the war ended, he noted.
The FEPC, he believed, should consider asking the president to outline
the administration's postwar plans so that white workers could be assured that a full employment economy would continue. Early in 1944
the National Urban League completed a survey on postwar industrial
jobs. Based on current performances, 253 plants employing 150,000
Afro-Americans in 120 cities would keep them on their jobs. Of these
responses, 154 came from firms with blacks working in skilled trades.
Despite stated concerns from 142 plants over absenteeism, race friction, "chip on the shoulder" attitudes, and high turnover, the National Urban League saw gains in postwar employment, but other observers were less sanguine. G. James Fleming found that when
personnel was reduced, black workers in Region III became victims of
trickery and other underhanded methods of getting them laid off or
fired. Typical was the practice of lowering efficiency ratings. A CIO
official in Los Angeles was also alarmed. By the summer of 1944 several local industries were already laying off African- and Mexican-
Americans and women ahead of other employees. Such policies would
"jeopardize the civic unity of the community" and "exacerbate
forces" of dissension, "which thrive on such situations," he warned.[3]

Congress provided little reassurance. In August, 1944, the Senate
passed a reconversion bill that turned over control of postwar unemployment insurance to the states. Authored by Georgia's senator Walter George, it was supported by Republicans and southern Democrats

2. Editorial, Chicago *Defender*, November 13, 1943, p.14.
3. John Davis to Will Maslow, August 21, 1943, in office files of George M. Johnson, John A. Davis file, R3HR, National Urban League Report, February 9, 1944,
cited in Weekly News Digest, February 18, 1944, in office files of Emanuel H. Bloch,
News Digest file, R6HR, and Philip M. Connelly to Malcolm Ross, July 27, 1944, in
Public Relations 5, R42HR, all in RG 228; Philadelphia *Tribune*, February 26, 1944,
p.15.

and gave "evidence of what Negroes can expect to be up against," noted the Norfolk *Journal and Guide.* The southern states, where 8,000,000 blacks resided, would "gyp the Negro out of his equitable share of the benefits . . . and use the opportunity to further depress the living standards of colored civilians and returned veterans in the postwar period." It was a "sorry picture," this army of black veterans "returned from fighting for democracy and forced into actual or virtual serfdom," noted this usually restrained and conservative southern black newspaper.[4]

In summer, 1944, the FEPC began discussing and planning for reconversion. A proposal to establish quotas for laying off blacks with little seniority appealed neither to the FEPC nor to Afro-American leaders. Labor unions would be a problem, observed the Chicago *Defender,* and other minority groups might try to use the plan to gain special treatment. John A. Davis wanted to get committee representation on the WPB's Production Executive Committee (PEC), a body that passed on all major cutbacks proposed by the procurement agencies and also determined the timing of such cutbacks and the plants to be affected. With or without the FEPC's physical presence on that body, Davis wrote, the PEC should be urged when it considered cutbacks to take into account special employment problems of minority workers and interracial tensions in war production centers. The PEC dealt only with major cutback programs, however. Minor changes could be authorized in the field by the procurement agencies themselves. Davis therefore urged the FEPC to prepare recommendations for the War and Navy departments and for the Maritime Commission.[5]

During September, 1944, Chairman Ross gave the committee a comprehensive set of staff proposals for action during the transition period. The procurement agencies were still writing new war contracts, he noted, and their volume would continue to be considerable until Japan surrendered. As cutbacks occurred after the defeat of Germany, the procurement agencies would have a greater choice among the qualified producers. The FEPC, he believed, should request that

4. Norfolk *Journal and Guide,* August 19, 1944, in Newspaper Clippings, Box 516, RG 228.

5. John Davis to Postwar Planning Committee, September 22, 1944, in office files of John A. Davis, All Other Members file, R68HR, RG 228; Chicago *Defender,* July 29, 1944, p. 3.

contracts be denied to firms practicing discrimination. At the same time, the procurement agencies should coordinate the placement of new war contracts to minimize the unemployment of minority workers. These agencies should also be asked to instruct their staffs to act without discrimination.[6]

In addition to the procurement agencies, the FEPC also targeted several others, including the Veterans Administration, which was responsible for overseeing the G.I. Bill; the WMC, whose USES and Veterans Employment Service should continue to report discrimination to the FEPC; the Selective Service System, whose enabling legislation contained a nondiscrimination clause; the Office of Vocational Rehabilitation, which distributed to the states funds for training the handicapped; the USO, which supervised the training of war workers; and the soon-to-be-created Office of War Mobilization and Reconversion, which would be in charge of planning war and civilian production during the transition period. With these agencies properly activated, the committee would be holding more regional hearings against parties charged with discrimination. The FEPC's plan for the reconversion period was well conceived. With cooperation from the other agencies, it was also workable.[7]

In pursuing this program, the committee wanted to approach the procurement, production, and manpower agencies through the president. In October, 1944, its staff prepared a letter from FDR to Ross requesting that the FEPC work with federal agencies in the formulation of peacetime antidiscrimination policies, copies of which would be sent to the targeted agencies. The White House refused, and Roosevelt, in fragile health and waging a reelection campaign, declined to meet with the committee to discuss reconversion. In January, 1945, the FEPC tried again. This time letters addressed to specific agency directors were sent to Roosevelt for his signature. They mentioned the president's concern about the utilization of minority workers, cited manpower shortages in several industries that could be traced to the refusal to employ minorities, and requested cooperation in ending discrimination. Roosevelt asked Office of War Mobilization director James F. Byrnes for advice. In his reply, Byrnes noted, "About a year

6. Malcolm Ross to Members of the Committee, September 29, 1944, in Records of George Johnson, Committee Materials file, R4HR, RG 228.
7. *Ibid.*

ago you assigned to Jonathan Daniels the task of considering the problems of the FEPC." It would be wise, he reminded FDR, "to have one person considering these questions." Byrnes himself had "consistently declined to discuss these matters either with the FEPC group or with the various Congressmen and Senators who [had] communicated" with him. In the end, Roosevelt declined to sign the letters. Apparently he did not consult Daniels, who reportedly favored some FEPC participation in the reconversion process.[8]

Daniels was no friend of the FEPC or of its often embattled chairman, however, and his negative influence was undoubtedly a factor in the administration's general failure to support the agency. When the Federal Council of Churches late in 1944 gave the White House the opportunity to nominate the FEPC for the Edward L. Bernays Award for Outstanding Achievement in White-Negro Relations, Daniels advised against it. The president was proud of the accomplishments of the whole administration in the civil rights field—accomplishments in which a number of government officials had been involved, Daniels noted. Although he realized such an award would benefit the administration, he based his advice on the possibility of the creation of a permanent FEPC: "Nothing should be done which would seem to assure the appointment of Malcolm Ross as its chairman. He has not done a very good job . . . and I think it would be a tragic thing if any [presidential recommendation] would seem to foreshadow his appointment as head of a permanent agency."[9]

After consulting Will Alexander, however, Daniels suggested nominating for the award a "combination of" a black (Ted Poston) and a white (Philleo Nash) for their careful "watching of the situation" during the summer of 1944 "to prevent the occurrence of any interracial clashes." Daniels alerted Alexander that he might be called on for such a suggestion. Although Poston and Nash were able wartime employees who performed valuable behind-the-scenes work in race re-

8. Draft of letter, President to Malcolm Ross, Documents file, October 11, 1944, R1HR, Malcolm Ross to Jonathan Daniels, October 16, 1944, in Public Relations 5, White House Correspondence file, R45HR, all in RG 228; Memorandum, James Byrnes to the President, January 18, 1945, Box 70–2, Byrnes Papers; Malcolm Ross to Julius Krug, October 16, 1944, Jonathan Daniels to Julius Krug, October 25, 1944, both in Daniels Papers.

9. Jonathan Daniels to the President, November 24, 1944, Jonathan Daniels to George E. Haynes, November 24, 1944, both in Box 33, Daniels Papers.

lations in the OWI, this Daniels-Alexander proposal from two white southern liberals whose own bland recipe for solving racial problems had turned sour, was small and mean-spirited in view of the considerable contributions and public service performed by the FEPC and its dedicated staff. In the end the administration did nothing.[10]

With Roosevelt's refusal to open doors for the agency, Ross made at least one other attempt to involve the FEPC directly in reconversion planning. In February, 1945, he asked Paul McNutt to permit an FEPC representative to attend the WMC's weekly meetings as an observer and to participate in discussions of proposed manpower policies when they affected the utilization of minority workers. Ross also wanted his field personnel to receive the same privileges on the WMC's local manpower priorities committees in selected areas, because "some of the regional [FEPC] men are now experts in this function." Finally, he requested an exchange of information between his Washington, D.C., staff and the WMC's director for program development. McNutt apparently granted none of these requests. Meanwhile, the FEPC's John Davis solicited whatever data was available from private groups such as the American Council on Race Relations and the National Urban League. Unfortunately, without White House and agency support the FEPC had no real input into reconversion.[11]

Not only was the FEPC cut off from reconversion discussions, but the staff also had no source for finding out what decisions had been made except through the bureaucratic grapevine. The FEPC's Max Berking learned about the activity of the important Production Readjustment Committee, the successor to the PEC, from a contact in the WPB whom he called "my informant." Berking's sleuthing was so successful that he recommended "our use of sympathetic experts" within other government agencies. Although the FEPC continued to send unsolicited recommendations to government agencies and their reconversion committees, its suggestions and requests appear to have been ignored.[12]

10. Jonathan Daniels to Will Alexander, December 5, 1944, in Box 33, Daniels Papers.

11. John Davis to Robert Weaver, December 2, 1944, in Public Relations 5, W file, R45HR, Malcolm Ross to Paul McNutt, February 9, 1945, in U.S. Govt., WMC, R67HR, and John Davis to Lester Granger, December 9, 1944, in office files of John A. Davis, G file, R68HR, all in RG 228.

12. Max Berking to John Davis, William Leland, Will Maslow, and Clarence Mitchell, January 8, 1945, Malcolm Ross to William Haber, OWMR, March 31, 1945,

So Ross and the staff tried to promote their ideas through press releases and other contracts with the general public. Some of the FEPC's agenda was carried late in December in a feature article in the Chicago *Sun*. African- and Mexican-Americans would be the first minority groups laid off when cutbacks occurred and the last to be taken into the civilian industries, the FEPC believed, and business would use this desperate situation to depress wage standards. The committee also feared an epidemic of race riots like those following World War I. The transfer to peacetime production would be even more difficult because larger numbers of minority workers had entered the job market. Labor unions must be encouraged to accept them, said the FEPC, if for no other reason than to protect the white workers from employers who would use African- and Mexican-Americans to break wage rates. By the same token, minority groups must avoid using the charge of racism as a solution to all of their problems.[13]

Reports during the spring of 1945 bore out some of the FEPC's fears, though race riots did not materialize. The number of layoffs was staggering even where discrimination was not a factor. At Curtiss-Wright in Buffalo, 9,000 female production workers lost their jobs, according to Edward Lawson in Region II. Black women were affected in a five-to-one ratio because discrimination forced them to be the last hired and trained. An IAM seniority agreement protected workers with greater longevity. By April, 4,000 mostly black women had registered with the USES. Of the others, many had little savings and believed they had earned a rest and deserved unemployment insurance. State investigators from Albany thought otherwise, cut off those who refused to report to the USES for job referrals, and demanded the return of unemployment compensation already paid.[14]

For many of these women, reconversion proved to be a shock. They had earned between $0.80 and $1.42 per hour at Curtiss-Wright, and though living costs had not declined, the USES expected them to interview for jobs that paid much less. Many turned down the referrals,

---

Malcolm Ross to Julius S. Krug, WPB, May 16, 1945, N–Z, Malcolm Ross to Brigadier General Frank T. Hines, March 23, 1945, A–M, all in U.S. Govt., Gen., R67HR, RG 228.

13. Chicago *Sun*, December 29, 1944, in Newspaper Clippings, Box 529, RG 228.

14. Edward Lawson to Will Maslow, April 17, 1945, in Reports, FEP, I file, R48HR, RG 228.

outraging a USES manager who had refused to accept discriminatory orders from employers in order to keep jobs available for black applicants. Flare-ups and tension were reported between African-American women and those of Polish and Italian descent. Thus was reconversion in the Buffalo area a tangle of disappointments, latent biases, and general confusion. In the South, state authorities took a different tack, according to Clarence Mitchell. Blacks were told they could not get unemployment compensation unless they agreed to accept service or laboring jobs when such work became available, a very effective approach in getting skilled and semiskilled blacks back into low-grade employment.[15]

Gloomy reports also circulated from St. Louis and Detroit, while in Houston the *Informer* advised its readers "to save, cut down on foolish spending, and invest in war bonds." Because of discrimination millions would not find jobs "after the war" even if a "big depression" did not occur. By November, 1945, the exodus of minority workers from wartime jobs had turned into a virtual rout, and discrimination was "rapidly approaching pre-war levels," columnist Ted Poston reported in the New York *Post*.[16]

Although the FEPC would be needed in peacetime as much as during the war, Congress, after bitter wrangling and lengthy filibusters throughout June and July, slashed the agency's budget by more than half, to $250,000. The cuts crippled operations. Shortly thereafter, Ross announced the August closing of five of the fifteen field offices and staff reductions from 114 to 51. A drastic reorganization of the central office and all of the remaining field offices got under way. Some important pending cases were sorted out for further attention, but the drastic cuts in personnel ended the case method of handling most complaints.[17]

Some staff members proposed seeking aid from the private sector. Advisory panels could be set up, first nationally and then locally. Outstanding citizens serving on these panels could give advice and assistance in negotiating and adjusting difficult cases. The panels could also

15. *Ibid.*; Clarence Mitchell to Will Maslow, May 18, 1945, in office files of George M. Johnson, C. M. Mitchell file, R3HR, RG 228.

16. Houston *Informer*, June 16, 1945, Box 514, and New York *Post*, November 26, 1945, Box 532, both in Newspaper Clippings, RG 228.

17. Proposals for reorganization, Documents file, July 21, 1945, R1HR, Frank L. Yates, acting comptroller general, to Malcolm Ross, July 23, 1945, in DJ-FOI, and news release, July 26, 1945, in Releases, II, F3FR, all in RG 228.

undertake public relations and community activities previously performed by FEPC staff, such as publishing surveys of economic opportunities for minority group members and projecting the impact of reconversion and demobilization. Information on the efficiency of minority group workers on production jobs was needed, as were studies of management and labor techniques for bringing about race adjustment within industry. Other studies could survey such community problems as bad housing and bad health resulting from unemployment. This type of work was already being performed by the National Urban League, the American Jewish Congress, and organizations like them. More to the point, however, prominent citizens on FEPC panels might encourage the donation of private funds and volunteer work to help defray the expenses of the regional offices. In San Francisco, Harry Kingman, who had resigned in May, returned to serve as an unpaid consultant. The Philadelphia regional office benefited from the volunteer efforts of Barbara Rex, a Wheaton College student who worked nearly full time for eight weeks purging the files, updating scrapbooks, typing cards, and taking telephone calls. Whereas Rex was most helpful, G. James Fleming reported that most volunteers were unpredictable. The proposal to rely on various contributions from private citizens proved to be impractical.[18]

Just as serious as the funding and staff cuts was the erosion of committee jurisdiction over war industries. After the victory over Japan, Evelyn Cooper warned, FEPC jurisdiction would be "reduced to the government and its contractors should war production cease at that time." The executive order would have to be amended to give the FEPC jurisdiction over reconverted peacetime industries whose government contracts had expired. Funding was "beside the point," Ross wrote to one well-wisher. The FEPC "must change its sights" to reconversion. Shortly after that, the staff prepared a new executive order, and Ross started it through the required administrative channels. In late August, he and five others met for ten minutes with President Truman and learned that no decision would be made about the FEPC before the president's September message to Congress.[19]

18. Proposals for reorganization, in Documents file, July 21, 1945, R1HR, news release, August 27, 1945, and monthly report, Fleming to Mitchell, September 17, 1945, both in office files of Maceo Hubbard, To Deputy Chairman files, R7HR, all in RG 228.

19. Evelyn Cooper to Malcolm Ross, August 11, 1945, in Records of George M.

To justify the need for a new executive order, the staff prepared a report to the president on the status of minorities in the work force. On Victory in Europe Day 1 in every 12 workers was African- or Mexican-American. The numbers of these minorities in skilled or semiskilled jobs had doubled during the war. Already hundreds of thousands were being released. By December, 450,000 blacks would be displaced in manufacturing alone. On the West Coast, thousands of Mexican-Americans were leaving the shipyards and aircraft plants, Truman was told. Hundreds of thousands of others would also have problems because they worked in the munitions industry, the one to cut back most drastically. Although their low seniority put them on the reconversion job market first, industries in transition from war production had not welcomed minorities, and the few retained had become janitors and caretakers. Both African- and Mexican-Americans faced wholesale discrimination in their search for work. Without remedial steps discrimination would be frozen as an industrial habit. Already, increasing numbers of hiring orders to the USES were specifying "white gentile only." Blacks in the government were in a somewhat better position because of civil service, even though most of their advances came in war agencies that were temporary. Indeed, 70 percent worked in the army service forces and in naval shore installations, establishments already demobilizing. Of those in government employment, 30 percent were in the civil service and constituted 7 percent of all civil service employees, but over 57 percent of those in civil service worked in temporary war agencies.[20]

The FEPC had processed over 12,000 cases since the beginning of the war and had settled 40 percent of them satisfactorily, the report noted. The agency's "wartime experience [had] demonstrated that discrimination in employment generally can be cured through persuasion if the authority were provided." During reconversion, minority problems required the same use of government activity as in wartime, the report concluded.[21]

Johnson, Committee Material file, R4HR, Malcolm Ross to A. A. Liveright, August 29, 1945, Malcolm Ross to Stuart Long, August 28, 1945, all in Public Relations 5, L file, R43HR, RG 228; Malcolm Ross to Harold D. Smith, August 21, 1945, in DJ-FOI; Chicago *Defender*, September 1, 1945, p. 1.

20. Malcolm Ross to Charles G. Ross, secretary to the president, August 28,1945, in Public Relations 5, White House Correspondence file, R45HR, RG 228.

21. *Ibid.*

Whether Truman read this condensed, but still lengthy, document is unknown. Nevertheless, he informed Congress on September 6 that the FEPC would continue during the reconversion period, and he urged the establishment of a permanent agency. Thus encouraged, the committee notified the president on September 18 of eight categories of pending cases for which decisions and directives were in preparation. Heading the list was the District of Columbia's Capital Transit Company, which had defied committee efforts to end its discrimination for over three years. The Cincinnati cases, in limbo since the FEPC's frustrating and unsuccessful attempt to resolve that situation at a hearing early in 1945, would also be reopened.[22]

In another memorandum to Truman, the FEPC tried to find out the extent of its jurisdiction in view of the president's endorsement to Congress. The committee wrote that it had "already received one pointed inquiry as to its authority to issue directives during this period," and its effectiveness required "clarification of its jurisdiction." The FEPC interpreted Truman's statement to Congress to mean that its authority over government contractors and industries, defined before Victory in Japan Day as both "war industries" and the unions of their employees, would continue whether they were engaged in war production or in reconversion. The committee admitted that achieving compliance would impose a heavy obligation on other agencies, such as the Office of War Mobilization and Reconversion, the WMC, and the War Shipping Administration, but this interpretation of the president's intent was obviously the committee's preference.[23]

There was, however, another interpretation of Truman's message and intent that was far less favorable to the FEPC. It would limit committee operations to government agencies, contractors, the remaining war industries, and the unions of their employees. If that interpretation were adopted, the FEPC would have to abandon docketed cases in industries in the process of reconversion. The FEPC maintained that failure to pursue pending cases would "greatly harm

22. Clarence Mitchell to Edward Lawson, September 6, 1945, in Teletype folder, II, R3HR, RG 228; memorandum to the President, Pending Decisions file, September 18, 1945, in DJ-FOI.

23. Memorandum to the President, Committee's Jurisdiction During the Transition Period, September 18, 1945, and William H. Rose to George T. Washington, memorandum, Continued Operation of the FEPC Under Executive Order 9346, October 15, 1945, both in DJ-FOI.

. . . [its] prestige and effectiveness." In addition, its inability to reach reconverted industries would open the door "for unrestrained discrimination in the field where minority groups most need protection." There would be a "serious loss of wartime gains in non-discrimination." Whatever was decided, the committee assumed that based on the president's ultimate enforcement authority, it would retain the power to issue directives against violators and to make recommendations to government agencies and the president on ways to carry out its mandate.[24]

For over three months the FEPC's proposed executive order moved slowly through various agencies and departments for comment. The committee received no word about its jurisdiction except in one case, Capital Transit. From the solicitor general's office came the opinion that "notwithstanding the surrender of Japan and the altered conditions in the labor market," Executive Order 9346 gave the committee jurisdiction over that public transportation system. Capital Transit, supported by southern congressmen, had refused since 1942 to hire blacks as platform workers (conductors and motormen) despite the FEPC's efforts, which included a public hearing in January, 1945, to change this policy. Transit systems in several cities had responded positively to the FEPC. Primarily through its insistence, blacks had been hired as platform workers and bus drivers in such major cities as New York, Chicago, Los Angeles, Detroit, and Philadelphia, the latter after a bitter strike by white operators and a takeover by the federal government. Persistent prodding and conferences had brought platform jobs for blacks in Albany, Syracuse, Buffalo, Flushing, Pittsburgh, Cleveland, Phoenix, San Diego, San Francisco, and Seattle, as well. Capital Transit and its white platform operators, however, were a model of resistance the FEPC hoped other carriers would not emulate.[25]

24. Memorandum to the President, Committee's Jurisdiction During the Transition Period, September 18, 1945, and Rose to Washington, memorandum, Continued Operation of the FEPC Under Executive Order 9346, October 15, 1945, both in DJ-FOI.

25. G. James Fleming to George Johnson, January 12, 1942, Elmer Henderson to Will Maslow, Annual Report, September 1, 1944, in Reports, Fleming file, R48HR, E. G. Cahill to Harry Kingman, November 4, 1943, in LARY Hearing Material file, R21HR, United Traction Co., in 6BR626, F21FR, Robert A. Brown to Will Maslow, December 4, 1944, in Region XII, Administrative Files, 1943–44, Correspondence with Other Offices, Brown file, F104FR, Region II weekly report, February 17, 1945, in Tension file, N.Y. Postwar Data, Syracuse, R76HR, Margaret A. Deane to Harry

Early in November, white workers illegally struck Capital Transit over a wage dispute. Advised by the Office of Defense Transportation (ODT) that United States soldiers would operate the cars and busses, the strikers returned after a brief walkout. But the strike resumed on November 21, and Truman ordered the ODT's head, Guy D. Richardson, to take over the system and operate it. In the meantime, the FEPC, having established its jurisdiction, was preparing findings and directives against the carrier. On November 23, two days after the government takeover, the committee voted unanimously to issue the directive unless countermanded by the president, in which case, some committee members wanted to request an immediate conference with Truman. It was a bold move and a direct challenge to an administration that had not responded to FEPC inquiries and that had passed the word unofficially that a new executive order was not needed. Such confrontational action by the FEPC could embarrass Truman's administration. How could a president who allegedly lacked the power to enforce the nondiscrimination clause seize the whole system and operate it when a labor contract was violated? Chairman Ross, confined to a hospital, was not a party to the action, but he opposed it and directed that the record show he was absent from the meeting.[26]

Before the FEPC directive went out, Charles Houston communicated the committee's intent to several administration officials. Richardson, now the federal manager of the transit company, "vehemently opposed" the directive because it would "embarrass the Government" and because it conflicted with the executive order of November 21 directing the takeover. Houston "found no such inconsistency." To conform with the order, Houston pointed out the "Federal Manager

Kingman, July 26, 1945, Region XII, Administrative Files, 1945, L and P files, F103FR, W. Hanes Beall to Will Maslow, April 30, 1945, in Indianapolis file, R15HR, Casper W. Clarke to Bernard Ross, May 17, 1945, in Region XII, Seattle Transit Co. file, F106FR, Alice Kahn to John A. Davis, September 13, 1943, in office files of John A. Davis, Capital Transit Co. file, R68HR, all in RG 228; Pittsburgh *Courier*, February 6, 1943; Winkler, "Philadelphia Transit Strike of 1944," 73–89.

26. Rose to Washington, memorandum, Continued Operation of the FEPC Under Executive Order 9346, October 15, 1945, in DJ-FOI; manuscript prepared by Charley Cherokee, Harry McAlpin, and Al Smith, November 12, 1945, in office files of Malcolm Ross, MS folder, R2HR, Charles Houston to Guy Richardson, November 24, 1945, in office files of Maceo Hubbard, To Deputy Chairman file, R7HR, all in RG 228; Charles Houston to Harry Truman, November 25, 1945, in Box 310–40, 1945, Truman Papers.

is required to operate the Capital Transit system under the non-discriminatory employment policy established" by Executive Orders 8802 and 9346, "even absent a Directive [from the FEPC] to the Capital Transit Company." [27]

The following day, on November 24, Presidential Assistant John Steelman telephoned Houston and ordered him not to issue the directive. The president, he reported, had "certain plans concerning the FEPC program with which the issuance of the Directive might interfere." Houston requested the order in writing. Although it was Saturday, Steelman said he would "see about that at two o'clock," but nothing was sent. Houston asked if "written instructions would be forthcoming on Monday," but Steelman was noncommittal. "It was my position," Houston wrote Truman the following day, "that the order to hold up the Capital Transit Decision involves grave public responsibility which must be properly established." Houston then requested a conference, but the White House refused. Houston's three-page letter went unanswered, though the president certainly had read it; hand-written at the bottom of the last page was the notation "Hold it up! Harry S. Truman." [28]

As days passed without a reply, reports circulated that committee members planned a blanket resignation to protest Truman's handling of the matter. Houston, after waiting seven days, resigned on December 3, but he did not depart meekly. "Without notice . . . or a chance for the Committee to present its views," he wrote Truman, "you ordered the Committee not to issue" the directive. When a conference was requested, not "even an acknowledgment of the letter" was received. "Since the effect of Truman's intervention in the Capital Transit case [was] not to eliminate the discrimination but to condone it," Houston concluded that Truman had repudiated the committee. "But more important," he accused the president, by such actions "you nullify the Executive Orders themselves." He then attacked the legal opinion reportedly "floating around the White House" that the government must honor "the existing terms and conditions of employ-

27. Houston to Truman, November 25, 1945, in Box 310–40, 1945, Truman Papers.

28. *Ibid.*; McNeil, *Charles Hamilton Houston*, 171–75; Barton J. Bernstein, "The Ambiguous Legacy: The Truman Administration and Civil Rights," in Barton J. Bernstein (ed.), *Politics and Policies of the Truman Administration* (Chicago, 1970), 274.

ment in effect on Capital Transit at the moment of seizure and that the nondiscriminatory employment policies" mandated in Executive Orders 8802 and 9346 could not be implemented during "government control." Houston insisted that the federal manager not only had the power "but must enforce the national policy of nondiscrimination." [29]

Neither the company management nor the union leaders "ever claimed that the exclusion of Negroes as platform workers and traffic checkers" was part of the labor contract, Houston wrote. They merely feared that if blacks were hired they could not control the reactions of rank-and-file white platform workers. Although this supposition was never put to a test, it was obvious, he thought, that "the union leadership could not prevent a rank and file walkout" over a wage dispute in violation of the collective bargaining agreement. "Your action in the Capital Transit case means that you do not hesitate to seize" a company when a private bargaining contract is violated "but will not move, or permit the Committee to move to effectuate the national nondiscriminatory employment policy," he accused. Houston noted further that Federal Manager Guy Richardson "did not oppose issuance of the Committee decision on jurisdictional grounds but purely on political considerations." Whether Richardson was stating official administration policy Houston did not know, but the FEPC's position had nonetheless become intolerable. The handling of the Capital Transit case had raised "the fundamental question of the basic government attitude toward minorities." [30]

Truman's response to Houston constituted a restatement of the administration's position that the law required the operation of the property "under the terms and conditions of employment" existing at the time of the government takeover. "The property was not seized for the purpose of enforcing the aims" of the FEPC, "laudable as these aims are, but to guarantee transportation for the citizens of Washington and vicinity." Contravening an act of Congress, Truman wrote, would be injurious to the goals desired "by all of us who are honestly interested in promoting the welfare of minority groups." He regretted their differences of viewpoint but not Houston's departure. The res-

29. Charles Houston to Harry Truman, December 3, 1945, in Box 310–40, 1945, Truman Papers; Chicago *Defender*, Chicago *Sun*, December 8, 1945, Philadelphia *Inquirer*, December 2, 1945, all in Newspaper Clippings, Box 532, RG 228.

30. Houston to Truman, December 3, 1945, in Box 310–40, 1945, Truman Papers.

ignation would "be effective immediately." Houston, who believed the Capital Transit case was extremely significant, distributed copies of his letter of resignation along with other materials to civil rights organizations and even to foreign embassies.[31]

The matter did not rest there. In a four-page missive to the president from the District of Columbia chapter of the National Lawyers Guild, the case for government implementation of the nondiscrimination policy during the seizure of Capital Transit was brilliantly put forth in a methodical presentation similar to a lawyer's brief. "My guess is that it was probably written by Houston himself for the Guild," declared a Justice Department attorney to his boss, Tom Clark. "I have no doubt if we refuse to reply to it they will make an issue of it." The Guild, while admitting that the War Labor Disputes Act required the maintenance of employment conditions that were in existence at the time of the government's intervention, argued that "the phrase means those terms and conditions of employment which were established by the collective bargaining process or which the parties themselves were unable to agree upon during that process." The labor agreement in effect at the time of the government seizure "reveals its silence on the utilization of Negroes as platform personnel." No provision in the labor contract excluding blacks from these jobs or confining "them to certain categories of jobs" existed. Consequently, "the employment of Negroes in platform work was not treated . . . as a term or condition of employment," a fact the company so stated at the FEPC hearing. Because the company's failure to hire blacks for platform jobs had no basis in the labor contract, the Guild concluded, "race was not a term or condition of employment within the meaning of the seizure order." Therefore, the ODT was not prohibited from altering employment situations that were discriminatory.[32]

Even if the exclusion of blacks were mandated by the collective bargaining agreement, the letter continued, the ODT would have to "disregard such practices" because they were illegal according to the United States Supreme Court in the recent *Steel* and *Tunstall* cases. Additionally, Executive Order 9346 had received "legislative approval" when Congress twice appropriated funds to carry out its pur-

31. Harry Truman to Charles Houston, December 7, 1945, in Box 310–40, 1945, Truman Papers; McNeil, *Charles Hamilton Houston*, 174.

32. National Lawyers Guild, District of Columbia Chapter, to the President, December 21, 1945, in DJ-FOI.

poses. Thus, it was "wholly untenable" to maintain that 9346 was not a part of "existing law." To do so would place the government "in the intolerable position of maintaining and condoning discrimination against Negroes" while it controlled and operated the transit system. The Guild professed to be "at a loss to comprehend" the president's statement that the company was not seized in order to pursue the aims of the FEPC. Did that mean that nondiscrimination applied "in some cases but not in others"? The jurisdiction of the committee ought to be unquestioned and interference with its "normal operations unwarranted."[33]

Two weeks after Houston's resignation, the committee met with the president, but the Capital Transit case was not discussed. Shortly, thereafter, on December 20, Truman issued Executive Order 9664 authorizing the FEPC to "investigate, make findings and recommendations [but not issue directives], and report . . . discrimination in industries" contributing to military production "or to the effective transition to a peacetime economy." Universally criticized by the black press, the order was branded as merely a gesture, a "last minute effort to remove the death rattle from the fundless FEPC." Indeed, it seemed to have meaning only in light of the earlier reopening in the Senate of the campaign for a permanent FEPC. In addition to the new executive order, Truman also sent letters to the heads of all government departments, agencies, and independent establishments requesting a careful analysis of personnel policies so that they could assure him that their practices were "in accord with national law and policy" involving the fair consideration of all qualified workers for regular appointments without discrimination.[34]

White House delay in issuing the new executive order certainly undermined the FEPC, but so did the agency's own miscalculation of its financial situation. When Congress cut its appropriation, the committee had initially planned to use part of the money for one more hearing. By early November, as field offices closed and their staffs

33. *Ibid.*
34. Memorandum, FEPC to the President, December 17, 1945, and Harry Truman to Heads of All Government Departments *et al.*, December 20, 1945, both in Box 310–40, 1945, Truman Papers; Executive Order 9664, December 20, 1945, in Legal Division, Indianapolis folder, R15HR, Baltimore *Afro-American*, December 29, 1945, Chicago *Sun*, December 21, 1945, in Newspaper Clippings, Box 532, all in RG 228; Chicago *Defender*, December 22, 1945, pp. 1,5.

departed, the FEPC discovered that its funds were inadequate. Either the hearing had to be dropped or more offices closed. Worse was to come. Many of the staff, particularly at the central office, had accumulated considerable annual leave, which had to be financed out of current appropriations. George Johnson, who had served since November, 1941, collected $2,500 as he returned to the Howard University Law School. In the agency as a whole, departing personnel would receive a total of $62,000. That, along with the practice of giving thirty days notice with pay, left the FEPC "practically without funds," Ross telegraphed Edward Lawson on November 15. Only $90,000 was left for the remainder of the fiscal year. By the time Truman issued the new executive order, the FEPC was financially strapped; on December 17, just before the order became effective, only $63,606 remained. At the beginning of 1946, only thirty-one persons worked for the FEPC, and all field offices were closed except Detroit, Chicago, and St. Louis.[35]

For a time, perhaps because of renewed efforts in Congress to pass legislation for a permanent FEPC, Malcolm Ross and the staff clung to the idea that another hearing would be possible. Single-mindedly and sometimes aimlessly, they collected data from such government agencies as the Census Bureau and the USES, from the remaining FEPC field offices, and from private organizations such as the National Urban League and the American Council on Race Relations. By mid-February, however, it had become obvious that neither the hearing nor the legislation was within reach, and the committee decided to wind up its affairs with a report that would give a picture of how fair employment had developed successfully during the previous four years. Produced by the Government Printing Office, the FEPC's *Final Report*, with nearly a hundred pages of text, was the committee's final contribution, and it was a valuable document.[36]

35. Memorandum, FEPC to the President, December 17, 1945, in Box 310–40, 1945, Truman Papers; John Davis and Clarence Mitchell to Malcolm Ross, November 2, 1945, in office files of John A. Davis, Mr. Ross folder, R68HR, and Malcolm Ross to Edward Lawson (teletype), November 15, 1945, Region II, Telegrams Received file, F3FR, both in RG 228; *Final Report*, x.

36. John A. Davis to A. A. Liveright, December 29, 1945, in Public Relations 5, L file, R43HR, Maceo Hubbard to Robert C. Weaver, January 21, 1946, Letters file, Malcolm Ross to J. C. Capt, Census Bureau, January 11, 1946, West Coast Material file, in office files of Malcolm Ross, R2HR, John Davis to Julius Thomas, National Urban League, February 12, 1946, in office files of John A. Davis, Mr. Davis file,

In the interim, the effort to get a permanent agency was going badly. Although in late December the NAACP seemed optimistic about securing a discharge petition to halt an expected Senate filibuster, there was little optimism in the black press. The network of support, so indispensable during earlier battles over the FEPC, was breaking down. The National Council for a Permanent FEPC would not admit it, columnist Ralph Matthews reported in the Baltimore *Afro-American*, "but they are having plenty of trouble behind the scenes trying to keep the other minority groups in line behind the measure." Catholics and Jews gave "a little lip service to the project," but they remained unenthusiastic, he declared. Many Catholic priests, "if cornered," would admit to being opponents of the bill despite previous Catholic encounters with the Ku Klux Klan. Catholics did not have an economic problem, and they resented "being lumped with colored people in America's thinking." Jews were also pulling back in the belief that their minority troubles were social, rather than economic, in origin. Both groups opposed "any statistics being published" that indicated they had been helped by the FEPC. Consequently, making the struggle for a permanent FEPC "an all inclusive thing, instead of specifically to protect colored workers" divided the groups that should have been fighting together to get the measure approved. For an FEPC bill ever to pass, the support had to come from "the man in the street" who knew what it meant to be "out of a job because of the color of his skin."[37]

As the 1946 sessions of the House and Senate were gaveled to order, some rays of hope appeared. The Republican House minority leader, Joseph Martin, under pressure from liberals in his party, belatedly predicted the passage of permanent FEPC legislation. In addition, some elements of the committee's network of support remained active. The UAW, which had an internal fair employment practice committee, announced that one thousand locals stood behind the national drive to get the bill passed. Other reports were sobering, however. By the middle of January, a poll was showing the American public nar-

---

R68HR, and John Davis to Collis Stocking, February 12, 1946, Publications file, II, R47HR, all in RG 228.

37. Walter White to Carl R. Johnson (telegram), December 20, 1945, in General Office File, FEPC-General, 1945, NAACP Papers; Baltimore *Afro-American*, December 29, 1945, in Newspaper Clippings, Box 532, RG 228.

rowly divided on the issue, with a slight plurality, 44 percent, opposing and 43 percent favoring the bill. The other 13 percent had no opinion.[38]

In his annual message to the Congress, Truman gave the agency only scant endorsement. A "sham battle" was about to begin, wrote columnist Elizabeth Donohue in New York's *PM*, "following President Truman's 14 words on [the FEPC] . . . in his 30,000-word message to Congress." The administration's "strategy against the anti-FEPC filibuster remained either a secret or a myth." Both Republicans and Southern Democrats were "able to formulate definite battle plans" because their fears of strong administration support for the measure "were obviously allayed." To win the battle for the agency, administration forces would have to try "to break the filibuster" by cloture and show "a determined effort to hold FEPC on the floor even though other bills [were] reported . . . for Senate action." Such administration resolve clearly did not exist. Southerners could now plan "a simple filibuster, uncomplicated by formidable opposition from the White House." The Republicans, believing the administration was ready to surrender on the FEPC, would use "every parliamentary strategem [*sic*] to embarrass" the divided Democrats by insisting that the "Senate remain in session beyond its usual hour" so that the Democratic bloodletting would be prolonged. Pursuing this strategy, the Republicans would oppose any administration attempt to bring in a weaker compromise bill.[39]

It was a relatively short battle in the Senate. FEPC forces lost to the southern filibuster within a week, though scattered sparring continued until the end of February. In accounting for the failure, pundits laid the blame on others as well as on the Truman administration. The liberals, for example, were lazy and never put their strength to the test. Consequently, filibustering against the FEPC was an easy exercise. Whereas such noted filibusterers as Senators Robert La-Follette and Huey Long had talked for eighteen and fifteen and a half hours, respectively, "no Senator in the present filibuster [had] held

---

38. Chicago *Defender*, January 5, 1946, Box 532, January 19, 1946, Box 533, Detroit *Michigan Chronicle*, January 19, 1946, Box 533, in Newspaper Clippings, RG 228.

39. New York *PM*, January 22, 1946, in Newspaper Clippings, Box 533, RG 228; Bernstein, "Ambiguous Legacy," 272–75.

the floor over three hours." When Senator Wayne Morse suggested keeping the Senate in continuous day-and-night session to break the filibuster, some supporters "who talk mighty big now" were terrified then. "So the gentlemanly farce goes on." In addition, Communists and their front organizations allegedly played a sly game by opposing the bill "to keep the issue unsettled for agitation purposes."[40]

Other writers saw the defeat of the FEPC as symbolic of the strong congressional resistance to nearly every liberal proposal from the administration. Late in January, a House bill had returned control of the USES to the states despite Truman's warning that the program to find jobs for war veterans and displaced war workers would be crippled. According to *PM*, Republicans wanted the patronage appointments for their governors, and southern Democrats sought local control of black workers so they could be forced into low-paying jobs. This conservative coalition also opposed the Office of Price Administration, a higher minimum wage, a national health bill, federal aid to education, and more public housing, all of which were measures supported by the administration.[41]

Both congressional liberals and the administration had shied away from a bitter FEPC battle. Senators Morse and Alexander Smith and Congressman Charles LaFollette, all liberal Republicans, vowed to introduce a new bill with amendments that would eliminate certain unspecified objectionable features, and Truman, in a letter to A. Philip Randolph, pledged his continued support. The National Council for a Permanent FEPC announced that a rally would be held in New York City's Madison Square Garden under the joint chairmanship of Eleanor Roosevelt and Lillian Smith, the southern-born author of *Strange Fruit*. A cast of radio and movie personalities had also signed up for the event. Smith's sponsorship was particularly appropriate. From her home in the north Georgia mountains, she had denounced caste, and unlike such typical white southern establishment liberals as Mark Ethridge, Jonathan Daniels, and Will Alexander, she rejected

40. Philadelphia *Record*, January 24, 1946, Box 532, Robert Roth, "FEPC Beaten by Southern Filibuster," *Record*, January 27, 1946, Box 533, and Thomas L. Stokes, "Behind the Lines," Washington, D.C., *News*, February 5, 1946, Box 534, all in Newspaper Clippings, RG 228.

41. *PM*, January 30, 1946, Box 533, and Dorothy Norman, "A World to Live in," New York *Post*, February 13, 1946, Box 534, both in Newspaper Clippings, RG 228.

the segregated society of her native South. For her and a small number of white Southerners, John Beecher and Witherspoon Dodge, for example, it was not an easy path. Dodge, particularly, had been libeled and vilified for his association with the CIO and his "anti-Southern" ideas. The FEPC's regional director in Atlanta in 1944 and a Congregational minister and pastor of the Radio Church, he espoused equality and justice for all and publicly advocated abolishing poll taxes.[42]

The Madison Square Garden rally, held early in March, attracted 17,000 participants who heard A. Philip Randolph threaten relentless war against senators voting against cloture. The struggle for the FEPC would go on, he promised. But this impressive demonstration was a last hurrah. Although Randolph believed a march on Washington should be held in June, organizations involved with the National Council for a Permanent FEPC opposed it. The CIO stated flatly that it could not get representation, as did the garment workers unions. The FEPC limped along until the end of April, when the remainder of its staff went on thirty-day termination furloughs. The funds were gone. The FEPC had to be liquidated.[43]

Earlier, in February, as the southern filibusterers triumphantly buried FEPC legislation in an avalanche of words, South Carolina senator Olin Johnston received a funeral spray of salmon-colored gladioli with a blue ribbon bearing the gold inscription "Rest in Peace." Because these flowers were graphically symbolic of death, his constituents thought them appropriate to grace the grave of the FEPC bill. Late in June a Florida congressman, still not believing that the strangled and

42. Administrative Files, Region VII, Dodge folder, RG 228; Philadelphia *Tribune*, November 27, 1943, p. 1; newspaper clipping, Greenville (S.C.) *Observer*, June 3, 1941, in Series X, Box 131, CR-FEPC folder, Correspondence, 1944, Russell Papers; St. Paul *Minnesota Pioneer Press*, February 13, 1946, Chicago *Sun*, February 19, 1946, Box 534, Atlanta *Daily World*, November 16, 1944, February 20, 1946, Box 515, Baltimore *Afro-American*, March 2, 1946, Box 535, New York *Herald Tribune*, February 24, 1946, Box 634, New York *Evening Post*, April 3, 1946, Box 536, all in Newspaper Clippings, RG 228; Anne C. Loveland, *Lillian Smith: a Southerner Confronts the South: A Biography* (Baton Rouge, 1986), 43, 45, 61, 83; Sosna, *In Search of the Silent South*, 172–97; John Kirby, *Black Americans and the Roosevelt Era: Liberalism and Race* (Knoxville, 1980), 63–68.

43. Memorandum, Roy Wilkins to Walter White, April 4, 1946, in General Office File, FEPC-General, 1946, NAACP Papers; Malcolm Ross to Committee (telegram), May 3, 1946, in office files of Malcolm Ross, Miscellaneous file, R3HR, and Baltimore *Afro-American*, March 9, 1946, in Newspaper Clippings, Box 535, both in RG 228.

lifeless federal body could really be dead, began shooting at it. On June 26, five days before the FEPC legally ended, the Honorable Joe Hendricks demanded to know "if the President [was] going to allocate any of the emergency fund to the F.E.P.C." He had heard reports that Truman intended to do just that and he was "considerably disturbed."[44]

44. Memorandum, MJC [Connally] to the President, June 26, 1946, in Office File, 40, Miscellaneous file (June, 1945), Box 210, 1946–51, Truman Papers.

Epilogue

World War II, with its massive social, demographic, and economic changes, was a watershed for the modern civil rights movement, and as scholars have recently demonstrated, the migration patterns it fostered through military service and work in war-related industries made a difference "in the lives of Black Americans."[1] As the first federal agency in history to deal exclusively with job discrimination, the FEPC became a focal point for much of the civil rights activity during the war years. Its hearings and investigations provided clear evidence of the importance of a federal presence even when the agency itself was weak and faltering. In this role, the FEPC gave aid and encouragement and also acted as a catalyst for change, while its supporters and beneficiaries, whose protests and mass action had led to the agency's creation in the first place, undertook new initiatives against discrimination. The FEPC's activity was unique. Never before had an agency of the federal government cooperated in such a way with minority groups and their organizations. Nevertheless, its stance by no means reflected the sentiments of the Roosevelt administration, which opposed its creation, gave it lip service instead of support, used it callously to defuse black protect, and blocked it when political expediency so dictated.

1. John Modell, Marc Goulden, and Sigurdur Magnusson, "World War II in the lives of Black Americans: Some Findings and an Interpretation," *Journal of American History*, LXXV (1989), 838–48.

Heading the list of administration concerns were the FEPC's investigations and public hearings. So long as the investigations focused on the private sector in regions politically receptive to such activity, the FEPC was left alone. By the spring of 1942, when the committee fixed its sights on government agencies such as the USOE, the administration soured and imposed a cloak of secrecy over revelations of discrimination in the bureaucracy. Political fallout from the Birmingham hearing strengthened the administration's resolve to muzzle the committee. Yet the government's reaction to the airing of its own discriminatory practices illustrates how effective the FEPC investigations and hearings could be.

In the private sector, there was even greater concern over the possibility of public exposure. The FEPC's condemnation at its Chicago hearing of the use of questions on race and religion in employment application forms led most midwestern defense contractors to avoid such practices, and FEPC investigations and threats of a hearing in Detroit aided in the easing of discriminatory hiring practices in that city.[2] Investigations and hearings were powerful tools that the FEPC used effectively throughout the war period, for most defense contractors were reluctant to face such scrutiny. Although the effect of the hearings upon their behavior as employers can never be fully known, it was undoubtedly significant.

Several other factors, not always apparent, provided the FEPC with clout. The robust wartime economy and the tight labor market gave credence to the agency's pleas to defense plants to hire minorities out of patriotism. Yet in the prewar job market, the mindset of the work place had reserved unskilled or helper jobs for African- and Mexican-Americans, and attitudes did not change when the defense plants opened up. Employers, white workers, and most of the unions initially resisted the entrance of minorities even into unskilled sectors of the plants, though labor shortages ultimately assured their influx. Skilled tasks and semiskilled production work generally remained closed to them, however. The FEPC's special contribution in the defense industries before Pearl Harbor, and in the war industries after-

2. Sarah Southall to Congressman Clarence Cannon, March 23, 1944, in Public Relations 5, Southall file, R45HR, RG 228; Meier and Rudwick, *Black Detroit and the Rise of the UAW*, 173–74; Dominic J. Capeci, Jr., *Race Relations in Wartime Detroit: The Sojourner Truth Housing Controversy of 1942* (Philadelphia, 1984), 70, 71, 162.

ward, was its emphasis on the qualifications of each worker and the quality of the job. All defense employment should be open to qualified applicants, regardless of race or religious preference, it insisted. In addition, decisions on upgrading, promotions, raises, seniority, and fringe benefits must be equally unbiased. This stress on qualifications and quality was a startling idea whose time had not come as far as the vast majority of white war workers and their employers were concerned, though its acceptance varied in the different regions. That market forces alone, in the absence of an FEPC, could have overcome prejudice and produced a similar emphasis upon quality is doubtful.

Extensive samplings of the several thousand complaints successfully adjusted by the FEPC suggest that the quality of work available to minorities would have been considerably lower without that agency's intervention. Barriers against skilled, semiskilled, and white-collar minority workers were breached in defense plants and government offices in the Northeast. Although stymied in cities such as Cincinnati and St. Louis, the FEPC was able to bring about some wartime changes in other areas of the Midwest. In the South, the agency was instrumental in getting defense training for many black workers, even though most trainees were forced to leave the region in order to find employment. Certainly Alabama Dry Dock of Mobile would not have put skilled black welders on an integrated shift without an FEPC stimulus. A settlement based on the establishment of a segregated way was distasteful to all of the members of the New Committee, yet the FEPC could not challenge segregation frontally in the South or anywhere else without first proving that segregation produced discrimination.[3]

After considerable prodding of the company by the Atlanta Urban League and the FEPC, blacks were trained and tried in skilled jobs at the Bell Bomber plant. At shipyards and oil refineries in Texas, African- and Mexican-Americans also received more consideration. Several urban rapid transit systems, including those in Philadelphia and in Los Angeles, hired minority platform workers as a result of the FEPC's efforts amid ugly reactions from angry white workers. Less obvious and completely unmeasurable, aside from the backlash, was the salutary ripple effect that these many changes at various work places may have had on workers and employers at other plants and

3. Merl Reed, "FEPC, Black Worker, and Southern Shipyards," 454–57.

industries. It is impossible to estimate the number of plants that might have been induced by FEPC pressure and appeals to patriotism to avoid discriminating against minority groups. Some employers feared the bad publicity that exposure of discriminatory practices would generate. Others undoubtedly developed a fatalism toward the inevitability of integrating the work force in the face of tight labor markets and FEPC appeals. One employer, Fowler McCormick of International Harvester, alerted to the problem of discrimination by the FEPC, reexamined his hiring policies during and after the war.[4]

It is also impossible to assess the activity and effectiveness of the various federal agencies and departments that assisted, willingly or otherwise, in the FEPC's work. Involved most deeply was the WMC, in conjunction with the USES, but the War and Navy departments, the CSC, and others also investigated complaints of discrimination at the behest of the FEPC. When Senator Richard B. Russell and the Atlanta *Journal* fretted and fumed over these insidious and sinister FEPC linkages to other federal agencies, they may have been more correct about the significance of FEPC prodding and pleading than even they knew. The FEPC's ties with the bureaucracy were usually formal and in writing. They involved not only the central office but most of the regional offices, which made interagency agreements of their own. Among these contracts, however, the ties with the WMC and the USES were the most important. There was real cooperation between the FEPC and the WMC on the regional level, particularly in the Northeast, in the Midwest, and on the West Coast. In the South, the FEPC had great difficulty getting cooperation from the regional WMC and USES offices. USES 510s, however, provided the FEPC with feedback only on failures to achieve compliance that were reported by the WMC. Obviously, the knowledge that the issuance of USES 510s was a certainty induced many employers to avoid submitting biased work orders, and alert USES officials persuaded others to stop discriminating. A USES 510 was issued, and a copy sent to the FEPC, only after an employer's refusal to change a discriminatory order.[5]

4. David W. Southern, *Gunnar Myrdal and Black-White Relations: The Use and Abuse of an American Dilemma* (Baton Rouge, 1987), 103.
5. Merl Reed, "FEPC and Federal Agencies," 46–53.

While the service agencies and depots trained men and performed support services on their far-flung bases and shore establishments, they also employed large numbers of civilians. Their agreements with the FEPC obligated them to make internal investigations of complaints of discrimination and to attempt to seek relaxation of any discriminatory practices found. If these efforts failed, the FEPC conducted its own investigation. The agency's field representatives settled cases of this type all over the country. The ripple effect from this activity and from the various service agencies' own investigations remains unknown and probably unknowable. Nevertheless, the FEPC's relationships with the federal bureaucracy in Washington, D.C., and in the field were of vital significance to its work.[6]

In addition to avoiding bias in their own hiring practices, the procurement agencies, as purveyors of defense contracts, had an additional obligation. All contracts contained the nondiscrimination clauses required under the executive orders. Every federal agency involved with the war effort, large or small, whether renting office space or purchasing utilities and services, wrote contracts that contained the nearly ubiquitous nondiscrimination clause. Although these agreements were enforced unevenly, many contractors and providers of services, by their frequent howls of protest, signaled their belief that these clauses were important. In addition, as one writer has pointed out, the clauses set a precedent for some kind of surveillance of government contracts in the future.[7]

The FEPC's influence over key agencies in the wide-ranging wartime bureaucracy, impossible to delineate precisely, was little short of amazing considering the committee's inherent weaknesses and insignificance. One of the smallest bodies in the bureaucratic establish-

6. Florence Bates to John Beecher, September 28, 1942, in Correspondence file, Region II, Bas-Cu, F4FR, Army Transport Command, 4GR280, F46FR, Brookley Field, Ala., Final Disposition Report, 7GR141, Closed Cases file, F83FR, Richmond Army Service Forces Depot, Final Disposition Report, 4GR326, 4GR328, F47FR, Final Disposition Report, 4GR410, Final Disposition Report, F48FR, Kelley Field, Tex., 10GR564, F99FR, Brooks Field, Tex., 10GR571, F97FR, Charleston (S.C.) Navy Yard, 7GR239, F83FR, Norfolk (Va.) Navy Yard, 4GR549, F43FR, and Baltimore Port of Embarkation, 4GR260, F46FR, all in RG 228.

7. Chicago *Defender*, November 6, 1943, p. 4; *Louisiana Weekly*, December 12, 1943, in Newspaper Clippings, Chronological, RG 228; Wilson Record, *Race and Radicalism: The NAACP and the Communist Party in Conflict* (Ithaca, 1964), 123.

ment, it carried a purposely vague mandate from the administration, and initially it had neither budgetary nor statutory congressional sanction. Despite the administration's political expediency, however, the FEPC functioned more effectively than anyone in the administrative establishment believed possible, though it constantly disappointed its most ardent supporters. Using as its authority a phrase from the executive order here, a presidential letter or statement there, and constantly applying pressure through its hearings and investigations, the committee and key leaders therein made the most of difficult and troublesome situations and at times wielded considerable influence. As time passed, the agency, propelled by the moral imperatives of its work and the support of its constituency, took on a bureaucratic life of its own despite administration efforts to dampen its activity.

Important in the FEPC's evolution was the development of its black leadership, a fact little appreciated. For many African-Americans, service with that agency certainly influenced and may even have changed the course of their lives. Some white employees were similarly affected. Unlike members of the much-touted Black Cabinet of the New Deal, blacks on the President's Committee served in policy-making positions, and others on the FEPC staff had influence on decisions. Moreover, armed with insider information about policy and agency activity, they could and did participate, sometimes with considerable glee, in that age-old Washington, D.C., game of leaking selected information to the press, a practice that infuriated political operatives in the Justice Department. More than any other Old Committee members except Lawrence Cramer, Earl Dickerson and Milton Webster influenced policy. On the New Committee, Webster, George Johnson, and Charles Houston were equally important. This extraordinary display of black leadership occurred in a city whose white establishment believed that blacks, allegedly having never worked with white people, did not know how to and could not do so. Thus, it was unthinkable that George Johnson, who many blacks believed should have been appointed the FEPC chairman, could even be considered for such a position. But blacks and whites, both in leadership positions, worked together in probably the most unusual interracial structure that the nation's capital had ever seen. To southerners, the FEPC's central and regional office arrangements, let alone its program, displayed some of their worst fears of race mixing. In the FEPC office itself, there was both individualism and cooperation but apparently little, if any, white noblesse oblige.[8]

If working arrangements sometimes produced confusion and inefficiency, serving the FEPC apparently was interesting and never dull. In October, 1945, Simon Stickgold, a young attorney who previously had completed nine months of service in the FEPC's Legal Division, wrote to Mike Ross apologetically over his failure "to walk into your office and formally complete my farewells." Because he saw how the committee thrived "on confusion," Stickgold thought his neglect could not have been "particularly devastating." He doubted he would "ever find as much excitement and aggravation packed into nine short months," and he "enjoyed every minute of it" even though, as he wrote, "our job is, at best, a thankless one." No matter what was done, "some group or the other is going to try to tear you apart." He appreciated Ross's "temperance and impartiality in administering [his] staff of *prima donnas* and of keeping as calm as [he] did under the thousands of conflicting pressures." Ross, in his reply, said that his nearly two years with the committee seemed "like a couple of lifetimes." Harry Kingman was also moved. Following his departure, he requested pictures of all the Region XII personnel to hang in his YMCA office at the University of California at Berkeley. Although Ross apparently did not receive flattering or congratulatory letters from others who served the agency, blacks or whites, both races appear to have regarded their experiences as something special.[9]

As chairman, Ross had his ups and downs as he faced attacks from the FEPC's enemies and as he attracted alternating praise and criticism from the black press. His refusal to support the committee's Capital Transit decision, reportedly out of reluctance to create ill will in the White House, would end his tenure, never clear of controversy, on an unusually sour note. The Chicago *Defender*, reviving old charges, thought that Ross acted from a "lack of national stature" that "forced him to be unsure of his ground" and led him "to take a week-kneed stand on basic issues." Columnist Louis Sautier thought Ross meant

8. Interviews with Will Maslow and Clarence M. Mitchell.
9. Simon Stickgold to Malcolm Ross, October 11, 1945, Malcolm Ross to Simon Stickgold, October 16, 1945, in Public Relations 5, S file, R44HR, Virginia R. Seymour to Robert E. Brown, October 2, 1945, in Region XII, Administrative Files, 1945, Los Angeles file, F103FR, all in RG 228; interviews with John Hope II and Clarence M. Mitchell; interview with Wilfred K. Leland, Washington, D.C., September 9, 1978.

well but was weak. The stature issue had haunted Ross from the beginning, and there was some truth to it. Yet the chairmanship, which became his after Francis Haas's unexpected departure, earlier had been rejected by numerous white men, some with less stature than Ross.

Given the administration's unwillingness even to entertain the thought of naming a black, another extended search for a white chairman following Haas's resignation might have harmed the agency. Although Ross, perceived as being Biddle's and the president's man, came with a heavy bag of liabilities, there is little evidence, except for his initial attempt to make policy without adequately consulting committee members and his later Capital Transit dissent, that as chairman he tried to shape the committee's actions to please the White House. Jonathan Daniels' continued displeasure with the committee makes it seem likely that Ross was faulted by the administration either for being too independent or for failing to keep the FEPC in line, or perhaps for both of the above. At the same time, the good-natured and likable chairman took a great deal of criticism and outright abuse from the White House, from Congress, from the boilermakers union, and from the black press, among others. A poor administrator, he was not the best chairman, but few questioned his dedication.

The FEPC's deputy chairman, George M. Johnson, was the epitome of organization and acted as the committee's "lash," keeping the heat on the staff. Serving also as director of the Legal Division, he attended all committee meetings and actively participated in the discussions. In short, he served as the cutting edge of committee action and had a hand in most of the activities of the staff. Proud, and to subordinates overly formal, Johnson had primary responsibility for evaluating staff performance. The phrase "George M. Johnson (M. stands for Mr.)," uttered mockingly by a former staff member, reveals not only Johnson's extreme sensitivity but also his search for dignity in a very imperfect world. In his participation at committee meetings, he exhibited a sharp legal mind and talents for both confrontation and compromise. His sense of order provided an organizational glue badly needed by committee and staff.[10]

Just as Earl Dickerson and Lawrence Cramer were the sparks on the Old Committee, Charles Houston provided brilliance and intellectual

10. Interviews with Wilfred K. Leland and John A. Davis.

vigor and the bright Boris Shishkin, considerable static, to the new one. Apparently sincere in opposing job discrimination, Shishkin, like his more limited AFL predecessor, Frank Fenton, had to serve another master, sometimes at the committee's expense. Too often the interests of the AFL, many of whose national craft unions were notorious opponents of the executive order, forced him to become the union bureaucrat on the committee. Since many of John Brophy's CIO unions had their own fair employment committees, this solid participant could make his contribution to the FEPC without having to play such cagey games. When Shishkin did not have to defend AFL interests, he articulated committee goals effectively and participated constructively, except for his frequent feuds with Chairman Ross, which mitigated the effectiveness of both men.

Charles Houston pursued a broad range of interests on the committee, from staff efficiency to program planning. At committee meetings and publicly as well, he was loyal to the chairman, once vigorously defending him against attacks from the black press. Besides Houston's energizing effect on the staff, his greatest contribution grew out of his avid participation in FEPC hearings. With the support of George Johnson, he brought to them more order and a stricter adherence to legal procedures. In the various shipyard rehearings on the West Coast, he proved a worthy match for the formidable legal talent sent forth by the shipbuilders. During the conflict with Truman over Capital Transit, he proved equally adept in argument with Justice Department attorneys over the president's powers.

Perhaps as few as three hundred or four hundred people served with the agency during the war years. These men and women were carefully selected individuals whose dedication was a known quantity. Most of them served the FEPC with distinction. As one of them recalled, the agency was a "tough outfit." Compared with "what was done in later times with more money, FEPC did a hell of a job." As these veterans of the war against job discrimination left the agency, most became involved in the civil rights struggle during the postwar years. Clarence M. Mitchell and Will Maslow joined two of the nation's most prominent minority organizations. In the NAACP, Mitchell served as head of the Washington, D.C., office until the late 1970s. Maslow left the FEPC to become general counsel for the American Jewish Congress and was its executive director between 1960 and

1972. Earl B. Dickerson returned to his law practice and his work with the Chicago Urban League.[11]

Sarah Southall, a member of the New Committee, remained with International Harvester, but she continued the FEPC's work in her own organization and elsewhere. Her book, published in 1950, constituted a plea for racial tolerance in the work place. From the field staff, Edward Rutledge, the white examiner-in-charge and regional director on the West Coast, looked back on his service with the FEPC as a moving experience that influenced the course of his life. After leaving the FEPC, he advised the Federal Housing Administration on race relations in the Los Angeles area and later went to the Northeast and the Middle Atlantic states with the Public Housing Administration. From 1955 to 1964, he served Governors W. Averell Harriman and Nelson Rockefeller of New York as director of housing. He also worked at the Metro Applied Research Center in New York City with black psychologist Kenneth Clark under a Ford Foundation grant and later became a member of the United States Commission on Civil Rights.[12]

Among black staff members whose activities could be traced, several made significant contributions in the postwar years. John Hope II, who had been teaching economics at Morehouse College when the war began, became a field investigator out of the Region VII office in Atlanta. According to Hope, his work with the FEPC made him aware of "whole new vistas" that ultimately influenced his "social and personal interests." At the University of Chicago before the war, he and his instructors had poorly understood the economics of race and how to become involved therein. After the war, with the FEPC experience behind him, he joined the Race Relations Institute at Fisk University, working under sociologist Charles S. Johnson. Hope authored two scholarly studies on black employment opportunities and found good use in the Office for Civil Rights during the 1960s and 1970s for some of the skills he had learned at the FEPC. He also served on the President's Committee for Equal Employment Opportunity, as did Marjorie Lawson of the FEPC's division of Review and Analysis. Lawson

11. Interviews with Earl B. Dickerson, John A. Davis, Clarence Mitchell, and Will Maslow.

12. Southall, *Industry's Unfinished Business*, 61; telephone interview with Edward Rutledge, January 14, 1987, interview with Edward Rutledge, Croton-on-Hudson, N.Y., August 6, 1987.

went on to a distinguished legal career, and in the 1960s she served as an associate judge on the District of Columbia's Juvenile Court and on the President's Task Force on Urban Renewal.[13]

Elmer Henderson, who directed the FEPC's Region VI in Chicago, worked for seven years as executive director of the American Council on Human Rights and then became general counsel for the House Committee on Government Operations. Maceo Hubbard, of the FEPC's Legal Division, served until the late 1970s in the Civil Rights Division of the Justice Department. Theodore Jones, the FEPC's budget officer, established his own Chicago accounting firm, served in the mid-1960s as regional director of the Office of Economic Opportunity, became a trustee of the University of Illinois, found time to work with the Chicago Commission on Human Relations, and in 1971 received the NAACP's outstanding service award.[14]

George M. Johnson remained as dean of the Howard University Law School until 1958, when briefly he headed the legal division of the United States Commission on Civil Rights. He also spent four years as vice-chancellor of the University of Nigeria. John A. Davis, head of the FEPC's Review and Analysis, earned a Ph.D. at Columbia University and became a political scientist at Brooklyn College. G. James Fleming, director of Region III, took a doctoral degree in political science and served with the Race Relations Committee of the American Friends until joining the faculty at Morgan State College.[15]

Frank D. Reeves, a young NAACP attorney and Howard University Law School instructor, worked in the FEPC's Legal Division throughout the war and had a distinguished career afterward. Involved in many civil rights cases, he successfully represented black children seeking to enroll in the Arlington, Virginia, public schools, an action that was upheld by the United States Supreme Court. In May, 1960,

13. Interview with John Hope II; telephone interview with John Hope II, January 2, 1987; John Hope II, "Negro Employment in Three Southern Plants of International Harvester Company," in *Selected Studies of Negro Employment in the South*, Report No. 6, NPA Committee of the South (Washington, D.C., 1953), and *Minority Access to Federal Grants-In-Aid: The Gap Between Policy and Performance* (New York, 1976); *Who's Who Among Black Americans, 1985* (4th ed., Lake Forest, Ill., 1985), 505.

14. Interview with Maceo Hubbard; telephone interview with Edward Rutledge; *Who's Who Among Black Americans, 1985*, p. 376.

15. Interview with John A. Davis; G. James Fleming, "The Administration of Fair Employment Practice Programs" (Ph.D. dissertation, University of Pennsylvania, 1948); *Who's Who Among Black Americans, 1985*, pp. 275, 449.

Reeves ran for Democratic national committeeman from the District of Columbia as a delegate for Senator Hubert Humphrey. Later, at the Democratic National Convention, he supported Senator John F. Kennedy, delivering one of the six seconding speeches, along with Governor Harriman of New York and gubernatorial candidate Terry Sanford of North Carolina. In January, 1961, President Kennedy appointed Reeves as an administrative assistant, the first black American to serve in that capacity. The following June, he declined a presidential nomination to the governing committee of the District of Columbia because of personal tax problems. Kennedy later gave Reeves two special assignments: in 1962, Reeves joined a three-person study group investigating a dispute between the Chicago Belt Railway Company and the Brotherhood of Locomotive Engineers; and the next year he served on an emergency board to investigate a dispute among the BSCP, the Pullman Company, and several railroads. After Reeves' death in 1973, a District of Columbia municipal building was named in his honor.[16]

These individuals and undoubtedly many others, mostly young professionals on ascending career curves, lived an exciting wartime experience. Much of what they did made a difference, partly because it involved a federal presence. After leaving the FEPC, they carried the message into the future in their individual pursuits. They had witnessed the implementation of FEPC procedures and policies that helped many individuals in minority groups aspire to better lives because of improvements in the quality of employment and in standard of living. In later decades, they would watch and participate as different organizations formed new networks of support for civil rights.

In the new agencies created by federal legislation in the 1960s, some of these FEPC veterans would help revive the struggle for fair employment practice. By this time the FEPC was part of the dim past and memories of its work and accomplishments were hazy and fading, but its veterans, now middle-aged, must have marveled in retrospect at what the agency had been able to accomplish in those earlier days. Although linkages between the President's Committee and the civil rights movement and legislation of the 1960s were blurred and indis-

16. Telephone interview with John Hope II; New York *Times*, April 11, 1943, p. 60, May 5, 1960, p. 27, July 14, 1960, p. 18, July 30, 1963, pp. 17, 32.

tinct, they could take comfort in the knowledge that the FEPC's near-revolutionary program of equal access to better employment opportunities and a better life, regardless of one's race or religion, was alive once again.

Bibliography

Primary Sources

UNPUBLISHED DOCUMENTS

The National Archives in Washington, D.C., and some of its regional archives branches hold the Records of the President's Committee on Fair Employment Practice, Record Group 228 (RG 228), more familiarly known as the Fair Employment Practice Committee (FEPC). All of the Headquarters Records (FEPC Central) are located at the National Archives, and some of the FEPC Field Records are in the regional archives branches (FEPC Region II in Bayonne, N.J.; Region III in Philadelphia; Region VII in East Point, Ga.; and Region XII in San Bruno, Calif.). Indispensable in using RG 228 is Charles Zaid (comp.), *Records of the Committee on Fair Employment Practice*, National Archives Preliminary Inventories, No. 147 (Washington, D.C., 1962), a finding aid that provides a brief history of the agency and a survey of the documents. Also useful, but of less value, are the Records of the War Manpower Commission (Record Group 211), an agency important in the enforcement of Executive Orders 8802 and 9346, whose records relative to the FEPC dovetail, but more often duplicate, those of the President's Committee.

In 1970, RG 228 was microfilmed and is now available in many libraries. The microfilming process was selective with the special goal of avoiding duplication. An excellent guide to the microfilmed material that provides a history of the agency and a description of the documents is Bruce I. Friend, *Guide to the Microfilm Record of Selected Documents of the Committee on Fair Employment Practice in the Custody of the National Archives* (Glen Rock, N.J., 1970). Omitted from the microfilming because of the copyright barrier was a wealth of material from newspapers gathered by the FEPC's various offices and by a clipping service. Newspaper clippings are scattered throughout the FEPC case files. Fortunately, the bulk of the newspaper items were collected at FEPC Central. They are available in Newspaper Clippings, RG 228.

Also in Washington, D.C., in the Manuscript Division of the Library of Congress, are the Records of the National Association for the Advancement of Colored People (NAACP). In its relationship with the FEPC, the NAACP did not generate an extensive body of records. Nevertheless, these records are important in filling in vital details not always provided in the FEPC files. The Records of the National Urban League, also at the Library of Congress, provide little information. In the archives at the Catholic University of America are the papers of Monsignor Francis J. Haas and John Brophy. The Haas Papers contain invaluable Justice Department internal communications provided to Haas when he became FEPC chairman. Finally, a few papers of Chairman Malcolm Ross, including photographs, were made available to me at the Washington, D.C., home of Ross's son, Sandy.

Besides research materials in the Washington, D.C., area, there are also important documents in the Franklin D. Roosevelt Library. The President's Office Files 4246-G have been mined extensively by historians of this period, and they were valuable to me as well. In addition, the Francis Biddle Papers and particularly the Harold D. Smith Papers have invaluable information on cabinet meetings and private conferences with Roosevelt.

Documents at the Harry S. Truman Library provide a clearer picture of the FEPC in its waning days. These include materials in the Harry S. Truman Papers and the File of Philleo Nash.

Other collections were also used, including the records of the Brotherhood of Sleeping Car Porters at the Chicago Historical Society, the Richard B. Russell Papers at the University of Georgia, the James F. Byrnes Papers at Clemson University, and the Jonathan Daniels Papers at the Southern Historical Collection at the University of North Carolina in Chapel Hill.

Finally, through Freedom of Information requests, I was able to obtain xeroxed copies of documents relating to the FEPC from the U.S. Department of Justice and the Federal Bureau of Investigation. These materials, presently in my possession, will eventually be deposited in Special Collections in the Pullen Library, Georgia State University.

NEWSPAPERS

Chicago *Defender* (1941–1946)
Philadelphia *Tribune* (selected periods)
Pittsburgh *Courier* (1941–1946)

In addition to the important Afro-American weeklies cited above, the newspaper clippings in RG 228 from a wide variety of the nation's daily and weekly press were useful. The following are cited, some extensively:

Amsterdam *Star News*
Atlanta *Constitution*

Atlanta *Daily World*
Atlanta *Journal*
Baltimore *Afro-American*
Baltimore *Sun*
Chicago *Journal of Commerce*
Chicago *Sun*
Chicago *Sunday Bee*
Christian Science Monitor
Cincinnati *Enquirer*
Cincinnati *Post*
Columbia *South Carolina Record*
Columbus *Ohio State News*
Detroit *Free Press*
Detroit *Michigan Chronicle*
Grand Rapids *Press*
Greenville (S.C.) *Observer*
Hartford *Courant*
Houston *Informer*
Indianapolis *Recorder*
Jackson (Miss.) *Clarion Ledger*
Kansas City *Black Dispatch*
Kansas City *Call*
Louisiana Weekly
Los Angeles *Sentinel*
Los Angeles *Times*
Miami *Herald*
Minneapolis *Spokesman*
Montgomery *Advertiser*
Newark *News*
New Orleans *Sentinel and Informer*
New York *Evening Post*
New York *Herald Tribune*
New York *PM*
New York *Post*
New York *Times*
New York *World Telegram*
Norfolk *Journal and Guide*
Philadelphia *Courier*
Philadelphia *Evening Bulletin*
Philadelphia *Record*
Pittsburgh *Post Gazette*
Richmond (Ind.) *Palladium Stem*
Salem (Ore.) *Journal*
St. Louis *Post-Dispatch*
St. Louis *Star Times*

St. Paul *Minnesota Pioneer Press*
St. Paul *Recorder*
San Francisco *Examiner*
San Francisco *People's World News*
Statesman (Ga.)
Tucson *Star*
Washington, D.C., *Afro-American*
Washington, D.C., *News*
Washington, D.C., *Post*
Washington, D.C., *Star*
Washington, D.C., *Times Herald*
Washington, D.C., *Tribune*

INTERVIEWS

John A. Davis, New Rochelle, N.Y., August 30, 1978.
Earl B. Dickerson, Chicago, December 11, 1978.
John Hope II, Washington, D.C., September 7, 1978, January 2, 1987 (tele
    phone).
Maceo Hubbard, Washington, D.C., August 25, 1978.
Wilfred C. Leland, Washington, D.C., September 9, 1978.
Will Maslow, New York, N.Y., August 29, 1978.
Clarence Mitchell, Washington, D.C., August 24, 1978.
Edward Rutledge, Croton-on-Hudson, N.Y., January 14, 1987 (telephone),
    August 6, 1987.

BOOKS

Archibald, Katherine. *Wartime Shipyard: A Study in Social Disunity.*
    Berkeley, 1947.
Committee on Fair Employment Practice. *Final Report.* Washington, D.C.,
    1947.
————. *First Report.* Washington, D.C., 1945.
Johnson, Charles S., et al. *To Stem This Tide: A Survey of Racial Tension
    Areas in the United States.* Boston, 1943.
Menefee, Seldon. *Assignment: U.S.A.* New York, 1943.
Myrdal, Gunnar. *An American Dilemma.* New York, 1944.
Northrup, Herbert R. *Organized Labor and the Negro.* New York, 1944.
Odum, Howard. *Race and Rumors of Race: Challenge to American Crisis.*
    Chapel Hill, 1943.
Ottley, Roi. *"New World A-Coming": Inside Black America.* Cleveland,
    1943.
Powell, Adam Clayton, Jr. *Marching Blacks: An Interpretive History of the
    Rise of the Black Common Man.* New York, 1945.
Weaver, Robert. *Negro Labor: A National Problem.* New York, 1946.
White, Walter Francis. *A Man Called White: The Autobiography of Walter
    White.* New York, 1948.

ARTICLES

Bailor, Lloyd. "The Automobile Unions and Negro Labor." *Political Science Quarterly,* LIX (1944), 548–77.

———. "The Negro Automobile Worker." *Journal of Political Economy,* LI (1943), 415—28.

Beecher, John. "8802 Blues." *New Republic,* February 22, 1943, p. 249.

———. "Problems of Discrimination." *Science and Society,* VII (1943), 6–44.

———. "S.S. Booker T. Washington." *New Republic,* October 2, 1944, pp. 421–23.

Branson, Herman. "The Training of Negroes for War Industries in World War II." *Journal of Negro Education,* XII (1943), 376–85.

Cherokee, Charley. "Twelve Rounds for the Championship." *Opportunity,* XXI (January, 1943), pp. 6–7.

Corey, Herbert. "Portrait of a Man with a Mission." *Nation's Business,* XXXII (February, 1944), p. 36.

Davis, John A. "Non-discrimination in the Federal Agencies." *Annals of the American Academy of Political and Social Science,* No. 244 (March, 1946), 64–74.

Davis, John A., and Cornelius A. Golightly. "Negro Employment in the Federal Government." *Phylon,* VI (1945), 337–46.

Davis, Ralph. "The Negro Newspaper and the War." *Sociology and Social Research,* XXVII (1943), 373–80.

"Fortune Management Poll." *Fortune,* XXVII (February, 1943), pp. 143–44.

Frazier, E. Franklin. "Ethnic and Minority Groups in Wartime." *American Journal of Sociology,* XLVIII (1942), 369–77.

Fuller, Helen. "The Ring Around the President." *New Republic,* October 25, 1943, pp. 563–65.

Granger, Lester. "Barriers to Negro War Employment." In *Black America: Accommodation and Confrontation in the Twentieth Century,* edited by Richard Resh. Lexington, Mass., 1967.

Graves, John Temple. "The Southern Negro and the War Crisis." *Virginia Quarterly Review,* XVIII (1942), 500–17.

Henderson, Elmer. "Employment of Negroes in the Federal Government." *Monthly Labor Review,* LVI (May, 1943), pp. 889–91.

———. "Negroes in Government Employment." *Opportunity,* XXI (1943), 113–21, 142–43.

"The Jim Crow Bloc." *New Republic,* February 22, 1943, pp. 240–41.

Johnson, Charles. "The Present Status of Race Relations in the South." *Social Forces,* XXIII (1944), 27–32.

Kesselman, Louis C. "The Fair Employment Practice Movement in Perspective." *Journal of Negro History,* XXXI (1946), 30–46.

Marshall, Thurgood. "Negro Status in the Boilermakers Union." *Crisis,* XLIV (March, 1944), pp. 77–78.

Murray, Florence. "The Negro and Civil Liberties During World War II." *Social Forces*, XXXV (1945), 211–16.

"The Negro in Industry." *New Republic*, October 18, 1943, pp. 538–41.

"The Negro's War." *Fortune*, XXV (June, 1942), pp. 77–80, 157–64.

Northrup, Herbert R. "Negroes in a War Industry: The Case of Shipbuilding." *Journal of Business*, XVI (1943), 160–72.

———. "Organized Labor and Negro Workers." *Journal of Political Economy*, LI (1943), 206–21.

———. "Unions and Negro Employment." *Annals of the American Academy of Political and Social Science*, No. 244 (1946), 42–47.

Randolph, A. Philip. "Keynote Address to the Policy Conference on the March on Washington Movement." In *Black Nationalism in America*, edited by John Bracey, Jr., August Meier, and Elliott Rudwick. Indianapolis, 1970.

Sancton, Thomas. "The Returning Tragic Era in the South." *New Republic*, January 4, 11, 18, 1943, pp. 11–14, 50–51, 81–82.

Thompson, Charles. "FEPC Hearings Reduce Race Problem to Lowest Terms—Equal Economic Opportunity." *Journal of Negro Education*, XII (1943), 585–89.

Wechsler, James A. "Pigeonhole for Negro Equality." *Nation*, January 23, 1943, pp. 121–22.

Wylie, Philip. "Memorandum on Anti-Semitism." *American Mercury*, LX (January, 1945), pp. 66–73.

Secondary Sources

BOOKS

Adams, Leonard P. *Wartime Manpower Mobilization: A Study of World War II Experience in the Buffalo-Niagara Area*. Ithaca, 1951.

Anderson, Jervis A. *Philip Randolph: A Biographical Portrait*. New York, 1972.

Baldwin, Sidney. *Poverty and Politics: The Rise and Decline of the Farm Security Administration*. Chapel Hill, 1968.

Bennett, Lerone, Jr. *Confrontation: Black and White*. Chicago, 1965.

Berman, Larry. *The Office of Management and Budget and the Presidency, 1921–1979*. Princeton, 1979.

Berman, William. *The Politics of Civil Rights in the Truman Administration*. Columbus, Ohio, 1970.

Biddle, Francis. *In Brief Authority*. Garden City, N.Y., 1962.

Blackman, John, Jr., *Presidential Seizure in Labor Disputes*. Cambridge, Mass., 1967.

Blantz, Thomas E. *A Priest in Public Service: Francis J. Haas and the New Deal*. Notre Dame, 1982.

Bloch, Herman. *The Circle of Discrimination: An Economic and Social Study of the Black Man in New York*. New York, 1969.

Blum, John. *V Was for Victory: Politics and American Culture During World War II*. New York, 1976.

Bodnar, John. *Immigration and Industrialization: Ethnicity in an American Mill Town*. Pittsburgh, 1977.

Brazeal, Brailsford. *The Brotherhood of Sleeping Car Porters: Its Origins and Development*. New York, 1946.

Brooks, Lester. *Blacks in the City: A History of the National Urban League*. Boston, 1971.

Brooks, Thomas. *Communications Workers of America: The Story of a Union*. New York, 1977.

Brophy, John. *A Miner's Life*. Madison, Wis., 1964.

Bunche, Ralph. *The Political Status of the Negro in the Age of FDR*. Chicago, 1973.

Buni, Andrew. *Robert L. Vann of the Pittsburgh Courier*. Pittsburgh, 1974.

Bureau of National Affairs. *State Fair Employment Laws and Their Administration: Texts, Federal-State Cooperation, Prohibited Acts*. Washington, D.C., 1964.

Burns, James. *Roosevelt: The Soldier of Freedom*. New York, 1970.

Cantril, Hadley, with Mildred Strunk, eds. *Public Opinion, 1935–1946*. Princeton, 1951.

Capeci, Dominic J., Jr. *The Harlem Riot of 1943*. Philadelphia, 1977.

———. *Race Relations in Wartime Detroit: The Sojourner Truth Housing Controversy of 1942*. Philadelphia, 1984.

Cavnes, Max Parvin. *The Hoosier Community at War*. Bloomington, Ind., 1961.

Chafe, William. *The Unfinished Journey: America Since World War II*. New York, 1986.

Chapman, Richard N. *Contours of Public Policy, 1939–1945*. New York, 1981.

Clive, Alan. *State of War: Michigan in World War II*. Ann Arbor, 1979.

Collins, Donald. *Native American Aliens: Disloyalty and the Renunciation of Citizenship by Japanese-Americans During World War II*. Westport, Conn., 1985.

Cox, Oliver. *Class, Caste, and Race*. New York, 1948.

Dalfiume, Richard. *Desegregation of the U.S. Armed Forces: Fighting on Two Fronts, 1939–1953*. Columbia, Mo., 1969.

Daniels, Jonathan. *White House Witness, 1942–1945*. New York, 1975.

Daniels, Roger. *Concentration Camps USA: Japanese-Americans and World War II*. New York, 1971.

Dickerson, Dennis C. *Out of the Crucible: Black Steelworkers in Western Pennsylvania, 1875–1980*. Albany, N.Y., 1986.

Dykeman, Wilma, and James Stokeley. *The Seeds of Southern Change: The Life of Will Alexander*. Chicago, 1962.

Eagles, Charles W. *Jonathan Daniels and Race Relations: The Evolution of a Southern Liberal*. Knoxville, 1982.

Fairchild, Bryon, and Jonathan Grossman. *The Army and Industrial Manpower*. Washington, D.C., 1959.

Fink, Gary M., ed. *Labor Unions*. Westport, Conn., 1977.

Finkle, Lee. *Forum for Protest: The Black Press During World War II*. Madison, N.J., 1975.

Flynn, George Q. *The Mess in Washington: Manpower Mobilization in World War II*. Westport, Conn., 1979.

Foner, Philip. *Organized Labor and the Black Worker, 1619–1973*. New York, 1974.

Franklin, John Hope. *From Slavery to Freedom: A History of Negro Americans*. New York, 1967.

Gann, L., and Peter Duignan. *The Hispanics in the United States: A History*. Boulder, 1986.

Garfinkel, Herbert. *When Negroes March: The March on Washington Movement in the Organizational Politics for FEPC*. Glencoe, Ill., 1959.

Girdner, Audrie, and Ann Loftis. *The Great Betrayal: The Evacuation of the Japanese-Americans During World War II*. London, 1969.

Greenberg, Jack. *Race Relations and American Law*. New York, 1959.

Hareven, Tamara. *Eleanor Roosevelt: An American Conscience*. New York, 1975.

Harris, William. *The Harder We Run: Black Workers Since the Civil War*. New York, 1982.

―――. *Keeping the Faith: A. Philip Randolph, Milton P. Webster, and the Brotherhood of Sleeping Car Porters, 1925–37*. Urbana, 1977.

Hartmann, Susan. *The Home Front and Beyond: American Women in the 1940s*. Boston, 1982.

Hiestand, Dale. *Economic Growth and Employment Opportunities of Minorities*. New York, 1964.

Hill, Herbert. *Black Labor and the American Legal System: Race, Work, and the Law*. Washington, D.C., 1977.

Hogan, Lawrence D. *A Black National News Service: The Associated Negro Press and Claude Barnett, 1919–1945*. London, c. 1984.

Hurst, James Willard. *Law and Social Order in the United States*. Ithaca, 1977.

Irons, Peter H. *The New Deal Lawyers*. Princeton, 1982.

Kammerer, Gladys. *Impact of the War on Federal Personnel Administration, 1939–1945*. Lexington, Ky., 1951.

Kesselman, Louis C. *The Social Politics of FEPC: A Study in Reform Pressure Movements*. Chapel Hill, 1948.

Kirby, John. *Black Americans and the Roosevelt Era: Liberalism and Race*. Knoxville, 1980.

Kirkendall, Richard. *The United States, 1929–1945: Years of Crisis and Change*. New York, 1974.

Kitano, Harry H. L. *Japanese-Americans: The Evolution of a Subculture*. London, 1969.

Konvitz, Milton. *A Century of Civil Rights*. New York, 1961.

Krueger, Thomas A. *And Promises to Keep: The Southern Conference for Human Welfare, 1938–1948*. Nashville, 1967.

Lee, Ulysses. *The Employment of Negro Troops in the United States Army in World War II: Special Studies*. Washington, D.C., 1966.

Lichtenstein, Nelson. *Labor's War at Home*. Chapel Hill, 1982.

Lingeman, Richard. *Don't You Know There's a War On? The American Home Front, 1941–45*. New York, 1970.

Loveland, Anne C. *Lillian Smith: a Southerner Confronts the South: A Biography*. Baton Rouge, 1986.

MacIver, R. *The More Perfect Union: A Program for the Control of Intergroup Discrimination in the United States*. New York, 1948.

Mangum, Charles, Jr. *The Legal Status of the Negro*. Chapel Hill, 1940.

Marshall, F. Ray. *The Negro Worker*. New York, 1967.

Marwick, Arthur. *War and Social Change in the Twentieth Century*. London, 1974.

Matthews, Donald, and James Prothro. *Negroes and the New Southern Politics*. New York, 1966.

Mazon, Mauricio. *The Zoot-Suit Riots: The Psychology of Symbolic Annihilation*. Austin, 1984.

McGill, Ralph. *The South and the Southerner*. Boston, 1963.

McGuire, Phillip. *He, Too, Spoke for Democracy: Judge Hastie, World War II, and the Black Soldier*. Westport, Conn., 1988.

McNeil, Genna Rae. *Groundwork: Charles Hamilton Houston and the Struggle for Civil Rights*. Philadelphia, 1983.

Meier, August, and Elliott Rudwick. *Black Detroit and the Rise of the UAW*. New York, 1979.

———. *Black History and the Historical Profession, 1915–1980*. Urbana, 1986.

———. *CORE: A Study in the Civil Rights Movement, 1942–1968*. New York, 1973.

Moon, Henry. *Balance of Power: The Negro Vote*. Garden City, N.Y., 1948.

Moore, Jesse Thomas, Jr., *A Search for Equality: The National Urban League, 1910–1961*. University Park, Pa., 1981.

Nash, Gerald D. *The American West Transformed: The Impact of the Second World War*. Bloomington, Ind., 1985.

———. *The Great Depression and World War II: Organizing America, 1933–1945*. New York, 1979.

Northrup, Herbert R. *The Negro in the Aerospace Industry*. Philadelphia, 1968.

———. *The Negro in the Automobile Industry*. Philadelphia, 1968.

———. *The Negro in the Rubber Tire Industry*. Philadelphia, 1969.

Ozanne, Robert. *A Century of Labor-Management Relations at McCormick and International Harvester*. Madison, Wis., 1967.

———. *The Negro in the Farm Equipment and Construction Machinery Industries*. Philadelphia, 1972.

Patterson, James. *America's Struggle Against Poverty, 1900–1985*. Cambridge, Mass., 1986.

Penton, M. James. *Apocalypse Delayed: The Story of Jehovah's Witnesses*. Toronto, 1985.

Perrett, Geoffrey. *Days of Sadness, Years of Triumph: The American People, 1939–1945*. New York, 1973.

Polenberg, Richard. *One Nation Divisible: Class, Race and Ethnicity in the United States Since 1938*. New York, 1980.

————. *War and Society: The United States, 1941–1945*. New York, 1972.

Program and Administration. New York, 1969. Vol. I of *Industrial Mobilization for War: History of the War Production Board and Predecessor Agencies, 1940–1945*. 3 vols. projected.

Quarles, Benjamin. *The Negro in the Making of America*. New York, 1964.

Record, Wilson. *Race and Radicalism: The NAACP and the Communist Party in Conflict*. Ithaca, 1964.

Riegelman, Carol. *Labour Management Cooperation in United States War Production*. Montreal, 1948.

Ross, Malcolm. *All Manner of Men*. New York, 1948.

Ruchames, Louis. *Race, Jobs, and Politics: The Story of FEPC*. New York, 1953.

Schlesinger, Arthur, Jr. *The Politics of Upheaval*. Boston, 1960. Vol. III of Schlesinger, *The Age of Roosevelt*. 4 vols. projected.

Seidman, Joel. *American Labor from Defense to Reconversion*. Chicago, 1953.

Silberman, Charles. *Crisis in Black and White*. New York, 1964.

Silvera, John, comp. *The Negro in World War II*. New York, 1969.

Sitkoff, Harvard. *The Depression Decade*. New York, 1978. Vol. I of Sitkoff, *A New Deal for Blacks: The Emergence of Civil Rights as a National Issue*. 3 vols. projected.

Somers, Herman. *Presidential Agency: OWMR, the Office of War Mobilization and Reconversion*. Cambridge, Mass., 1950.

Sosna, Morton. *In Search of the Silent South: Southern Liberals and the Race Issue*. New York, 1977.

Southall, Sarah E. *Industry's Unfinished Business*. New York, 1950.

Southern, David W. *Gunnar Myrdal and Black-White Relations: The Use and Abuse of an American Dilemma*. Baton Rouge, 1987.

Spicer, Edward, et al. *Impounded People: Japanese-Americans in the Relocation Centers*. Tucson, 1969.

Stanfield, John. *Philanthropy and Jim Crow in American Social Science*. Westport, Conn., 1985.

Stiller, Jesse H. *George S. Messersmith: Diplomat of Democracy*. Chapel Hill, 1987.

Strickland, Arvarh E. *History of the Chicago Urban League*. Urbana, 1966.

Tindall, George B. *The Emergence of the New South, 1913–1945*. Baton Rouge, 1967.

Van Riper, Paul. *History of the United States Civil Service*. Evanston, Ill., 1958.

Vatter, Harold. *The United States Economy in World War II*. New York, 1985.

Ware, Gilbert. *William Hastie: Grace Under Pressure*. New York, 1984.

Washburn, Patrick S. *A Question of Sedition: The Federal Government's Investigation of the Black Press During World War II*. New York, 1986.

Weglyn, Michael. *Years of Infamy: The Untold Story of America's Concentration Camps*. New York, 1976.

Weiss, Nancy. *Farewell to the Party of Lincoln: Black Politics in the Age of FDR*. Princeton, 1983.

———. *The National Urban League, 1910–1940*. New York, 1974.

Winkler, Allan M. *The Politics of Propaganda: The Office of War Information, 1942–1945*. New Haven, 1978.

Wolters, Raymond. *Negroes and the Great Depression: The Problem of Economic Recovery*. Westport, Conn., 1970.

Wynn, Neil A. *The Afro-American and the Second World War*. New York, 1976.

ARTICLES

Adams, Patricia L. "Fighting for Democracy in St. Louis: Civil Rights During World War II." *Missouri History Review*, LXXX (1985), 58–75.

Anderson, Karen. "Last Hired, First Fired: Black Women Workers During World War II." *Journal of American History*, LXIX (1982), 82–97.

Arroyo, Luis L. "Chicano Participation in Organized Labor: The CIO in Los Angeles, 1938–1950. An Extended Research Note." *Aztlan*, VI (1975), 277–303.

Bailey, Robert. "Theodore G. Bilbo and the Fair Employment Practices Controversy: A Southern Senator's Reaction to a Changing World." *Journal of Mississippi History*, XLII (1980), 27–42.

Bernstein, Barton J. "The Ambiguous Legacy: The Truman Administration and Civil Rights." In *Politics and Policies of the Truman Administration*, edited by Barton J. Bernstein. Chicago, 1970.

———. "America in War and Peace: The Test of Liberalism." In *Towards a New Past: Dissenting Essays in American History*, edited by Barton J. Bernstein. New York, 1968.

———. "The New Deal: The Conservative Achievements of Liberal Reform." In *Towards a New Past: Dissenting Essays in American History*, edited by Barton J. Bernstein. New York, 1968.

Blum, John. "World War II." In *A Comparative Approach to American History*, edited by C. Vann Woodward. New York, 1968.

Brody, David. "The Emergence of Mass-Production Unionism." In *Change and Continuity in Twentieth Century America*, edited by John Braeman, Robert H. Bremner, and Everett Walters. Columbus, Ohio, 1964.

————. "The New Deal and World War II." In *Change and Continuity in Twentieth Century America,* edited by John Braeman, Robert H. Bremner, and Everett Walters. Columbus, Ohio, 1964.

Broussard, Albert S. "Strange Territory, Familiar Leadership: The Impact of World War II on San Francisco's Black Community." *California History,* LXV (1986), 18–25, 71–73.

Capeci, Dominic J., Jr. "Wartime Fair Employment Practices Committees: The Governor's Committee and the First FEPC in New York City, 1941–1943." *Afro-Americans in New York Life and History,* IX (1985), 45–63.

Chafe, William. "The Civil Rights Revolution, 1945–1960: The Gods Bring Threads to Webs Begun." In *Reshaping America: Society and Institutions, 1945–1960,* edited by Robert H. Bremner and Gary W. Rechard. Columbus, Ohio, 1982.

Cripps, Thomas. "Movies, Race, and World War II: 'Tennessee Johnson' as an Anticipation of the Strategies of the Civil Rights Movement." *Prologue,* XIV (1982), 49–67.

Critchlow, Donald. "Communist Unions and Racism: A Comparative Study of the United Electrical, Radio and Machine Workers and the National Maritime Union to the Black Question During World War II." *Labor History,* XVII (1976), 230–44.

Culley, John. "World War II and a Western Town: The Internment of the Japanese Railroad Workers of Clovis, New Mexico." *Western Historical Quarterly,* XIII (1982), 43–61.

Dalfiume, Richard. "The 'Forgotten Years' of the Negro Revolution." *Journal of American History,* LV (June, 1968), 90–106.

Dewing, Donald. "Negro Employment in Southern Industry." *Journal of Political Economy,* LX (August, 1952), 279–93.

Dickerson, Dennis C. "Fighting on the Domestic Front: Black Steelworkers in Western Pennsylvania During World War II." In *Life and Labor: Dimensions of Working-Class History,* edited by Charles Stephenson and Robert Asher. Albany, N.Y., 1986.

Eagles, Charles. "Two 'Double V's': Jonathan Daniels, FDR, and Race Relations During World War II." *North Carolina Historical Review,* LIX (1982), 252–70.

Finkle, Lee. "The Conservative Aims of Militant Rhetoric: Black Protest During World War II." *Journal of American History,* LX (1973), 692–713.

Fox, Daniel. "Black Americans and the Politics of Poverty, 1900–1970." In *Key Issues in the Afro-American Experience,* edited by Nathan Huggins, Martin Kilson, and Daniel Fox. New York, 1971.

Garcia, Mario. "Americans All: The Mexican American Generation and the Politics of Wartime Los Angeles, 1941–45." *Social Science Quarterly,* LXV (1984), 278–89.

Goodenow, Ronald. "Paradox in Progressive Educational Reform: The South and the Education of Blacks in the Depression Years." *Phylon,* XXXIX (1978), 49–65.

Gottlieb, Peter. "Migration and Jobs: The New Black Workers in Pittsburgh, 1916–1930." *Western Pennsylvania Historical Magazine,* LXI (1978), 1–16.

Harris, William H. "Federal Intervention in Union Discrimination: FEPC and West Coast Shipyards During World War II." *Labor History,* XXII (1981), 325–47.

Hastie, William. "Charles Hamilton Houston, 1895–1950." *Journal of Negro History,* XXXV (1950), 355–58.

Henderson, Alexa B. "FEPC and the Southern Railway Case: An Investigation into the Discriminatory Practices of Railroads During World War II." *Journal of Negro History,* LXI (1976), 173–87.

Hill, Herbert. "Racial Inequality in Employment: The Patterns of Discrimination." *Annals of the American Academy of Political and Social Science,* No. 357 (1965), 30–47.

———. "Whose Law—Whose Order? The Failure of Federal Contract Compliance." In *The Black Experience in American Politics,* edited by Charles Hamilton. New York, 1973.

Hope, John II. "Negro Employment in Three Southern Plants of International Harvester Company." Report No. 6, NPA Committee of the South. Washington, D.C., 1953.

Johnson, Charles. "The Army, the Negro, and the Civilian Conservation Corps, 1933–1942." *Military Affairs,* XXXVI (1972), 82–87.

Kalmar, Karen. "Southern Black Elites and the New Deal: A Case Study of Savannah, Georgia." *Georgia Historical Quarterly,* LXV (1981), 341–55.

Kellogg, Peter. "Civil Rights Consciousness in the 1940s." *Historian,* XLII (1979), 18–41.

Koistinen, A. C. "Mobilizing the World War II Economy: Labor and the Industrial Military Alliance." *Pacific Historical Review,* XLII (1973), 443–78.

Koppes, Clayton, and Gregory Black. "Blacks, Loyalty, and Motion Picture Propaganda in World War II." *Journal of American History,* LXXIII (1986), 383–406.

———. "What to Show the World: The Office of War Information and Hollywood, 1942–1945." *Journal of American History,* LXIV (1977), 87–105.

Korstad, Robert, and Nelson Lichtenstein. "Opportunities Found and Lost: Labor, Radicals, and the Early Civil Rights Movement." *Journal of American History,* LXXV (1988), 786–811.

Leonard, Walter. "The Development of the Black Bar." *Annals of the American Academy of Political and Social Science,* No. 407 (1973), 134–43.

McGuire, Phillip. "Judge Hastie, World War II, and the Army Air Corps." *Phylon,* XLII (1981), 157–67.

Meier, August. "Civil Rights Strategies for Negro Employment." In *Employment, Race, and Poverty*, edited by Arthur M. Ross and Herbert Hill. New York, 1967.

Meier, August, and Elliott Rudwick. "Communist Unions and the Black Community: The Case of the Transport Workers Union, 1934–1944." *Labor History*, XXIII (1982), 165–97.

————. "How CORE Began." *Social Science Quarterly*, XLIX (1969), 789–99.

————. "The Origins of Non-violent Direct Action in Afro-American Protest: A Note on Historical Discontinuities." In *Along the Color Line: Explorations in the Black Experience*, edited by August Meier and Elliott Rudwick. Urbana, 1976.

Miyamoto, S. Frank. "Forced Evacuation of the Japanese Minority During World War II." *Journal of Social Issues*, XXIX (1973), 11–31.

Modell, John, Marc Goulden, and Sigurdur Magnusson. "World War II in the Lives of Black Americans: Some Findings and an Interpretation." *Journal of American History*, LXXVI (1989), 838—48.

Monroy, Douglas. "Essay on Understanding the Work Experience of Mexicans in Southern California, 1900–1939." *Aztlan*, XII (1981), 59–74.

Neuchterlein, James A. "The Politics of Civil Rights: The FEPC, 1941–1946." *Prologue*, X (1978), 171–91.

Norrell, Robert J. "Caste in Steel: Jim Crow Careers in Birmingham, Alabama." *Journal of American History*, LXXIII (1986), 669–94.

Okamura, Raymond Y. "American Concentration Camps: A Cover-up Through Euphemistic Terminology." *Journal of Ethnic Studies*, X (1982), 95–109.

Okihiro, Gary Y., and Julie Sly. "The Press, Japanese-Americans, and the Concentration Camps." *Phylon*, XLIV (1983), 66–83.

Parks, Robert. "Development of Segregation in the U.S. Army Hospitals, 1940–42." *Military Affairs*, XXXVII (1973), 145–50.

Radosh, Ronald. "The Myth of the New Deal." In *A New History of Leviathan*, edited by Ronald Radosh and Murray N. Rothbard. New York, 1972.

Rayack, Elton. "Discrimination and the Occupational Progress of Negroes." *Review of Economics and Statistics*, XLIII (1961), 209–14.

Reed, Bernice. "Accommodation Between Negro and White Employees in a West Coast Aircraft Industry, 1942–44." *Social Forces*, XXVI (1947), 76–84.

Reed, Christopher. "Black Chicago Political Realignment During the Depression and New Deal." *Illinois Historical Journal*, LXXVIII (1985), 242–56.

Reed, Merl E. "FEPC and the Federal Agencies in the South." *Journal of Negro History*, LXV (1980), 43–56.

————. "The FEPC, the Black Worker and the Southern Shipyards." *South Atlantic Quarterly*, LXXIV (1973), 446–67.

————. "Pennsylvania's Black Workers, the Defense Industries, and the Federal Agencies, 1941–1945." *Labor History*, XXVII (1986), 356–84.

Sitkoff, Harvard. "Racial Militancy and Interracial Violence in the Second World War." *Journal of American History*, LVIII (1971), 661–81.

Suggs, H. "Black Strategy and Ideology in the Segregation Era: P. B. Young and the *Norfolk Journal and Guide*, 1910–1954." *Virginia Magazine of History and Biography*, XCI (1983), 161–90.

Thornbrough, Emma. "Breaking Racial Barriers to Public Accommodations in Indiana, 1935–1963." *Indiana Magazine of History*, LXXXIII (1987), 301–43.

Winkler, Allan M. "The Philadelphia Transit Strike of 1944." *Journal of American History*, LXIX (1972), 73–89.

Wynn, Neil. "The Impact of the Second World War on the American Negro." *Journal of Contemporary History*, VI (1971), 42–54.

UNPUBLISHED SOURCES

Bradbury, William Chapman, Jr. "Racial Discrimination in the Federal Service." Ph.D. dissertation, Columbia University, 1952.

Ellis, Ann Wells. "The Commission on Interracial Cooperation, 1919–1944: Its Activities and Results." Ph.D. dissertation, Georgia State University, 1976.

Fleming, G. James. "The Administration of Fair Employment Practice Programs." Ph.D. dissertation, University of Pennsylvania, 1948.

Jenkins, Lou Ella. "The Fair Employment Practice Committee and Mexican-Americans in the Southwest." M.A. thesis, Georgia State University, 1974.

Potenziani, David D. "Look to the Past: Richard B. Russell and the Defense of Southern White Supremacy." Ph.D. dissertation, University of Georgia, 1981.

Straub, Eleanor F. "Government Policy Toward Civilian Women During World War II." Ph.D. dissertation, Emory University, 1973.

Sullivan, Patricia A. "Gideon's Southern Soldiers: New Deal Politics and Civil Rights Reform, 1933–1948." Ph.D. dissertation, Emory University, 1983.

Wright, Kennard Harry. "Sun Shipyard Number Four—The Story of a Major Negro Homefront Defense Effort During the Second World War." M.A. thesis, Morgan State College, 1972.

Index

Kaiser Shipyards: nationwide recruiting
campaign, 270–71; mentioned, 272, 277,
280, 283, 284, 285, 294, 301, 307, 308,
309, 313
Kansas City *Call*, 163
Kansas City *Star*, 147
Keenan, Joseph: negotiates with FEPC for
IBB, 292–94; mentioned, 296, 298
Kelly, Mayor Edward, 34, 100
Kelly, Emmett, 275, 277
Kennedy, Senator John F., 356
Kesselman, Louis G., 2
Kingman, Harry L.: director of Region XII,
228–29; mentioned, 128, 151, 247, 248,
250, 251, 275, 283, 294, 301, 307, 308,
329, 351
Kobata, Ruby, 249
Ku Klux Klan, 38

Labor Department, 244
Labor Division, 13, 25, 26, 27, 51, 52, 69,
74, 77, 78, 80, 81–82, 83, 86, 87, 96, 97,
125, 176, 269
La Follette, Congressman Charles, 147, 163,
341
La Follette, Senator Robert, 340
LaGuardia, Fiorello, 14, 21
Landes, Dr. Ruth, 25
Langsdale, Cliff, 311–13, 316
Lasseter, Dillard B., 201, 202
Lawson, Edward: director of Region II, 209–
11; mentioned, 119, 125, 205, 210, 246,
327, 338
Lawson, Marjorie, 152, 154, 161, 354
Lazarus, Judge Sylvan J., 272
Le Flore, J. L., 179, 182
Lehman, Governor Herbert, 16
Lemire, Virginia, 306
Lewis, C. R., 196
Library of Congress, 89
Lockheed Aircraft Company, 39, 238
Long, Senator Huey, 340
Los Angeles hearing, 36–39, 41, 177–78,
238
Los Angeles *Sentinel*, 161, 289
Los Angeles *Times*, 248
Louisville *Courier-Journal*, 22, 48

McAplin, Harry, 90, 119, 130, 132, 153, 158,
159, 160
McClellan, Senator John, 160
McCormick, Fowler, 348
McDaniel, J. E., 199–200, 201
McGill, Ralph, 171, 225
MacGowan, Charles: elected president of
IBB, 288; mentioned, 275, 286, 287, 292,

293, 294, 296, 297, 298, 300, 301, 302,
311–13, 314
McIntyre, Marvin, 49, 50, 53, 70, 73, 78,
82, 94, 98, 101, 104, 105, 113, 122, 188
McKeller, Senator Kenneth, 169
McKenzie, Marjorie, 16
McKessen and Robbins Company, 253
McKnight, William T.: appointed director of
Region V, 215; mentioned, 218, 219, 221
MacLean, Malcolm: appointed FEPC chair-
man, 49; and public relations, 49–51; on
reorganization, 58–60; on Birmingham
hearing, 66–67, 72; on merger with
WMC, 78–79, 81, 87; appraisal of, 115–
16; mentioned, 50–51, 53, 54, 68, 74, 85,
96, 101–102, 114, 187, 188, 190, 232
McNutt, Paul, 52, 53, 74, 77, 78, 79, 80, 81,
83, 84, 85, 86–87, 88, 89, 91, 92–93, 96,
99, 102, 106, 108, 109, 110, 111, 122, 123,
156, 206, 214, 215, 326
McSherry, General Frank L., 81, 83, 86, 88
Mahoney Act, 16–17, 31, 209, 211
Manly, Milo, 211, 212
Marcantonio, Congressman Vito, 158, 161
March on Washington Movement
(MOWM), 3, 4, 6, 13, 14, 21, 199, 315
Marinship Corporation, 283, 284, 309, 310
Maritime Commission, 28, 30, 118, 184,
267, 303, 323
Marlin Rockwell Company, 211
Marshall, Larkin, 202
Martin, Congressman Joseph, 166, 339
Maslow, Will: appointed director of Field
Operations, 207–208; mentioned, 124,
133, 135, 141, 150–51, 153, 154, 201,
242, 257, 258, 353
Matthews, Ralph, 339
Maybank, Senator Burnet, 169
Meier, August, 4, 7, 8
Merrill, E. D., 127
Messersmith, Ambassador George, 235, 237
Mexican-Americans, 177, 227, 229, 231–38
Miami *Herald*, 160
Milledgeville, Ga.: suppression of black citi-
zens' committees, 196–98
Miller, Frieda, 31
Minorities Group branch, 13, 78, 86, 96, 97,
176
Mitchell, Clarence, 25, 118, 119, 120–21,
150–51, 154, 200, 250–51, 258, 328, 353
Miyakawa, T. Scott, 243–44
Mobile Metal Trades Council (AFL), 71, 120
Mobley, M. D., 187, 188, 190, 191, 197
Moley, Raymond, 163
Montgomery *Advertiser*, 156–57
Moore Dry Dock Company, 284, 316